CAEC Test Prep

Canadian Adult Education Credential Study Guide and Practice Test Questions

Copyright © 2024 by Complete Test Preparation Inc. ALL RIGHTS RESERVED. No part of this book may be reproduced or transferred in any form or by any means, graphic, electronic, or mechanical, including photocopying, recording, web distribution, taping, or by any information storage retrieval system, without the written permission of the author.

Notice: Complete Test Preparation Inc. makes every reasonable effort to obtain from reliable sources accurate, complete, and timely information about the tests covered in this book. Nevertheless, changes can be made in the tests or the administration of the tests at any time and Complete Test Preparation Inc. makes no representation or warranty, either expressed or implied as to the accuracy, timeliness, or completeness of the information contained in this book. Complete Test Preparation Inc. makes no representations or warranties of any kind, express or implied, about the completeness, accuracy, reliability, suitability or availability with respect to the information contained in this document for any purpose. Any reliance you place on such information is therefore strictly at your own risk.

The author(s) shall not be liable for any loss incurred as a consequence of the use and application, directly or indirectly, of any information presented in this work. Sold with the understanding, the author(s) is not engaged in rendering professional services or advice. If advice or expert assistance is required, the services of a competent professional should be sought.

The company, product and service names used in this publication are for identification purposes only. All trademarks and registered trademarks are the property of their respective owners. Complete Test Preparation Inc. is not affiliated with any educational institution.

Complete Test Preparation is not affiliated with the makers of the Canadian Adult Education Credential, who do not endorse this product and are not involved in the production.

Version 8.5 November 2024

ISBN: 9781772454390

We strongly recommend that students check with exam providers for up-to-date information regarding test content.

Published by
Complete Test Preparation Inc.
Victoria BC Canada

Visit us on the web at https://www.test-preparation.ca
Printed in the USA

About Complete Test Preparation Inc.

Why Us?
The Complete Test Preparation Team has been publishing high quality study materials since 2005, with a catalogue of over 145 titles, in English, French and Chinese, as well as ESL curriculum for all levels.

To keep up with the industry changes, we update everything all the time!

And the best part?
With every purchase, you're helping people all over the world improve themselves and their education. So thank you in advance for supporting this mission with us! Together, we are truly making a difference in the lives of those often forgotten by the system.

Charities that we support -
https://www.test-preparation.ca/charities-and-non-profits/

You have definitely come to the right place.
If you want to spend your valuable study time where it will help you the most - we've got you covered today and tomorrow.

The Environment and Sustainability

Environmental consciousness is important for the continued growth of our company. Besides eco-balancing each title, as a print on demand publisher, we only print units as orders come in, which greatly reduces excess printing and waste. This revolutionary printing technology also eliminates carbon emissions from trucks hauling boxes of books everywhere to warehouses. We also maintain a commitment to recycling any waste materials that may result from the printing process. We continue to review our manufacturing practices on an ongoing basis to ensure we are doing our part to protect and improve the environment.

Feedback

We welcome your feedback. Email us at feedback@test-preparation.ca with your comments and suggestions. We carefully review all suggestions and often incorporate reader suggestions into upcoming versions. As a Print on Demand Publisher, we update our products frequently.

Contents

6 Getting Started
How this study guide is organized ... 6
The CAEC Study Plan ... 7
Making a Study Schedule ... 7

12 Social Studies
Social Studies Self-Assessment ... 12
Answer Key ... 26
Milestones in Canadian History ... 32
Canadian Government - Overview ... 33
Canadian History - An Overview ... 34
Overview of Concepts in Basic Economics ... 40

42 Reading
Reading Self-Assessment ... 42
Answer Key ... 52
Help with Reading Comprehension ... 54
Common Reading Comprehension Mistakes ... 59

60 Mathematics
Mathematics Self-Assessment ... 62
Answer Key ... 74
Basic math Video Tutorials ... 85
Fraction Tips, Tricks and Shortcuts ... 85
Most Common Fraction Mistakes on a Test ... 89
Decimal Tips, Tricks and Shortcuts ... 89
Converting Decimals to Fractions ... 90
Percent Tips, Tricks and Shortcuts ... 91
How to Answer Basic Math Multiple Choice ... 92
How to Solve Word Problems ... 94
Types of Word Problems ... 96
Ratios ... 102
Solving One-Variable Linear Equations ... 106
Solving Two-Variable Linear Equations ... 106
Adding and Subtracting Polynomials ... 108
Multiplying and Dividing Polynomials ... 108
Simplifying Polynomials ... 109
Factoring Polynomials ... 109
Quadratic equations ... 110
Cartesian Plane, Coordinate Plane and Coordinate Grid ... 111
Quadrilaterals ... 120
Data and Statistics ... 123
Permutations and Combinations - A Quick Review ... 123
Inferences from Data ... 124
Simple Probability ... 125
Mode, Mean and Median ... 126
Dependent and Independent Variables ... 127

128 Language Arts Writing
    Writing Tips and Common Mistakes   145
    Redundancy   145
    Common English Usage Mistakes - A Quick Review   150
    Subject Verb Agreement   156

161 How to Write an Essay
    Example Essay 2   164
    Example Essay 3   167
    Common Essay Mistakes - Example 1   170
    Common Essay Mistakes - Example 2   171
    Example Essay Prompts   173
    Writing Concisely   174

176 Science
    Science Self-Assessment   178
    Answer Key   184
    Science Tutorials   186
    Scientific Method   186
    Biology   188
    Classification   200
    Chemistry   202
    How to Solve Molarity Questions   214
    Basic Physics   215
    Energy: Work and Power   218
    Force and Newton's Three Laws   220
    Fundamental Forces   223
    States of Matter   228
    Oxidation and Reduction   230
    Speed, Acceleration and Force Problems   231

234 Practice Test Questions Set 1
    Answer Key   319
    Analyzing your practice tests   355

356 Practice Test Questions Set 2
    Answer Key   443

481 Conclusion

483 Online Resources

Getting Started

CONGRATULATIONS! By deciding to take the CAEC Exam, you have taken the first step toward a great future! Of course, there is no point in taking this important examination unless you intend to do your best to earn the highest grade you possibly can. That means getting yourself organized and discovering the best approaches, methods and strategies to master the material. Yes, that will require real effort and dedication, but if you are willing to focus your energy and devote the study time necessary, before you know it you will be on you will be opening that letter of acceptance to the school of your dreams!

We know that taking on a new endeavour can be scary, and it is easy to feel unsure of where to begin. That's where we come in. This study guide is designed to help you improve your test-taking skills, show you a few tricks of the trade and increase both your competency and confidence.

The CAEC Exam

The CAEC exam has four sections, reading, mathematics, sentence skills and writing. The reading section consists of reading comprehension questions. The mathematics section contains three sections, arithmetic, algebra and college level math. The sentence skills section contains questions on sentence structure and rewriting sentences. The writing section contains an essay question.

While we seek to make our guide as comprehensive as possible, note that like all exams, the CAEC exam might be adjusted at some future point. New material might be added, or content that is no longer relevant or applicable might be removed. It is always a good idea to give the materials you receive when you register to take the CAEC a careful review.

How this study guide is organized

This study guide is divided into three sections. The first section, Self-Assessments, which will help you recognize your areas of strength and weaknesses. This will be a boon when it comes to managing your study time most efficiently; there is not much point of focusing on material you have already got firmly under control. Instead, taking the self-assessments will show you where that time could be much better spent. In this area you will begin with a few questions to evaluate quickly your understanding of material that is likely to appear on the CAEC. If you do poorly in certain areas, simply work carefully through those sections in the tutorials and then try the self-assessment again.

The second section, Tutorials, offers information in each of the content areas, as well as strategies to help you master that material. The tutorials are not intended to be a complete course, but cover general principles. If you find that you do not understand the tutorials, it is recommended that you seek out additional instruction.

Third, we offer two sets of practice test questions, similar to those on the CAEC exam.

The CAEC Study Plan

Now that you have made the decision to take the CAEC, it is time to get started. Before you do another thing, you will need to figure out a plan of attack. The very best study tip is to start early! The longer the time period you devote to regular study practice, the more likely you will retain the material and access it quickly. If you thought that 1 x 20 is the same as 2 x 10, guess what? It really is not, when it comes to study time. Reviewing material for just an hour per day over the course of 20 days is far better than studying for two hours a day for only 10 days. The more often you revisit a particular piece of information, the better you will know it. Not only will your grasp and understanding be better, but your ability to reach into your brain and quickly and efficiently pull out the tidbit you need, will be greatly enhanced as well.

The great Chinese scholar and philosopher Confucius believed that true knowledge could be defined as knowing what you know and what you do not know. The first step in preparing for the CAEC is to assess your strengths and weaknesses. You may already have an idea of what you know and what you do not know, but evaluating yourself using our Self- Assessment modules for each of the three areas, Math, Writing and Reading Comprehension, will clarify the details.

Making a Study Schedule

To make your study time most productive, you will need to develop a study plan. The purpose of the plan is to organize all the bits of pieces of information in such a way that you will not feel overwhelmed. Rome was not built in a day, and learning everything you will need to know to pass the CAEC is going to take time, too. Arranging the material you need to learn into manageable chunks is the best way to go. Each study session should make you feel as though you have accomplished your goal, or at least are closer, and your goal is simply to learn what you planned to learn during that particular session. Try to organize the content in such a way that each study session builds on previous ones. That way, you will retain the information, be better able to access it, and review the previous bits and pieces at the same time.

Self-assessment

The Best Study Tip! The very best study tip is to start early! The longer you study regularly, the more you will retain and 'learn' the material. Studying for 1 hour per day for 20 days is far better than studying for 2 hours for 10 days.

What don't you know?

The first step is to assess your strengths and weaknesses. You may already have an idea of where your weaknesses are, or you can take our Self-assessment modules for each of the areas, Reading Comprehension, Arithmetic, Essay Writing, Algebra and College Level Math.

Exam Component	Rate 1 to 5
Reading Comprehension	
Making Inferences	
Main idea	
Arithmetic	
Decimals Percent and Fractions	
Problem solving (Word Problems)	
Basic Algebra	
Simple Geometry	
Problem Solving	
Essay Writing	
Sentence Skills	
Sentence Correction	
Sentence Shift	
Basic English Grammar and Usage	
Algebra	
Exponents	
Linear Equations	
Quadratics	
Polynomials	
College Level	
Coordinate Geometry	

Making a Study Schedule

The key to a successful study plan is to divide the material you need to learn into manageable size and learn it, while at the same time reviewing the material that you already know.

Using the table above, any scores of three or below, mean you need to spend time learning, reviewing and practicing this subject area. A score of four means you need to review the material, but you don't have to re-learn. A score of five and you are OK with just an occasional review before the exam.

A score of zero or one means you really do need to work on this and you should allocate the most time and give it the highest priority. Some students prefer a 5-day plan and others a 10-day plan. It also depends on how much time until the exam.

Here is an example of a 5-day plan based on an example from the table above:

Main Idea: 1   Study 1 hour everyday – review on last day
Fractions: 3   Study 1 hour for 2 days then ½ hour and then review
Algebra: 4   Review every second day
Grammar & Usage: 2 Study 1 hour on the first day – then ½ hour everyday
Reading Comprehension: 5   Review for ½ hour every other day
Geometry: 5 Review for ½ hour every other day

Using this example, geometry and reading comprehension are good and only need occasional review. Algebra is good and needs 'some' review. Fractions need a bit of work, grammar and usage needs a lot of work and Main Idea is very weak and need most of time. Based on this, here is a sample study plan:

Day	Subject	Time
Monday		
Study	Main Idea	1 hour
Study	Grammar & Usage	1 hour
	½ hour break	
Study	Fractions	1 hour
Review	Algebra	½ hour
Tuesday		
Study	Main Idea	1 hour
Study	Grammar & Usage	½ hour
	½ hour break	
Study	Fractions	½ hour
Review	Algebra	½ hour
Review	Geometry	½ hour
Wednesday		
Study	Main Idea	1 hour
Study	Grammar & Usage	½ hour
	½ hour break	
Study	Fractions	½ hour
Review	Geometry	½ hour
Thursday		
Study	Main Idea	½ hour
Study	Grammar & Usage	½ hour
Review	Fractions	½ hour
	½ hour break	
Review	Geometry	½ hour
Review	Algebra	½ hour
Friday		
Review	Main Idea	½ hour
Review	Grammar & Usage	½ hour
Review	Fractions	½ hour
	½ hour break	
Review	Algebra	½ hour
Review	Grammar & Usage	½ hour

Using this example, adapt the study plan to your own schedule. This schedule assumes 2 ½ - 3 hours available to study everyday for a 5 day period.

First, write out what you need to study and how much. Next figure out how many days before the test. Note, do NOT study on the last day before the test. On the last day before the test, you won't learn anything and will probably only confuse yourself.

Make a table with the days before the test and the number of hours you have available to study each day. We suggest working with 1 hour and ½ hour time slots.

Start filling in the blanks, with the subjects you need to study the most, getting the most time, and the most regular time slots (i.e. everyday) and the subjects that you know getting the least time (i.e. ½ hour every other day, or every 3rd day).

Tips for making a schedule

Once you make a schedule, stick with it! Make your study sessions reasonable. If you make a study schedule and don't stick with it, you set yourself up for failure. Instead, schedule study sessions that are a bit shorter and set yourself up for success! Make sure your study sessions are do-able. Studying is hard work, but after you pass, you can party and take a break!

Schedule breaks. Breaks are just as important as study time. Work out a rotation of studying and breaks that works for you.

Build up study time. If you find it hard to sit still and study for 1 hour straight through, build up to it. Start with 20 minutes, and then take a break. Once you get used to 20-minute study sessions, increase the time to 30 minutes. Gradually work you way up to 1 hour.

How to Make a Study Plan and Schedule
https://www.test-preparation.ca/make-study-plan/

40 minutes to 1 hour is optimal. Studying for longer than this is tiring and not productive. Studying for shorter isn't long enough to be productive.

Studying Math. Studying Math is different from studying other subjects because you use a different part of your brain. The best way to study math is to practice everyday. This will train your mind to think in a mathematical way. If you miss a day or days, the mathematical mind-set is gone, and you have to start all over again to build it up.

More Info on Making a Study Plan

How to study math

https://www.test-preparation.ca/study-math/

How to Study
For more information, see our How to Study Guide at
https://www.test-preparation.ca/learning-study/

Flash Cards - The Complete Guide

https://www.test-preparation.ca/flash-cards/

Social Studies

THIS SECTION CONTAINS A SELF-ASSESSMENT AND READING TUTORIAL. The tutorials are designed to familiarize general principles and the self-assessment contains general questions similar to the questions likely to be on the CAEC, but are not intended to be identical to the exam questions. The tutorials are not designed to be a complete reading course, and it is assumed that students have some familiarity with social studies questions. If you do not understand parts of the tutorial, or find the tutorial difficult, it is recommended that you seek out additional instruction.

Note that these questions are for skill practice only.

Tour of the CAEC Social Studies Content

The CAEC social studies section has 50 social studies questions. Below is a detailed list of the types of social studies questions that generally appear on the CAEC.

- Draw logical conclusions
- Identify the main idea
- Identify secondary ideas
- Identify the author's intent

The questions below are not the same as you will find on the CAEC - that would be too easy! And nobody knows what the questions will be and they change all the time. Mostly the changes consist of substituting new questions for old, but the changes can be new question formats or styles, changes to the number of questions in each section, changes to the time limits for each section and combining sections. Below are general reading questions that cover the same areas as the CAEC. So, while the format and exact wording of the questions may differ slightly, and change from year to year, if you can answer the questions below, you will have no problem with the reading section of the CAEC.

Social Studies Self-Assessment

The purpose of the self-assessment is:

- Identify your strengths and weaknesses.
- Develop your personalized study plan (above)
- Get accustomed to the CAEC format
- Extra practice – the self-assessments are almost a full 3rd practice test!
- Provide a baseline score for preparing your study schedule.

Since this is a Self-assessment, and depending on how confident you are with social studies, timing is optional. The self-assessment has 24 questions, so allow about 20 minutes to complete this assessment.

Once complete, use the table below to assess your understanding of the content, and prepare your study schedule described in chapter 1.

80% - 100%	Excellent – you have mastered the content
60 – 79%	Good. You have a working knowledge. Even though you can just pass this section, you may want to review the tutorials and do some extra practice to see if you can improve your mark.
40% - 59%	Below Average. You do not understand social studies problems. Review the tutorials , and retake this quiz again in a few days, before proceeding to the practice test questions.
Less than 40%	Poor. You have a very limited understanding of social studies problems. Please review the tutorials , and retake this quiz again in a few days, before proceeding to the practice test questions.

Answer Sheet

	A B C D E		A B C D E
1	○ ○ ○ ○ ○	21	○ ○ ○ ○ ○
2	○ ○ ○ ○ ○	22	○ ○ ○ ○ ○
3	○ ○ ○ ○ ○	23	○ ○ ○ ○ ○
4	○ ○ ○ ○ ○	24	○ ○ ○ ○ ○
5	○ ○ ○ ○ ○	25	○ ○ ○ ○ ○
6	○ ○ ○ ○ ○	26	○ ○ ○ ○ ○
7	○ ○ ○ ○ ○	27	○ ○ ○ ○ ○
8	○ ○ ○ ○ ○	28	○ ○ ○ ○ ○
9	○ ○ ○ ○ ○	29	○ ○ ○ ○ ○
10	○ ○ ○ ○ ○	30	○ ○ ○ ○ ○
11	○ ○ ○ ○ ○	31	○ ○ ○ ○ ○
12	○ ○ ○ ○ ○	32	○ ○ ○ ○ ○
13	○ ○ ○ ○ ○	33	○ ○ ○ ○ ○
14	○ ○ ○ ○ ○	34	○ ○ ○ ○ ○
15	○ ○ ○ ○ ○	35	○ ○ ○ ○ ○
16	○ ○ ○ ○ ○	36	○ ○ ○ ○ ○
17	○ ○ ○ ○ ○	37	○ ○ ○ ○ ○
18	○ ○ ○ ○ ○	38	○ ○ ○ ○ ○
19	○ ○ ○ ○ ○	39	○ ○ ○ ○ ○
20	○ ○ ○ ○ ○	40	○ ○ ○ ○ ○

Passage I - Languages

Questions 1 - 4 refer to the following passage

Canada consists of two major languages, English and French. Stemming from the early English and French-speaking Christian populations migrating from Europe, the dual-language system is at the center of Canadian education, business, and government. In fact, the Canadian government must, by law, provide all services in both English and French.

The 18 million Anglophone, those with English as their first language, make up most of Canada's population. Most of the 7 million Francophone, (about 10-15 percent of the population) those whose first language is French, live in Quebec, though many make their homes in Ontario, New Brunswick, and Manitoba. New Brunswick is the only officially bilingual province, where English and French serve as official languages.

1. What are the two official languages of Canada?

    a. Inuktitut and Michif
    b. English and Michif
    c. English and French
    d. French and Inuktitut

2. Who are the Anglophones?

    a. People whose first language is English
    b. People whose first language is French
    c. People whose first language is French and English
    d. People whose first language is neither French nor English

3. Who are Francophones?

    a. People whose first language is French
    b. People whose first language is English
    c. People whose first language is French and English
    d. People whose first language is neither French nor English

4. Where do most Francophones live?

    a. Quebec
    b. Ontario
    c. New Brunswick
    d. Manitoba

Passage 2 - The Intolerables Act

Questions 5 - 7 refer to the following passage

The Intolerable Acts were the American Patriots' term for a series of punitive laws passed by the British Parliament in 1774 after the Boston Tea Party. They were meant to punish the Massachusetts colonists for their defiance of throwing a large tea shipment into Boston Harbor in reaction to being taxed by the British. In Great Britain, these laws were called the Coercive Acts.

The acts took away Massachusetts' self-government and historic rights, triggering outrage and resistance in the Thirteen Colonies. They were key developments in the outbreak of the American Revolution in 1775.

Four of the acts were issued in direct response to the Boston Tea Party of December 1773; the British Parliament hoped these punitive measures would, by making an example of Massachusetts, reverse the trend of colonial resistance to parliamentary authority that had begun with the 1764 Sugar Act. A fifth act, the Quebec Act, enlarged the boundaries of what was then the Province of Quebec and instituted reforms generally favorable to the French Catholic inhabitants of the region; although unrelated to the other four Acts, it was passed in the same legislative session and seen by the colonists as one of the Intolerable Acts. The Patriots viewed the acts as an arbitrary violation of the rights of Massachusetts, and in September 1774 they organized the First Continental Congress to coordinate a protest. As tensions escalated, the American Revolutionary War broke out in April 1775, leading in July 1776 to the declaration of an independent United States of America.

5. Which one of these was not part of the Intolerable Acts?

    a. The Stamp Act

    b. The Townshed Acts

    c. The Tea Act

    d. The Foreign Trade Act

6. The British American colonists revolted because

    a. most colonists wanted to be free from British rule.

    b. most colonists wanted to be represented in Parliament.

    c. most colonists did not want to be taxed.

    d. All of the Above

7. Why did the British Parliament impose the first of the Intolerable Acts?

    a. To raise revenue for British Parliamentary salaries

    b. To pay for the British military in the American Colonies

    c. To make trade with non-British countries more expensive

    d. To fund the British military's ongoing war in India

Passage 3 - Structure of Government

Questions 8 - 10 refer to the following passage

Canada holds the traditional values of a *constitutional monarchy*, in which the Head of State is the Sovereign (King or Queen). The current Sovereign is Queen Elizabeth II. This individual rules according the Canada's Constitution, which is the document outlining the rule of law. The Sovereign's role varies, but generally Her Majesty is a symbol of Canadian heritage and a reflection of Canada's rich history.

A distinction must be made between the Sovereign, who is the head of state, and the Prime Minister, who is the head of government. Canada's Governor General serves as the Sovereign's representative, and his or her term is usually limited to five years. Lieutenant Governors serve as Sovereign representatives in each of the ten provinces.

Canada's government has three levels: federal, provincial and territorial/municipal. The interaction of these three branches, the Federal, Judicial, and Legislative branches is critical to Canadian democratic policy, and by working together they are able to secure the rights and freedoms of Canadian citizens.

8. What type of government does Canada have?

    a. Parliamentary Democracy
    b. Democratic Parliament
    c. House of Commons
    d. Federalism

9. What are the three branches of parliament?

    a. The Sovereign, Congress and Senate
    b. The Senate, Prime Minister and House of Commons
    c. The House of Commons, Senate and Sovereign
    d. President, Senate and House of Commons

10. Who serves as the Sovereign's representative in Canada?

    a. The Commissioner
    b. The Premier
    c. The Prime Minister
    d. Canada's Governor General

Questions 11 - 14 refer to the following cartoon

11. What is the author's purpose in this political cartoon?

a. The author wants to inform the audience that the president is working to put the union back together but that his actions might not be enough to heal the rift

b. The author wants to persuade the audience to forgive President Lincoln for splitting the union because he's working hard to put it back together.

c. The author wants to entertain the audience with a silly image of the President and Vice President

d. The author wants to inform the audience that the President and Vice President are plotting against the southern states and tying their fate to the union.

12. Published in 1865, what is the historical context for this political cartoon?

a. This cartoon depicts President Abe Lincoln and his Vice President trying the mend the rifts in the union to prevent Civil War.

b. This cartoon depicts President Abe Lincoln and his Vice President intentionally splitting the union to cause a civil war.

c. This cartoon depicts President Abe Lincoln intentionally splitting the union to cause a civil war while his Vice president works to keep that war from happening.

d. This cartoon depicts President Abe Lincoln and his Vice President attempting to repair the union after the civil war has ended.

13. What is the author's tone toward their subject?

a. The author is buoyant

b. The author is satirical

c. The author is elated

d. The author is accusatory

14. What is meant by the author's use of "The Rail-Splitter" in the title?

a. The author is using the term to point out the role that President Lincoln's election had in splitting the union.

b. The author is using the term to antagonize Lincoln and blame him for the Civil War

c. The author is using the term to refer to Lincoln's hard work in fighting the Civil War

d. The author is using the term to capitalize on the irony of the "rail-splitter" putting things back together.

Questions 15 - 16 refer to the following map

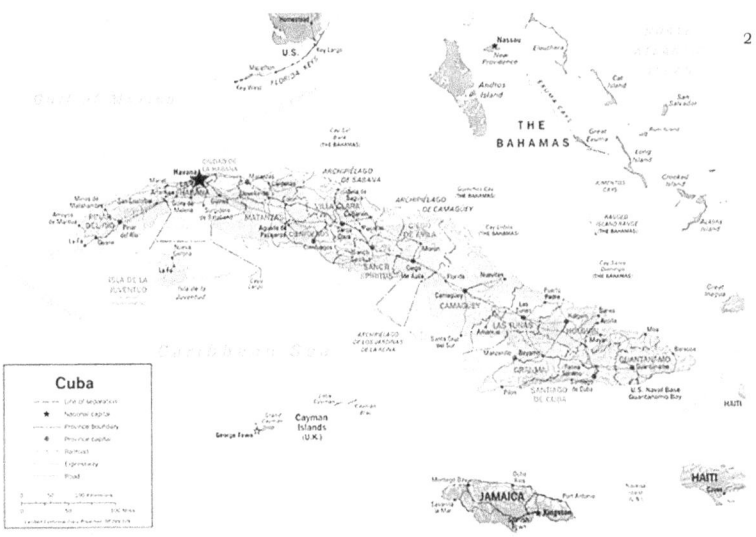

15. Where are the Cayman Islands located?

a. Windward Passage

b. Yucatan Channel

c. Gulf of Mexico

d. Caribbean Sea

16. Based on the map above, how is the Cuban Island separated

a. Into individual Nations

b. Into separate states

c. Into Providence States

d. Into Cities

Passage 4 - The Study of Geography

Questions 17 - 18 refer to the following passage

The systematic study of the Earth and the features within is known as geography. Geography is usually associated with place names and cartography. While it is true that most geographers receive training in cartography and toponymy, it is wrong to assume those are the main preoccupation of geographers. Geography includes the study of space, distribution of phenomena, the temporal database, processes and features. It is also a study of how man interacts with his physical environment. Geography is considered to be highly interdisciplinary because the subject of place and space affects several topics, such as health, animals, economics, climate and plants. The attentiveness paid to the relationship between human and physical phenomena and its spatial patterns would determine the interdisciplinary nature of the geographical approach. [3]

17. Based on the passage above what does a geographer study?

   a. Animal populations in the areas surrounding human settlements
   b. Crop production and yield
   c. Average rainfall yields over one year
   d. All of the above

18. Based on a context of the passage what is cartography?

   a. The study and creation of maps
   b. The study of rocks and where specific rock types can be found
   c. The study of the annual weather patterns for a specific place
   d. The study of the elevation

Microeconomics 1

Questions 19 - 20 refer to the following passage

Microeconomics studies how units that make up a market structure interact within that structure to form a market system. These units that make up a market structure would include public and private players under various classifications. The markets operate under governmental regulation and is characterized by a scarcity of tradable units. Items traded can be tangible such as furniture and cars, or can be a service rendered such as entertainment or repair services.

Theoretically, the aggregate quantity supplied would equal the aggregate quantity demanded in any free market. Over time, such a market would reach economic equilibrium as it reacts to changes in price. In the real world, however, several issues can prevent a market from reaching equilibrium, and even when reached the equilibrium may be morally inequitable. For example, external factors could limit the supply of health care services making the equilibrium price far too expensive for many who need it.[4]

19. Based on the text above, define equilibrium:

   a. Equilibrium is the base state, how a system exists when there are no external forces acting on it.

   b. Equilibrium is a state of balance achieved when opposite forces act with equal strength.

   c. Equilibrium is the idea that all the forces acting on a system must be equal for the system to be fair.

   d. Equilibrium is not achievable and therefore unnecessary to define

20. Which of the following best explains the relationship between supply and demand?

   a. As supply increases demand also increases

   b. As supply decreases demand increases

   c. Supply and demand differ based on the product

   d. Supply and demand differ based on the type of economy

21. Which group of people are considered the original inhabitants of Canada?

   a. Colonizers

   b. Immigrants

   c. Indigenous Peoples

   d. Explorers

22. When did Canada officially become a country through confederation?

   a. 1800s

   b. 1900s

   c. 1700s

   d. 1600s

23. Which major event led to a period of economic hardship known as the Great Depression in the 1930s?

   a. World War I
   b. World War II
   c. Cold War
   d. Stock Market Crash

24. Which social movement advocated for equal rights and opportunities for women in Canada?

   a. Civil Rights Movement
   b. Women's Liberation Movement
   c. Labor Movement
   d. Environmental Movement

25. Which historical period saw significant advancements in women's suffrage and labor laws in Canada?

   a. Victorian Era
   b. Industrial Revolution
   c. Roaring Twenties
   d. Progressive Era

26. Which document outlines the basic rights and freedoms of Canadian citizens?

   a. The Magna Carta
   b. The Canadian Charter of Rights and Freedoms
   c. The Declaration of Independence
   d. The Bill of Rights

27. What level of government deals with national matters like defense and immigration?

   a. Municipal Government
   b. Provincial Government
   c. Federal Government
   d. Parliamentary Government

28. Who is the head of government in Canada and leads the federal Cabinet?

    a. Mayor

    b. Premier

    c. Prime Minister

    d. Governor General

29. What type of democracy is practiced in Canada where citizens elect representatives to make decisions on their behalf?

    a. Direct Democracy

    b. Participatory Democracy

    c. Constitutional Monarchy

    d. Parliamentary Democracy

30. What responsibilities do Canadian citizens have that contribute to the wellbeing of the community?

    a. Paying Taxes

    b. Voting in Elections

    c. Obeying Laws

    d. All of the Above

31. What is the capital city of Canada?

    a. Toronto

    b. Vancouver

    c. Ottawa

    d. Montreal

32. Which province is known for its oil sands?

    a. Ontario

    b. Quebec

    c. Alberta

    d. British Columbia

33. What is the largest industry in Canada?

   a. Fishing

   b. Mining

   c. Technology

   d. Forestry

34. Which Canadian province or territory is the smallest in terms of land area?

   a. Yukon

   b. Prince Edward Island

   c. Nova Scotia

   d. Newfoundland and Labrador

35. What environmental issue is Canada actively working to address?

   a. Deforestation

   b. Water pollution

   c. Climate change

   d. Air pollution

36. Which international organization is Canada a member of?

   a. NATO

   b. United Nations

   c. ASEAN

   d. EU

37. What is a key aspect of Canada's foreign policy?

   a. Isolationism

   b. International cooperation

   c. Warfare

   d. Territorial expansion

38. Which Canadian province is the largest by land area?

   a. Ontario
   b. Quebec
   c. British Columbia
   d. Alberta

39. Who was the first prime minister of Canada?

   a. John A. Macdonald
   b. Wilfrid Laurier
   c. Pierre Trudeau
   d. Stephen Harper

40. When did Canada become a country?

   a. 1867
   b. 1901
   c. 1982
   d. 1957

Answer Key

1. C
Canada has two official languages, English and French.

2. A
Anglophones, or English speaking people, make up most Canada's population.

3. A
Francophones, or French speaking people, make up about 10-15 percent of Canada's population.

4. A
Most of the 7 million Francophone, those whose first language is French, live in Quebec.

5. D
The Foreign Trade Act did not take place until centuries after the American Revolutionary War. All the Intolerable Acts took place in the lead-up to the American Revolutionary War.

Choice A is incorrect; the Stamp Act imposed a tax on the colonies by forcing them to use paper produced in Britain for many printed materials. This was the first of the Intolerable Acts or taxes that were placed on British American subjects without their consent.

Choice B is incorrect; the Townshed Acts were also part of the Intolerable Acts that were meant to raise revenue in the colonies for the employment of judges and governors. These were also used to punish colonists and force compliance with the numerous other taxes being levied against the colonies.

Choice C is incorrect; the Tea Act allowed the British East India Company to sell tea directly to the colonies, thus making it cheaper. Many colonists hated this act because a small tax was added without their consent, which resulted in the Boston Tea Party.

6. B
The British imposed taxes through the Intolerable Acts either without representation from the colonies at all, or with representatives that effectively had no say in the matter.

Choice A is incorrect; even during the American Revolutionary War, most of the colonists did not decisively want to be free from British rule; they either wanted to stay under British rule, or were undecided.

Choice C is incorrect; while Colonists and people everywhere do not like to be taxed, most realized taxes were what allowed government to function and the colonists made no statements against ALL taxes, just some of them.

Social Studies

7. B

After the Seven Years War with France, Great Britain had a lot of debt and Parliament wanted the colonies to pay for some of the military expenditures and the cost of maintaining a military presence in the colonies.

Choice A is incorrect; None of the Intolerable Acts were used to raise revenue for the British Parliament salaries. The Intolerable Acts were used to pay off war debt, punish the colonies, and a variety of other things.

Choice C is incorrect; the Navigation Acts kept most trade in the British Colonies strictly between the colonies and Great Britain.

Choice D is incorrect; while the East India Company was fighting in India at this time, the British military was not involved there yet.

8. A

Canada's government is known as a Parliamentary Democracy.

9. C

These three branches of government are the Sovereign (King or Queen), the Senate, and the House of Commons.

10. D

Canada's Governor General serves as the Sovereign's representative, for a term, usually limited to five years.

11. A

While the author has some concerns about its effectiveness, this political cartoon was created as a commentary on the success of reconstruction efforts, like the Ten Percent Plan.
Choice B is incorrect because the tone of the piece is not forgiving and the piece is focused on satirizing the reconstruction efforts.
Choice C is incorrect because the purpose of political cartoons is not for entertainment
Choice D is incorrect because the tone of the caricatures is not malicious or plotting.

12. D

In 1865 the Civil War was drawing to a close and the President and Vice President were already working on the implementation of Reconstruction legislation to bring the southern states back into the union, depicted here as sewing the rift in the union back together.
Choice A is incorrect because the war had already occurred by 1865 and therefore cannot be prevented.
Choice B is incorrect because the President and Vice President are clearly depicted attempting to fix a tear that already exists, not to create one themselves.
Choice C is incorrect because the President is not creating new tears, but holding the country steady so that they can be repaired, as indicated by the Vice President's dialogue.

13. B
While the author is perhaps hopeful for the future of the union, he's created this piece to point out the flaws in the reconstruction legislation (the messy stitches) and the struggle that will exist in rejoining the union (Lincoln needing the keep the country steady). He's also capitalizing on irony in the title of the piece by noting that Lincoln was called the Rail-Splitter President but instead of splitting the union he's trying to mend it.
Choice A is incorrect because buoyant is often used to indicate those who recover quickly from setbacks, the author's tone is not entirely hopeful that the Reconstruction measures will work, as signified by the messy stitches on the jagged tear in the union.
Choice C is incorrect because the author is hopeful, perhaps, for the future of the union, he recognizes that there are problems ahead and he's definitely capitalizing on the irony surrounding the President, not distracted by his own joy.
Choice D is incorrect because the author has some doubts about the future of the union there isn't a wrong he's accusing the President of having committed.

14. D
The author is capitalizing on the irony of President Lincoln's election moniker to highlight the issues that will exist in reconstruction.
Choice A is incorrect because the focus of this piece is on the reconstruction of the union, not its demise.
Choice B is incorrect because the author of the political cartoon notes issues ahead, he's not attempting to directly antagonize the president. Instead he's reminding the president that he must keep the union steady if progress is to be made.
Choice C is incorrect because rail splitting is hard work, the focus of this piece is on reconstruction, not the war itself.

15. D
The Cayman Islands are located in the Caribbean Sea.

16. C
Choice C is correct based on the map key.
Choice A is incorrect. The map key indicates that Cuba is separated into provinces.
Choice B is incorrect. While the division may look like states, students need to reference the map key for appropriate terminology.
Choice D is incorrect because cities are clearly distinguished in other ways.

17. D
Based on the passage all these topics might interest a geographer, therefore the best answer is choice D, All of the above

18. A
Cartography is the study of map making.
Choice B is incorrect. The study of rock types and where specific rock types can be found is called geology
Choice C is incorrect. The study of weather is called meteorology.
Choice D is incorrect. The study of elevation is called topography.

19. B
Equilibrium is a state of balance achieved when opposite forces act with equal strength.

20. B
As supply decreases there is less product to fill demand, so demand increases.
Choice A is incorrect. Supply and demand forms a curve. One increasing will always meant that the other decreases.
Choice C is incorrect. The idea of supply and demand are not impacted by the type of product.
Choice D is incorrect. Supply and Demand are a constant. While certain economies can artificially impact supply and demand (Communism for example) those impacts don't change the relationship between supply and demand.

21. C
The correct answer is Indigenous Peoples because they were the first people to live in Canada, with a rich history and culture that predates colonization.

22. A
The correct answer is 1800s as Canada became a country through confederation in 1867.

23. D
The correct answer is Stock Market Crash as it triggered the Great Depression by causing widespread unemployment and economic instability.

24. B
The correct answer is Women's Liberation Movement as it aimed to achieve gender equality and address issues such as workplace discrimination and reproductive rights.

25. D
The correct answer is Progressive Era as it was marked by reforms that improved working conditions, expanded voting rights, and promoted social justice.

26. B
The correct answer is The Canadian Charter of Rights and Freedoms. It is a part of the Canadian Constitution that guarantees fundamental rights and freedoms to all Canadians.

27. C
The correct answer is Federal Government. It has the authority to make decisions on issues that affect the whole country, such as defense and immigration.

28. C

The correct answer is Prime Minister. The Prime Minister is the head of government in Canada and leads the federal Cabinet in making important decisions for the country.

29. D

The correct answer is Parliamentary Democracy. In this system, citizens elect representatives to Parliament who then make decisions and pass laws on behalf of the people.

30. D

The correct answer is All of the Above. Canadian citizens have responsibilities like paying taxes, voting in elections, and obeying laws, which collectively contribute to the wellbeing of the community.

31. C

The correct answer is Ottawa. Ottawa is the capital city of Canada where the Parliament of Canada is located.

32. C

The correct answer is Alberta. Alberta is known for its oil sands, which are a major natural resource in the province.

33. B

The correct answer is Mining. Mining is one of the major industries in Canada, contributing significantly to the economy.

34. B

The correct answer is Prince Edward Island. Prince Edward Island is the smallest province in Canada in terms of land area.

35. C

The correct answer is Climate change. Canada has been focusing on efforts to address climate change through various policies and initiatives.

36. B

The correct answer is the United Nations. Canada has been a member of the United Nations since its establishment in 1945, playing an active role in global affairs through this organization.

37. B

The correct answer is International cooperation. Canada's foreign policy emphasizes diplomacy, peacekeeping, and working collaboratively with other nations to address global challenges.

38. C

The correct answer is British Columbia because it covers a total land area of approximately 944,735 square kilometers.

39. A

The correct answer is John A. Macdonald as he served as the prime minister from 1867 to 1873 and again from 1878 to 1891.

40. A

The correct answer is 1867 because that is when the Constitution Act united the three colonies into the Dominion of Canada.

Milestones in Canadian History

The Canadian Confederation (1867): The Confederation of Canada brought together the provinces of Ontario, Quebec, New Brunswick, and Nova Scotia to form the Dominion of Canada, laying the foundation for the country we know today.

The Completion of the Canadian Pacific Railway (1885): The completion of the CPR connected the east and west coasts of Canada, facilitating transportation and trade across the vast country and significantly impacting Canada's economic development.

The Battle of Vimy Ridge (1917): In World War I, Canadian forces achieved a significant victory at the Battle of Vimy Ridge in France, where they displayed exceptional skill and bravery, helping to forge a stronger sense of national identity among Canadians.

The Statute of Westminster (1931): The Statute of Westminster granted Canada greater independence from Britain, giving it more control over its own affairs and paving the way for the evolution of Canada as a fully sovereign nation.

The Quiet Revolution (1960s): A period of rapid social, cultural, and political change in Quebec, the Quiet Revolution saw significant shifts in areas such as education, healthcare, and language, leading to a redefinition of Quebec's role within Canada.

The Patriation of the Constitution (1982): With the passage of the Constitution Act, 1982, Canada gained full control over its constitution, including the Charter of Rights and Freedoms, marking a crucial milestone in the country's journey towards greater autonomy and self-governance.

The Official Recognition of Indigenous Rights (2016): The Truth and Reconciliation Commission called for the recognition of Indigenous rights, leading to the official acknowledgment of Indigenous peoples' inherent rights and the need for reconciliation, marking a significant step towards addressing historical injustices in Canada.

Canadian Government - Overview

Introduction
In this chapter, we will cover the key aspects of the Canadian government system, including its structure, constitution, levels of government, political system, laws, and citizenship.

Canadian Government and Politics
The Canadian government operates within a framework that combines elements of parliamentary democracy and constitutional monarchy. It is based on the principles of representative democracy, where elected officials make decisions on behalf of the people.

Constitution and Charter of Rights and Freedoms
The Canadian Constitution outlines the country's fundamental laws and principles. It includes the Charter of Rights and Freedoms, which guarantees certain rights and freedoms to all Canadians, such as freedom of speech, religion, and assembly.

Levels of Government
Canada has three main levels of government: federal, provincial, and municipal. Each level has its own responsibilities and functions. The federal government deals with national issues, while provincial governments handle matters within their respective provinces. Municipal governments focus on local community needs.

Political System
Canada operates under a parliamentary democracy, where the government is elected by the people and accountable to the elected representatives in Parliament. The Prime Minister is the head of government, while the Governor General represents the monarch. The electoral process involves regular elections to choose representatives at the federal, provincial, and municipal levels.

Laws and Citizenship
Canadian citizens have certain rights and responsibilities under the law. These include the right to vote, freedom of expression, and the obligation to obey the law. Understanding these rights and responsibilities is essential for active participation in the democratic process.

Canadian History - An Overview

The Aboriginals

The earliest settlers of Canada, the First Peoples, were dependant on the land for their livelihood. Hunters, fisherman, and farmers by trade, the First Nations were masters of their environment. As they sought more resources for growing populations, war became common as tribes came into contact. Groups competed, and tribes grew, but when the Europeans arrived, everything changed.

The arrival of the Europeans brought new products and the possibility of trade, but it also brought disease. Early on, huge populations of the First Nations died. As their interactions continued, however, the onset of diseases decreased and the bonds of trade were formed. European traders, missionaries, and soldiers arrived year after year, laying the foundation for the future of Canada.

The Europeans

The Vikings were the first Europeans to land on what was to become Canadian shores. The remains of their first settlements can still be seen today. These seafarers, who also likely settled Greenland, landed in Labrador and Newfoundland. The Vikings were only the beginning.

European exploration of Canada began in 1497. John Cabot was the first to map Canada's Eastern shore, and less than a century later, another famous explorer, Jacques Cartier, led three more expeditions across the Atlantic to what is today Eastern Canada. Cartier claimed the land for King Francis I of France and on hearing the Iroquois word, *kanata,* ('village'), the land came to be known as Canada.

Royal New France

The first European settlement of what is now Canada, was established by French explorers Pierre de Monts and Samuel de Champlain. These settlements, built in the Bay of Fundy on Île Ste-Croix (Dochet Island) on what's now the Maine-New Brunswick border. This settlement did not survive the harsh winter, and was followed by a settlement at Port-Royal, in Acadia, today, Nova Scotia.

These settlements were followed in 1608 by a fortress in what is now Québec City. With the allegiance of several local Aboriginal tribes, the Algonquin, Montagnais, and Huron, the French colonists were able to survive harsh conditions and establish a healthy trade with the First Nations. This alliance allowed the French to expand, and eventually, gaining control of vast tracts of lands stretching from the Hudson Bay to the Gulf of Mexico.

Early Struggles

While France controlled trade near the Hudson Bay area, England was encroaching into their territory. Tensions were high as the Hudson's Bay Trading Company, given exclusive rights by the King Charles the II of England in 1670, began competing with other trading companies in Montreal. England's hold on the East coast grew quickly and it was soon too powerful for the struggling New France. Tensions build, and in the 18th century, things finally reached a head.

England won a decisive victory in the Battle of the Plains of Abraham at Québec city in 1759, ending the reign of France in Canada and North America. The British renamed the (French) colony at Québec City, now under British administration, "The Province of Quebec," and the French who lived there, Canadiens.

British Accommodation

After their defeat at the hands of the British, the French population in Québec City was still a majority in the new province. To govern this population, most whom were also Catholic, the British government passed the Quebec Act in 1774. This act served as a middle ground and gave the French Catholics religious freedom and allowed them to run for public office, which was not even possible in Great Britain. The Quebec Act also gave the French the opportunity to exercise civil law, while still being governed by British criminal law.

The American Revolution

In 1776, 13 British colonies to the south of Quebec declared independence from the British. Those who were still loyal to Great Britain, called *Loyalists*, fled to Nova Scotia and Quebec. This group of more than 40,000, consisted of a variety of ethnic, linguistic, and religious backgrounds. 3,000 black Loyalists also moved north, fleeing the ongoing conflict. Some of these black Loyalists, former slaves, founded Freetown, Sierra Leone, a West African colony for freed slaves.

Democracy: The beginning

Establishing democracy, normally a long and bloody process, was for Canada gradual and peaceful. 1758 saw the first representative assembly elected in Halifax, Nova Scotia. Similar elections took place shortly thereafter, including Prince Edward Island (1773) and New Brunswick (1785). Later, the Province of Quebec was split by the *Constitutional Act* (1791) into Lower Canada (present-day Ontario) and Upper Canada (present-day Quebec). In Lower Canada, English-speaking Protestant Loyalists made their homes, and in Upper Canada, French-speaking Catholics. The *Constitutional Act* also formalized the name *Canada*, and gave the people the power to elect legislative assemblies.

The End of Slavery

The process of putting an end to slavery, known as Abolition, began in Canada in the late 18th century. General John Graves Simcoe, a Loyalist military officer, began the push toward Abolition in Upper Canada in 1793. In the following years, the British Parliament would prohibit the buying and selling of slaves and 1883 slavery was abolished in the British Empire. As a result, thousands of slaves from America escaped and headed north into Canada.

Economic Growth

Early on, the fur trade was the most prominent form of business in Canada. The demand for beaver pelts was especially high for Europeans, and the only supply came from North America. The Hudson's Bay Company was largely in command of this lucrative trade, with outposts from Fort Garry (Winnipeg) to Fort Langley (Vancouver). In the 18th and 19th centuries, financial institutions were opened, and in 1832 the Montreal Stock Exchange was established. These new economic developments helped Canada grow, but most people still depended on farming, fishing, and logging to make a living.

The War of 1812

By the 19th century, Canada was becoming an increasingly powerful part of the British Empire. While the British were fighting off Napoleon Bonaparte, the Americans were devising a plan to conquer Canada. Angry at Britain's interference with trade lanes to Europe, the Americans launched an attack on Canada in 1812. Canada was ready, however, and with the help of the First Nations and, in particular, Shawnee chief Tecumseh, the Canadians defeated the Americans. Over the next few years the Canadians and Americans led brief raids into each other's territory, but the Americans eventually came to respect the Canada's resilience.

Rebellion

Canadian democracy was growing, but not fast enough for some. In 1837-8, rebels attacked areas near Montreal and Toronto. Many of these rebels demanded the republican values of America, and some even wanted to become a part of their southern neighbor. These rebels were unable to overcome British soldiers and Canadian volunteers, however, and many of them were exiled or hanged for their crimes.
The reformer Lord Durham, an Englishman sent to relay news of the rebellion, suggested that Upper and Lower Canada become one, governed by what he termed a "responsible government." This meant that British rule must have the support of most representatives to govern. He also believed that uniting the people in common language (English) and religion (Protestant) were the keys to growing the new country of Canada.

Responsible Government

Upper and Lower Canada were united in 1840, forming the Province of Canada. The reformers Sir Louis-Hippolyte La Fontaine, Robert Baldwin, and Nova Scotia's Joseph Howe, were important figures in developing responsible government. Nova Scotia was the first British North American colony to adopt full responsible government (1847-8). The same system is alive today, wherein the assembly must hold full confidence in the government, which would otherwise be forced to resign.

Confederation

From 1864 to 1867, Canadian representatives were working hard to establish a new country. Known as the Fathers of Confederation, these men advanced with the full support of the British government. Two levels of government, federal and provincial, were formed, and the Province of Canada was divided into Ontario and Quebec. Along with New Brunswick and Nova Scotia, these newly independent provinces formed the Dominion of Canada. Each province had control over its own legislature, but major democratic issues would be dealt with together.

On July 1, 1867 the British Parliament passed the *Constitution Act* - formerly known as the *British North America Act*, which officially named the Dominion of Canada an independent country. Canada Day, formerly Dominion Day, is a national statutory holiday celebrated in all provinces and territories and a day off for most businesses.

Canada's first prime minister was named in 1867. Scotland-born Sir John Alexander Macdonald had come to Canada as a child. A lawyer and a gifted politician, Macdonald was known for his colorful personality and if you have a $10 bill, you will see his portrait.

The West

In 1869, soon after the Dominion of Canada was formed, Métis tribes from the interior captured Fort Garry and threatened the newly formed country of Canada. Because they were not consulted when Canada took over the Northwest region from the Hudson's Bay Company, these 12,000 Aboriginals prepared for battle. Ottawa met the challenge in 1870, sending soldiers to retake Fort Garry and to restore the West. The leader of the uprising, Louis Riel, was defeated and Canada formed a new province, Manitoba. When the rights of the Métis and Indigenous tribes were again threatened in the late 19th century, Riel again staged a revolt. Louis Riel was executed for high treason in 1885. He is still seen as defender of Métis and Indigenous rights.

The Métis uprising forced Prime Minister Macdonald to fortify the Western frontier. As a result, the North West Mounted Police (NWMP) was formed in 1873. Their goal was to negotiate and establish peace, and in the process, the NWMP established forts that have since grown into major cities and towns. Today, the Royal Canadian Mounted Police (RCMP) are Canada's national police force and one of the most recognizable symbols of Canadian authority.

Along with a national police force, joining the East and West by railroad was another major development of the late 19th century. Ottawa promised to construct a railroad that reached to the West Coast, and this agreement prompted British Columbia to join Canada in 1871. British and American investors financed the new railroad, and European and Chinese labor built it. The Canadian Pacific Railway was finished in 1885. The CPR is a symbol of Canadian unification and the work of the laborers who built it is still remembered today.

Into the West

The end of the 19th century and the beginning of the 20th century were periods of extreme growth in Canada. An estimated 2 million British and American immigrants made their way into Canada over a period of roughly twenty years. Sir Wilfrid Laurier, the first French-Canadian Prime Minister, whose portrait is on the $5 bill, encouraged a westward migration. The railway made it possible for hundreds of thousands to move West, and it did not take long for a thriving agricultural center to develop.

World War I

When Britain declared war on Germany in 1914, Ottawa formed the Canadian Expeditionary Force of over 600,000 men, mostly volunteers. These Canadian forces proved their valor and in April of 1917, they were instrumental in capturing Vimy Ridge in France. This great victory showed the world that Canada was truly united.

The Canadian Corps, formerly the Canadian Expeditionary Force, was also a major contributor in other major victories throughout the final stages of the World War I. When the war ended in 1918, Canada had gained loyalty from its allies and a new-found national pride from its citizens. Canadians remember veterans each year on November 11th, called "Remembrance Day."

Voting Rights for Women

Early on, voting in the Confederation was the right of white male property owners only. This was common in all democracies in the early 20th century. The right to vote, or women's suffrage, was initiated by Dr. Emily Stowe, the first woman to practice the medicine in Canada. Through her determination, Manitoba granted women the right to vote in 1916.

In the years following, women continued to gain further voting rights. By 1918, most women over the age of 21 were allowed to vote in federal elections. In 1921, the first female Member of Parliament, Agnes Macphail, a farmer and a teacher, was elected.

Post-World War I

Following World War I, the British Empire became the British Commonwealth of Nations, an association of free states. Canada continues to play a key role in this association, along with other states of the Empire such as India and Australia.

The 1920's were a time of great success in Canada, with low unemployment and booming business. The Stock Market Crash of 1929, however, had a devastating effect on Canada's economy and led to the Great Depression. In 1933 over a quarter of the population was unemployed and many businesses were forced to close. Furthermore, in the West, a terrible drought coupled with low grain prices destroyed commerce.

These difficulties set the stage for widespread demands for a government instituted program that would serve as a safety net. A set minimum wage, unemployment insurance, and a central bank were all part of this plan. The Bank of Canada was established in 1934, which brought stability to the failing economy.

World War II

When Hitler forced the world into war in 1939, Canada joined its allies in a fight against tyranny and oppression. Over one million Canadians served in the war, and about 44,000 of these died. The Royal Canadian Air Force (RCAF) provided bombers and fighter planes in the Battle of Britain, and the Royal Canadian Navy (RCN) played a key role in the war at sea. By the end of the war, Canada's Navy had grown into the third largest in the world.

In the Pacific, Japan attacked Canadian occupied Vancouver and British Columbia. After four years of war in the Pacific, Japan eventually surrendered in 1945. Following the war, Canadians of Japanese descent were treated harshly and many were forced to relocate. In 1988, the Government of Canada apologized for this wartime treatment.

Overview of Concepts in Basic Economics

Basic Economics
Economics is the study of how individuals and societies manage scarce resources. It helps us understand decision-making processes and the allocation of resources to meet needs and wants.

Example:
When a person decides between buying a new phone or saving for a vacation, they are making an economic decision based on limited money.

Supply and Demand
Supply and demand are fundamental concepts that describe how goods and services are allocated in a market.

Example:
If a new video game console is released (increased demand) but the manufacturer can only produce a limited number (limited supply), the price of the console will likely rise due to high demand and low supply.

Recessions and Depressions
A recession is a period of economic decline typically defined as two consecutive quarters of negative GDP growth. A depression is a more severe and prolonged downturn.

Example:
During the 2008 financial crisis, many people lost their jobs, businesses closed, and the economy shrank significantly. This was a recession; if it had lasted longer and caused deeper economic pain, it could have been classified as a depression.

Market Failure
Market failure occurs when the allocation of goods and services is not efficient, often due to externalities, public goods, or monopolies.

Example:
Pollution from factories is a negative externality. If a factory pollutes a river, it affects everyone living nearby, but the factory does not bear the full cost of this damage, leading to overproduction of harmful goods.

The Firm
A firm is an organization that produces goods or services to sell them in the market. Firms aim to maximize profits by efficiently utilizing resources.

Example:
A local bakery decides to increase production of cookies because they are selling well, thus maximizing its profits by meeting consumer demand.

Basic Concepts in Macroeconomics
Macroeconomics studies the economy as a whole, focusing on large-scale economic factors like national productivity, unemployment rates, and inflation.

Example:
Governments track unemployment rates to understand how many people are without jobs and to formulate policies to stimulate job creation.

Basic Concepts in Microeconomics
Microeconomics focuses on individual consumers and businesses, analyzing how they make decisions and interact in markets.

Example:
If the price of apples rises, consumers may decide to buy fewer apples and substitute them with oranges, demonstrating how price changes affect individual purchasing behavior.

Reading

This section contains a self-assessment and reading tutorial. The tutorials are designed to familiarize general principles and the self-assessment contains general questions similar to the reading questions likely to be on the CAEC, but are not intended to be identical to the exam questions. The tutorials are not designed to be a complete reading course, and it is assumed that students have some familiarity with social studies questions. If you do not understand parts of the tutorial, or find the tutorial difficult, it is recommended that you seek out additional instruction.

Note that these questions are for skill practice only.

Tour of the CAEC Reading Content

Below is a detailed list of the types of questions that generally appear on the CAEC.

- Draw logical conclusions
- Identify the main idea
- Identify secondary ideas
- Identify the author's intent

The questions below are not the same as you will find on the CAEC - that would be too easy! And nobody knows what the questions will be and they change all the time. Mostly the changes consist of substituting new questions for old, but the changes can be new question formats or styles, changes to the number of questions in each section, changes to the time limits for each section and combining sections. Below are general reading questions that cover the same areas as the CAEC. So, while the format and exact wording of the questions may differ slightly, and change from year to year, if you can answer the questions below, you will have no problem with the reading section of the CAEC.

Reading Self-Assessment

The purpose of the self-assessment is:

- Identify your strengths and weaknesses.
- Develop your personalized study plan (above)
- Get accustomed to the CAEC format
- Extra practice – the self-assessments are almost a full 3rd practice test!
- Provide a baseline score for preparing your study schedule.

Reading

Since this is a Self-assessment, and depending on how confident you are with reading comprehension, timing is optional. The self-assessment has 24 questions, so allow about 20 minutes to complete this assessment.

Once complete, use the table below to assess your understanding of the content, and prepare your study schedule described in chapter 1.

Self Assessment Answer Sheet

	A	B	C	D
1	○	○	○	○
2	○	○	○	○
3	○	○	○	○
4	○	○	○	○
5	○	○	○	○
6	○	○	○	○
7	○	○	○	○
8	○	○	○	○
9	○	○	○	○
10	○	○	○	○
11	○	○	○	○
12	○	○	○	○
13	○	○	○	○
14	○	○	○	○
15	○	○	○	○

Passage 1

Questions 1 - 2 refer to the following passage

Howard's End

E. M. Forster

This long letter is because I'm writing before breakfast. Oh, the beautiful vine leaves! The house is covered with a vine. I looked out earlier, and Mrs. Wilcox was already in the garden. She evidently loves it. No wonder she sometimes looks tired. She was watching the large red poppies come out. Then she walked off the lawn to the meadow, whose corner to the right I can just see.

Trail, trail, went her long dress over the sopping grass, and she came back with her hands full of the hay that was cut yesterday--I suppose for rabbits or something, as she
kept on smelling it. The air here is delicious. Later on I heard the noise of croquet balls, and looked out again, and it was Charles Wilcox practicing; they are keen on all games. Presently he started sneezing and had to stop. Then I hear more clicketing, and it is Mr. Wilcox practising, and then, 'a-tissue, a-tissue': he has to stop too. Then Evie comes out, and does some calisthenic exercises on a machine that is tacked on to a greengage-tree--they put everything to use--and then she says 'a-tissue,' and in she goes.

And finally Mrs. Wilcox reappears, trail, trail, still smelling hay and looking at the flowers. I inflict all this on you because once you said that life is sometimes life and sometimes only a drama, and one must learn to distinguish t'other from which, and up to now I have always put that down as 'Meg's clever nonsense.' But this morning, it really does seem not life but a play, and it did amuse me enormously to watch the W's. Now Mrs. Wilcox has come in.

1. The most compelling evidence the narrator gives that his environment "does seem not life but a play" is:

    a. Mrs. Wilcox's love of the garden.

    b. The bucolic, natural scenery.

    c. The activities of the Wilcox family.

    d. His persistent focus on smells.

2. In his letter, the narrator's tone is mainly:

    a. Romantic

    b. Ecstatic

    c. Apologetic

    d. Cheerful

Passage 2 - The Thirty-Nine Steps

John Buchan

Questions 3 - 5 refer to the following passage

I did not give him very close attention. The fact is, I was more interested in his own adventures than in his high politics. I reckoned that Karolides and his affairs were not my business, leaving all that to him. So a lot that he said slipped clean out of my memory.

I remember that he was very clear that the danger to Karolides would not begin till he had got to London, and would come from the very highest quarters, where there would be no thought of suspicion. He mentioned the name of a woman--Julia Czechenyi--as having something to do with
the danger. She would be the decoy, I gathered, to get Karolides out of the care of his guards. He talked, too, about a Black Stone and a man that lisped in his speech, and he described very particularly somebody that he never referred to without a shudder--an old man with a young voice who could hood his eyes like a hawk.

He spoke a good deal about death, too. He was mortally anxious about winning through with his job, but he didn't care a rush for his life.

'I reckon it's like going to sleep when you are pretty well tired out, and waking to find a summer day with the scent of hay coming in at the window. I used to thank God for such mornings way back in the Blue-Grass country, and I guess I'll thank Him when I wake up on the other side of Jordan.'

Next day he was much more cheerful, and read the life of Stonewall Jackson much of the time. I went out to dinner with a mining engineer I had got to see on business, and came back about half-past ten in time for our game of chess before turning in.

3. What does the following line analogize? "I reckon it's like going to sleep when you are pretty well tired out, and waking to find a summer day with the scent of hay coming in at the window."

 a. What the narrator imagines the experience of death to be like.

 b. The sensation of "winning through" with one's job.

 c. The speaker is describing his fluctuating mood as the danger to Karolides approaches.

 d. What the narrator's companion imagines the experience of death to be like.

4. It can be inferred from the passage that Karolides:

   a. Is a woman

   b. Is the narrator's companion

   c. Is presently in danger

   d. Will be threatened by surreptitious forces

5. The narrator's greater interest in his companion's "adventures than in his high politics" suggests that:

   a. The narrator is not a political man.

   b. The narrator is indifferent to his companion.

   c. The narrator is a man of action.

   d. More can be learned from the companion's description of events than his personal beliefs for committing to a cause.

Passage 3 - A Man of Means

P. G. Wodehouse and C. H. Bovill

Questions 6 - 9 refer to the following passage

For some months after his arrival, Muriel had been to Roland Bleke a mere automaton, a something outside himself that was made only for neatly-laid breakfast tables and silent removal of plates at dinner.

Gradually, however, when his natural shyness was soothed by use sufficiently to enable him to look at her when she came into the room, he discovered that she was a strikingly pretty girl, bounded to the North by a mass of auburn hair and to the South by small and shapely feet. She also possessed what, we are informed--we are children in these
matters ourselves--is known as the R. S. V. P. eye. This eye had met Roland's one evening, as he chumped his chop, and before he knew what he was doing he had remarked that it had been a fine day.

From that wonderful moment matters had developed at an incredible speed. Roland had a nice sense of the social proprieties, and he could not bring himself to ignore a girl with whom he had once exchanged easy conversation about the weather. Whenever she came to lay his table, he felt bound to say something. Not being an experienced gagger, he found
it more and more difficult each evening to hit on something bright, until finally, from sheer lack of inspiration, he kissed her.

If matters had progressed rapidly before, they went like lightning then. It was as if he had touched a spring or pressed a button, setting vast machinery in motion. Even as he reeled back stunned at his audacity, the room became suddenly full of Coppins of every variety known to science.

Through a mist he was aware of Mrs. Coppin crying in a corner, of Mr. Coppin drinking his health in the remains of sparkling limado, of Brothers Frank and Percy, one on each side trying to borrow simultaneously half-crowns, and of Muriel, flushed but demure, making bread-pellets and throwing them in an abstracted way, one by one, at the Coppin cat, which had wandered in on the chance of fish.

6. Muriel's R.S.V.P. eye impels Roland to:

   a. Speak

   b. Fall in love with her

   d. Gradually see her in a different light

   d. Kiss her

7. Which of the following best summarizes the reason Roland and Muriel's first kiss comes about?

   a. Roland is not experienced at kissing, and wants to practice.

   b. Roland is a man not of words, but of action.

   c. Roland intends to marry her.

   d. Roland is unimaginative.

8. What best describes the "machinery" that Roland sets in motion?

   a. The complexity of his relationship with Muriel.

   b. The course of his relationship with Muriel, independent of his own agency.

   c. The Coppins' scheme for Roland and Muriel's marriage.

   d. The speed at which Roland is integrated into the Coppins' family.

9. An appropriate summary of this passage would be:

   a. A man changes his dreams and aligns himself with a powerful, if dysfunctional, family.

   b. Without particular direction or intent, a man stumbles into a bizarre relationship.

   c. An astute girl helps a shy man overcome his awkwardness.

   d. The unwillingness of the protagonist is used to exemplify the dangers of marriage.

   e. An ordinary man is vexed by the seductive qualities of a country girl.

Passage 4 - Low Blood Sugar

Questions 10 - 13 refer to the following passage

As the name suggest, low blood sugar is low sugar levels in the bloodstream. This can occur when you have not eaten properly and undertake strenuous activity, or when you are very hungry. When Low blood sugar occurs regularly and is ongoing, it is a medical condition called hypoglycemia. This condition can occur in diabetics and in healthy adults.

Causes of low blood sugar can include excessive alcohol consumption, metabolic problems, stomach surgery, pancreas, liver or kidneys problems, as well as a side-effect of some medications.

Symptoms

There are different symptoms depending on the severity of the case.

Mild hypoglycemia can lead to feelings of nausea and hunger. The patient may also feel nervous, jittery and have fast heart beats. Sweaty skin, clammy and cold skin are likely symptoms.

Moderate hypoglycemia can result in a short tempered, confusion, nervousness, fear and blurring of vision. The patient may feel weak and unsteady.

Severe cases of hypoglycemia can lead to seizures, coma, fainting spells, night-mares, headaches, excessive sweats and severe tiredness.

Diagnosis of low blood sugar

A doctor can diagnosis this medical condition by asking the patient questions and testing blood and urine samples. Home testing kits are available for patients to monitor blood sugar levels. It is important to see a qualified doctor though. The doctor can administer tests to ensure that will safely rule out other medical conditions that could affect blood sugar levels.

Treatment

Quick treatments include drinking or eating foods and drinks with high sugar contents. Good examples include soda, fruit juice, hard candy and raisins. Glucose energy tablets can also help. Doctors may also recommend medications and well as changes in diet and exercise routine to treat chronic low blood sugar.

10. Based on the article, which of the following is true?

    a. Low blood sugar can happen to anyone.

    b. Low blood sugar only happens to diabetics.

    c. Low blood sugar can occur even.

    d. None of the statements are true.

11. Which of the following are the author's opinion?

a. Quick treatments include drinking or eating foods and drinks with high sugar contents.

b. None of the statements are opinions.

c. This condition can occur in diabetics and in healthy adults.

d. There are different symptoms depending on the severity of the case

12. What is the author's purpose?

a. To inform
b. To persuade
c. To entertain
d. To analyze

13. Which of the following is not a detail?

a. A doctor can diagnosis this medical condition by asking the patient questions and testing.

b. A doctor will test blood and urine samples.

c. Glucose energy tablets can also help.

d. Home test kits monitor blood sugar levels.

Passage 5 - Email

Questions 14 – 15 refer to the following email.

Subject: Medical Staff Changes

To all staff:

This email is to advise you of a paper on recommended medical staff changes has been posted to the Human Resources website.

The contents are of primary interest to medical staff, other staff may be interested in reading it, particularly those in medical support roles.

The paper deals with several major issues:

1. Improving our ability to attract top quality staff to the hospital, and retain our existing staff. These changes will make our position and departmental names internationally recognizable and comparable with North American and North Asian departments and positions.

2. Improving our ability to attract top quality staff by introducing greater flexibility in the departmental structure.

3. General comments on issues to be further discussed relative to research staff.

The changes outlined in this paper are significant. I encourage you to read the document and send to me any comments you may have, so that it can be enhanced and improved.

Gordon Simms
Administrator,
Seven Oaks Regional Hospital

14. Are all hospital staff required to read the document posted to the Human Resources website?

    a. Yes all staff are required to read the document.
    b. No, reading the document is optional.
    c. Only medical staff are required to read the document.
    d. None of the above are correct.

15. Have the changes to medical staff been made?

    a. Yes, the changes have been made.
    b. No, the changes are only being discussed.
    c. Some of the changes have been made.
    d. None of the choices are correct.

Answer Key

1. C
The author writes, "it did amuse me enormously to watch the W's." It is no single character that evokes the drama of life, but their collectively taken appearances and actions. Choice D is irrelevant, choice B is not conveyed, for example, through allusion to drama or the stage, and choice A belongs to the host of activities the narrator observes.

2. D
Choices A and B are inaccurate: the narrator writes with amusement and an eye for detail, but inflects little passion in his observation. He does not write with deep sympathy or affection. The narrator does seem to apologize for his lengthy description, but most of his writing is descriptive and observational, not repentant.

3. D
Choice A is clearly incorrect. It is the narrator's companion, not the narrator, who says this line. Choice B is also incorrect: the narrator mentions his companion's concern about "winning through with his job," but the analogy connects to and follows the observation that the companion "didn't care a rush for his life." Evidence for choices C is not strong, as there is no obvious connection to mood, Karolides's danger, or political beliefs or opinion. Therefore, choice D is the best answer, supported by the preceding line's idea that the companion does not care for his own life. Readers should also pick up on allusion to death when the companion mentions he will thank God when he wakes up on the other side of the Jordan (a biblical river, the crossing of which signifies the transition from life to death).

4. D
The narrator recollects the information that the danger to Karolides "would come from the very highest quarters, where there would be no thought of suspicion," e.g. that those plotting against Karolides would do so with utmost stealth. Choice A can be eliminated right away, absent any proof. The reader must reject choice B once they identify that the narrator's companion frets the danger to Karolides, but is not himself that man. Choice C is incorrect, as the reader will recall that Karolides's danger is to begin only once he is in London.

5. B
Choices A and D are subjective interpretations and not supported by evidence. Choice C is somewhat implied, but there is little action in the passage and hence no direct evidence to support this assumption. This leaves the reader with choice B as the best choice.

6. A
The greatest clue to this answer is, "before he knew what he was doing he had remarked that it had been a fine day." Choice A is thus the correct answer, the R. S. V. P. eye compels Roland to speak. The reader will note that Roland has already begun to see Muriel differently (Choice C can be eliminated), and it is only once he speaks and runs out of things to say that he is prompted to kiss her. The kiss is not the immediate consequence of the R. S. V. P. eye, and choice D as well can be eliminated. Choice B is impossible to prove; it is nowhere mentioned if Roland loves Muriel, it is only suggested he is attracted to her.

7. D
Choice D is the best answer, which the text directly supports: "from sheer lack of inspiration, he kissed her." There is no evidence, direct or otherwise, for choice A, B, or C.

8. D
Perhaps a more difficult problem. The readers can eliminate choice C, as there is no mention, explicitly or implicitly, of any plot to have Raymond and Muriel wed. "Vast machinery" does connote complexity, but here, the reader must remember the preceding sentence: "If matters had progressed rapidly before, they went like lightning then." The function of the machine imagery is to express some element of speed in Roland's relationship with Muriel — not necessarily complexity. On these grounds, choice A is eliminated. Choice B is a tempting choice, as Roland is clearly not the figurative operator of such machinery, however, Roland's active role in kissing Muriel, correlating to the pressing of a button, cannot be forgotten. Choice D is thus the best choice, and is captured by the sudden materialisation of all the Coppins.

9. B
Choice A can be eliminated immediately: there are no grounds on which to understand that joining the Coppins has been Roland's intent, nor that he has changed his mind from some other path. Choices C and E are both similarly persuasive: Roland does overcome his shyness with Muriel, and he does find her vexing. Be it so, they each fail on several counts. There is no indication that Muriel is astute, nor that it is her intent to help Roland overcome his shyness. Likewise, auburn hair and shapely feet are not sufficient to classify Muriel as a country girl, and there is no evidence she is attempting to seduce Roland. Roland's unwillingness makes choice D plausible, yet it cannot be concluded that the authors are detractors of marriage. Choice B captures Roland's unwillingness, and provides the best summary.

10. B
Low blood sugar occurs both in diabetics and healthy adults.

11. B
None of the statements are the author's opinion.

12. A
The author's purpose is to inform.

13. A

The only statement that is **not** a detail is, "A doctor can diagnosis this medical condition by asking the patient questions and testing."

14. B

Reading the document posted to the Human Resources website is optional.

15. B

The document is recommended changes and have not be implemented yet.

Help with Reading Comprehension

At first sight, reading comprehension tests look challenging especially if you are given long essays to answer only two to three questions. While reading, you might notice your attention wandering, or you may feel sleepy. Do not be discouraged because there are various tactics and long-range strategies that make comprehending even long, boring essays easier.

Your friends before your foes. It is always best to start with passages with familiar subjects rather than those with unfamiliar ones. This approach applies the same logic as tackling easy questions before hard ones. Skip passages that do not interest you and leave them for later.

Don't use 'special' reading techniques. This is not the time for speed-reading or anything like that – just plain ordinary reading – not too slow and not too fast.

Read through the entire passage and the questions before you do anything. Many students try reading the questions first and then looking for answers in the passage thinking this approach is more efficient. What these students do not realize is that it is often hard to navigate in unfamiliar roads. If you do not familiarize yourself with the passage first, looking for answers become not only time-consuming but also dangerous because you might miss the context of the answer you are looking for. If you read the questions first you will only confuse yourself and lose valuable time.

Familiarize yourself with reading comprehension questions. If you are familiar with the common types of reading questions, you are able to take note of important parts of the passage, saving time. There are six major kinds of reading questions.

- **Main Idea**- Questions that ask for the central thought or significance of the passage.

- **Specific Details** - Questions that asks for explicitly stated ideas.

- **Drawing Inferences** - Questions that ask for a logical extension of statements.

- **Tone or Attitude** - Questions that test your ability to sense the emotional state of the author.

- **Context Meaning** – Questions that ask for the meaning of a word depending on the context.

- **Technique** – Questions that ask for the method of organization or the writing style of the author.

Read. Read. Read. The best preparation for reading comprehension tests is always to read, read and read. If you are not used to reading lengthy passages, you will probably lose concentration. Increase your attention span by making a habit out of reading. Read everyday and increase the time slowly each day.

Reading Comprehension tests become less daunting when you have trained yourself to read and understand fast. Always remember that it is easier to understand passages you are interested in. Do not read through passages hastily. Make mental notes of ideas you may be asked.

Reading Strategy

When facing the reading comprehension section of a standardized test, you need a strategy to be successful. You want to keep several steps in mind:

- **First, make a note of the time and the number of sections.** Time your work accordingly. Typically, four to five minutes per section is sufficient. Second, read the directions for each selection thoroughly before beginning (and listen carefully to any additional verbal instructions, as they will often clarify obscure or confusing written guidelines). You must know exactly how to do what you're about to do!

- **Now you're ready to begin reading the selection.** Read the passage carefully, noting significant characters or events on scrap paper or underlining on the test sheet. Many students find making a basic list in the margins helpful. Quickly jot down or underline one-word summaries of characters, notable happenings, numbers, or key ideas. This will help retain information and focus wandering thoughts. Remember, however, that your goal is to find the information that answers the questions. Even if you find the passage interesting, stay on track.

- **Now read the question and all the choices.** Now you have read the passage, have a general idea of the main ideas, and have marked the important points. Read the question and all the choices. Never choose an answer without reading them all! Questions are often designed to confuse – stay focussed and clear. Usually the choices will focus on one or two facts or inferences from the passage. Keep these clear in your mind.

- **Search for the answer.** With a very general idea of what the different choices are, go back to the passage and scan for the relevant information. Watch for big words, unusual or unique words. These make your job easier as you can scan the text for the particular word.

- **Mark the Answer.** Now you have the key information the question is looking for. Go back to the question, quickly scan the choices and mark the correct one.

Typically, there will be several questions dealing with facts from the selection, a couple more inference questions dealing with logical consequences of those facts, and periodically an application-oriented question surfaces to force you to make connections with what you already know. Some students prefer to answer the questions as listed, and feel classifying the question and then ordering is wasting precious time. Other students prefer to answer the different types of questions in order of how easy or difficult they are. The choice is yours and do whatever works for you. If you want to try answering in order of difficulty, here is a recommended order, answer fact questions first; they're easily found within the passage. Tackle inference problems next, after re-reading the question(s) as many times as you need to. Application or 'best guess' questions usually take the longest, so, save them for last.

Use the practice tests to try out both ways of answering and see what works for you.

Main Idea and Supporting Details

Identifying the main idea, topic and supporting details in a passage can feel like an overwhelming task. The passages used for standardized tests can be boring and seem difficult - Test writers don't use interesting passages or ones that talk about things most people are familiar with. Despite these obstacles, all passages and paragraphs will have the information you need to answer the questions.

The topic of a passage or paragraph is its subject. It's the general idea and can be summed up in a word or short phrase. Sometimes, there is a short description of the passage if it's taken from a longer work. Make sure you read the description as it might state the topic of the passage. If not, read the passage and ask yourself, "Who or what is this about?" For example:

> Over the years, school uniforms have been hotly debated. Arguments are made that students have the right to show individuality and express themselves by choosing their own clothes. However, this brings up social and academic issues. Some kids cannot afford to wear the clothes they like and might be bullied by the "better dressed" students. With attention drawn to clothes and the individual, students will lose focus on class work and the reason they are in school. School uniforms should be mandatory.

Ask: What is this paragraph about?

Topic: school uniforms

Once you have the topic, it's easier to find the main idea. The main idea is a specific statement telling what the writer wants you to know. Writers usually state the main idea as a thesis statement. If you're looking for the main idea of a single paragraph, the main idea is called the topic sentence and will probably be the first or last sentence. If you're looking for the main idea of an entire passage, look for the thesis statement in either the first or last paragraph. The main idea is usually restated in the conclusion. To find the main idea of a passage or paragraph, follow these steps:

1. Find the topic.

2. Ask yourself, "What point is the author trying to make about the topic?"

3. Create your own sentence summarizing the author's point.

4. Look in the text for the sentence closest in meaning to yours.

Look at the example paragraph again. It's already established that the topic of the paragraph is school uniforms. What is the main idea/topic sentence?

Ask: "What point is the author trying to make about school uniforms?"

Summary: Students should wear school uniforms.

Topic sentence: School uniforms should be mandatory.

Main Idea: School uniforms should be mandatory.

Each paragraph offers supporting details to explain the main idea. The details could be facts or reasons, but they will always answer a question about the main idea. What? Where? Why? When? How? How much/many? Look at the example paragraph again. You'll notice that more than one sentence answers a question about the main idea. These are the supporting details.

Main Idea: School uniforms should be mandatory.

Ask: Why? Some kids cannot afford to wear clothes they like and could be bullied by the "better dressed" kids. Supporting Detail

With attention drawn to clothes and the individual, Students will lose focus on class work and the reason they are in school. Supporting Detail

What if the author doesn't state the main idea in a topic sentence? The passage will have an implied main idea. It's not as difficult to find as it might seem. Paragraphs are always organized around ideas. To find an implied main idea, you need to know the topic and then find the relationship between the supporting details. Ask yourself, "What is the point the author is making about the relationship between the details?"

> Cocoa is what makes chocolate good for you. Chocolate comes in many varieties. These delectable flavors include milk chocolate, dark chocolate, semi-sweet, and white chocolate.

Ask: What is this paragraph about?
Topic: Chocolate

Ask: What? Where? Why? When? How? How much/many?

Supporting details: Chocolate is good for you because it is made of cocoa, Chocolate is delicious, Chocolate comes in different delicious flavors

Ask: What is the relationship between the details and what is the author's point?

Main Idea: Chocolate is good because it is healthy and it tastes good.

Testing Tips for Main Idea Questions

1. Skim the questions – not the answer choices - before reading the passage.

2. Questions about main idea might use the words "theme," "generalization," or "purpose."

3. Save questions about the main idea for last. Questions can often be found in order in the passage.

3. Underline topic sentences in the passage. Most tests allow you to write in your test booklet.

4. Answer the question in your own words before looking at the choices. Then match your answer with a choice.

5. Cross out incorrect choices immediately to prevent confusion.

6. If two of the choices mean the same thing but use different words, they are BOTH incorrect.

7. If a question asks about the whole passage, cross out the choices that apply only to part of it.

8. If only part of the information is correct, that choice is incorrect.

9. An choice that is too broad is incorrect. All information needs to be backed up by the passage.

10. Choices with extreme wording are usually incorrect.

Common Reading Comprehension Mistakes

Skimming or not reading the passage carefully enough.

Not fully understanding the question being asked.

Assuming you know the answer before reading the passage.

Focusing on small details and missing the main idea.

Not using the context of the passage to infer meaning.

Jumping to conclusions without considering all the information provided.

Not eliminating clearly incorrect answer choices.

Reading Comprehension Video Tutorials

https://www.test-preparation.ca/making-inferences/

Mathematics

THIS SECTION CONTAINS A SELF-ASSESSMENT AND MATH TUTORIALS. The tutorials are designed to familiarize general principles and the self-assessment contains general questions similar to the math questions likely to be on the CAEC exam, but are not intended to be identical to the exam questions. The tutorials are not designed to be a complete math course, and it is assumed that students have some familiarity with math. If you do not understand parts of the tutorial, or find the tutorial difficult, it is recommended that you seek out additional instruction.

Tour of the CAEC Math Content

Below is a list of the likely math topics likely to appear on the CAEC.

- Solve word problems

- Calculate percent and ratio

- Operations using fractions, percent and fractions

- Simple geometry and measurement

- Data analysis, basic statistics and probability

- Operations with polynomials

- Exponents

- Solving Inequalities

- Linear equations with one variable

- Solving quadratic equations

- Solving Binomials

- Coordinate geometry

- Solutions of inequalities

- Area, perimeter and volume

- Pythagorean geometry

The questions in the self-assessment are not the same as you will find on the CAEC - that would be too easy! And nobody knows what the questions will be and they change all the time. Mostly, the changes consist of substituting new questions for old, but the changes also can be new question formats or styles, changes to the number of questions in each section, changes to the time limits for each section, and combining sections. So, while the format and exact wording of the questions may differ slightly, and changes from year to year, if you can answer the questions below, you will have no problem with the math section of the CAEC.

Mathematics Self-Assessment

The purpose of the self-assessment is:

- Identify your strengths and weaknesses.
- Develop your personalized study plan (above)
- Get accustomed to the CAEC format
- Extra practice – the self-assessments are almost a full 3rd practice test!
- Provide a baseline score for preparing your study schedule.

Since this is a Self-assessment, and depending on how confident you are with math, timing yourself is optional.
Once complete, use the table below to assess your understanding of the content, and prepare your study schedule described in chapter 1.

80% - 100%	Excellent – you have mastered the content
60 – 79%	Good. You have a working knowledge. Even though you can just pass this section, you may want to review the tutorials and do some extra practice to see if you can improve your mark.
40% - 59%	Below Average. You do not understand basic math concepts. Review the tutorials, and retake this quiz again in a few days, before proceeding to the practice test questions.
Less than 40%	Poor. You have a very limited understanding of the math content. Please review the tutorials, and retake this quiz again in a few days, before proceeding to the practice test questions.

Answer Sheet

	A	B	C	D	E		A	B	C	D	E
1	○	○	○	○	○	26	○	○	○	○	○
2	○	○	○	○	○	27	○	○	○	○	○
3	○	○	○	○	○	28	○	○	○	○	○
4	○	○	○	○	○	29	○	○	○	○	○
5	○	○	○	○	○	30	○	○	○	○	○
6	○	○	○	○	○	31	○	○	○	○	○
7	○	○	○	○	○	32	○	○	○	○	○
8	○	○	○	○	○	33	○	○	○	○	○
9	○	○	○	○	○	34	○	○	○	○	○
10	○	○	○	○	○	35	○	○	○	○	○
11	○	○	○	○	○	36	○	○	○	○	○
12	○	○	○	○	○	37	○	○	○	○	○
13	○	○	○	○	○	38	○	○	○	○	○
14	○	○	○	○	○	39	○	○	○	○	○
15	○	○	○	○	○	40	○	○	○	○	○
16	○	○	○	○	○	41	○	○	○	○	○
17	○	○	○	○	○	42	○	○	○	○	○
18	○	○	○	○	○	43	○	○	○	○	○
19	○	○	○	○	○	44	○	○	○	○	○
20	○	○	○	○	○	45	○	○	○	○	○
21	○	○	○	○	○	46	○	○	○	○	○
22	○	○	○	○	○	47	○	○	○	○	○
23	○	○	○	○	○	48	○	○	○	○	○
24	○	○	○	○	○	49	○	○	○	○	○
25	○	○	○	○	○	50	○	○	○	○	○

Mathematics

1. Brad has agreed to buy everyone a Coke. Each drink costs $1.89, and there are 5 friends. Estimate Brad's cost.

   a. $7
   b. $8
   c. $10
   d. $12

2. Sarah weighs 25 pounds more than Tony. If together they weigh 205 pounds, how much does Sarah weigh approximately in kilograms? Assume 1 pound = 0.4535 kilograms.

   a. 41
   b. 48
   c. 50
   d. 52

3. A building is 15 m long and 20 m wide and 10 m high. What is the volume of the building?

   a. 45 m^3
   b. 3,000 m^3
   c. 1500 m^3
   d. 300 m^3

4. 15 is what percent of 200?

   a. 7.5%
   b. 15%
   c. 20%
   d. 17.50%

5. A boy has 5 red balls, 3 white balls and 2 yellow balls. What percent of the balls are yellow?

   a. 2%
   b. 8%
   c. 20%
   d. 12%

6. Add 10% of 300 to 50% of 20

   a. 50
   b. 40
   c. 60
   d. 45

7. What is 10% of 30 multiplied by 75% of 200?

   a. 450
   b. 750
   c. 20
   d. 45

8. Convert 4/20 to percent.

   a. 25%
   b. 20%
   c. 40%
   d. 30%

9. Convert 0.55 to percent.

   a. 45%
   b. 15%
   c. 75%
   d. 55%

10. A man buys an item for $420 and has a balance of $3000.00. How much did he have before?

   a. $2,580
   b. $3,420
   c. $2,420
   d. $342

11. What is the best approximate solution for 1.135 - 113.5?

   a. -110
   b. 100
   c. -90
   d. 110

12. Solve 3/4 + 2/4 + 1.2

    a. 1 1/7
    b. 2 3/4
    c. 2 9/20
    d. 3 1/4

13. The average weight of 13 students in a class of 15 (two were absent that day) is 42 kg. When the remaining two are weighed, the average became 42.7 kg. If one of the remaining students weighs 48 kg., how much does the other weigh?

    a. 44.7 kg.
    b. 45.6 kg.
    c. 46.5 kg.
    d. 47.4 kg.

14. A fence around a square field costs $2000, at a rate of $5 per meter. What is the length of one side?

    a. 40 meters
    b. 80 meters
    c. 100 meters
    d. 320 meters

15. There were some oranges in a basket. By adding 8/5 of the total to the basket, the new total is 130. How many oranges were in the basket?

    a. 60
    b. 50
    c. 40
    d. 35

16. 3 boys are asked to clean a surface that is 4 ft^2. If the surface is divided equally among the boys, how much will each clean?

    a. 1 ft 6 $inches^2$
    b. 14 $inches^2$
    c. 1 ft 2 $inches^2$
    d. 1 ft^2 48 $inches^2$

17. **A person earns $25,000 per month and pays $9,000 income tax per year. The Government increased income tax by 0.5% per month and his monthly earning was increased $11,000. How much more income tax will he pay per month?**

   a. $1260
   b. $1050
   c. $750
   d. $510

18. **Estimate 2009 x 108**

   a. 110,000
   b. 2,0000
   c. 21,000
   d. 210,000

Exponents

19. **Express in 3^4 standard form**

   a. 81
   b. 27
   c. 12
   d. 9

20. **Simplify $4^3 + 2^4$**

   a. 45
   b. 108
   c. 80
   d. 48

21. **If x = 2 and y = 5, solve $xy^3 - x^3$**

   a. 240
   b. 258
   c. 248
   d. 242

Mathematics

22. $X^3 \times X^2 =$

   a. 5^x
   b. x^{-5}
   c. x^{-1}
   d. X^5

23. Express 100000^0 in standard form.

   a. 1
   b. 0
   c. 100000
   d. 1000

24. Solve $\sqrt{144}$

   a. 14
   b. 72
   c. 24
   d. 12

Linear Equations

25. Solve the linear equation: $-x - 7 = -3x - 9$

   a. -1
   b. 0
   c. 1
   d. 2

26. Solve the system: $4x - y = 5 \quad x + 2y = 8$

   a. (3,2)
   b. (3,3)
   c. (2,3)
   d. (2,2)

Polynomials

27. Add $-3x^2 + 2x + 6$ and $-x^2 - x - 1$.

    a. $-2x^2 + x + 5$
    b. $-4x^2 + x + 5$
    c. $-2x^2 + 3x + 5$
    d. $-4x^2 + 3x + 5$

28. Simplify the following expression:

$3x^3 + 2x^2 + 5x - 7 + 4x^2 - 5x + 2 - 3x^3$

    a. $6x^2 - 9$
    b. $6x^2 - 5$
    c. $6x^2 - 10x - 5$
    d. $6x^2 + 10x - 9$

29. Multiply $x - 1$ and $x^2 + x + 2$.

    a. $x^3 + x - 2$
    b. $x^2 + x - 2$
    c. $x^3 + x^2 - 2$
    d. $x^3 + 2x^2 - 2$

30. Factor the polynomial $9x^2 - 6x + 12$.

    a. $3(x^2 - 2x + 9)$
    b. $3(3x^2 - 3x + 4)$
    c. $9(x^2 - 3x + 3)$
    d. $3(3x^2 - 2x + 4)$

Quadratics

31. Find 2 numbers that sum to 21 and the sum of the squares is 261.

    a. 14 and 7
    b. 15 and 6
    c. 16 and 5
    d. 17 and 4

32. Using the factoring method, solve the quadratic equation:
$x^2 + 4x + 4 = 0$

    a. 0 and 1
    b. 1 and 2
    c. 2
    d. -2

33. Using the quadratic formula, solve the quadratic equation: $x - 31/x = 0$

    a. $-\sqrt{13}$ and $\sqrt{13}$
    b. $-\sqrt{31}$ and $\sqrt{31}$
    c. $-\sqrt{31}$ and $2\sqrt{31}$
    d. $-\sqrt{3}$ and $\sqrt{3}$

34. Using the factoring method, solve the quadratic equation: $2x^2 - 3x = 0$

    a. 0 and 1.5
    b. 1.5 and 2
    c. 2 and 2.5
    d. 0 and 2

35. Using the quadratic formula, solve the quadratic equation:
$x^2 - 9x + 14 = 0$

    a. 2 and 7
    b. -2 and 7
    c. -7 and -2
    d. -7 and 2

Geometry

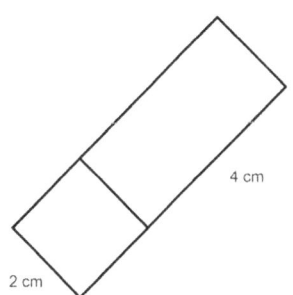

Note: Figure not drawn to scale

36. Assuming the shape with 2 cm side is square, what is the perimeter of the above shape?

   a. 12 cm
   b. 16 cm
   c. 6 cm
   d. 20 cm

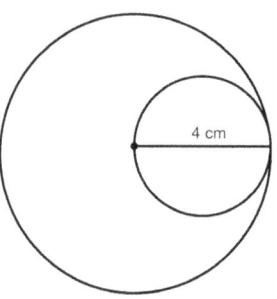

Note: Figure not drawn to scale

37. Assuming the diameter of the small circle is equal to the radius of the large circle, what is (area of large circle) - (area of small circle) in the figure above?

   a. 8 π cm²
   b. 10 π cm²
   c. 12 π cm²
   d. 16 π cm²

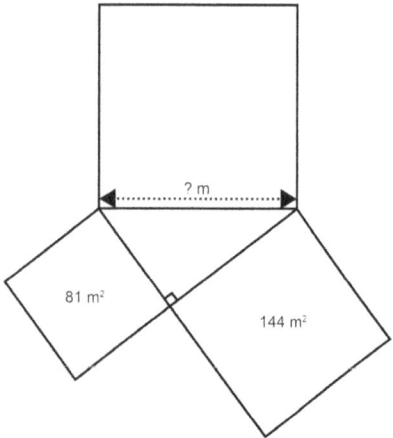

Note: Figure not drawn to scale

38. Assuming the shapes around the right triangle are square, what is the length of each side of the square above?

    a. 10
    b. 15
    c. 20
    d. 5

Inequalities

39. Solve the inequality: -7x - 1 ≥ 13

    a. [2, + ∞)
    b. (7, + ∞)
    c. (-∞, -2]
    d. [2, + ∞)

40. Solve the inequality: 2x - 1 ≥ x + 10

    a. (-∞, 9)
    b. [9, +∞)
    c. (-∞, -9)
    d. [11, +∞)

Data and Statistics

41. There are 3 blue, 1 white and 4 red identical balls inside a bag. If it is aimed to take two balls out of the bag consecutively, what is the probability to have 1 blue and 1 white ball?

    a. 3/28
    b. 1/12
    c. 1/7
    d. 3/7

42. Claire is playing a dart game and throwing the dart for 6 times. The probability to hit the board is 1/6. What is the probability to strike 4 times?

    a. 0.008
    b. 0.08
    c. 0.8
    d. 0.2

43. A boy has 4 red, 5 green and 2 yellow balls. He chooses two balls randomly for play. What is the probability that one is red and other is green?

   a. 2/11
   b. 19/22
   c. 20/121
   d. 9/11

44. A company, surveys a random sample of 120 employees about the number of days next month they prefer to eat out, instead of at the company cafeteria. 80 expected to eat out 5 days next month. There are 450 employees in the company. Based on the data, find the most reasonable estimate for the number of employees who expect to eat out 5 days next month.

   a. 240
   b. 300
   c. 360
   d. 390

45. There are 5 blue, 5 green and 5 red books on a shelf. Two books are selected randomly. What is the probability of choosing two books of different colors?

   a. 1/3
   b. 2/5
   c. 4/7
   d. 5/7

46. There are 3 blue, 1 white and 4 red identical balls inside a bag. If it is aimed to take two balls out of the bag consecutively, what is the probability to have 1 blue and 1 white ball?

   a. 3/28
   b. 1/12
   c. 1/7
   d. 3/7

47. Find the mean of these set of numbers: 100, 1050, 320, 600 and 150

   a. 333
   b. 444
   c. 440
   d. 320

Mathematics

48. A boy has 4 red, 5 green and 2 yellow balls. He chooses two balls randomly for play. What is the probability that one is red and other is green?

    a. 2/11

    b. 19/22

    c. 20/121

    d. 9/11

49. Find the median of the set of numbers: 1, 2, 3, 4, 5, 6, 7, 8, 9 and 10

    a. 55

    b. 10

    c. 1

    d. 5.5

50. The following represents the age distribution of students in an elementary class. Find the mode of the values: 7, 9, 10, 13, 11, 7, 9, 19, 12, 11, 9, 7, 9, 10, 11

    a. 7

    b. 9

    c. 10

    d. 11

Answer Key

1. C
If there are 5 friends and each drink costs $1.89, we can round up to $2 per drink and estimate the total cost at, 5 X $2 = $10.
The actual cost is 5 X $1.89 = $9.45.

2. D
Let us denote Sarah's weight by "x." Then, since she weighs 25 pounds more than Tony, so Tony will be x-25. They together weigh 205 pounds which means that the sum of the two representations will be equal to 205:

Sarah : x

Tony : x - 25

x + (x - 25) = 205 ... by arranging this equation we have:

x + x - 25 = 205

2x - 25 = 205 ... we add 25 to each side to have x term alone:

2x - 25 + 25 = 205 + 25

2x = 230

x = 230/2

x = 115 pounds → Sarah weighs 115 pounds. Since 1 pound is 0.4535 kilograms, we need to multiply 115 by 0.4535 to have her weight in kilograms:

x = 115 * 0.4535 = 52.1525 kilograms → this is equal to 52 when rounded to the nearest whole number.

3. B
Formula for volume of a shape is L x W x H = 15 x 20 x 10 = 3,000 m³

4. A
15/200 = X/100
200X = (15 * 100)
1500/20 Cancel zeros in the numerator and denominator
15/2 = 7.5%.

Notice that the questions asks, What 15 is what percent of 200? The question does not ask, what is 15% of 200! The answers are very different.

5. C
Total no. of balls = 10, no. of yellow balls = 2, answer = 2/10 X 100 = 20%.

6. B
10% of 300 = 30 and 50% of 20 = 10 so 30 + 10 = 40.

7. A
10% of 30 = 3 and 75% of 200 = 150, 3 X 150 = 450

8. B
4/20 X 100 = 1/5 X 100 = 20%

9. D
0.55 X 100 = 55%

10. B
(Amount Spent) $420 + $3000 (Balance) = $3420

11. A
1.135 -113.5 = -112.37. Best approximate = -110

12. C
3/4 + 2/4 + 1.2, first convert the decimal to fraction, = 3/4 + 2/4 + 1 1/5 = ¾ + 2/4 + 6/5 = (find common denominator) (15 + 10 + 24)/20 = 49/20 = 2 9/20

13. C
Total weight of 13 students with average 42 will be = 42 * 13 = 546 kg.

The total weight of the remaining 2 will be found by subtracting the total weight of 13 students from the total weight of 15 students: 640.5 - 546 = 94.5 kg.

94.5 = the total weight of two students. One of these students weigh 48 kg, so;

The weight of the other will be = 94.5 – 48 = 46.5 kg

14. C
Total expense is $2000 and we are informed that $5 is spent per meter. Combining these two information, we know that the total length of the fence is 2000/5 = 400 meters.

The fence is built around a square-shaped field. If one side of the square is "a," the perimeter of the square is "4a." Here, the perimeter is equal to 400 meters. So,

400 = 4a

100 = a → this means that one side of the square is equal to 100 meters

15. B
Let the number of oranges in the basket before additions = x
Then: X + 8x/5 = 130
5x + 8x = 650
650 = 13x
X = 50

16. D
1 foot is equal to 12 inches. So 1 ft² = 12 * 12 in²

4 ft² = 4 * 12 * 12 in² = 576 in²

The total surface area is divided equally among 3 boys.

Each boy will clean 576/3 = 192 in²

192 in² = 144 in² + 48 in²; 144 in² = 1 ft²

So, each boy will clean 1 ft² and 48 in²

17. D
The income tax per year is $9,000. So, the income tax per month is 9,000/12 = $750.

This person earns $25,000 per month and pays $750 income tax. We need to find the rate of the income tax:

Tax rate: 750 * 100/25,000 = 3%

Government increased this rate by 0.5% so it became 3.5%.

The income of the person per month is increased $11,000 so it became: $25,000 + $11,000 = $36,000.

The new monthly income tax is: 36,000 * 3.5/100 = $1260.

Amount of increase in tax per month is: $1260 - $750 = $510.

18. D
2009 x 108 = 210,000

Exponents

19. A
3 x 3 x 3 x 3 = 81

20. C
(4 x 4 x 4) + (2 x 2 x 2 x 2) = 64 + 16 = 80

21. D
$2(5)^3 - (2)^3 = 2(125) - 8 = 250 - 8 = 242$

22. D
$X^3 \times X^2 = X^{3+2} = X^5$
To multiply exponents with like bases, add the exponents.

23. A
Any value (except 0) raised to the power of 0 equals 1.

24. D
√144 = 12

Linear Equations

25. A
We should collect similar terms on the same side. Here, we can collect x terms on left side, and the constants on the right side:

-x - 7 = -3x - 9 .... Let us add 3x to both sides:

-x - 7 + 3x = -3x - 9 + 3x

2x - 7 = - 9 ... Now, we can add + 7 to both sides:

2x - 7 + 7 = -9 + 7

2x = -2 ... Dividing both sides by 2 gives us the value of x:

x = -2/2

x = -1

26. C
First, we need to write two equations separately:
4x - y = 5 (I)

x + 2y = 8 (II) ... Here, we can use two ways to solve the system. One is substitution method, the other one is linear elimination method:

Method 1 - Substitution Method

Equation (I) gives us that y = 4x - 5. We insert this value of y into equation (II):

x + 2(4x - 5) = 8

x + 8x - 10 = 8

9x - 10 = 8

9x = 18

x = 2

But knowing x = 2, we can find the value of y by inserting x = 2 into either of the equations. Let us choose equation (I):

4(2) - y = 5

8 - y = 5

8 - 5 = y

y = 3 → solution is (2, 3)

Method 2 - Linear Elimination Method

2•/ 4x - y = 5 ... by multiplying equation (I) by 2, we see that -2y will form; and y terms

    x + 2y = 8 ... will be eliminated when summed with +2y in equation (II):

2•/ 4x - y = 5

+   x + 2y = 8

    8x - 2y = 10

 + x + 2y = 8 ... Summing side-by-side:

8x + x - 2y + 2y = 10 + 8 ... -2y and +2y cancel:

9x = 18

x = 2

By knowing x = 2, we can find the value of y by inserting x = 2 into either of the equations. Let us choose equation (I):

4(2) - y = 5

8 - y = 5

8 - 5 = y

y = 3 → solution is (2, 3)

Polynomials

27. B
$(-3x^2 + 2x + 6) + (-x^2 - x - 1)$

$= -3x^2 + 2x + 6 - x^2 - x - 1$ ... we write similar terms together:

$= -3x^2 - x^2 + 2x - x + 6 - 1$ ... we operate within the same terms:

$= -4x^2 + x + 5$

28. B
$3x^3 + 2x^2 + 5x - 7 + 4x^2 - 5x + 2 - 3x^3$ ... we write similar terms together:

$= 3x^3 - 3x^3 + 2x^2 + 4x^2 + 5x - 5x - 7 + 2$ ... we operate within the same terms. $3x^3$ and $-3x^3$, 5x and -5x cancel:

$= 6x^2 - 5$

29. A
We are asked to multiply $(x - 1)(x^2 + x + 2)$.
Each term in the parenthesis (x - 1) should be multiplied to each term in the parenthesis $(x^2 + x + 2)$:

$= x(x^2 + x + 2) - 1(x^2 + x + 2) = x^3 + x^2 + 2x - x^2 - x - 2$ ... we write terms together:

$= x^3 + x^2 - x^2 + 2x - x - 2$ ... we operate within the same terms. x^2 and $-x^2$ cancel:

$= x^3 + x - 2$

30. D
First, we need to search for a constant common factor in each of the terms. If there is any, we need to take it out of the equation and write it as a coefficient in front:
$9x^2 - 6x + 12 = 3(3x^2 - 2x + 4)$

We cannot go further from this point, so this is the factored form of the polynomial.

Quadratics

31. B
There are two statements made. This means that we can write two equations according to these statements:
The sum of two numbers are 21: $x + y = 21$

The sum of the squares is 261: $x^2 + y^2 = 261$

We are asked to find x and y.

Since we have the sums of the numbers and the sums of their squares; we can use the square formula of $x + y$, that is:

$(x + y)^2 = x^2 + 2xy + y^2$ ... Here, we can insert the known values $x + y$ and $x^2 + y^2$:

$(21)^2 = 261 + 2xy$ ... Arranging to find xy:

$441 = 261 + 2xy$

$441 - 261 = 2xy$

$180 = 2xy$

$xy = 180/2$

$xy = 90$

We need to find two number which multiply to 90. Checking the answer choices, we see that in (b), 15 and 6 are given. 15 * 6 = 90. Also their squares sum up to 261 ($15^2 + 6^2 = 225 + 36 = 261$). So these two numbers satisfy the equation.

32. D
$x^2 + 4x + 4 = 0$ ... We try to separate the middle term 4x to find common factors with x^2 and 4 separately:

$x^2 + 2x + 2x + 4 = 0$ ... Here, we see that x is a common factor for x^2 and 2x, and 2 is a common factor for 2x and 4:

$x(x + 2) + 2(x + 2) = 0$ ... Here, we have x times $x + 2$ and 2 times $x + 2$ summed up. This means that we have $x + 2$ times $x + 2$:

$(x + 2)(x + 2) = 0$

$(x + 2)^2 = 0$ ... This is true if only if $x + 2$ is equal to zero.

$x + 2 = 0$

$x = -2$

33. B

To solve the equation, first we need to arrange it to appear in the form $ax^2 + bx + c = 0$ by removing the denominator:

$x - 31/x = 0$ ... First, we enlarge the equation by x:

$x * x - 31 * x/x = 0$

$x^2 - 31 = 0$

The quadratic formula to find the roots of a quadratic equation is:

$x_{1,2} = (-b \pm \sqrt{\Delta}) / 2a$ where $\Delta = b^2 - 4ac$ and is called the discriminant of the quadratic equation.

In our question, the equation is $x^2 - 31 = 0$. By remembering the form $ax^2 + bx + c = 0$:

$a = 1, b = 0, c = -31$

So, we can find the discriminant first, and then the roots of the equation:

$\Delta = b^2 - 4ac = 0^2 - 4 * 1 * (-31) = 124$

$x_{1,2} = (-b \pm \sqrt{\Delta}) / 2a = (\pm\sqrt{124}) / 2 = (\pm\sqrt{4 * 31}) / 2 = (\pm 2\sqrt{31}) / 2$ ... Simplifying by 2:

$x_{1,2} = \pm\sqrt{31}$ ... This means that the roots are $\sqrt{31}$ and $-\sqrt{31}$.

34. A

$2x^2 - 3x = 0$ ... we see that both of the terms contain x; so we can take it out as a factor:

$x(2x - 3) = 0$ ... two terms are multiplied and the result is zero. This means that either of the terms or both of the terms can be equal to zero:

$x = 0$ ... this is one solution

$2x - 3 = 0 \rightarrow 2x = 3 \rightarrow x = 3/2 \rightarrow x = 1.5$ ... this is the second solution.

So, the solutions are 0 and 1.5.

35. A

To solve the equation, we need the equation in the form $ax^2 + bx + c = 0$.

$x^2 - 9x + 14 = 0$ is already in this form.

The quadratic formula to find the roots of a quadratic equation is:

$x_{1,2} = (-b \pm \sqrt{\Delta}) / 2a$ where $\Delta = b^2 - 4ac$ and is called the discriminant of the quadratic equation.

In our question, the equation is $x^2 - 9x + 14 = 0$. By remembering the form $ax^2 + bx + c = 0$:

$a = 1, b = -9, c = 14$

So, we can find the discriminant first, and then the roots of the equation:

$\Delta = b^2 - 4ac = (-9)^2 - 4 * 1 * 14 = 81 - 56 = 25$

$x_{1,2} = (-b \pm \sqrt{\Delta}) / 2a = (-(-9) \pm \sqrt{25}) / 2 = (9 \pm 5) / 2$

This means that the roots are,

$x_1 = (9 - 5) / 2 = 2$ and $x_2 = (9 + 5) / 2 = 7$

Geometry

36. B
We see that there is a square with side 2 cm and a rectangle adjacent to it, with one side 2 cm (common side with the square) and the other side 4 cm. The perimeter of a shape is found by summing up all sides surrounding the shape, not adding the ones inside the shape. Three 2 cm sides from the square, and two 4 cm sides and one 2 cm side from the rectangle contribute the perimeter.

So, the perimeter of the shape is: $2 + 2 + 2 + 4 + 2 + 4 = 16$ cm.

37. C
In the figure, we are given a large circle and a small circle inside it; with the diameter equal to the radius of the large one. The diameter of the small circle is 4 cm. This means that its radius is 2 cm. Since the diameter of the small circle is the radius of the large circle, the radius of the large circle is 4 cm. The area of a circle is calculated by: πr^2 where r is the radius.

Area of the small circle: $\pi(2)^2 = 4\pi$

Area of the large circle: $\pi(4)^2 = 16\pi$

The difference area is found by:

Area of the large circle - Area of the small circle = $16\pi - 4\pi = 12\pi$

38. B

We see that there are three squares forming a right triangle in the middle. Two of the squares have the areas 81 m² and 144 m². If we denote their sides a and b respectively:

a² = 81 and b² = 144. The length which is asked is the hypotenuse; a and b are the opposite and adjacent sides of the right angle. By using the Pythagorean Theorem, we can find the value of the asked side:

Pythagorean Theorem:
(Hypotenuse)² = (Perpendicular)² + (Base)²
h² = a² + b²

a² = 81, b² = 144
h² = a² + b²
h² = 81+144
h² = 225
h = 15

Inequalities

39. C
To solve an inequality, we aim to leave x alone; without factors on one side, and the other numbers on the other side of the inequality sign:
-7x - 1 ≥ 13 ... first, we add 1 to both sides:

-7x - 1 + 1 ≥ 13 + 1

-7x ≥ 14 ... second, we divide both sides by 7:

-7x/7 ≥ 14/7

-x ≥ 2 ... last, we multiply both sides by -1 to obtain a positive x. It is important not to forget that if we divide or multiply an inequality by a negative number, the inequality changes its direction:

x ≤ -2 ... This is the solution. This means that x can be equal to -2 or a smaller value. So, (-∞, -2] is the solution.

40. D
2x - 1 ≥ x + 10 ... first, we need to collect similar terms in the same side:

2x - x - 1 ≥ 10

x - 1 ≥ 10

x ≥ 10 + 1

x ≥ 11 ... this means that x can be 11 or a higher value; there is no upper limit for x, but lower limit is 11; including 11. This is shown as [11, +∞).

Data and Statistics

41. A
There are 8 balls in the bag in total. It is important that two balls are taken out of the bag one by one. We can first take the blue then the white, or first white, then the blue. So, we will have two possibilities to be summed up. Since the balls are taken consecutively, we should be careful with the total number of balls for each case:

First blue, then white ball:

There are 3 blue balls; so, having a blue ball is 3/8 possible. Then, we have 7 balls left in the bag. The possibility to have a white ball is 1/7.

P = (3/8) * (1/7) = 3/56

First white, then blue ball:

There is only 1 white ball; so, having a white ball is 1/8 possible. Then, we have 7 balls left in the bag. The possibility to have a blue ball is 3/7.

P = (1/8) * (3/7) = 3/56

Overall probability is:

3/56 + 3/56 = 3/28

42. A
Here, we can use binomial distribution - probability mass function:

$C(n, x) * p^x * q^{n-x}$

where n is the number of hits, x is the successful number of hits, p is the success probability and q is the failure probability. Since the success probability is 1/6, failure probability is 1 - 1/6 = 5/6:

$C(n, x) * p^x * q^{n-x}$ = C(6, 4) * (1/6)^4 * (5/6)^2 = (6! / (2! * 4!)) * (25 / 6^6) = 0.008

43. A
Probability that the 1st ball is red: 4/11
Probability the 2nd ball is green: 5/10

Combined probability is 4/11 * 5/10 = 20/110 = 2/11

44. B
80 out of 120 expect to eat out 5 days next month. This information gives the proportion of people expecting to eat out to total number of people. However, not all employees participated the survey; so we accept that the random sample represents all employees:

If 80 out of 120 expect to eat out next month, how many employees out of 450 expect to eat out next month?

450 * 80 / 120 = 300 employees

45. D
Assume that the first book chosen is red. Since we need to choose the second book in green or blue, there are 10 possible books to be chosen out of 15 - 1(that is the red book chosen first) = 14 books. There are equal number of books in each color, so the results will be the same if we think that blue or green book is the first book.

So, the probability will be 10/14 = 5/7.

46. A
There are 8 balls in the bag in total. It is important that two balls are taken out of the bag one by one. We can first take the blue then the white, or first white, then the blue. So, we will have two possibilities to be summed up. Since the balls are taken consecutively, we should be careful with the total number of balls for each case:

First blue, then white ball:

There are 3 blue balls; so, having a blue ball is 3/8 possible. Then, we have 7 balls left in the bag. The possibility to have a white ball is 1/7.

P = (3/8) * (1/7) = 3/56

First white, then blue ball:

There is only 1 white ball; so, having a white ball is 1/8 possible. Then, we have 7 balls left in the bag. The possibility to have a blue ball is 3/7.

P = (1/8) * (3/7) = 3/56

Overall probability is:

3/56 + 3/56 = 3/28

47. B
First add all the numbers 100 + 1050 + 320 + 600 + 150 = 2220. Then divide by 5 (the number of data provided) = 2220/5 = 444.

48. A
Probability that the 1st ball is red: 4/11

Probability the 2nd ball is green: 5/10

Combined probability is 4/11 * 5/10 = 20/110 = 2/11

49. D
First arrange the numbers in a numerical sequence - 1,2,3,4,5,6,7,8,9, 10. Then find the middle number or numbers. The middle numbers are 5 and 6. The median = 5 + 6/2 = 11/2 = 5.5

50. B
The mode, or most occurring number in the series (7, 9, 10, 13, 11, 7, 9, 19, 12, 11, 9, 7, 9, 10, 11) is 9.

Basic math Video Tutorials

https://www.test-preparation.ca/math-videos/

Fraction Tips, Tricks and Shortcuts

When you are writing an exam, time is precious, so anything you can do to answer questions faster is a real advantage.

Here are some ideas, shortcuts, tips and tricks that can speed up answering fraction problems.

Remember that a fraction is just a number which names a portion of something. For instance, instead of having a whole pie, a fraction says you have a part of a pie--such as a half of one or a fourth of one.

Two numbers make up a fraction. The number on top is the numerator. The number on the bottom is the denominator.

To remember which is which, just remember that "denominator" and "down" both start with a "d." And the "downstairs" number is the denominator. So for instance, in ½, the numerator is 1, and the denominator (or "downstairs") number is 2.

Adding Fractions

It's easy to add two fractions if they have the same denominator. Just add the digits on top and leave the bottom one the same: 1/10 + 6/10 = 7/10.

It's the same with subtracting fractions with the same denominator: 7/10 - 6/10 = 1/10.

Adding and subtracting fractions with different denominators is a little more complicated.

First, you have to arrange the fractions so they have the same denominators.

The easiest way to do this is to multiply the denominators: For 2/5 + 1/2 multiply 5 by 2. Now you have a denominator of 10.

But now you have to change the top numbers too. Since you multiplied the 5 in 2/5 by 2, you also multiply the 2 by 2, to get 4. So the first fraction is now 4/10.

In the second fraction, you multiplied the denominator by 5, you have to multiply the numerator by 5 also, to get 5/10.

Now you have 4/10 + 5/10 and you can add 5 and 4 to get 9/10.

Simplest Form

To reduce a fraction to its simplest form, you have to arrange the numerator and denominator so the only common factor is 1.

Think of it this way:

Let's take an example: The fraction 2/10.

This is not reduced to its simplest terms because there is a number that will divide evenly into both: 2. We want to make it so that the only number that will divide evenly into both is 1.

Divide the top and bottom by 2 to get the new, reduced fraction - 1/5.

Multiplying Fractions

This is the easiest of all: Just multiply the two top numbers and then multiply the two bottom numbers.

Here is an example,

2/5 X 2/3

First, multiply the numerators: 2 X 2 = 4

then multiply the denominators: 5 X 3 = 15

Your answer is 4/15.

Dividing Fractions

Dividing fractions is easy if you remember a simple trick - first turn the second fraction upside down - then multiply!

Here is an example:

7/8 X 1/2

Turn the second fraction upside down:

7/8 X 2/1

then multiply:

(7 X 2) / (8 X 1) = 14/8

Converting Fractions to Decimals

There are a couple of ways to become good at converting fractions to decimals. One -- the one that will make you the fastest in basic math skills -- is to learn some basic fraction facts. It's a good idea, if you're good at memory, to memorize the following:

1/100 is one hundredth, or .01.

1/50 is two hundredths, or .02.

1/25 is one twenty-fifths or four hundredths, or .04.

1/20 is one twentieth or five hundredths, or .05.

1/10 is one tenth, or .1.

1/8 is one eighth, or one hundred twenty-five thousandths, or. 125.

1/5 is one fifth, or two tenths, or .2.

1/4 is one fourth or twenty-five hundredths, or .25.

1/3 is one third or thirty-three hundredths, or .33.

1/2 is one half or five tenths, or .5.

3/4 is three fourths, or seventy-five hundredths, or .75.

Of course, if you're no good at memorization, another good technique for converting a fraction to a decimal is to manipulate it so that the fraction's denominator is 10, 10, 1000, or some other power of 10. Here's an example: We'll start with ¾. What is the first number in the 4 "times table" that you can multiply and get a multiple of 10? Can you multiply 4 by something to get 10? No. Can you multiply it by something to get 100? Yes! 4 X 25 is 100. So let's take that 25 and multiply it by the numerator in our fraction ¾. The numerator is 3, and 3 X 25 is 75. We'll move the decimal in 75 all the way to the left, and we find that ¾ is .75.

We'll do another one: 1/5. Again, we want to find a power of 10 that 5 goes into evenly. Will 5 go into 10? Yes! It goes 2 times. So we'll take that 2 and multiply it by our numerator, 1, and we get 2. We move the decimal in 2 all the way to the left and find that 1/5 is equal to .2.

Converting Fractions to Percent

Here is a quick method to convert fraction to percent and a strategy for answering on a multiple choice test that will save you valuable exam time.

First, remember that a fraction is a division problem: you're dividing the bottom number into the top.

Taking an example, convert 2/3 into percent.

The first method is to multiple the numerator by 100 and divide. So,

(2 X 100) / 2 = 100/3 = 66.66

Add a % sign and you have the answer, 66.66%

If you're doing these conversions on a multiple-choice test, here's an idea that might be even easier and faster. Let's say you have a fraction of 1/8 and you're asked to convert to percent.

Since we know that "percent" means hundredths, ask yourself what number we can multiply 8 by to get 100. Since there is no number, ask what number gets us close to 100.

That number is 12: 8 X 12 = 96. So it gets us a little less than 100. Now, whatever you do to the denominator, you have to do to the numerator. Let's multiply 1 X 12 and we get 12. However, since 96 is a little less than 100, we know that our answer will be a little MORE than 12%.

Look at the choices and eliminate the obvious wrong choices. So if your possible answers on the multiple-choice test are these:

a) 8.5% b) 19% c) 12.5% d) 25%

then we know the answer is c) 12.5%, because it's a little MORE than the 12 we got in our math problem above.

Here all the choices except choice C 12.5% can be eliminated.

You don't have to know the exact correct answer, just enough to estimate, then eliminate the obviously wrong answers.

This was an easy example to demonstrate the strategy, but don't be fooled! You probably won't get such an easy question on your exam. By estimating your answer quickly, then eliminating obviously incorrect choices immediately, you save precious exam time.

Mathematics

Most Common Fraction Mistakes on a Test

1. Not simplifying fractions first. Always simplify fractions to the simples form before adding, subtracting or other operations.

2. Not understanding common denominators.

To add or subtract fractions, they must have the same denominator. For example, to add 1/2 and 3/4, a common denominator is needed. The common denominator 4, because 4 is a multiple of both 2 and 4.

So, you would convert 1/2 to 2/4 and add it to 3/4 to get 2/4 + 3/4 = 5/4

3. Errors with mixed numbers and converting to improper fractions or vice versa.

Referring to the problem above, 5/4 is an improper fraction, since 5 (the numerator) is larger than 4 (the denominator). This can be converted to a mixed number – 5/4 = 4/4 + 1/4, and we know 4/4 = 1

so – 1 + 1/4 = 1 1/4.

4. Errors with equivalent fractions and reducing to the simplest form.

Here is question – Does 2/4 = 1/2 ?   YES! we can reduce 2/4 by dividing the numerator (top) and the denominator (bottom) by 2. so 2/4 divided by 2/2 = 1/2.

5. Errors canceling common factors in fractions.

Cancelling out common factors works like this – 2/4 X 4/8   These are divisible by 2 so we divide by 2 in the top of one side and bottom of the other – 1/4 X 4/4

We can do the same again with the bottom of the first fraction and the top of the second – 1/1 X 1/4   and since 1/1 = 1 we have 1 X 1/4 = 1/4.

6. Errors with basic arithmetic operations (addition, subtraction, multiplication, and division) with fractions.

Decimal Tips, Tricks and Shortcuts

Converting Decimals to Fractions

Converting decimals to fractions is easy if you say it the right way! If you say "point one" or "point 25," you'll have trouble.

But if you say, "one tenth" and "twenty-five hundredths," then you have already solved it! That's because, if you know your fractions, you know that "one tenth" looks like this: 1/10. And "twenty-five hundredths" looks like this: 25/100.

Even if you have digits before the decimal, such as 3.4, learning how to say the word will help you with the conversion into a fraction. It's not "three point four," it's "three and four tenths." Knowing this, you know that the fraction which looks like "three and four tenths" is 3 4/10.

The conversion is not complete until you reduce the fraction to its lowest terms: It's not 25/100, but 1/4.

Converting Decimals to Percent

Changing a decimal to a percent is easy if you remember one thing: multiply by 100.

For example, if you start with .45, simply multiply it by 100 for 45. Then add the % sign to the end - 45%.

Think of it this way: take out the decimal point, add a percent sign on the opposite side. In other words, the decimal on the left is replaced by the % on the right.

It doesn't work quite that easily if the decimal is in the middle of the number. For example, 3.7. Here, take out the decimal in the middle and replace it with a 0 % at the end. So 3.7 converted to decimal is 370%.

Percent Tips, Tricks and Shortcuts

Percent problems are not nearly as scary as they appear, if you remember this neat trick:

Draw a cross as in:

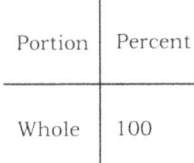

In the upper left, write PORTION. In the bottom left, write WHOLE. In the top right, write PERCENT and in the bottom right, write 100. Whatever your problem is, you will leave blank the unknown, and fill in the other four parts. For example, let's suppose your problem is: Find 10% of 50. Since we know the 10% part, we put 10 in the percent corner. Since the whole number in our problem is 50, we put that in the corner marked whole. You always put 100 underneath the percent, so we leave it as is, which leaves only the top left corner blank. This is where we'll put our answer. Now simply multiply the two corner numbers that are NOT 100. Here, it's 10 X 50. That gives us 500. Now divide by the remaining corner, or 100, to get a final answer of 5. 5 is the number that goes in the upper-left corner, and is your final solution.

Another hint to remember: Percents are the same thing as hundredths in decimals. So .45 is the same as 45 hundredths or 45 percent.

Converting Percents to Decimals

Percents are a type of decimal, so it should be no surprise that converting between the two is actually fairly simple. Here are a few tricks and shortcuts to keep in mind:

- Remember that percent literally means "per 100" or "for every 100." So when you speak of 30% you're saying 30 for every 100 or the fraction 30/100. In basic math, you learned that fractions that have 10 or 100 as the denominator can easily be turned to a decimal. 30/100 is thirty hundredths, or expressed as a decimal, .30.
- Another way to look at it: To convert a percent to a decimal, simply divide the number by 100. So for instance, if the percent is 47%, divide 47 by 100. The result will be .47. Get rid of the % mark and you're done.
- Remember that the easiest way of dividing by 100 is by moving your decimal two spots to the left.

Converting Percents to Fractions

Converting percents to fractions is easy. After all, a percent is just a type of fraction; it tells you what part of 100 that you're talking about. Here are some simple ideas for making the conversion from a percent to a fraction:

- If the percent is a whole number -- say 34% -- then simply write a fraction with 100 as the denominator (the bottom number). Then put the percentage itself on top. So 34% becomes 34/100.
- Now reduce as you would reduce any percent. Here, by dividing 2 into 34 and 2 into 100, you get 17/50.
- If your percent is not a whole number -- say 3.4% --then convert it to a decimal expressed as hundredths. 3.4 is the same as 3.40 (or 3 and forty hundredths). Now ask yourself how you would express "three and forty hundredths" as a fraction. It would, of course, be 3 40/100. Reduce this and it becomes 3 2/5.

How to Answer Basic Math Multiple Choice

The time allowed on the math portion of a standardized test is typically so short that there's no room for error. You have to be fast and accurate.

Math strategy is very helpful, but nothing beats knowing your stuff! Make sure that you have learned all the important formulas that will be used.

If you don't know the formulas, strategy won't help you.

How to Answer Basic Math Questions - the Basics

First, read the problem, but not the answers.

Work through the problem first and come up with your own answers. Hopefully, you should find your answer among the choices.

If no answer matches the one you got, re-check your math, but this time, use a different method. In math, there are different ways to solve a problem.

Math Multiple Choice Strategy

The two strategies for working with basic math multiple choice are Estimation and Elimination.

Estimation is just as it sounds - try to estimate an approximate answer first. Then look at the choices.

Elimination is probably the most powerful strategy for answering multiple choice.

Eliminate obviously incorrect answers and narrowing the possible choices.

Here are a few basic math examples of how this works.

Solve 2/3 + 5/12

    a. 9/17

    b. 3/11

    c. 7/12

    d. 1 1/12

First estimate the answer. 2/3 is more than half and 5/12 is about half, so the answer is going to be very close to 1.

Next, Eliminate. Choice A is about 1/2 and can be eliminated, choice B is very small, less than 1/2 and can be eliminated. Choice C is close to 1/2 and can be eliminated. Leaving only choice D, which is just over 1.

Work through the solution, find a common denominator and add. The correct answer is 1 1/12, so Choice D is correct.

Let's look at another example:

Solve 4/5 − 2/3

    a. 2/2

    b. 2/13

    c. 1

    d. 2/15

First, quickly estimate the answer. 4/5 is very close to 1, and 2/3 more than half, so the answer is going to be less than 1/2.

Choice A can be eliminated right away, because it is 1. Choice C can be eliminated for the same reason.

Next, look at the denominators. Since 5 and 3 don't go into 13, choice B can be eliminated as well.

That leaves choice D. Checking the answer, the common denominator will be 15. So the answer is 2/15 and choice D is correct.

How to Solve Word Problems

Do you know what the biggest tip for solving word problems is?

Practice regularly and systematically.

Sounds simple and easy right? Yes it is, and yes it really does work.

Word problems are a way of thinking and require you to translate a real-world problem into mathematical terms.

Some math teachers say that learning how to think mathematically is the main reason for teaching word problems.

So what does that mean?

Studying word problems and math in general requires a logical and mathematical frame of mind. The only way you can get this is by practicing regularly, which means every day.

It is critical that you practice word problems every day for the 5 days before the exam as the absolute minimum.

If you practice and miss a day, you have lost the mathematical frame of mind and the benefit of your previous practice is gone. You must start all over again.

Everything is important.

All the information given in the problem has some purpose. There is no unnecessary information! Word problems are typically around 50 words in 2 or 3 sentences.

Often, the relationships are complicated. To explain everything, every word counts.

Make sure that you use every piece of information.

7 steps to solving word problems.

Step 1 – Read through the problem at least three times. The first reading should be a quick scan, and the next two readings should be done slowly to find answers to these questions:

What does the problem ask? (Usually located at the end)

Mark all information and underline all important words or phrases.

Step 2 – Draw a picture. Use arrows, circles, lines, whatever works for you. This makes the problem real.

A favorite word problem is something like, 1 train leaves Station A travelling at 100 km/hr and another train leaves Station B travelling at 60 km/hr. ...

Draw a line, the two stations, and the two trains at either end.

Depending on the question, make a table with a blank portion to show information you don't know.

Step 3 – Assign a single letter to represent each unknown.

You may want to note the unknown that each letter represents so you don't get confused.

Step 4 – Translate the information into an equation.

Remember that the main problem with word problems is that they are not expressed in regular math equations. Your ability to identify correctly the variables and translate the information into an equation determines your ability to solve the problem.

Step 5 – Check the equation to see if it looks like regular equations that you are used to seeing and whether it looks sensible.

Does the equation appear to represent the information in the question? Take note that you may need to rewrite some formulas needed to solve the word problem equation.

Step 6 – Use algebra rules to solve the equation.

Simplify each side of the equation by removing parentheses and combining like terms.

Use addition or subtraction to isolate the variable term on one side of the equation. If a number crosses to the other side of the equation, the sign changes to the opposite -- for example positive to negative.

Use multiplication or division to solve for the variable. What you to once side of the equation you must do for the other.

Where there are multiple unknowns you will need to use elimination or substitution methods to resolve all the equations.

Step 7 – Check your final answers to see if they make sense with the information given in the problem.

For example, if the word problem involves a discount, the final price should be less or if a product was taxed then the final answer has to cost more.

Types of Word Problems

Word problems can be classified into 12 types. Below are examples of each type with a complete solution. Some types of word problems can be solved quickly using multiple choice strategies and some cannot. Always look for ways to estimate the answer and then eliminate choices.

1. Age

A girl is 10 years older than her brother. By next year, she will be twice the age of her brother. What are their ages now?

   a. 25, 15
   b. 19, 9
   c. 21, 11
   d. 29, 19

Solution: B

We will assume that the girl's age is "a" and her brother's is "b." This means that based on the information in the first sentence,
$a = 10 + b$

Next year, she will be twice her brother's age, which gives
$a + 1 = 2(b + 1)$

We need to solve for one unknown factor and then use the answer to solve for the other. To do this we substitute the value of "a" from the first equation into the second equation. This gives

$10 + b + 1 = 2b + 2$
$11 + b = 2b + 2$
$11 - 2 = 2b - b$
$b = 9$

$9 = b$ this means that her brother is 9 years old. Solving for the girl's age in the first equation gives $a = 10 + 9$. $a = 19$ the girl is aged 19. So, the girl is aged 19 and the boy is 9

2. Distance or speed

Two boats travel down a river towards the same destination, starting at the same time. One boat is traveling at 52 km/hr, and the other boat at 43 km/hr. How far apart will they be after 40 minutes?

   a. 46.67 km
   b. 19.23 km
   c. 6.4 km
   d. 14.39 km

Solution: C

After 40 minutes, the first boat will have traveled = 52 km/hr x 40 minutes/60 minutes = 34.66 km
After 40 minutes, the second boat will have traveled = 43 km/hr x 40/60 minutes = 28.66 km
Difference between the two boats will be 34.66 km – 28.66 km = 6.04 km.

Multiple Choice Strategy

First estimate the answer. The first boat is travelling 9 km. faster than the second, for 40 minutes, which is 2/3 of an hour. 2/3 of 9 = 6, as a rough guess of the distance apart.

Choices A, B and D can be eliminated right away.

3. Ratio

The instructions in a cookbook states that 700 grams of flour must be mixed in 100 ml of water, and 0.90 grams of salt added. A cook however has just 325 grams of flour. What is the quantity of water and salt that he should use?

   a. 0.41 grams and 46.4 ml
   b. 0.45 grams and 49.3 ml
   c. 0.39 grams and 39.8 ml
   d. 0.25 grams and 40.1 ml

Solution: A

The Cookbook states 700 grams of flour, but the cook only has 325. The first step is to determine the percentage of flour he has 325/700 x 100 = 46.4%
That means that 46.4% of all other items must also be used.
46.4% of 100 = 46.4 ml of water
46.4% of 0.90 = 0.41 grams of salt.

Multiple Choice Strategy

The recipe calls for 700 grams of flour but the cook only has 325, which is just less than half, the quantity of water and salt are going to be about half.

Choices C and D can be eliminated right away. Choice B is very close so be careful. Looking closely at choice B, it is exactly half, and since 325 is slightly less than half of 700, it can't be correct.
Choice A is correct.

4. Percent

An agent received $6,685 as his commission for selling a property. If his commission was 13% of the selling price, how much was the property?

   a. $68,825
   b. $121,850
   c. $49,025
   d. $51,423

Solution: D

Let's assume that the property price is x
That means from the information given, 13% of x = 6,685
Solve for x,
x = 6685 x 100/13 = $51,423

Multiple Choice Strategy

The commission, 13%, is just over 10%, which is easier to work with. Round up $6685 to $6700, and multiple by 10 for an approximate answer. 10 X 6700 = $67,000. You can do this in your head. Choice B is much too big and can be eliminated. Choice C is too small and can be eliminated. Choices A and D are left and good possibilities.

Do the calculations to make the final choice.

5. Sales & Profit

A store owner buys merchandise for $21,045. He transports them for $3,905 and pays his staff $1,450 to stock the merchandise on his shelves. If he does not incur further costs, how much does he need to sell the items to make $5,000 profit?

    a. $32,500
    b. $29,350
    c. $32,400
    d. $31,400

Solution: D

Total cost of the items is $21,045 + $3,905 + $1,450 = $26,400

Total cost is now $26,400 + $5000 profit = $31,400

Multiple Choice Strategy

Round off and add the numbers up in your head quickly.
21,000 + 4,000 + 1500 = 26500. Add in 5000 profit for a total of 31500.

Choice B is too small and can be eliminated. Choices C and A are too large and can be eliminated.

6. Tax/Income

A woman earns $42,000 per month and pays 5% tax on her monthly income. If the Government increases her monthly taxes by $1,500, what is her income after tax?

    a. $38,400
    b. $36,050
    c. $40,500
    d. $39, 500

Solution: A

Initial tax on income was 5/100 x 42,000 = $2,100
$1,500 was added to the tax to give $2,100 + 1,500 = $3,600
Income after tax left is $42,000 - $3,600 = $38,400

7. Interest

A man invests $3000 in a 2-year term deposit that pays 3% interest per year. How much will he have at the end of the 2-year term?

    a. $5,200
    b. $3,020
    c. $3,182.7
    d. $3,000

Solution: C

This is a compound interest problem. The funds are invested for 2 years and interest is paid yearly, so in the second year, he will earn interest on the interest paid in the first year.

3% interest in the first year = 3/100 x 3,000 = $90
At end of first year, total amount = 3,000 + 90 = $3,090
Second year = 3/100 x 3,090 = 92.7.
At end of second year, total amount = $3090 + $92.7 = $3,182.7

8. Averaging

The average weight of 10 books is 54 grams. 2 more books were added and the average weight became 55.4. If one of the 2 new books added weighed 62.8 g, what is the weight of the other?

    a. 44.7 g
    b. 67.4 g
    c. 62 g
    d. 52 g

Solution: C
Total weight of 10 books with average 54 grams will be = 10 × 54 = 540 g
Total weight of 12 books with average 55.4 will be = 55.4 × 12 = 664.8 g
So total weight of the remaining 2 will be= 664.8 – 540 = 124.8 g
If one weighs 62.8, the weight of the other will be= 124.8 g – 62.8 g = 62 g

Multiple Choice Strategy

Averaging problems can be estimated by looking at which direction the average goes. If additional items are added and the average goes up, the new items much be greater than the average. If the average goes down after new items are added, the new items must be less than the average.
Here, the average is 54 grams and 2 books are added which increases the average to 55.4, so the new books must weight more than 54 grams.

Choices A and D can be eliminated right away.

9. Probability

A bag contains 15 marbles of various colors. If 3 marbles are white, 5 are red and the rest are black, what is the probability of randomly picking out a black marble from the bag?

    a. 7/15
    b. 3/15
    c. 1/5
    d. 4/15

Solution: A

Total marbles = 15
Number of black marbles = 15 − (3 + 5) = 7
Probability of picking out a black marble = 7/15

10. Two Variables

A company paid a total of $2850 to book for 6 single rooms and 4 double rooms in a hotel for one night. Another company paid $3185 to book for 13 single rooms for one night in the same hotel. What is the cost for single and double rooms in that hotel?

    a. single= $250 and double = $345
    b. single= $254 and double = $350
    c. single = $245 and double = $305
    d. single = $245 and double = $345

Solution: D

We can determine the price of single rooms from the information given of the second company. 13 single rooms = 3185.
One single room = 3185 / 13 = 245
The first company paid for 6 single rooms at $245. 245 x 6 = $1470

Total amount paid for 4 double rooms by first company = $2850 - $1470 = $1380

Cost per double room = 1380 / 4 = $345

11. Simple Geometry

The length of a rectangle is 5 in. more than its width. The perimeter of the rectangle is 26 in. What is the width and length of the rectangle?

    a. width = 6 inches, Length = 9 inches
    b. width = 4 inches, Length = 9 inches
    c. width =4 inches, Length = 5 inches
    d. width = 6 inches, Length = 11 inches

Solution: B

Formula for perimeter of a rectangle is 2(L + W)
p=26, so 2(L+W) = p
The length is 5 inches more than the width, so
2(w+5) + 2w = 26
2w + 10 + 2w = 26
2w + 2w = 26 - 10
4w = 16

W = 16/4 = 4 inches

L is 5 inches more than w, so L = 5 + 4 = 9 inches.

12. Totals and fractions

A basket contains 125 oranges, mangos and apples. If 3/5 of the fruits in the basket are mangos and only 2/5 of the mangos are ripe, how many ripe mangos are there in the basket?

   a. 30
   b. 68
   c. 55
   d. 47

Solution: A
Number of mangos in the basket is 3/5 x 125 = 75
Number of ripe mangos = 2/5 x 75 = 30

Ratios

In mathematics, a ratio is a relationship between two numbers of the same kind (e.g., objects, persons, students, spoonfuls, units of whatever identical dimension), usually expressed as "a to b" or a:b, sometimes expressed arithmetically as a dimensionless quotient of the two which explicitly indicates how many times the first number contains the second (not necessarily an integer). In layman's terms a ratio represents, simply, for every amount of one thing, how much there is of another thing. For example, suppose I have 10 pairs of socks for every pair of shoes then the ratio of shoes:socks would be 1:10 and the ratio of socks:shoes would be 10:1.

Notation and terminology

The ratio of numbers A and B can be expressed as:
the ratio of A to B
A is to B
A:B

A rational number which is the quotient of A divided by B
The numbers A and B are sometimes called terms with A being the antecedent and B being the consequent.

The proportion expressing the equality of the ratios A:B and C:D is written A:B=C:D or A:B::C:D. This form, when spoken or written in the English language, is often expressed as
A is to B as C is to D.

Again, A, B, C, D are called the terms of the proportion. A and D are called the extremes, and B and C are called the means. The equality of three or more proportions is called a continued proportion.

Ratios are sometimes used with three or more terms. The dimensions of a two by four that is ten inches long are 2:4:10.

Examples

The quantities being compared in a ratio might be physical quantities such as speed or length, or numbers of objects, or amounts of particular substances. A common example of the last case is the weight ratio of water to cement used in concrete, which is commonly stated as 1:4. This means that the weight of cement used is four times the weight of water used. It does not say anything about the total amounts of cement and water used, nor the quantity of concrete being made. Equivalently it could be said that the ratio of cement to water is 4:1, that there is 4 times as much cement as water, or that there is a quarter (1/4) as much water as cement..
Older televisions have a 4:3 "aspect ratio," which means that the width is 4/3 of the height; modern widescreen TVs have a 16:9 aspect ratio.

Fractional

If there are 2 oranges and 3 apples, the ratio of oranges to apples is 2:3, and the ratio of oranges to the total number of pieces of fruit is 2:5. These ratios can also be expressed in fraction form: there are 2/3 as many oranges as apples, and 2/5 of the pieces of fruit are oranges. If orange juice concentrate is to be diluted with water in the ratio 1:4, then one part of concentrate is mixed with four parts of water, giving five parts total; the quantity of orange juice concentrate is 1/4 the amount of water, while the amount of orange juice concentrate is 1/5 of the total liquid. In both ratios and fractions, it is important to be clear what is being compared to what, and beginners often make mistakes for this reason.

Number of terms

In general, when comparing the quantities of a two-quantity ratio, this can be expressed as a fraction derived from the ratio. For example, in a ratio of 2:3, the amount/size/volume/number of the first quantity will be that of the second quantity. This pattern also works with ratios with more than two terms. However, a ratio with more than two terms cannot be completely converted into a single fraction; a single fraction represents only one part of the ratio since a fraction can only compare two numbers. If the ratio deals with objects or amounts of objects, this is often expressed as "for every two parts of the first quantity there are three parts of the second quantity."

Percent and ratio

If we multiply all quantities involved in a ratio by the same number, the ratio remains valid. For example, a ratio of 3:2 is the same as 12:8. It is usual either to reduce terms to the lowest common denominator, or to express them in parts per hundred (percent).

If a mixture contains substances A, B, C & D in the ratio 5:9:4:2 then there are 5 parts of A for every 9 parts of B, 4 parts of C and 2 parts of D. As 5+9+4+2=20, the total mixture contains 5/20 of A (5 parts out of 20), 9/20 of B, 4/20 of C, and 2/20 of D. If we divide all numbers by the total and multiply by 100, this is converted to percentages: 25% A, 45% B, 20% C, and 10% D (equivalent to writing the ratio as 25:45:20:10).

Proportion

If the two or more ratio quantities encompass all the quantities in a particular situation, for example two apples and three oranges in a fruit basket containing no other types of fruit, it could be said that "the whole" contains five parts, made up of two parts apples and three parts oranges. Here, or 40% of the whole are apples or 60% of the whole are oranges. This comparison of a specific quantity to "the whole" is sometimes called a proportion. Proportions are sometimes expressed as percentages as demonstrated above.

Reduction

Note that ratios can be reduced (as fractions are) by dividing each quantity by the common factors of all the quantities. This is often called "cancelling." As for fractions, the simplest form is considered to be that in which the numbers in the ratio are the smallest possible integers.

Thus, the ratio 40:60 may be considered equivalent in meaning to the ratio 2:3 within contexts concerned only with relative quantities.

Mathematically, we write: "40:60" = "2:3" (dividing both quantities by 20).
Grammatically, we would say, "40 to 60 equals 2 to 3."
An alternative representation is: "40:60::2:3"
Grammatically, we would say, "40 is to 60 as 2 is to 3."
A ratio that has integers for both quantities and that cannot be reduced any further (using integers) is said to be in simplest form or lowest terms.
Sometimes it is useful to write a ratio in the form 1:n or n:1 to enable comparisons of different ratios.

For example, the ratio 4:5 can be written as 1:1.25 (dividing both sides by 4). Alternatively, 4:5 can be written as 0.8:1 (dividing both sides by 5). Where the context makes the meaning clear, a ratio in this form is sometimes written without the 1 and the colon, though, mathematically, this makes it a factor or multiplier.

Exponents: Tips, Shortcuts & Tricks

Exponents seem like advanced math to most—like some mysterious code with a complicated meaning. In fact, though, an exponent is just short hand for saying that you're multiplying a number by itself two or more times. For instance, instead of saying that you're multiplying 5 x 5 x 5, you can show that you're multiplying 5 by itself 3 times if you just write 5^3. We usually say this as "five to the third power" or "five to the power of three." In this example, the raised 3 is an "exponent," while the 5 is the "base." You can even use exponents with fractions. For instance, $1/2^3$ means you're multiplying 1/2 x 1/2 x 1/2. (The answer is 1/8). Some other helpful hints for working with exponents:

- Here's how to do basic multiplication of exponents. If you have the same number with a different exponent (For instance 5^3 X 5^2) just add the exponents and multiply the bases as usual. The answer, then, is 5^5.
- This doesn't work, though, if the bases are different. For instance, in 5^3 X 3^2 we simply have to do the math the long way to figure out the final solution: 5 x 5 x 5, multiplying that result times the result for 3 X 3. (The answer is 1125).
- Looking at it from the opposite side, to divide two exponents with the same base (or bottom number), subtract the smaller exponent from the larger one. If we were dividing the problem above, we would subtract the 2 from the 3 to get 1. 5 to the power of 1 is simply 5.
- One time when thinking of exponents as merely multiplication doesn't work is when the raised number is zero. Any number raised to the "zeroth" power is 1 (Not, as we tend to think, zero).

Number (x)	X^2	X^3
1	1	1
2	4	8
3	9	27
4	16	64
5	25	125
6	36	216
7	49	343
8	64	512
9	81	729
10	100	1000
11	121	1331
12	144	1728
13	169	2197
14	196	2744
15	225	3375
16	256	4096

Solving One-Variable Linear Equations

Linear equations with variable x is an equation with the following form:
$$ax = b$$

where a and b are real numbers. If a=0 and b is different from 0, then the equation has no solution.

Let's solve one simple example of a linear equation with one variable:
$$4x - 2 = 2x + 6$$

When we are given this type of equation, we are always moving variables to the one side, and real numbers to the other side of the equals sign. Always remember: if you are changing sides, you are changing signs. Let's move all variables to the left, and real number to the right side:

4x - 2 = 2x + 6
4x - 2x = 6 + 2
2x = 8
x = 8/2
x = 4

When 2x goes to the left it becomes -2x, and -2 goes to the right and becomes +2. After calculations, we find that x is 4, which is a solution of our linear equation.

Let's solve a little more complex linear equation:

2x - 6/4 + 4 = x
2x - 6 + 16 = 4x
2x - 4x = -16 + 6
-2x = -10
x = -10/-2
x = 5

We multiply whole equation by 4, to lose the fractional line. Now we have a simple linear equation. If we change sides, we change the signs.

Solving Two-Variable Linear Equations

If we have 2 or more linear equations with 2 or more variables, then we have a system of linear equations. The idea here is to express one variable using the other in one equation, and then use it in the second equation, so we get a linear equation with one variable. Here is an example:
x - y = 3
2x + y = 9
From the first equation, we express y using x.

y = x - 3

In the second equation, we write x-3 instead of y. And there we get a linear equation with one variable x.

2x + x - 3 = 9
3x = 9 + 3
3x = 12
x = 12/3
x = 4

Now that we found x, we can use it to find y.

y = x - 3
y = 4 - 3
y = 1

So, the solution of this system is (x,y) = (4,1).

Let's solve one more system using a different method:

Solve:

5x - 3y = 17
x + 3y = 11

5x - 3y + x + 3y = 17 - 11

Notice that we have -3y in the first equation and +3y in the second. If we add these 2, we get zero, which means we lose variable y. So, we add these 2 equations and we get a linear equation with one variable.

6x = 6
x = 1

Now that we have x, we use it to find y.

5 - 3y = 17
-3y = 17 - 5
-3y = 12
y = 12/(-3)
y = -4

Adding and Subtracting Polynomials

When we are adding or subtracting 2 or more polynomials, we have to first group the same variables (arguments) that have the same degrees and then add or subtract them. For example, if we have ax^3 in one polynomial (where a is some real number), we have to group it with bx^3 from the other polynomial (where b is also some real number). Here is one example with adding polynomials:

$(-x^2 + 2x + 3) + (2x^2 + 4x - 5) =$
$-x^2 + 2x + 3 + 2x^2 + 4x - 5 =$
$x^2 + 6x - 2$

We remove the brackets, and since we have a plus in front of every bracket, the signs in the polynomials don't change.
We group variables with the same degrees. We have -1 + 2, which is 1 and that's how we got x^2. For the first degree, where we have 2 + 4 which is 6, and the constants (real numbers) where we have 3 - 5 which is -2.

The principle is the same with subtracting, only we have to keep in mind that a minus in front of the polynomial changes all signs in that polynomial. Here is one example:

$(4x^3 - x^2 + 3) - (-3x^2 - 10) =$
$4x^3 - x^2 + 3 + 3x^2 + 10 =$
$4x^3 + 2x^2 + 13$

We remove the brackets, and since we have a minus in front of the second polynomial, all signs in that polynomial change. We have -3 x 2 and with minus in front, it becomes a plus and same goes for -10.

Now we group the variables with same degrees: there is no variable with the third degree in the second polynomial, so we just write 4 x 3. We group other variables the same way as adding polynomials.

Multiplying and Dividing Polynomials

If we have two polynomials that we need to multiply, then multiply each member of the first polynomial with each member of the second. Let's see in one example how this works:

$(x-1)(x-2) = x^2 - 2x - x + 2 = x^2 - 3x + 2$

The first member of the first polynomial is multiplied with the first member of the second polynomial and then with the second member of the second polynomial. Continue the process with the second member of the first polynomial, then simplify.

To multiply more polynomials, multiply the first 2, then multiply that result with next polynomial and so on. Here is one example:

$(1 - x)(2 - x)(3 - x) = (2 - x - 2x + x^2)(3 - x)$
$= (2 - 3x + x^2)(3 - x)$
$= 6 - 2x - 9x + 3x^2 + 3x^2 - x^3 = 6 - 11x + 6x^2 - x^3$

Simplifying Polynomials

Let's say we are given some expression with one or more variables, where we have to add, subtract and multiply polynomials. We do the calculations with variables and constants and then we group the variables with the appropriate degrees. As a result, we would get a polynomial. This process is called simplifying polynomials, where we go from a complex expression to a simple polynomial.

Example:

Simplify the following expression and arrange the degrees from bigger to smaller:

$4 + 3x - 2x^2 + 5x + 6x^3 - 2x^2 + 1 = 6x^3 - 4x^2 + 8x + 5$

We can have more complex expressions such as:

$(x + 5)(1 - x) - (2x - 2) = x - x^2 + 5 - 5x - 2x + 2 = -x^2 - 6x + 7$

Here, first we multiply the polynomials and then we subtract the result and the third polynomial.

Factoring Polynomials

If we have a polynomial that we want to write as multiplication of a real number and a polynomial or as a multiplication of 2 or more polynomials, then we are dealing with factoring polynomials.

Let's see an example for a simple factoring:

$12x^2 + 6x - 4 =$
$2 * 6x^2 + 2 * 3x - 2 * 2 =$
$2(6x^2 + 3x - 2)$

We look at every polynomial member as a product of a real number and a variable. Notice that all real numbers in the polynomial are even, so they have the same number (factor). We pull out that 2 in front of the polynomial, and we write what is left.

What if have a more complex case, where we can't find a factor that is a real number? Here is an example:

$x^2 - 2x + 1 =$
$x^2 - x - x + 1 =$
$x(x - 1) - (x - 1) =$
$(x - 1)(x - 1)$

We can write -2x as –x-x . Now we group first 2 members and we see that they have the same factor x, which we can pull in front of them. For the other 2 members, we pull the minus in front of them, so we can get the same binomial that we got with the first 2 members. Now we have that this binomial is the factor for x(x-1) and (x-1).

If we pull x-1 in front (underlined), from the first member we are left with x, and from the second we have -1.

And that is how we transform a polynomial into a product of 2 polynomials (here, binomials).

Quadratic equations

A. Factoring

Quadratic equations are usually called second degree equations, which mean that the second degree is the highest degree of the variable that can be found in the quadratic equation. The form of these equations is:

$$ax^2 + bx + c = 0$$

where a, b and c are some real numbers.

One way for solving quadratic equations is the factoring method, where we transform the quadratic equation into a product of 2 or more polynomials. Let's see how that works in one simple example:

$x^2 + 2x = 0$

$x(x+2) = 0$

$(x=0) \vee (x+2=0)$

$(x=0) \vee (x=-2)$

Notice that here we don't have parameter c, but this is still a quadratic equation, because we have the second degree of variable x. Our factor here is x, which we put in front, and we are left with x+2. The equation is equal to 0, so either x or x+2 are 0, or, both are 0.

So, our 2 solutions are 0 and -2.

B. Quadratic formula

If we are unsure how to rewrite quadratic equations so we can solve it using factoring method, we can use the formula for quadratic equation:

$$x_{1,2} = \frac{-b \pm \sqrt{b^2 - 4ac}}{2a}$$

We write $x_{1,2}$ because it represents 2 solutions of the equation. Here is one example:

$3x^2 - 10x + 3 = 0$

$x_{1,2} = \dfrac{-b \pm \sqrt{b^2 - 4ac}}{2a}$

$x_{1,2} = \dfrac{-(-10) \pm \sqrt{(-10)^2 - 4 \cdot 3 \cdot 3}}{2 \cdot 3}$

$x_{1,2} = \dfrac{10 \pm \sqrt{100 - 36}}{6}$

$x_{1,2} = \dfrac{10 \pm \sqrt{64}}{6}$

$x_{1,2} = \dfrac{10 \pm 8}{6}$

$x_1 = \dfrac{10 + 8}{6} = \dfrac{18}{6} = 3$

$x_2 = \dfrac{10 - 8}{6} = \dfrac{2}{6} = \dfrac{1}{3}$

We see that a is 3, b is -10 and c is 3.
We use these numbers in the equation and do some calculations.

Notice that we have + and -, so x_1 is for + and x_2 is for -, and that's how we get 2 solutions.

Cartesian Plane, Coordinate Plane and Coordinate Grid

To locate dots and draw lines and curves, we use the coordinate plane. It also called Cartesian coordinate plane. It is a two-dimensional surface with a coordinate grid in it, which helps us to count the units. For the counting of those units, we use x-axis (horizontal scale) and y-axis (vertical scale).

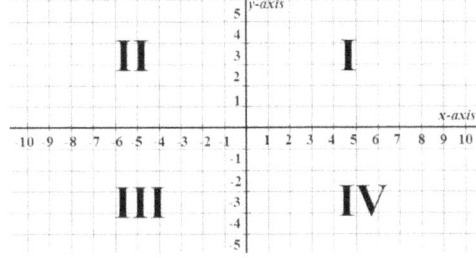

The whole system is called a coordinate system which is divided into 4 parts, called quadrants. The quadrant where all numbers are positive is the 1st quadrant (I), and if we go counterclockwise, we mark all 4 quadrants.

The location of a dot in the coordinate system is represented by coordinates. Coordinates are represented as a pair of numbers, where the 1st number is located on the x-axis and the 2nd number is located on the y-axis. So, if a dot A has coordinates a and b, then we write:

A=(a,b)   or   A(a,b)

The point where x-axis and y-axis intersect is called an origin. The origin is the point from which we measure the distance along the x and y axes.

In the Cartesian coordinate system we can calculate the distance between 2 given points. If we have dots with coordinates:
A=(a,b)
B=(c,d)
Then the distance d between A and B can be calculated by the following formula:

$$d = \sqrt{(c-a)^2 + (d-b)^2}$$

Cartesian coordinate system is used for the drawing of 2-dimensional shapes, and is also commonly used for functions.

Example:

Draw the function   y = (1 - x)/2

To draw a linear function, we need at least 2 points.
If we put that x=0 then value for y would be:

$$y = \frac{1-x}{2} = \frac{1-0}{2} = \frac{1}{2}$$

We found the 1st point, let's name it A, with following coordinates:

A = (0,1/2)

To find the 2nd point, we can put that x=1. Here,, the value for y would be:

$$y = \frac{1-x}{2} = \frac{1-1}{2} = \frac{0}{2} = 0$$

If we denote the 2nd point with B, then the coordinates for this point are:

B=(1,0)

Since we have 2 points necessary for the function, we find them in the coordinate system and we connect them with a line that represents the function,

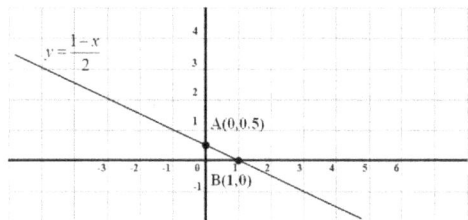

Perimeter Area and Volume

Definitions

Perimeter - the linear distance around a figure

Area - the number of square units to completely cover a 2-D face

Surface Area - the combined areas of all faces of a 3-D solid

Volume - The number of cube units to completely fill a 3-D solid

Perimeter and Area (2-dimensional shapes)

Perimeter of a shape determines the length around that shape, while the area includes the space inside the shape.

Example Problems

Determine the Perimeter of a 2-D Shape
To determine the perimeter of any figure, simply add the lengths of every side. Be sure to write you final answer with linear units.

Rectangles have opposite sides that are congrucnt (exactly the same), so an alternate method is to double the sum of the length and width.

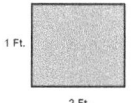

Identify if the opposite sides are congruent.

Add all sides.

P = 2 + 1 + 2 + 1 = 6 ft

Determine the Area of a 2-D Shape

Specific equations exist to determine the areas of basic 2-D figures. When multiple figures are present, select the equation appropriate to your figure, and then substitute values and solve. Be sure that your final answer has square units.

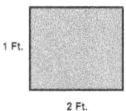

Area$_{Rectangle}$ = Length * Width
Area$_{Rectangle}$ = (2 ft)·(1 ft)
Area$_{Rectangle}$ = 2 ft^2

Area and Perimeter of Common Shapes

Rectangle:

P = 2a + 2b
A = ab

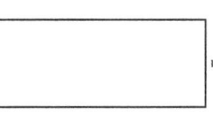

Square

P = 4a
A = a^2

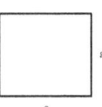

Parallelogram

P = 2a + 2b
A = ah$_a$ = bh$_b$

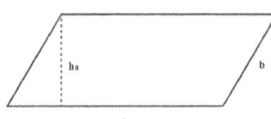

Rhombus

P = 4a
A = ah = $d_1 d_2 / 2$

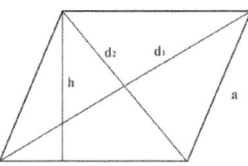

Triangle

P = a + b + c
A = $ah_a/2$ = $bh_b/2$ = $ch_c/2$

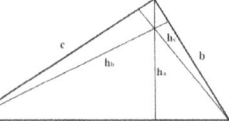

Equilateral Triangle

P = 3a
A = $(a^2 \sqrt{3})/4$

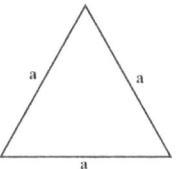

Trapezoid

P = a + b + c + d
A = ((a + b)/2)h

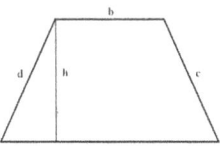

Circle

P = 2r $\prod$
A = $r^2 \prod$

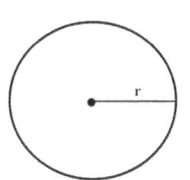

Area and Volume - 3-dimensional shapes

To calculate the area of a 3-dimensional shape, we calculate the areas of all sides and then we add them all.

To find the volume of a 3-dimensional shape, we multiply the area of the base (B) and the height (H) of the 3-dimensional shape.

$$V = BH$$

In case of a pyramid and a cone, the volume would be divided by 3.

$$V = BH/3$$

Here are some of the 3-dimensional shapes with formulas for their area and volume:

Cuboids

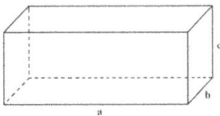

$A = 2(ab + bc + ac)$
$V = abc$

Cube

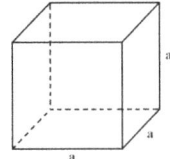

$A = 6a^2$
$V = a^3$

Pyramid

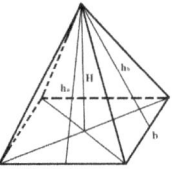

$A = ab + ah_a + bh_b$

$V = abH/3$

Cylinder

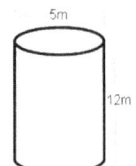

$A = 2r^2\Pi + 2r\Pi H$
$V = r^2\Pi H$

Cone

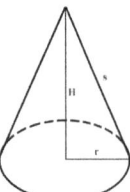

$A = (r + s)r\Pi$
$V = (r^2\Pi H)/3$

Area of Complex 2-D and 3-D Shapes

A complex figure is a combination of 2 or more basic shapes.

Area of a Composite 2-D Shape

To determine the area of any composite figure, simply add the areas of each component basic figure. Be sure to write you final answer with square units.

Mathematics

Example Problem

Determine the area of the given shape.

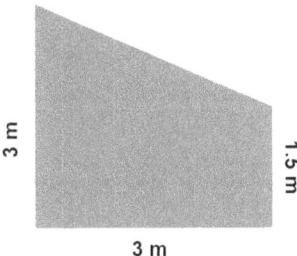

Redraw the original shape as a rectangle and a triangle. Rectangles have opposite sides that are congruent (exactly the same).

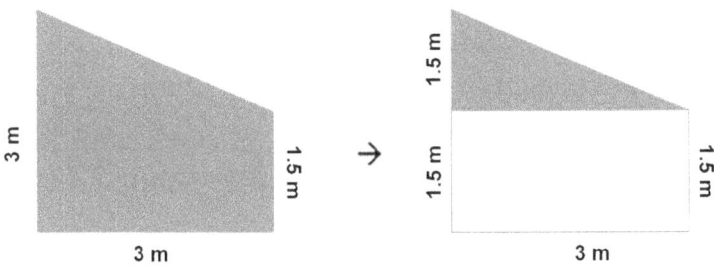

$\text{Area}_{Composite} = \text{Area}_{Triangle} + \text{Area}_{Rectangle}$
$\text{Area}_{Triangle} = (1/2)(\text{Base})(\text{Height}) = (1/2)(3m)(1.5m) = 2.25 \text{ m}^2$
$\text{Area}_{Rectangle} = (\text{Base})(\text{Height}) = (3m)(1.5m) = 4.5 \text{ m}^2$
$\text{Area}_{Composite} = (2.25m^2) + (4.5m^2) = 6.75 \text{ m}^2$

Determine the Surface Area of a Composite 3-D Solid

To determine the surface area of any composite solid, simply add the surface areas of each component basic solid. you must also subtract the area of any internal face. Be sure to write you final answer with square units.

Example Problem

Determine the surface area of the given shape. Leave the final answer in terms of pi.

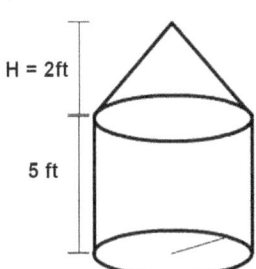

Redraw the original shape as a cylinder and a cone. We will have to subtract the area of the circle where the figures meet from each surface area equation because they are "inside" the solid.

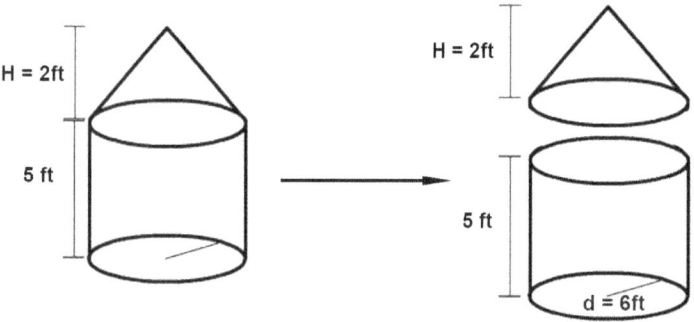

SurfaceArea $_{Composite}$ = S.Area $_{Cone}$ + S.Area $_{Cylinder}$

S.Area $_{Cone}$ = ~~(Base Area)~~+(1/2)(Perimeter)(Height) = (1/2)(dπ)(h) = (1/2)(6π)(2) = 6π ft²

S.Area $_{Cylinder}$ = ~~2~~(Base Area)+(Perimeter)(Height) = (πr²)+(dπ)(h) = (π3²)+(6π)(5) = 39π ft²

S.Area $_{Composite}$ = (6π ft²) + (39π ft²) = 45π ft²

Pythagorean Geometry

If we have a right triangle ABC, where its sides (legs) are a and b and c is a hypotenuse (the side opposite the right angle), then we can establish a relationship between these sides using the following formula:

$c^2 = a^2 + b^2$

This formula is proven in the Pythagorean Theorem. There are many proofs of this theorem, but we'll look at just one geometrical proof:

If we draw squares on the right triangle's sides, then the area of the square on the hypotenuse is equal to the sum of the areas of the squares that are on other two sides of the triangle. Since the areas of these squares are a², b² and c², that is how we got the formula above.

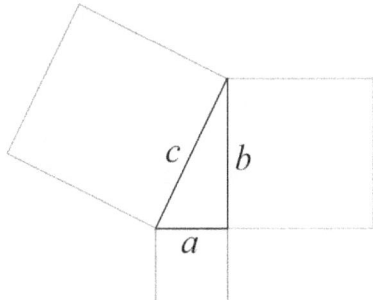

One of the famous right triangles is one with sides 3, 4 and 5. And we can see here that:

$3^2 + 4^2 = 5^2$
$9 + 16 = 25$
$25 = 25$

Example Problem:

The isosceles triangle ABC has a perimeter of 18 centimeters, and the difference between its base and legs is 3 centimeters. Find the height of this triangle.

We write the information we have about triangle ABC and draw a picture for a bet-

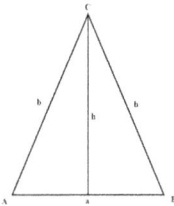

ter understanding of the relationship between its elements:

P = 18 cm
a - b = 3 cm
h = ?

We use the formula for the perimeter of the isosceles triangle, since that is what is given to us:
P = a + 2b = 18 cm

Notice that we have 2 equations with 2 variables, so we can solve it as a system of equations:

a + 2b = 18
a − b = 3 / a + 2b = 18
2a − 2b = 6 / a + 2b + 2a − 2b = 18 + 6
3a = 24
a = 24/3 = 8 cm

Now we go back to find b:
a - b = 3
8 - b = 3
b = 8 - 3
b = 5 cm

Using Pythagorean Theorem, we can find the height using a and b, because the height falls on the side at a right angle. Notice that height cuts side a exactly in half, and that's why we use in the formula a/2. Here, b is our hypotenuse, so we have:

$b^2 = (a/2)^2 + h^2$
$h^2 = b^2 - (a/2)^2$
$h^2 = 5^2 - (8/2)^2$
$h^2 = 5^2 - (8/2)^2$
$h^2 = 25 - 4^2$
$h^2 = 26 - 16$
$h^2 = 9$
h = 3 cm.

Quadrilaterals

Quadrilaterals are 2-dimensional geometrical shapes that have 4 sides and 4 angles. There are many types of quadrilaterals, depending on the length of its sides and if they are parallel and also depending on the size of its angles. All quadrilaterals have the following properties:

>Sum of all interior angles is 360^0

>Sum of all exterior angles is 360^0

A quadrilateral is a parallelogram is it fulfills at least one of the following conditions:

>Angles on each side are supplementary
>Opposite angles are equal
>Opposite sides are equal
>Diagonals intersect each other exactly in half

Here are some of the quadrilaterals:

Square

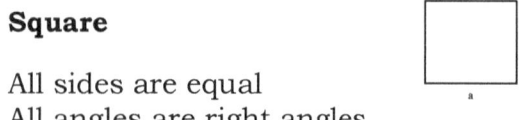

All sides are equal
All angles are right angles

Rectangle

2 pairs of equal sides
All angles are right angles

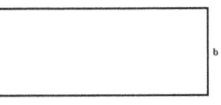

Parallelogram

2 pairs of equal sides
Opposite angles are equal

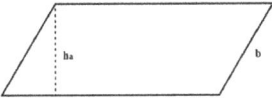

Rhombus

All sides are equal
Opposite angles are equal

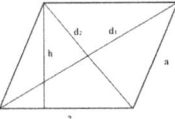

Trapezoid

One pair of parallel sides

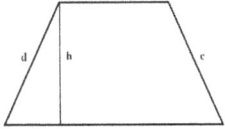

Example Problem

Find all angles of a parallelogram if one angle is greater than the other one by 400.

First, we draw an image of a parallelogram:

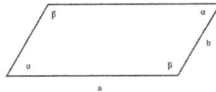

We denote angles by α and β, Since this is a parallelogram, the opposite angles are equal.

We are given that one angle is greater than the other one by 40^0, so we can write:

$β = α + 40^0$

We solve this problem in two ways:
1) The sum of all internal angles of every quadrilateral is 360^0. There are 2 α and 2 β. So we have:
$2α + 2β = 360^0$

Now, instead of β we write α + 40:
$2α + 2(α + 40^0) = 360^0$
$2α + 2α + 80^0 = 360^0$

4 α = 360⁰ - 80⁰
4 α = 280⁰
α = 280⁰ / 4
α = 70⁰
Now we can find β from α:
β = α + 40⁰
β = 70⁰ + 40⁰
β = 110⁰
2) One of the conditions for parallelogram is "Angles on each side are supplementary" and we can use that to find these angles:
α + β = 180⁰
α + α + 40⁰ = 180⁰
2 α = 180⁰ - 40⁰
2 α = 140⁰
α = 70⁰

Now we find β:
β = α + 40⁰
β = 70⁰ + 40⁰
β = 110⁰

Solving inequalities

Basic linear inequalities have one of the following form:

ax + b > 0
ax + b < 0
ax + b $\geq$ 0
ax + b $\leq$ 0

where a and b are some real numbers. Our solution to any of these inequalities would be some interval. Let's see one simple example:

2x - 10 > 16
2x > 16 + 10
2x > 26/2
x > 13

So, the interval here is:

(3, + ∞)

If we have a case where –x is lesser or greater than some number, then we multiply the whole inequality by -1, where the sign of inequality also changes:

-3x + 9 $\leq$ 12
-3x $\leq$ 12 - 9

-3x ≤ 3
-x ≤ 3/-1
x ≤ -3

So, the interval here is: (3, + ∞) Notice the difference in the brackets. This is because this interval contains number 3.

Let's see a little more complex example:

X/X + 1 > 0

Whenever we have a fraction, we have to make a table:

	-1		0	
x	-		-	+
x+1	-		+	+
x/ X + 1	+		-	+

x is positive on the right of the 0, negative on the left of the 0. x+1 is positive on right of the -1, and negative on the left of the -1. If we multiply the signs, we get the signs for the function. We are interested in the positive sign (because we need it to be greater than 0), so the interval is:

(-∞, -1) U (0, +∞)

Data and Statistics

Permutations and Combinations - A Quick Review

Permutations are a series of items where the order is important, such the winners in a race, where there is a first, second and third.

Combinations are where the order is not important, such as a plate of vegetables. There may be carrots, peas and potatoes on a plate and the order doesn't matter.

A key factor in both combination and permutations is with repetition, or with no repetition.

Permutations

There are two types, permutations with repetition and without repetition.

Permutations with Repetition

If there are n items, then there will be n choices. To choose c items, there will be n number of choices for the first choice, and n number of choices for the second choice, repeated c times, or n^c.

Permutation without Repetition

Without repetition the formula gets more complicated. If c items are chosen from n items, for the first choice, there will be n possibilities. For the second choice, since 1 choice has been taken out, there will be n-1 choices available, and with each choice, the possible choices is reduced.

This is a factorial function. For example, if there are 10 balls in a bag and 10 choices are made without repetition, then the number of possible choices will be,

10 X 9 X 8 X 7 X 6 X 5 X 4 X 3 X 2 X 1 = 3,628,800

If there are 2 balls taken out then the number of possibilities will be,

10 X 9 = 90

which gives the formula,

P(n,c) = n!/(n-c)!

Combinations without Repetition

Let say I have 3 chocolates to give to 3 children. I can give one to Brian, one to Peter and one to Laura. Or, I can reverse the order or mix up the order and the result is the same - each child gets a chocolate. This is the same as a permutation - the number of ways I can do this is 3!

If the order does matter, it gets quite a bit more complex.

If there are 10 balls in a bag, and we choose 3, the number of combinations will be

10! / (10 - 3)!

3,628,800 / 5040 = 720 possible combinations

If the order does matter the number of combinations will be less, giving the formula,

n! / (n - c)! * c!

Inferences from Data

Lets say there are 100 people and 30 are chosen randomly. Of those 30, 15 say they will leave early this Friday.

Note that the people are chosen randomly, and also that a person cannot be chosen twice.

This gives the proportion of people that will leave early. We can use this random sample to predict the number of people in the entire population that will leave early, based on the random sample.
This gives a very simple equation:

$15/30 = x/100$

$x = 50$

So we can infer that 50 people in the entire population will leave early on Friday.

Simple Probability

Probability of an event is given by

The Number Of Ways Event A Can Occur
The total number Of Possible Outcomes

So for example if there are 4 red balls and 3 yellow balls in a bag, the probability of choosing a red ball will be

$4/7$

Another example:

21. In a certain game, players toss a coin and roll a dice. A player wins if the coin comes up heads, or the dice with a number greater than 4. In 20 games, how many times will a player win?

    a. 13
    b. 8
    c. 11
    d. 15

Correct Answer: A
First determine the possible number of outcomes, the sample space of this event will be

S = { (H,1),(H,2),(H,3),(H,4),(H,5),(H,6)
(T,1),(T,2),(T,3),(T,4),(T,5),(T,6) }

So there are a total of 12 outcomes and 8 winning outcomes. The probability of a win in a single event is P (W)
=8/12=2/3. In 20 games the probability of a win
= 2/3 × 20 = 13

Mode, Mean and Median

The Mode, Mean and Median, are types of averages.

The mean is the average calculated by adding the numbers and dividing by the number of items in the data set. The median is the middle value in a data set. To calculate the median, put the numbers in order, and the median will be the middle number. If there is an even number of items in the data set, then the median is found by taking the mean (average) of the two middle-most numbers.

See the example below. The mode is the most frequently occurring number. If no number is repeated, then there is no mode.
Examples

Find the median, mode and mean of the following list: 6, 7, 8, 12, 14, 6, 7, 10

Find the mean

First add the numbers

6 + 7 + 8 + 12 + 14 + 6 + 7 + 10 = 70

There are 8 numbers in the list, so divide by 9
70/8 = 8.75 = mean

Find the median

First put the numbers in order

6, 6, 7, 7, 8, 10, 12, 14,

The data set has an even number of numbers, so the median is the average of 7 and 8. (7 + 8)/2 = 7.5

Find the mode

The mode is the most frequently occurring number. Here 6 and 7 both occur twice, so they are both considered the mode.

Dependent and Independent Variables

Independent variables are exactly just what you would think - a variable that is "independent" and therefore isn't changed by the other variables. For example, someone's age might be an independent variable. Other factors (such as what they eat or what school they go to) has no effect on their age.

When setting up a test, you are trying to see of the independent variable has an effect on the other (dependent) variable.

A *dependent* variable is just what you would think. It is something that depends on other factors. For example, a test score could be a dependent variable because it could change depending on several factors such as how much you studied, how much sleep you got the night before you took the test, or even how hungry you were when you took it. Usually when you are looking for a relationship between two things you are trying to find out what makes the dependent variable change the way it does.

Language Arts Writing

This section contains a self-assessment and Language Arts tutorials. The tutorials are designed to familiarize general principles and the self-assessment contains general questions similar to the Language Arts questions likely to be on the CAE^C exam, but are not intended to be identical to the exam questions. The tutorials are not designed to be a complete course, and it is assumed that students have some familiarity with Language Arts. If you do not understand parts of the tutorial, or find the tutorial difficult, it is recommended that you seek out additional instruction.

Tour of the CAE^C Language Arts Content

The CAE^C Language Arts section has 20 questions. Below is a list of the likely Language Arts topics likely to appear on the CAE^C.

- English grammar

- English usage

- Punctuation

- Capitalization

- Subject - verb agreement

- Sentence structure - run-on sentences, fragments etc.

- Unity and Coherence in a passage

- Identify topic sentences

The questions in the self-assessment are not the same as you will find on the CAE^C - that would be too easy! And nobody knows what the questions will be and they change all the time. Mostly, the changes consist of substituting new questions for old, but the changes also can be new question formats or styles, changes to the number of questions in each section, changes to the time limits for each section, and combining sections. So, while the format and exact wording of the questions may differ slightly, and changes from year to year, if you can answer the questions below, you will have no problem with the Language Arts section of the CAE^C.

Language Arts Self-Assessment

The purpose of the self-assessment is:

- Identify your strengths and weaknesses.
- Develop your personalized study plan (above)
- Get accustomed to the CAEC format
- Extra practice – the self-assessments are almost a full 3rd practice test!
- Provide a baseline score for preparing your study schedule.

Since this is a Self-assessment, and depending on how confident you are with Language Arts, timing yourself is optional. The CAE^C has 20 questions. This self-assessment has 30 questions, so allow about 30 minutes to complete.

Once complete, use the table below to assess your understanding of the content, and prepare your study schedule described in chapter 1.

80% - 100%	Excellent – you have mastered the content
60 – 79%	Good. You have a working knowledge. Even though you can just pass this section, you may want to review the tutorials and do some extra practice to see if you can improve your mark.
40% - 59%	Below Average. You do not understand the Language Arts content. Review the tutorials , and retake this quiz again in a few days, before proceeding to the practice test questions.
Less than 40%	Poor. You have a very limited understanding of the Language Arts content. Please review the tutorials , and retake this quiz again in a few days, before proceeding to the practice test questions.

Language Arts Answer Sheet

1. A B C D   11. A B C D   21. A B C D
2. A B C D   12. A B C D   22. A B C D
3. A B C D   13. A B C D   23. A B C D
4. A B C D   14. A B C D   24. A B C D
5. A B C D   15. A B C D   25. A B C D
6. A B C D   16. A B C D   26. A B C D
7. A B C D   17. A B C D   27. A B C D
8. A B C D   18. A B C D   28. A B C D
9. A B C D   19. A B C D   29. A B C D
10. A B C D   20. A B C D   30. A B C D

Passage 1 - A Personal Satellite?

Questions 1 - 4 refer to the following passage

Many of us are already so loaded with technology, we don't have time to think about integrating even more! [1] In fact at this point it seems impossible to think about personal satellites now, just as we once thought about smart phones. [2] The reality of personal spacecraft is still in the realm of Star Trek and geeky space fantasies. [3]

However, the days when each of us will have our own personal satellite are not far away! [4] And what is even more exciting is they will be available for the cost of an iPhone! [5] At least, according to Zach Manchester, the inventor of the nano-satellite KickSat. [6] "I'd like to think of it as the people's satellite," says Manchester. [7] "We're pushing towards a personal satellite, where you can afford to put your own thing in space." [8]

The KickSat, a 30 cm. long hardware pack, is a space enthusiast's dream. [9] It contains the basics of a fully functional satellite. [10] Inside its compact design, the KickSat itself contains 200 more tinier satellites of cubic shape called "Sprites." [11] The Sprites are engineered and programmed so that they can be tracked and communicate via radio signals with a ground station on earth. [12] Each Sprite is available for purchase and is uniquely named after the sponsors who support Zach's project. [13] Anyone who has sponsored a Sprite will be able to track their personal satellite from a ground station installed in their balcony or roof! [14]

1. Which sentence from the passage is an example of a sentence fragment?

    a. 4
    b. 7
    c. 6
    d. 10

2. Which of the following sentences should be edited to reduce redundancy?

    a. 5
    b. 4
    c. 10
    d. 16

3. Which of the following changes are needed to sentence 2?

a. In fact at this point it seems impossible to think about personal satellites now - just as we once thought about smart phones.

b. In fact, at this point, it seems impossible to think about personal satellites now, just as we once thought about smart phones.

c. In fact, at this point, it seems impossible to think about personal satellites now - just as we once thought about smart phones.

d. In fact at this point, it seems impossible to think about personal satellites now, just as we once thought about smart phones.

4. Which of the following changes are needed to sentence 11?

a. Under its compact design, the KickSat itself contains 200 more tiny satellites of cubic shape called "Sprites."

b. Under its compact design, the KickSat itself contains 200 more tiny satellites of cubic shapes called "Sprites."

c. Inside its compact design, the KickSat itself contains 200 tinier satellites of cubic shapes called "Sprites."

d. With its compact design, the KickSat contains 200 tiny cube-shaped satellites called "Sprites."

Passage 2 - Alvin Lee's Guitar

Questions 5 - 8 refer to the following passage

Only a few of his contemporaries rocked the rock n' roll era with their guitars like Alvin Lee. [1] Even at the age of 67, just a year before his demise, he produced one of the finest albums of his five-decade long career with *Still on the Road to Freedom*. [2] Strikingly flamboyant with his guitar, Lee gained millions of admirers around the world with hits like "*I'd Love to Change the World,*" "*On the Road to Freedom*" and "*Freedom for the Stallion*" which reflected popular worldviews at the time of their release. [3]

Alvin Lee began playing guitar at an early age, and was influenced by his parents' passion for music and inspired by the likes of Chuck Berry and Scotty Moore. [4] Lee started his career as the lead vocalist and guitarist in a band named the Jaybirds at the famous Marquee Club in London in 1962. [5] A few years later the band changed its name to *Ten Years After* and released its debut album under the new name. [6] Lee's lightning fast guitar playing at the Woodstock Festival gained him instant stardom and Lee was asked to tour the US. [7]

In the coming years, he worked with rock legends like Mylon LeFevre, George Harrison, Steve Winwood, Ronnie Wood and Mick Fleetwood and released the country rock masterpiece *On the Road to Freedom* which brought him overwhelming trans-Atlantic popularity. [8] In subsequent years, he continued addressing social and global issues in albums like *A Space in Time, Pump Iron!, Let It Rock* and *Rocket Fuel*. [9] With many of his songs, such as, "*I'd Love to Change the World,*" Lee used the power of rock music to show his solidarity with ordinary people and their worldviews. [10] He also went on with inspiring the upcoming generations of rock stars by producing expressive and tasteful guitar performances in his 1980s albums *Free Fall*, *RX5* and *Detroit Diesel*. [11]

5. Which sentence in the second paragraph is the least relevant to the main idea of the second paragraph?

    a. 4
    b. 5
    c. 6
    d. 7

6. Which of the following changes is/are needed in sentence 6?

    a. A few years later, the band changed its name to *Ten Years After* and released its debut album under the new name.

    b. A few years later, the band changed its name to *Ten Years After*, and released its debut album under the new name.

    c. A few years later the band changed its name to *Ten Years After*, and released its debut album under the new name.

    d. A few years later, the band changed its name to *Ten Years After* and, released its debut album under the new name.

7. Which of the following sentences, if inserted before sentence 11, would best illustrate the main idea of the passage?

    a. His charismatic personality earned him more fame and led him to perform even better for the sake of his admirers.

    b. As he gained popularity because of his artistic creations he tried to implant political motives into his music.

    c. At the same time, he thought of doing something for the future generations.

    d. With the creative songs he composed, he established himself as an exemplary figure among fellow guitarists and the generations that followed.

8. Which of the following changes are needed to sentence 11?

    a. He also went on inspiring the upcoming generations of rock stars by producing expressive and tasteful guitar performances in his 1980s albums *Free Fall*, *RX5* and *Detroit Diesel*.

    b. He also went on to inspire the upcoming generations of rock stars by producing expressive and tasteful guitar performances in his 1980s albums *Free Fall*, *RX5* and *Detroit Diesel*.

    c. He also went with inspiring the upcoming generations of rock stars by producing expressive and tasteful guitar performances in his 1980s albums *Free Fall*, *RX5* and *Detroit Diesel*. .

d. He also went on to inspiring the upcoming generations of rock stars by producing expressive and tasteful guitar performances in his 1980s albums *Free Fall*, *RX5* and *Detroit Diesel*.

Passage 3 - Baseball in Uganda

Questions 9 - 12 refer to the following passage

They were denied participation the year earlier, but the Ugandan kids made their mark at the 2012 Little League World Series. [1] The Lugazi Little League team members were the darlings of the world baseball stage when they participated in their dream tournament. [2] This time, they made sure all their participants were age-qualified; all of the new stars were 11 years old. [3] No, not really forged to any extent. [4] And what is more interesting, they are all native Ugandans; a fact that points to the huge baseball talent in Uganda. [5]

Baseball talent isn't appreciated in the East African country dominated by soccer athletes, however. [6] And that is what has captured the attention of the sponsors interested in investing on the emerging generation of players. [7] After their disappointing disqualification for alleged forging of documents in 2011, many investors had already offered financial commitments to develop the sport in the country. [8] Proposals for infrastructure development had already been made and organizers were looking to boost government support for the new sport. [9]

The Uganda Baseball and Softball Association has started construction of its first ever home diamond thanks to funding by the government of Japan. [10] Apart from that, some organizations and professional players are helping the Lugazi Little League with equipment, coaching, support staff organization of events and so on. [11] Many NGOs are offering academic scholarships to native Ugandans who wish to pursue their higher studies and become a baseball professional in the USA. [12]

After their remarkable appearance in the 2012 event, youngsters in Uganda are turning their attention to this new game. [13] With the new season of the World Series only a few months away, we will soon witness if young Ugandans are really interested in the sport. [14]

9. What sentence from the passage is an example of a sentence fragment?

    a. 2
    b. 3
    c. 4
    d. 5

Writing

10. Which sentence is not consistent with the author's purpose?

    a. 3

    b. 5

    c. 12

    d. 14

11. Which of the following changes to sentence 11 would focus attention on the main idea of the third paragraph?

    a. Apart from that, some organizations and professional players are organizing charity matches for raising funds for helping the sport develop in the country.

    b. Apart from that, some non-profit organizations are donating money to improve the infrastructure of the country by building roads and highways to promote the sport.

    c. Apart from that, the Lugazi League has been receiving substantial funding from non-governmental organizations and fellow baseball pros who provide assistance with equipment, coaching, support staff and organization of events.

    d. Apart from that, some professional players are promoting the Lugazi Little League by participating in them directly or indirectly.

12. Which of the following changes are needed to sentence 7?

    a. And that is what has attracted the attention of the sponsors interested in investing on the emerging generation of players.

    b. And that is what has attracted the attention of the sponsors to invest in the emerging generation of players.

    c. And that is what has captured the attention of the sponsors for investing on the emerging generation of players.

    d. And that is what has attracted the attention of the sponsors who are interested in investing on the emerging generation of players.

Passage 4 - Bhutan: Happiness is a Place

Questions 13 - 16 refer to the following passage

Imagine an artist painting a canvas of a light blue sky touching emerald hills at the foot of the majestic Himalayas. [1] Its valleys carpeted with thick meadows of green, and shades of dark green woods upright like sky high walls around you - leaving you calm and serene. [2] And in a short distance, little houses made from coffee-brown bark of Himalayan wood, with reddish clay rooftops and limestone-painted radiant snow-white walls. [3]

And as you watch his brush delicately stroke the blue shades onto the canvas, and then adding the flock of grey swans flying overhead, you are perplexed as to whether you are seeing the beauty mother nature has spread before you, or some mystical union of the artist's impression and your mind in another mysterious realm. [4] You become more puzzled with the distant bleat of lambs and wild goats and yet again are overwhelmed with the fragrance of wild jasmine, drifting on the breeze tempting you to follow. [5] It is as if the gentle, direction less wind is teasing you, inviting you to play your favorite childhood game "catch me if you can" and lift you up into the heavens; high above the peaks of the Himalayas. [6] You remain bewildered. [7] Stunned by the scenery, you are left astonished, by the beauty of nature. [8]

13. What sentence from the passage is an example of a sentence fragment?

    a. 1 and 4
    b. 2 and 3
    c. 5
    d. 6

14. Which of the following sentences should be deleted to reduce redundancy?

    a. 4
    b. 5
    c. 7
    d. 8

15. Which of the following changes are needed in sentence 2?

    a. Its valleys carpeted with thick meadows of green, and shades of dark green woods standing like sky high walls around you- leaving you calm and serene.
    b. Its valleys carpeted with thick meadows of green, and shades of dark green woods standing like sky high walls around you- leaving you calm and serene; an eternal sense of association and security.
    c. Its valleys carpeted with thick meadows of green, and shades of dark green woods standing like sky high walls around you- leaving you calm and serene.; an eternal sense of association and security.
    d. Its valleys carpeted with thick meadows of green, and shades of dark green woods standing like sky high walls around you- leaving you calm and serene.; an eternal sense of belonging and security.

16. Which of the following sentences contains non-standard usage?

    a. 2
    b. 3
    c. 6
    d. 7

17. Ted and Janice <u>who had been friends for years went on vacation together</u> every summer.

   a. Ted and Janice, who had been friends for years, went on vacation together every summer.
   b. Ted and Janice who had been friends for years, went on vacation together every summer.
   c. Ted, and Janice who had been friends for years, went on vacation together every summer.
   d. None of the choices are correct.

18. None of us want to go to the <u>party not even</u> if there will be live music.

   a. None of us want to go to the party not even, if there will be live music.
   b. None of us want to go to the party, not even if there will be live music.
   c. None of us want to go to the party; not even if there will be live music.
   d. None of the choice are correct.

19. <u>John, Maurice, and Thomas,</u> quit school two months before graduation.

   a. John, Maurice, and Thomas quit school two months before graduation.
   b. John, Maurice and Thomas quit school two months before graduation.
   c. John Maurice and Thomas, quit school two months before graduation.
   d. None of the choice are correct.

20. "My father said that he would be there on <u>Sunday," Lee</u> explained.

   a. "My father said that he would be there on Sunday" Lee explained.
   b. None of the choices are correct.
   c. "My father said that he would be there on Sunday," Lee explained.
   d. "My father said that he would be there on Sunday." Lee explained.

21. I own two <u>dogs, a cat, named Jeffrey and Henry, the goldfish.</u>

   a. I own two dogs, a cat named Jeffrey, and Henry, the goldfish.
   b. I own two dogs a cat, named Jeffrey, and Henry, the goldfish.
   c. I own two dogs, a cat named Jeffrey; and Henry, the goldfish.
   d. None of the choices are correct.

22. Choose the sentence below with the correct punctuation.

a. Marcus who won the debate tournament, is the best speaker that I know.
b. Marcus, who won the debate tournament, is the best speaker that I know.
c. Marcus who won the debate tournament is the best speaker that I know.
d. Marcus who won the debate tournament is the best speaker, that I know.

23. The ceremony had an emotional <u>affect</u> on the groom, but the bride was not <u>affected</u>.

a. The ceremony had an emotional effect on the groom, but the bride was not affected.
b. The ceremony had an emotional affect on the groom, but the bride was not affected.
c. The ceremony had an emotional effect on the groom, but the bride was not effected.

24. Anna was taller <u>than Luis, but then</u> he grew four inches in three months.

a. None of the choices are correct.
b. Anna was taller then Luis, but than he grew four inches in three months.
c. Anna was taller than Luis, but than he grew four inches, in three months.
d. Anna was taller than Luis, but then he grew four inches in three months.

25. <u>There</u> second home is in Boca Raton, but <u>they're</u> not <u>there</u> for most of the year.

a. Their second home is in Boca Raton, but there not their for most of the year.
b. They're second home is in Boca Raton, but they're not there for most of the year.
c. Their second home is in Boca Raton, but they're not there for most of the year.
d. None of the choices are correct.

26. <u>Their</u> going to graduate in June; after that, <u>their</u> best option will be to go <u>there.</u>

a. They're going to graduate in June; after that, their best option will be to go there.
b. There going to graduate in June; after that, their best option will be to go there.
c. They're going to graduate in June; after that, there best option will be to go their.
d. None of the choices are correct.

27. Your mistaken; that is not you're book.

   a. You're mistaken; that is not you're book.
   b. Your mistaken; that is not your book.
   c. You're mistaken; that is not your book.
   d. None of the choices are correct.

28. You're classes are on the west side of campus, but you're living on the east side.

   a. You're classes are on the west side of campus, but you're living on the east side.
   b. Your classes are on the west side of campus, but your living on the east side.
   c. Your classes are on the west side of campus, but you're living on the east side.
   d. None of the choices are correct.

29. The Chinese lives in one of the world's most populous nations, while a citizen of Bermuda lives in one of the least populous.

   a. The Chinese live in one of the world's most populous nations, while a citizen of Bermuda lives in one of the least populous.
   b. The Chinese lives in one of the world's most populous nations, while a citizen of Bermuda live in one of the least populous.
   c. The Chinese live in one of the world's most populous nations, while a citizen of Bermuda live in one of the least populous.
   d. None of the choices are correct.

30. You shouldn't sit in that chair wearing black pants; I sit the white cat there just a moment ago.

   a. You shouldn't sit in that chair wearing black pants; I set the white cat there just a moment ago.
   b. You shouldn't set in that chair wearing black pants; I sit the white cat there just a moment ago.
   c. You shouldn't set in that chair wearing black pants; I set the white cat there just a moment ago.
   d. None of the choices are correct.

Answer Key

1. B
Sentence 6 is a fragment. "At least, according to Zach Manchester, the inventor of the nano-satellite KickSat."

This sentence fails to complete the thought, even though it is somewhat consistent with the previous sentence. Sentence 6 does not have a subject and thus does not form any main clause which is essential for constructing a complete thought. This fragment can be revised as "At least, <u>this is</u> according to Zach Manchester, the inventor of the nano-satellite KickSat."

2. B
Suggested changes to Sentence 4 to reduce redundancy, "However, the days when each of us will have our own personal spacecraft are truly not far away!"

The adjectives "own" and "personal" are used simultaneously. Either of them can be used, and the other must be eliminated. The correct form will be either one of the following:

- However, the days when each of us will have our own spacecraft are truly not far away!
- However, the days when each of us will have our personal spacecraft are truly not far away!

3. C
The revised version of sentence 2 is, "In fact, at this point, it seems impossible to think about personal satellites now - just as we once thought about smart phones."

This choice uses the correct punctuation; two commas, one before and one after the subordinate conjunction "at this point" which bridges the adverbial clause after it with the adjective at the start of the sentence. Also the use of a hyphen to express extended thought is correct in choice C.

4. D
The only choice with correct grammar is choice D. It replaces "more tiny" with "tiny" as well as "cubic shaped" with "cube-shaped." Tinier is the correct comparative form of "tiny" and "cubic" is the adjective that must describe the singular noun "shape," not "shapes" or any of its verbal forms. Two word adjectives, such as "a 3-mile race" are hyphenated.

"Under its compact design" is incorrect. Replace with, "with its compact design ... "

5. A
Sentence 4 is least relevant, "Alvin Lee began playing guitar at an early age, and was influenced by his parents' passion for music and inspired by the likes of Chuck Berry and Scotty Moore."

This sentence talks about Lee's source of motivation rather than his achievements, which is actually the main topic of the paragraph. Other sentences are related to a significant extent, but this sentence deviates from the main idea the most.

6. A
The edited version of sentence 6 is, "A few years later, the band changed its name to Ten Years After and released its debut album under the new name."

Choice A places a comma after the prepositional phrase "A few years later" that expresses time. No other punctuation is necessary for a coordinate conjunction "and" as proposed by choices B and C since the clause "released its debut album under the new name" is a subordinate rather than an independent one. Choice D offers an incorrect suggestion, placing a comma after "and."

7. D
The following sentence, if inserted after sentence 11, "With the songs he composed, he established himself as an exemplary figure among fellow guitarists and the immediate generation that followed" best illustrates the main idea of the passage.

This sentence best complements the other sentences and the main idea of the passage which concentrates on the impact Alvin Lee has made on his admirers and contemporaries with his skills and creations. The emphasis of the passage is on how he influenced them with his guitar work and that is complemented best if the sentence by choice D before sentence 11.

8. B
Suggested changes to sentence 11 are, "He also went on to inspire upcoming generations of rock stars by producing expressive and tasteful guitar performances in his 1980s albums. *Free Fall*, *RX5* and *Detroit Diesel*."

The correction offered in choice B is the only appropriate one since the gerund form of "inspire" is not appropriate when starting the action. Here,, the author expresses initiation of the process of inspiring more than one generation. So, rather than continuing an already started process, this sentence refers to beginning of an additional process of inspiring as indicated by "also." The gerund form is used rather when the action represented by the verb is in a continuous process already in motion. Therefore, the to-infinitive must be used. As a result choice A can be eliminated. Choices C and D offer no valid gerund or infinitive.

9. C
Sentence 4 is a fragment, "No, not really forged to any extent."

This sentence does not contain a subject and therefore has no main clause. A correct revision would be, "No, they didn't forge their registration documentation."

10. D
Sentence 14 is not consistent with the author's purpose. "With the new season of the World Series only a few months away, we will soon witness if young Ugandans are really interested in the sport."

This sentence is totally inconsistent with the theme of the passage. The author intends to portray the sport in Uganda mentioning the presence of young talent and their rising interest in the sport on several occasions yet in the 14th sentence, their interest in playing baseball is questioned with the if clause; and this is not consistent with the author's purpose. Other choices present no real inconsistencies. Choice A is a sentence fragment, but it is consistent with the previous sentence as an extended thought.

11. C
The changes to sentence 11 are, "Apart from that, the Lugazi League has been receiving substantial funding from non-governmental organizations and fellow baseball pros who provide assistance with equipment, coaching, support staff and organization of events."

When the sentence is updated to this form, it remains consistent with the factual information provided in the original sentence, and at the same time, better expresses the main idea of the paragraph. Choices A and B do not have any factual basis as compared to choice C and can be eliminated. Choice D does not have any factual basis either and it is irrelevant to the main idea of the paragraph as it talks about promoting the sport rather than funding it.

12. B
Changes to sentence 7 are, "And that is what has attracted the attention of the sponsors to invest in the emerging generation of players."

Choice B offers the correct English usage as well as grammar. The synonym "attract" is more appropriate and also omission of a redundant "interested in" along with "the attention of sponsors" is correctly suggested. In addition, to-infinitive form of "invest" is used rather than the gerund in the original form. Choice A contains the redundant expression "interested in" and so is inappropriate. Choice C still has the synonym "capture" and the gerund noun form "investing" is disputable. Choice D once again has the redundant expression as in choice A.

13. B
There are two answers - sentence 2 and 3 are fragments.

Sentence 2- Its valleys carpeted with thick meadows of green, and shades of dark green woods upright like sky high walls around you- installing within your being an in illimitable bliss and serenity.

This is an intentional, or stylistic fragment used in conjunction with the thought in the previous sentence, especially to emphasize the inspiring aspects of the place. Though a fragment that does not complete the thought, it is in perfect harmony with the first sentence. See question 15 for suggested changes to sentence 2.

Sentence 3 And in a short distance, little houses made from coffee-brown bark of Himalayan wood, with reddish clay rooftops and limestone-painted radiant snow-white walls.

This is a continuation of the thought in the first sentence. It also has an intentional fragment similar to sentence 2 and is in fact, an extension of it. This sentence does not have a verb or verbal clause and therefore clearly a sentence fragment.

14. D
Sentence 8 can be deleted. "Stunned by the scenery, you are left astonished, by the beauty of nature."

Sentence 8 is effectively the summary of sentences 4 through 7 which among themselves express the astonishment of the observer cohesively without exaggerating. Sentence 8 overlaps with the description in the previous sentences unnecessarily and should be removed.

15. D
Suggested changes to sentence 2 are, "Its valleys carpeted with thick meadows of green, and shades of dark green woods standing like sky high walls around you- leaving you calm and serene."

The choices seem to make the correct changes in the sentence as we move progressively from choice A to choice D. The changes are related to usage of words in the right context. In choice A, the word "upright" is replaced with its gerund synonym "standing."

16. C
Sentence 6 contains the non-standard usage, "catch me if you can."

Normally, the expression "catch me if you can" is the name given to a child's game. However, here,, it has been used with quotation marks to express a special sense in the behavior of the breeze; emphasizing it by personalization with a child. This can therefore be considered as a non-standard use of the quotation marks.

17. A
Use a comma to separate phrases.

18. B
Use a comma separates independent clauses. None of us wants to go to the party, not even if there will be live music.

19. B
Don't use a comma before 'and' in a list.

20. C
Commas always go with a quote and the use of said, explained etc.

21. A
This is an example if a comma which appears before 'and,' but is disambiguating. Without the comma, the sentence would be "I own two dogs, a cat named Jeffrey and Henry, the goldfish." This means there is a cat named Jeffrey and Henry, and a goldfish with no name mentioned. The comma appears to show the distinction.

I own two dogs, a cat named Jeffrey, and Henry, the goldfish.

22. B
Comma separate phrases.

23. A
Affect vs. Effect - Affect is a verb (action) and effect is a noun (thing).

24. D
Than vs. Then – Than is used for comparison, as in, taller than, and then is used for time, as in, but then...

25. C
There vs. their vs. they're. There indicates existence as in, "there are." Their is to indicate possession, as in, "their book." They're is the contraction form of "they are."

26. A
There vs. their vs. they're. There indicates existence as in, "there are." Their is to indicate possession, as in, "their book." They're is the contraction form of "they are."

27. C
Your vs. you're. Your is the possessive form of you. You're is the contraction form of you are.

28. C
Your vs. you're. Your is the possessive form of you. You're is the contraction form of you are.

29. A
Singular subjects. "The Chinese" is plural, and "a citizen of Bermuda" is singular.

30. A
Sit vs. Set. Set requires an object – something to set down. Sit is something that you do, like sit on the chair.

Writing Tips and Common Mistakes

Redundancy

Duplication and verbosity in English is the use of two or more words that clearly mean the same thing, making one of them unnecessary. It is easy to do use redundant expressions or phrases in a conversation where speech is spontaneous, and common in spoken English. In written English, however, redundancy is more serious and harder to ignore. Here are list of redundant phrases to avoid.

1. Suddenly exploded.

An explosion is instantaneous or immediate and that is sudden enough. No need to use 'suddenly' along with exploded.

2. Final outcome.

An outcome refers to the result. An outcome is intrinsically final and so no need to use final along with outcome.

3. Advance notice/planning/reservations/warning.

A warning, notice, reservation or plan is made before an event. Once the reader sees any of these words, they know that they were done or carried out before the event. These words do not need to be used with advance.

4. Began, new beginning.

Beginning signals the start or the first time, and therefore the use of "new" is superfluous.

5. Add an additional.

The word 'add' indicates the provision of another something, and so "additional" is superfluous.

6. For a period/number of days.

The word "days" is already in plural and clearly signifies more than just one day. It is thus redundant to use "a number of," or "a period of" along with days. Simply state the number of days or of the specific number of days is unknown, you say 'many days.'

7. Foreign imports.

Imports are foreign as they come from another country, so it is superfluous to refer to imports as "foreign."

8. Forever and ever.

Forever indicates eternity and so there is no need for "ever" as it simply duplicated forever.

9. Came at a time when.

"At a time" is not necessary in this phrase because the 'when' already provides a temporal reference to the action, coming.

10. Free gift.

It cannot be a gift if it is paid for. A gift, by nature, is free and so referring to a gift is free is redundant.

11. Collaborate/join/meet/merge together.

The words merge, join, meet and collaborate already suggest people or things coming together. It is unnecessary to use any of these words with together, such as saying merge together or join together. The correct expression is to simply say join or merge, omitting the together.

12. Invited guests.

Guests are those invited for an event. Since they had to be invited to be guests, there is no need to use invited with guests.

13. Major breakthrough.

A breakthrough is significant by nature. It can only be described as a breakthrough when there is a notable progress. The significant nature of the progress is already implied when you use the word "breakthrough," so "major" is redundant.

14. Absolutely certain or sure/essential/ guaranteed.

When someone or something is said to be sure or certain it indicates that it is without doubt. Using "absolutely" in addition to certain or sure is unnecessary. Essential or guaranteed is used for something that is absolute and so also does not need the word absolutely to accompany them.

15. Ask a question.

Ask means to present a question. Using "question" in addition to "ask" is redundant.

16. Basic fundamentals/essentials.

Using basic here is redundant. Essentials and fundamental suggest an elementary nature.

17. [Number] a.m. in the morning/p.m. in the evening.

When you write 8 a.m. the reader knows you mean 8 o'clock in the morning. It is not necessary to say 8 a.m. in the morning. Simply write 8 a.m. or 8 p.m.

18. Definite decision.

A decision is already definite even if it can be reversed later. A decision is a definite course of action has been chosen. No need to use the word definite along with the word decision.

19. Past history/record.

A record or history by definition refers to past events or occurrences. Using past to qualify history or record is unnecessary.

20. Consensus of opinion.

Consensus means agreement over something that may be or not be an opinion. So it may look that using the phrase 'consensus of opinion' is appropriate, but it is better to omit "opinion."

21. Enter in.

Enter means going in, as no one enters out. There fore no need to add "in," simply use "enter."

22. Plan ahead.

You cannot plan for the past. Planning can only be done for the future. When you use "plan," the future is already implied.

23. Possibly might.

The words might and possibly signify probability, so just use one at a time.

24. Direct confrontation.

A confrontation is a head-on conflict, and does not need to be modified with "direct."

25. Postpone until later.

Something postponed is delayed or moved to a later time, and does not need to be modified with "later."

26. False pretense.

The word pretense is only used to describe a deception, so a "false" pretense is redundant.

27. Protest against.

Protest involves showing opposition; there is no need to use against.

28. End result.

Result only comes at the end. The reader who sees the word 'result' already knows that it occurs at the end.

29. Estimated at about/roughly.

Estimates are approximations that are not expected to be accurate, and do not need to be modified with "roughly" or "about."

30. Repeat again.

Repeat refers to something repeated and does not need to be modified with "again."

31. Difficult dilemma.

A dilemma is a situation that is complicated or difficult, and does not need to be modified with "difficult."

32. Revert back.

Revert indicates returning to a former or earlier state. Something that reverts goes back to how it used to be. No need to add back.

33. (During the) course (of).

During means "in or throughout the duration of," and doesn't require the use of the word "course."

34. Same identical.

Same and identical means the same thing and should not be used together.

35. Completely filled/finished/opposite.

Completely indicates thoroughness. However, the words finished and filled already indicate something thoroughly filled or finished to the extent possible. The words filled and finished thus do not need to be qualified with "completely."

36. Since the time when.

In this phrase, 'the time when' is not necessary as 'since' already indicates sometime in the past.

37. Close proximity/scrutiny.

Proximity means being close, in respect to location. Scrutiny means studying something closely. Both words suggest close, whether in respect to location as with proximity, or in respect to study, as with scrutiny. It is therefore unnecessary to use the words together.

38. Spell out in detail.

'Spell out' involves providing details, so no need to add "in detail."

39. Written down.

Anything written can be said to be taken down. Written should therefore be used on its own.

40. (Filled to) capacity.

Anything that is filled has reached its capacity and so the word capacity does not need to be used along with filled.

41. Unintended mistake.

Something is a mistake because it is not intended. The lack of intention is plain and so there is no need to qualify with "unintended."

42. Still remains.

"Remains" signifies that something is still as it is, and so using 'still' is superfluous.

43. Actual experience/fact.

Something becomes an experience after it has occurred. If it didn't occur it is not an experience. A fact can only be a fact when it is sure or confirmed. Both experience and fact thus do not need to be modified with "actual."

44. Therapeutic treatment.

Therapeutic refers to the healing or curing of illness. All medical treatment is therapeutic in that it aims to heal or cure. When speaking of medical treatment, there is thus no need to use therapeutic to qualify treatment.

45. At the present time.

"At present" alone indicates the present time or "at this time." Using "at the present time" is the verbose version. Better to just use "at present."

46. Unexpected surprise.

A surprise is unexpected by nature. The unexpected nature is assumed once the word surprised is read or heard. No need to use unexpected to qualify it.

47. As for example.

"As" indicates the use of an example and so it is redundant to say "an example."

48. Usual custom.

A custom refers to something that is observed or done repeatedly or routinely. The use of 'usual' along with custom is not necessary.

49. Added bonus.

Bonus already shows something extra, in addition to the ordinary. Using "added" to describe the bonus is not necessary.

50. Few in number.

Something is few because it is small in number. No need to use number with few.

Common English Usage Mistakes - A Quick Review

Like some parts of English grammar, usage is definitely going to be on the exam and there isn't any tricky strategies or shortcuts to help you get through this section.
Here is a quick review of common usage mistakes.

1. May and Might

'May' can act as a principal verb, which can express permission or possibility.

Examples:

Lets wait, the meeting may have started.
May I begin now?

'May' can act as an auxiliary verb, which an expresses a purpose or wish

Examples:

May you find favour in the sight of your employer.

May your wishes come true.
People go to school so that they may be educated.

The past tense of may is might.

Examples:

I asked if I might begin

'Might' can be used to signify a weak or slim possibility or polite suggestion.

Examples:

You might find him in his office, but I doubt it.
You might offer to help if you want to.

2. Lie and Lay

The verb lay should always take an object. The three forms of the verb lay are: laid, lay and laid.

The verb lie (recline) should not take any object. The three forms of the verb lie are: lay, lie and lain.

Examples:

Lay on the bed.
The tables were laid by the students.
Let the little kid lie.
The patient lay on the table.

The dog has lain there for 30 minutes.

Note: The verb lie can also mean "to tell a falsehood." This verb can appear in three forms: lied, lie, and lied. This is different from the verb lie (recline) mentioned above.

Examples:

The accused is fond of telling lies.
Did she lie?

3. Would and should

The past tense of shall is 'should', and so "should" generally follows the same principles as "shall."

The past tense of will is "would," and so "would" generally follows the same principles as "will."

The two verbs 'would and should' can be correctly used interchangeably to signify obligation. The two verbs also have some unique uses too. Should is used in three persons to signify obligation.

Examples:

I should go after work.
People should exercise everyday.
You should be generous.

"Would" is specially used in any of the three persons, to signify willingness, determination and habitual action.

Examples:

They would go for a test run every Saturday.
They would not ignore their duties.
She would try to be punctual.

4. Principle and Auxiliary Verbs

Two principle verbs can be used along with one auxiliary verb as long as the auxiliary verb form suits the two principal verbs.

Examples:

Several people have been employed and some promoted.

A new tree has been planted and the old has been cut down.
Again note the difference in the verb form.

5. Can and Could

A. Can is used to express capacity or ability.

Examples:

I can complete the assignment today
He can meet his target.

B. Can is also used to express permission.

Examples:

Yes, you can begin

In the sentence below, "can" was used to mean the same thing as "may." However, the difference is that the word "can" is used for negative or interrogative sentences, while "may" is used in affirmative sentences to express possibility.

Examples:

They may be correct.   Positive sentence - use may.
Can this statement be correct? A question using "can."
It cannot be correct. Negative sentence using "can."

The past tense of can is could. It can serve as a principal verb when it is used to express its own meaning.

Examples:

Despite the difficulty of the test, he could still perform well.
"Could" here is used to express ability.

6. Ought

The verb ought should normally be followed by the word to.

Examples:

I *ought to* close shop now.
The verb 'ought' expresses:

A. Desirability

You ought to wash your hands before eating.   It is desirable to wash your hands.

B. Probability

She ought to be on her way back by now.   She is probably on her way.

C. Moral obligation or duty

The government ought to protect the oppressed.   It is the government's duty to protect the oppressed.

7. Raise and Rise

Rise
The verb rise means to go up, or to ascend.
The verb rise can appear in three forms, rose, rise, and risen. The verb should not take an object.

Examples:

The bird rose very slowly.
The trees rise above the house.
My aunt has risen in her career.

Raise
The verb raise means to increase, to lift up.
The verb raise can appear in three forms, raised, raise and raised.

Examples:

He raised his hand.
The workers requested a raise.
Do not raise that subject.

8. Past Tense and Past Participle

Pay attention to the proper use of these verbs: sing, show, ring, awake, fly, flow, begin, hang and sink.

Mistakes usually occur when using the past participle and past tense of these verbs as they are often mixed up.

Each of these verbs can appear in three forms:

Sing, Sang, Sung.
Show, Showed, Showed/Shown.
Ring, Rang, Rung.
Awake, awoke, awaken
Fly, Flew, Flown.
Flow, Flowed, Flowed.
Begin, Began, Begun.
Hang, Hanged, Hanged (a criminal)
Hang, Hung, Hung (a picture)
Sink, Sank, Sunk.

Examples:

The stranger rang the door bell. (simple past tense)
I have rung the door bell already. (past participle - an action completed in the past)

The stone sank in the river. (simple past tense)
The stone had already sunk. (past participle - an action completed in the past)

The meeting began at 4:00.
The meeting has begun.

9. Shall and Will

When speaking informally, the two can be used interchangeably. In formal writing, they must be used correctly.

"Will" is used in the second or third person, while "shall" is used in the first person. Both verbs are used to express a time or even in the future.

Examples:

I shall, We shall (First Person)
You will (Second Person)
They will (Third Person)

This principle however reverses when the verbs are to be used to express threats, determination, command, willingness, promise or compulsion. In these instances, will is now used in first person and shall in the second and third person.

Examples:

I will be there next week, no matter what.
This is a promise, so the first person "I" takes "will."

You shall ensure that the work is completed.
This is a command, so the second person "you" takes "shall."

I will try to make payments as promised.
This is a promise, so the first person "I" takes "will."

They shall have arrived by the end of the day.
This is a determination, so the third person "they" takes shall.

Note
A. The two verbs, shall and will should not occur twice in the same sentence when the same future is being referred to

Example:

I shall arrive early if my driver is here on time.

B. Will should not be used in the first person when questions are being asked

Examples:

Shall I go ?
Shall we go?

Subject Verb Agreement

Verbs in any sentence must agree with the subject of the sentence in person and number. Problems usually occur when the verb doesn't correspond with the right subject or the verb fails to match the noun close to it.

Unfortunately, there is no easy way around these principals - no tricky strategy or easy rule. You just have to memorize them.

Here is a quick review:

The verb to be, present (past)

Person	Singular	Plural
First	I am (was)	we are (were)
Second	you are (were)	you are (were)
Third	he, she, it is (was)	they are (were)

The verb to have, present (past)

Person	Singular	Plural
First	I have (had)	we have (had)
Second	you have (had)	you have (had)
Third	he, she, it has (had)	they have (had)

Regular verbs, e.g. to walk, present (past)

Person	Singular	Plural
First	I walk (walked)	we walk (walked)
Second	you walk (walked)	you walk (walked)
Third	he, she, it walks (walked)	they work (walked)

1. Every and Each

When nouns are qualified by "every" or "each," they take a singular verb even if they are joined by 'and'

Examples:

Each mother and daughter *was* a given separate test.
Every teacher and student *was* properly welcomed.

2. Plural Nouns

Nouns like measles, tongs, trousers, riches, scissors etc. are all plural.

Examples:

The trousers *are* dirty.
My scissors *have* gone missing.
The tongs *are* on the table.

3. With and As Well

Two subjects linked by "with" or "as well" should have a verb that matches the first subject.

Examples:

The pencil, with the papers and equipment, *is* on the desk.
David as well as Louis is coming.

4. Plural Nouns

The following nouns take a singular verb:

> politics, mathematics, innings, news, advice, summons, furniture, information, poetry, machinery, vacation, scenery

Examples:

The machinery *is* difficult to assemble
The furniture *has* been delivered
The scenery *was* beautiful

5. Single Entities

A proper noun in plural form that refers to a single entity requires a singular verb. This is a complicated way of saying; some things appear to be plural, but are really singular, or some nouns refer to a collection of things but the collection is really singular.

Examples:

The United Nations Organization *is* the decision maker in the matter.

Here the "United Nations Organization" is really only one "thing" or noun, but is made up of many "nations."

The book, "The Seven Virgins" *was* not available in the library.
Here there is only one book, although the title of the book is plural.

6. Specific Amounts are always singular

A plural noun that refers to a specific amount or quantity that is considered as a whole (dozen, hundred, score etc) requires a singular verb.

Examples:

60 minutes *is* quite a long time.
Here "60 minutes" is considered a whole, and therefore one item (singular noun).

The first million is the most difficult.

7. Either, Neither and Each are always singular

The verb is always singular when used with: either, each, neither, every one and many.

Examples:

Either of the boys *is* lying.
Each of the employees *has* been well compensated
Many a police officer *has* been found to be courageous
Every one of the teachers *is* responsible

8. Linking with Either, Or, and Neither match the second subject

Two subjects linked by "either," "or," "nor" or "neither" should have a verb that matches the second subject.

Examples:

Neither David nor Paul *will* be coming.
Either Mary or Tina *is* paying.

Note
If one subject linked by "either," "or," "nor" or "neither" is in plural form, then the verb should also be in plural, and the verb should be close to the plural subject.

Examples:
Neither the mother *nor* her kids *have* eaten.
Either Mary *or* her *friends are* paying.

9. Collective Nouns are Plural

Some collective nouns such as poultry, gentry, cattle, vermin etc. are considered plural and require a plural verb.

Examples:

The *poultry are* sick.
The *cattle are* well fed.

Note
Collective nouns involving people can work with both plural and singular verbs.

Examples:

Nigerians are known to be hard working
Europeans live in Africa

10. Nouns that are Singular and Plural

Nouns like deer, sheep, swine, salmon etc. can be singular or plural and require the same verb form.

Examples:

The swine is feeding. (singular)
The swine are feeding. (plural)

The salmon is on the table. (singular)
The salmon are running upstream. (plural)

11. Collective Nouns are Singular

Collective nouns such as Army, Jury, Assembly, Committee, Team etc should carry a singular verb when they subscribe to one idea. If the ideas or views are more than one, then the verb used should be plural.

Examples:

The committee is in agreement in their decision.

The committee were in disagreement in their decision.
The jury has agreed on a verdict.
The jury were unable to agree on a verdict.

12. Subjects links by "and" are plural.

Two subjects linked by "and" always require a plural verb

Examples:

David and John are students.

Note
If the subjects linked by "and" are used as one phrase, or constitute one idea, then the verb must be singular

The color of his socks and shoe is black.
Here "socks and shoe" are two nouns, however the subject is "color" which is singular.

How to Write an Essay

Writing an essay can be a difficult process, especially under time constraints in an exam. Here are three simple steps to help you to write a solid, well thought out essay:

1. **Brainstorm** potential themes and general ideas for your essay.

2. **Outline** your essay step by step, including subheadings for ease of understanding.

3. **Write** your essay carefully being aware of proper grammar and sentence structure.

Brainstorming

You should first spend some time thinking about the general subject of the essay. If the essay is asking a question, you must make sure to answer this fully in your essay. You may find it helpful to highlight key words in your assignment or use a simple spider diagram to jot down key ideas.

Example

Read the following information and complete the following assignment:

Joseph Conrad is a Polish author who lived in England for most of his life and wrote a huge amount of English literature. Much of his work was completed during the height of the British Empire's colonial imperialism.

Assignment: What impact has Joseph Conrad had on modern society? Present your point of view on the matter and support it with evidence. Your evidence may include reasoning, logic, examples from readings, your own experience, and observations.

Joseph Conrad

> **Background?** sailor, adventure, Polish immigrant, Youth, Nostromo, Heart of Darkness
> **Themes in his works?** ivory, silver trading, colonialism, corruption, greed
> **Thoughts?** descent into madness, nature of evil

Outlining (or planning)

An outline or plan is critical to organize your thoughts and ideas fully and logically. There are many ways to do this; the easiest is to write down the following headings:

1. Title
2. Introduction
3. Body
4. Conclusion

You should then jot down key ideas and themes that fit logically under the appropriate heading. This plan is now the backbone of your essay.

Tip: Even if you are not required to produce an outline or plan for the assignment, you should always leave it with your essay in the exam booklet or the back of the assignment paper. Simply draw a line across it and write 'plan' or 'outline'. This demonstrates to the reader the approach you use in formulating and finally writing your essay.

Writing the Essay

Your introduction is what will help the reader to decide whether they want to read the rest of your essay. The introduction also introduces the subject matter and allows you to provide a general background to the reader. The first sentence is very important and you should avoid starting the essay with openers such as 'I will be comparing…'

Example

> Born as Józef Teodor Konrad Korzeniowski on December 3rd, 1857, Joseph Conrad led an adventurous life. As a Polish immigrant, Conrad never quite fit into England where he spent most of his adult life. As a younger man, Conrad made a living off sailing voyages. These swashbuckling experiences soon had him writing tales of the high seas such as one of his first works, Youth. While his early, adventurous work was of high quality, Conrad is best remembered for shedding light on the exploitative side of colonialism. Age and experience led him to start writing about (and challenging) the darker side of the imperial way of thinking. Conrad's work has forever soured words such as colonialism and imperialism.

In the main, or body of your essay, you should always be yourself and be original.

Avoid using clichés.
- Be aware of your tone.
- Consider the language that you use. Avoid jargon and slang. Use clear prose and imagery.
- Your writing should always flow; remember to use transitions, especially between paragraphs. Read aloud in your head to make sure a paragraph sounds right.
- Always try to use a new paragraph for new ideas.

Example

Conrad's written fiction focused on themes such as greed and power. He portrayed these two concepts as purveyors of evil. Greed and power may take on different guises, but the end result would always be the same.

Perhaps his most famous piece, The Heart of Darkness, is about the descent of an English ivory trader, Mr. Kurtz, into madness. We are taken up a river resembling the Congo by a narrator, Marlow, who is sent to retrieve Mr. Kurtz. Marlow eventually finds that Kurtz has been diluted by power and greed, the two things that spurred on colonialism in Africa. Kurtz has taken charge of a large tribe of natives (that he brutalizes) and has been hoarding ivory for himself.

Much of Conrad's later work was cut from the same vein as The Heart of Darkness. His crowning achievement is considered Nostromo where he takes an idealistic hero and corrupts him with colonial greed. Only this time the greed is for silver, not ivory.

Conrad's work resonates with readers partly because it was semi-autobiographical. Where his experience sailing the high seas helped bring his adventure stories to light, likewise did his experience witnessing atrocities in Africa reverberate through his writing.

The conclusion is your last chance to impress your reader and brings your entire essay to a logical close. You may want to link your conclusion back to your introduction or provide some closing statements. Do not panic if you cannot close your essay off completely. Few subjects offer closure.

Your conclusion should always be consistent with the rest of the essay and you should never introduce a new idea in your conclusion. It is also important to remember that a weak conclusion can diminish the impact of a good essay.

Example

In sum, Joseph Conrad's life experiences and masterful writing left a lasting impact on the image of progress and what it meant to "move forward." He brought to light the cost in human lives that was required for Europe to continue mining natural resources from foreign lands. Joseph Conrad had a permanent impact on imperial culture, and colonial brutality has been on the decline ever since his work was published.

Presentation

Poor grammar and punctuation can ruin an otherwise good essay. You should always follow any requirements about the presentation of your essay, such as word count. You should also make sure that your writing is legible. Always allow time for one final read-through before submission.

Tip: If you are able to, write with double spacing. If you make a mistake, you can cross it out and write the correction on the blank line above.

Some final points to think about for writing a solid, well thought out essay:

- A good essay will contain a strong focus.

- There is no set essay structure but you can use subheadings for better readability.

- Avoid particularly sensitive or controversial material. If you must write about something controversial, always make sure to include counter arguments.

- Your essay may have little to do with the subject itself; it is about what you make of the subject.

- Your essay can include examples from your readings, experience, studies or observations.

- Spend time doing practice essays and looking at sample essays beforehand.

Example 2

How Community Service Benefits Both Individuals and Society

Introduction
Community service plays a crucial role in developing strong and supportive communities. Not only does it benefit the people who receive help, but it also offers numerous personal growth opportunities for those who volunteer. In this essay, I will discuss how community service provides benefits to both individuals and society, fostering a culture of giving and growth.

Commentary:

Thesis Statement: The thesis is clear and states the essay's main point, setting up the reader for the discussion of both individual and societal benefits of community service.

Hook/General Introduction: The first sentence grabs attention by introducing the broad topic of community service. It also offers a sense of why this subject matters.

Body Paragraph 1: The Personal Benefits of Community Service

One of the most significant advantages of community service for individuals is personal development. Volunteering can enhance a person's empathy, patience, and understanding of different social issues. For instance, by working at a homeless shelter, a volunteer gains insight into the challenges of homelessness and is better equipped to understand the importance of supporting social services. Additionally, community service can improve various skills, including communication, teamwork, and leadership. This is particularly true for high school students who participate in volunteer activities, as they often find themselves in leadership roles that challenge them to grow personally and professionally.

Commentary:

Topic Sentence: The paragraph starts with a clear topic sentence that introduces the focus on the personal benefits of community service.

Supporting Details and Examples: Specific examples, like volunteering at a homeless shelter, are used to support the topic sentence and add depth to the argument. Explanation and Analysis: The paragraph analyzes the benefits, explaining how community service leads to skill-building and personal growth.

Body Paragraph 2: The Societal Benefits of Community Service
In addition to benefiting individuals, community service also strengthens society as a whole. When people engage in community service, they help build a more connected and caring society. For example, food banks and donation drives can help reduce hunger in local communities, leading to a healthier and more stable population. Furthermore, when citizens give their time and effort to support community projects, it creates a sense of unity and shared responsibility. As a result, communities become stronger and more resilient, as members feel they have a role in shaping their surroundings.

Commentary:

Topic Sentence: This paragraph transitions to societal benefits with a clear topic sentence.

Supporting Details: Concrete examples, such as food banks and donation drives, are provided to support the argument.

Explanation and Analysis: **The societal effects of community service are analyzed,** showing how collective action leads to stronger communities.

Body Paragraph 3: The Interconnectedness of Personal and Societal Benefits
It is important to note that the personal and societal benefits of community service are interconnected. As individuals grow through volunteer work, they become more engaged and empathetic citizens, which in turn leads to greater societal improvement. For instance, a student who volunteers in environmental clean-up efforts may develop a passion for sustainability, eventually influencing policies or initiatives that benefit the environment. In this way, community service acts as a cycle: personal development leads to greater social contribution, which in turn fosters more opportunities for personal growth.

Commentary:

Topic Sentence: This paragraph serves as a bridge, showing the connection between individual and societal benefits.

Supporting Details and Analysis: The example of environmental clean-up is used to illustrate how personal growth can lead to societal change. The analysis reinforces the thesis by showing how these two elements are interconnected.

Conclusion
In conclusion, community service provides valuable benefits for both individuals and society. On a personal level, it allows people to grow and develop important life skills. At the same time, it fosters stronger, more united communities. By volunteering, people not only improve themselves but also contribute to the well-being of society. It is clear that community service is a powerful force for good, creating a cycle of positive change that benefits everyone involved.

Commentary:

Restatement of Thesis: The conclusion restates the thesis, bringing the essay full circle.

Summary of Main Points: The personal and societal benefits are briefly summarized to remind the reader of the key arguments.

Closing Thought: The essay ends with a strong closing sentence that emphasizes the importance and power of community service, leaving the reader with something to think about.

Final Commentary on the Essay Writing Process:

Prewriting: Before writing, think about your topic and thesis. In this case, we decided to explore how community service benefits both individuals and society.

Drafting: Start with an introduction that presents your thesis clearly. In the body, use separate paragraphs to explore different aspects of your thesis, making sure each has its own topic sentence and supporting details.

Revising: Look for areas where you can improve clarity, coherence, or add stronger examples. Ensure that each paragraph logically connects to the next.
Editing: Correct any grammar or punctuation errors, and make sure your wording is precise and formal.

Final Review: Read your essay one more time to check for flow and impact.
This is an example of how to structure a well-organized essay, from introduction to conclusion, using evidence and clear analysis to support your thesis.

Example Essay 3

The Impact of Technology on Modern Education
Introduction

Technology has revolutionized many aspects of our daily lives, and education is no exception. In modern classrooms, technology has transformed the way students learn, how teachers teach, and how educational content is delivered. From digital learning tools and virtual classrooms to online research and collaboration platforms, technology has made education more accessible, personalized, and engaging. In this essay, I will discuss the profound impact that technology has had on modern education, focusing on its ability to enhance learning experiences, increase access to education, and prepare students for a technology-driven world.

Commentary:

Thesis Statement: The thesis clearly outlines the three main areas of focus—enhancing learning, increasing access, and preparing students for the future.
Hook/General Introduction: The opening sentence establishes the importance of technology in modern life, creating relevance for the topic. The introduction gives a general sense of how technology has reshaped education.

Body Paragraph 1: Enhancing Learning Experiences

One of the most significant ways technology has impacted modern education is by enhancing the learning experience for students. Digital tools such as interactive whiteboards, educational apps, and online simulations provide students with more engaging and dynamic learning environments. For instance, students studying biology can now participate in virtual dissections, allowing them to explore complex systems in a detailed, hands-on manner without the limitations of physical resources. Additionally, platforms like Khan Academy and Duolingo allow students to learn at their own pace, offering personalized learning experiences that cater to individual needs and learning styles. By making learning more interactive and adaptable, technology improves students' understanding and retention of information.

Commentary:

Topic Sentence: The paragraph introduces the idea that technology enhances the learning experience, setting up a detailed discussion.

Supporting Details and Examples: Concrete examples such as virtual dissections and online learning platforms provide evidence to support the topic sentence. Explanation and Analysis: The explanation connects the examples to the overall argument, showing how technology makes learning more interactive and effective.

Body Paragraph 2: Increasing Access to Education
Technology has also dramatically increased access to education, particularly for students who live in remote or underserved areas. With the rise of online courses, students can access high-quality education from anywhere in the world. Platforms such as Coursera, edX, and Google Classroom have made it possible for learners to participate in classes that were once only available at prestigious universities. Moreover, technology has made education more inclusive, with tools like speech-to-text software and screen readers enabling students with disabilities to participate more fully in the learning process. By breaking down geographic and physical barriers, technology has democratized education, making it more accessible to a broader range of students.

Commentary:

Topic Sentence: This paragraph shifts the focus to how technology increases access to education, with a clear and direct topic sentence.

Supporting Details: Specific examples of platforms and tools (Coursera, Google Classroom) are provided to illustrate how access has expanded.

Explanation and Analysis: The analysis explains how these technological advances have opened up educational opportunities for students who were previously excluded or limited by their circumstances.|

Body Paragraph 3: Preparing Students for a Technology-Driven World
In addition to enhancing learning and increasing access, technology plays a crucial role in preparing students for a future that is increasingly technology-driven. As automation and artificial intelligence continue to transform industries, students need to develop digital literacy and technical skills to succeed in the workforce. Schools and universities now integrate coding, robotics, and data science into their curriculums, ensuring that students are equipped with the tools they need to thrive in modern workplaces. Furthermore, collaborative platforms such as Google Drive and Microsoft Teams teach students how to work effectively in remote teams, a skill that is becoming essential in today's globalized job market. By incorporating technology into education, schools are preparing students to meet the demands of the future.

Commentary:

Topic Sentence: This paragraph focuses on how technology prepares students for the future, with a clear link to the essay's overall thesis.

Supporting Details and Examples: Examples of coding, robotics, and collaborative platforms are used to show how students are gaining practical skills for future careers.

Explanation and Analysis: The analysis connects these examples to the larger argument, demonstrating that technology is not just a tool for learning but also a preparation for real-world challenges.

Conclusion

In conclusion, the impact of technology on modern education is profound and far-reaching. It has enhanced the learning experience by making it more interactive and personalized, increased access to education by breaking down geographic and physical barriers, and prepared students for a future dominated by technological advancements. While technology poses some challenges, such as the need for digital equity, its overall effect on education has been overwhelmingly positive. As technology continues to evolve, so too will the possibilities for improving education, creating new opportunities for students and educators alike.

Commentary:

Restatement of Thesis: The conclusion reiterates the essay's main points, summarizing the benefits of technology in education.

Summary of Main Points: The personal and societal impacts of technology on education are restated to remind the reader of the key points discussed.

Closing Thought: The essay ends with a forward-looking statement about the continued evolution of technology and its potential to further improve education. This leaves the reader with a sense of ongoing progress.

Final Commentary on the Essay Writing Process:
Prewriting: Before beginning, we brainstormed the different ways technology impacts education, then developed a thesis that tied these ideas together.

Drafting: In the drafting stage, we organized our ideas into body paragraphs that each focused on one main point, supported by specific examples and analysis. Revising: As we revised, we ensured that each paragraph was clear and flowed logically from one to the next, with transitions connecting the ideas.

Editing: We checked for any grammatical or structural issues, ensuring the essay is polished and easy to read.

Final Review: Finally, we gave the essay a thorough read to make sure the argument was cohesive, the evidence was strong, and the writing was engaging.

This essay demonstrates the importance of technology in modern education, structured with a clear thesis, supporting details, and thoughtful analysis throughout.

Common Essay Mistakes - Example 1

Whether the topic is love or action, reality television shows damage society. Viewers witness the personal struggles of strangers and they experience an outpouring of emotions in the name of entertainment. This can be dangerous on many levels. Viewers become numb to real emotions and values. Run the risk of not interpreting a dangerous situation correctly. 1 The reality show participant is also at risk because they are completely exposed. 2 The damage to both viewers and participants leads to the destruction of our healthy societal values.

Romance reality shows are dangerous to the participants and contribute to the emotional problems witnessed in society today as we set up a system built on equality and respect, shows like "The Bachelor" tear it down. 3 In front of millions of viewers every week, young women compete for a man. Twenty-five women claim to be in love with a man they just met. The man is reduced to an object they compete for. There are tears, fights, and manipulation aimed at winning the prize. 4 Imagine a young woman's reality when she returns home and faces the scrutiny of viewers who watched her unravel on television every Monday night. These women objectify themselves and have learned 5 that relationships are a combination of hysteria and competition. This does not give hope to a society based on family values and equality.

6 While incorporating the same manipulations and breakdown of relationships offered on "The Bachelor," shows like "Survivor" add another level of danger. Not only are they building a society based on lying to each other, they are competing in physical challenges that become dangerous. In the name of entertainment, these challenges become increasingly physical and are usually held in a hostile environment. The viewer's ability to determine the safety of an activity is **messed up**. 7 To entertain and preserve their pride, participants continue in competitions regardless of the danger level. For example, 8 participants on "Survivor" have sustained serious injuries as heart attack and burns. Societal rules are based on the safety of its citizens, not on hurting yourself for entertainment.

Reality shows of all kinds are dangerous to participants. They damage society. 9

1. Correct sentence fragments. Who/what runs the risk? Add a subject or combine sentences. Try: "Viewers become numb to real emotions and run the risk of not interpreting a dangerous situation correctly."
2. Correct redundant phrases. Try: "The reality show participant is also at risk because they are exposed."

3. Correct run-on sentences. Decide which thoughts should be separated. Try: "Romance reality shows are dangerous to participants and contribute to the emotional problems of society today. As we support a system built on equality and respect, shows like "The Bachelor" tear it down."

4. Vary sentence structure and length. Try: "Twenty-five women claim to be in love with a man who is reduced to being the object of competition. There are tears, fights, and manipulation aimed at winning the prize."

5. Use active voice. Try: These women objectify themselves and learned that relationships are a combination of hysteria and competition.

6. Use transitions to tie paragraphs together. Try: Start the paragraph with, "Action oriented reality shows are equally as dangerous to the participants."

7. Avoid casual language/slang. Try: "The viewer's ability to determine the safety of an activity is compromised."

8. Don't address the essay. Avoid phrases like "for example" and "in conclusion." Try: "Participants on "Survivor" have sustained serious injuries as heart attack and burns.

9. Leave yourself time to write a strong conclusion! Try: Designate 3-5 minutes for writing your conclusion.

Common Essay Mistakes - Example 2

Questioning authority makes society stronger. In every aspect our society, there is an authoritative person or group making rules. There is also the group underneath them who are meant to follow. 1 This is true of our country's public schools as well as our federal government. The right to question authority at both of these levels is guaranteed by the United States Declaration of Independence. People are given the ability to question so that authority figures are kept in check 2 and will be forced to listen to the opinions of other people. Questioning authority leads to positive changes in society and preserves what is already working well.

If students never question the authority of a principal's decisions, the best interest of the student body is lost. Good things 3 may not remain in place for the students and no amendment to the rules are sought. Change requires that authority be questioned. An example of this is Silver Head Middle School in Davie, Florida. Last year, the principal felt strongly about enforcing the school's uniform policy. Some students were not bothered by this. 4 Many students felt the policy disregarded their civil rights. A petition voicing student dissatisfaction was signed and presented to the principal. He met with a student representative to discuss the petition. Compromise was reached as a monthly "casual day." The students were able to promote change and peace by questioning authority.

Even at the level of federal government, our country's ultimate authority, the ability to question is the key to the harmony keeping society strong. Most government officials are elected by the public so they have the right to question their authority. 5 If there's a mandate, law, or statement that citizens aren't 6 happy with, they have recourse. Campaigning for or against a political platform and participating in the electoral process give a voice to every opinion. I think elections are very important. 7 Without this questioning and examination of society's laws, the government will represent only the voice of the authority figure. The success of our society is based on the questioning of authority. 8

    Society is strengthened by those who question authority. Dialogue is created between people with different visions and change becomes possible. At both the level of public school and of federal government, the positive effects of questioning authority can be witnessed. Whether questioning the decisions of a single principal or the motives of the federal government, it is the willingness of people to question and create change that allows society to grow. A strong society is inspired by many voices, all at different levels. 9 These voices keep society strong.

1. Write concisely. Combine the sentences to improve understanding and cut unnecessary words. Try: "In every aspect of society, there is an authority making rules and a group of people meant to follow them."

2. Avoid slang. Re-word "kept in check." Try: "People are given the ability to question so that authority figures are held accountable and will be forced to listen to the opinions of other people.

2-2. Cut unnecessary words. Try: "People are given the ability to question so that authority figures are held accountable and will listen to other opinions."

3. Use precise language. What are "good things?" Try: "Interesting activities may not remain in place for the students and no amendment to the rules are sought."

Use correct subject-verb agreement. Be careful to identify the correct subject of your sentence. Try: "Interesting activities may not remain in place for the students and no amendment to the rules is sought."

4. Don't add information that doesn't add value to your argument. Cut: "Some students weren't bothered by this."

5. Check for parallel structure. Who has the right to question whose authority? Try: "Having voted them in, the people have the authority to question public officials."
6. Don't use contractions in academic essays. Try: "If there is a mandate, law, or statement that citizens are not happy with, they have recourse."

7. Don't use the pronoun "I" in persuasive essays. Cut opinions. Cut:"I think elections are very important."
8. Use specific examples to prove your argument. Try: Discuss a particular election in depth.

9. Cut redundant sentences. Cut: "A strong society is inspired by many voices, all at different levels."

Example Essay Prompts

Describe a person who has had a significant impact on your life and explain why.

Discuss the importance of teamwork in achieving success.

Analyze the effects of social media on relationships and communication.

Explain how community service can benefit individuals and society as a whole.

Compare and contrast two different cultures and discuss how they influence one another.

Describe a challenge you have faced and how you overcame it.

Discuss the impact of technology on modern education.

Explain the benefits of reading for personal growth and development.

Analyze the causes of climate change and propose potential solutions.

Reflect on a moment that changed your perspective on life.

Writing Concisely

Concise writing is direct and descriptive. The reader follows the writer's thoughts easily. If your writing is concise, a four paragraph essay is acceptable for standardized tests. It's better to write clearly about fewer ideas than to write poorly about many.

This doesn't always mean using fewer words. It means that every word you use is important to the message. Unnecessary or repetitive information dilutes ideas and weakens your writing. The meaning of the word concise comes from the Latin, "to cut up." If it isn't necessary information, don't waste precious testing minutes writing it down.

Being redundant is a quick way to lengthen a sentence or paragraph, but it takes away your power during a timed essay. While many writers use repetition of phrases and key words to make their point, it's important to remove words that don't add value. Redundancy can confuse and lead you away from your subject when you need to write quickly. Be aware that many redundant phrases are part of our daily language and need to be cut from your essay.

For example, "bouquet of flowers" is a redundant phrase as only the word "bouquet" is necessary. Its definition includes flowers. Be especially careful with words you use to stress a point, such as "completely," "totally," and "very."

First of all, I'd like to thank my family.
Revised: First, I'd like to thank my family.

The school *introduced a new* rule.
Revised: The school introduced a rule.

I am *completely full*.
Revised: I am full.

Your glass is *totally empty*!
Revised: Your glass is empty!

Her artwork is *very unique*.
Revised: Her artwork is unique.

Other ways to cut bulk and time include avoiding phrases that have no meaning or power in your essay. Phrases like "in my opinion," "as a matter of fact," and "due to the fact that" are space and time wasters. Also, change passive verbs to active voice.

In my opinion, the paper is well written.
Revised: The paper is well written.

The book *was written* by the best students.
Revised: The best students wrote the book.

The teacher *is listening* to the students.
The teacher listens to the students.

This assigns action to the subject, shortens, and clarifies the sentence. When time is working against you, precise language is on your side.

Not only should you remove redundant phrases, whole sentences without value should be cut too. Replacing general nouns with specific ones is an effective way to accomplish this.

She screamed as the thing came closer. It was a sharp-toothed dog.

Revised: She screamed as the sharp-toothed dog came closer.

The revised sentence is precise and the paragraph is improved by combining sentences and varying sentence structure. When editing, ask yourself which thoughts should be connected and which need to be separated. Skim each paragraph as you finish writing it and cut as you go.

Leave three to four minutes for final editing. While reading, make a point to pause at every period. This allows you to "hear" sentences the way your reader will, not how you meant them to sound. This will help you find the phrases and sentences that need to be cut or combined. The result is an essay a grader will appreciate.

Science

This section contains a self-assessment and basic science tutorials. The tutorials are designed to familiarize general principles and the self-assessment contains general questions similar to the science likely to be on the CAEC exam, but are not intended to be identical to the exam questions. The tutorials are not designed to be a complete course, and it is assumed that students have some familiarity with basic science. If you do not understand parts of the tutorial, or find the tutorial difficult, it is recommended that you seek out additional instruction.

Tour of the CAEC Science Content

The CAEC Science section has 20 questions. Below is a list of the likely science topics likely to appear on the CAEC.

- Physics
- Chemistry
- Life Science
- Earth Science
- Space Science

The questions in the self-assessment are not the same as you will find on the CAEC - that would be too easy! And nobody knows what the questions will be and they change all the time. Mostly, the changes consist of substituting new questions for old, but the changes also can be new question formats or styles, changes to the number of questions in each section, changes to the time limits for each section, and combining sections. So, while the format and exact wording of the questions may differ slightly, and changes from year to year, if you can answer the questions below, you will have no problem with the science section of the CAEC .

Science Self-Assessment

The purpose of the self-assessment is:

- Identify your strengths and weaknesses.
- Develop your personalized study plan (above)
- Get accustomed to the CAEC format
- Extra practice – the self-assessments are almost a full 3rd practice test!
- Provide a baseline score for preparing your study schedule.

Since this is a Self-assessment, and depending on how confident you are with Language Arts, timing yourself is optional. The CAEC has 20 questions. This self-assessment has 15 questions, so allow about 15 minutes to complete.

Once complete, use the table below to assess your understanding of the content, and prepare your study schedule described in chapter 1.

80% - 100%	Excellent – you have mastered the content
60 – 79%	Good. You have a working knowledge. Even though you can just pass this section, you may want to review the tutorials and do some extra practice to see if you can improve your mark.
40% - 59%	Below Average. You do not understand the science content. Review the tutorials, and retake this quiz again in a few days, before proceeding to the practice test questions.
Less than 40%	Poor. You have a very limited understanding of the science content. Please review the tutorials, and retake this quiz again in a few days, before proceeding to the practice test questions.

Science Answer Sheet

1. A B C D   11. A B C D

2. A B C D   12. A B C D

3. A B C D   13. A B C D

4. A B C D   14. A B C D

5. A B C D   15. A B C D

6. A B C D

7. A B C D

8. A B C D

9. A B C D

10. A B C D

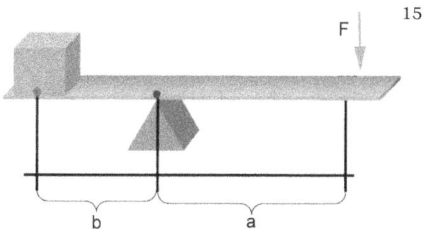

1. Consider the illustration above and the corresponding data:

Weight = W = 200 pounds
Distance from fulcrum to Weight = b = 10 feet
Distance from fulcrum to point where force is applied = a = 20 feet
How much force (F) must be applied to lift the weight?

    a. 80
    b. 100
    c. 150
    d. 200

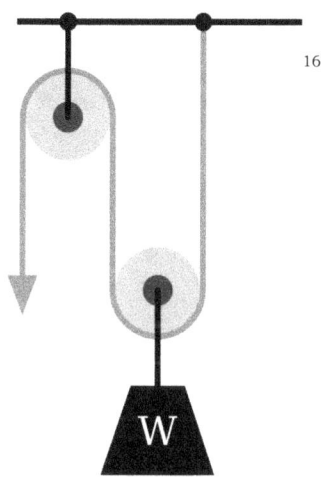

2. Consider the pulley arrangement above. If the weight, W, is 50 pounds, how much force is required to lift it?

    a. 10 pounds
    b. 20 pounds
    c. 25 pounds
    d. 50 pounds

3. If a 100-pound object is sitting on a 10-square-inch plate, what is the PSI?

   a. 5
   b. 10
   c. 15
   d. 20

Proteins

Questions 4 - 9 refer to the following passage

Proteins are large molecules consisting of many joined amino acids. They form the basis of many different body tissues and play an essential role in a variety of biological processes such as catalyzing chemical reactions, transporting molecules such as oxygen, our immune system and transmitting messages between cells. Some proteins have a structural role, for instance, movements of the proteins actin and myosin are responsible for the contraction of skeletal muscle. A property of many proteins is that they specifically bind to a certain molecule or class of molecules. Antibodies are an example of globular proteins that attach to one particular type of molecule. In fact, the enzyme-linked immunosorbent assay (ELISA), uses antibodies to detect various biomolecules in the blood, making it one of the most sensitive tests in modern medicine. Enzymes, however are probably the most important group of proteins. Virtually every reaction in a living cell requires an enzyme to lower the activation energy of the reaction.

4. Which of the following is not an example of a protein?

   a. Actin
   b. Myosin
   c. Amino acid
   d. Antibodies

5. Enzymes are known to catalyze reactions in the body. What does this mean?

   a. They create a chemical reaction
   b. They speed up chemical reactions
   c. They are involved in chemical reactions
   d. Provide energy for the reaction to occur

6. Which of the following is not a feature of enzymes?

   a. They lower the energy needed to begin a reaction
   b. They are specific
   c. They are proteins
   d. They are antibodies

7. Which of the following is another example of a structural protein that can be found in the human body?

   a. Haemoglobin

   b. Keratin

   c. Insulin

   d. Estrogen

8. Which of the following is not true of atomic theory?

   a. Originated 2500 years ago with Greek philosopher, Leucippus and his pupil Democritus

   b. Is the field of physics that describes the characteristics and properties of atoms that make up matter.

   c. Explains temperature as the momentum of atoms.

   d. Explains macroscopic phenomenon through the behavior of microscopic atoms.

9. Which of these statements about atoms is/are correct?

   a. Atoms are the largest unit of matter that can take part in a chemical reaction.

   b. Atoms can be chemically broken down into much simpler forms.

   c. Atoms are composed of protons and neutrons in a central nucleus surrounded by electrons.

   d. Atoms do not differ in terms of atomic number or atomic mass.

The Effect of Insulin on Glucose Uptake and Metabolism

Questions 9 - 15 refer to the following passage

The hormone insulin is another example of a protein. It plays several roles in the body's metabolism helping it to control blood glucose levels. Insulin signals the liver, muscle and fat cells to remove glucose from the blood, helping cells to take up glucose to use as energy. If the body has sufficient energy, insulin signals the liver to take up glucose and store it as glycogen.

To regulate glucose, insulin binds to its receptor, which in turn starts many protein activation cascades. These include translocation of the Glut-4 transporter to the plasma membrane and influx of glucose, glycogen synthesis (4), glycolysis (5) and fatty acid synthesis.

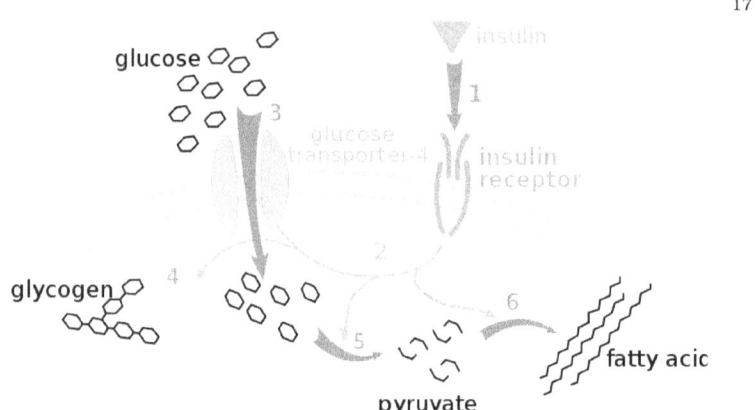

10. The process above shows how glucose is controlled in a healthy individual. What would be the outcome if this process failed to operate correctly?

   a. Heart Disease
   b. Cancer
   c. Diabetes
   d. Pancreatitis

11. Name the organ responsible for making the hormone insulin.

   a. Small intestine
   b. Gall Bladder
   c. Liver
   d. Pancreas

12. Insulin is another example of a protein. Which of the following statements best describes the role of insulin in the body?

   a. Insulin regulates how the body stores and uses glucose and fat.
   b. Insulin turns glucose into glycogen
   c. Insulin triggers the formation of fatty acids
   d. Insulin allows glucose transporter-4 to move glucose through the plasma membrane

13. Name the cellular process that all cells require glucose as a reactant for:

    a. Photosynthesis

    b. Cell division

    c. Respiration

    d. Reproduction

14. Which of the following conclusions are correct, relating to insulin's effect on glucose uptake:

    a. When blood glucose levels are low, insulin causes the liver as well as muscle and fat cells to remove glucose from the blood.

    b. Insulin prevents glucose from moving through the glucose transporter molecule when glucose levels are high

    c. The more glucose is in the blood; the more insulin is released to control it

    d. Insulin triggers the muscle cells to take up excess glucose and store it as glycogen.

15. Protons, neutrons, and electrons differ in that:

    a. Protons and neutrons form the nucleus of an atom, while electrons are found in fixed energy levels around the nucleus of the atom.

    b. Protons and neutrons are charged particles and electrons are neutral.

    c. Protons and neutrons form fixed energy levels around the nucleus of the atom and electrons are located near the surface of the atom.

    d. Protons, neutrons and electrons are charged particles.

Answer Key

1. B
To solve for F, Weight X b (distance from fulcrum to weight) = Force X a (distance from fulcrum to point where force is applied)
200 X 10 = F X 20
2000/20 = F
F = 100

2. C
Since the weight is only attached to one pulley, the force required will be 50/2 = 25 pounds.

3. B
Calculate the PSI by taking the weight divided by the size of the object the weight is bearing on. 100/10 = 10 PSI.

4. C
Choice C is correct as amino acids are the subunits which join together to make a protein. Choices A and B are incorrect as the text tells us they are structural proteins.
Choice D is also incorrect as the text tells us that they are globular proteins.

5. B
Choice B is correct - the definition of a catalyst "speeding up a chemical reaction by lowering the amount of energy needed." Choices A and D are incorrect - enzymes reduce the amount of energy needed, they do not create the reaction or provide the energy.
Choice C is incorrect - enzymes are not involved in reactions, they are not a reactant nor become a product, which is why they can be reused again once a reaction has finished.

6. D
Choice D is the correct choice. Enzymes lower the energy needed to begin the reaction; they are specific, meaning that each enzyme only catalyzes one reaction. The text also tells us that they are proteins; therefore choices A, B and C are incorrect. Enzymes are not antibodies.

7. B
Choice B is correct as keratin is a protein found in skin and nails, a building material for the body. Choice A - hemoglobin is a globular protein, carrying oxygen in red blood cells and is therefore incorrect. Choice C is incorrect - insulin controls blood glucose levels
Choice D is incorrect - estrogen is the female reproductive hormone

8. C
Choice C is incorrect because atomic theory explains temperature as the motion of atoms (faster = hotter), not the momentum. The momentum of atoms explains the outward pressure that they exert.

9. C
The only correct statement about atoms is they "Are composed of protons and neutrons in a central nucleus surrounded by electrons."

10. C
An inability to make or produce sufficient levels of insulin results in diabetes.

11. D
The pancreas is responsible for producing insulin. Choice A is incorrect; this is where food is digested before it enters the bloodstream. Choice B is incorrect, this where bile is stored. Choice C is incorrect; the liver does store excess glucose taken out of the blood as glycogen.

12. A
Insulin helps control blood glucose levels by signaling the liver and muscle and fat cells to absorb glucose from the blood. If the body has enough energy, insulin signals the liver to take up glucose and store it as glycogen. Choice B is incorrect; insulin does not turn glucose into glycogen; this is the product that the liver turns glucose into for storage. Choice C is incorrect as it only gives a partial answer. Choice D is incorrect as this is a partial answer.

13. C
Glucose is an essential reactant needed for respiration. Choice A is incorrect as glucose is a product of photosynthesis and only occurs in plants. Choice B is incorrect as glucose is not used directly in cell division. Choice D is incorrect as glucose is not a primary reactant needed for reproduction.

14. C
The concentration of glucose directly correlates to the amount of insulin needed. Choice A is incorrect as this occurs when blood glucose levels are high. Choice B is incorrect as insulin will allow glucose to cross the plasma membrane removing excess glucose from the bloodstream. Choice D is incorrect as this process occurs in the liver.

15. A
Protons and neutrons form the nucleus of an atom, while electrons are found in fixed energy levels around the nucleus of the atom.

Science Tutorials

Scientific Method

The scientific method is a set of steps that allow people who ask "how" and "why" questions about the world to go about finding valid answers that accurately reflect reality.

Were it not for the scientific method, people would have no valid method for drawing quantifiable and accurate information about the world.

There are four primary steps to the scientific method:

1. Analyzing an aspect of reality and asking "how" or "why" it works or exists
2. Forming a hypothesis that explains "how" or "why"
3. Making a prediction about the sort of things that would happen if the hypothesis were true
4. Performing an experiment to test your prediction.

These steps vary somewhat depending on the field of science you happen to be studying. (In astronomy, for instance, experiments are generally eschewed in favor of observational evidence confirming predictions are true.) But for the most part, this is the model scientists follow.

Observation and Analysis

The first step in the scientific method requires you to determine what it is about reality that you want to explore.

You might notice that your friends who eat regular servings of fruits and vegetables are healthier and more athletic than your friends who live off red meat and meals covered in cheese and gravy. This is an observation and, noting it, you are likely to ask yourself "why" it seems to be true. At this stage of the scientific method, scientists will often do research to see if anyone else has explored similar observations and analyze what other people's findings have been. This is an important step not only because it can show what others have found to be true about their observation, but because it can show what others have found to be false, which can be equally as valuable.

Hypothesis

After making your observation and doing some research, you can form your hypothesis. A hypothesis is an idea you formulate based on the evidence you have already gathered about "how" your observation relates to reality.

Using the example of your friends' diets, you may have found research discussing vitamin levels in fruits and vegetables and how certain vitamins will effect a person's health and athleticism. This research may lead you to hypothesize that the foods your healthy friends are eating contain specific types of vitamins, and it is the vitamins making them healthy. Just as importantly, however, is applying research that shows hypotheses that were later proven wrong. Scientists need to know this information, too, as it can help keep them from making errors in their thinking. For instance, you could come across a research paper in which someone hypothesized that the sugars in fruits and vegetables gave people more energy, which then helped them be more athletic. If the paper were to go on to explain that no such link was found, and that the protein and carbohydrates in meat and gravy contained far more energy than the sugar, you would know that this hypothesis was wrong and that there was no need for you to waste time exploring it.

Prediction

The third step in the scientific method is making a prediction based on your hypothesis.

Forming predictions is vital to the scientific method because if your prediction turns out to be correct, it will demonstrate that your hypothesis can accurately explain some aspect of the world. This is important because one aspect of the scientific method is its ability to prove objectively that your way of understanding the world is valid. We can take the simple example of a car that will not start. If you notice the fuel gauge is pointing towards empty, you can announce your prediction to the other passengers that a careful test of the gas tank will show the car has no fuel. While this seems obvious, it is still important to note since a prediction like this is the only way to really *prove* to your friends that you understand how a fuel gauge works and what it means.

In the same way, a prediction made by a hypothesis is the only way to show that it represents reality. For instance, based on your vitamin hypothesis you may predict people can be healthy and athletic while eating whatever they want, as long as they take vitamin supplements. If these prediction ends being true, it will show that it is in fact the vitamins, and only the vitamins, in fruits and vegetables that make people healthy and athletic. It will prove that your hypothesis shows how vitamins work.

Experiment

The final step is to perform an experiment that tests your prediction.

You may decide to separate your healthy friends into three groups, give one group vitamin supplements and prohibit them from eating vegetables, give another fake supplements and prohibit them from eating vegetables and have the third act normally as the control group. It is always important to have a control group so you have someone acting "normally" to compare your results against. If this experiment shows the real supplement group and the control group maintaining the same level of health and athleticism, while the fake supplement group grows weak and sickly, you will know your hypothesis is true. If, on the other hand, you get unexpected results, you will need to go back to step one, analyze your results, make new observations and try again with a different hypothesis.

Any hypothesis that cannot be confirmed with experiment (or for fields such as astronomy, with observation) cannot be considered true and must be altered or abandoned. It is in this stage where scientists—being humans, with human beliefs and prejudices—are most likely to abandon the scientific method. If an experiment or observation gives a scientist results that he or she does not like, the scientist may be inclined to ignore the results rather than reexamine the hypothesis. This was the case for nearly a thousand years in astronomy with astronomers attempting to form accurate models of the solar system based on circular orbits of the planets and on Earth being in the center. For philosophical reasons they believed that circles were "perfect" and that the Earth was "important," so no model that had the correct elliptical orbits or the sun properly in the center was accepted until the 16th century, even though those models more accurately described all astronomers' observations.

Biology

Biology is a natural science concerned with the study of life and living organisms, including their structure, function, growth, origin, evolution, distribution, and taxonomy.

Biology is a vast subject containing many subdivisions, topics, and disciplines. Among the most important topics are five unifying principles that can be said to be the fundamental axioms of modern biology:

- Cells are the basic unit of life

- New species and inherited traits are the product of evolution

- Genes are the basic unit of heredity

- An organism regulates its internal environment to maintain a stable and constant condition

- Living organisms consume and transform energy.

Sub-disciplines of biology are recognized on the scale at which organisms are studied and the methods used to study them: biochemistry examines the rudimentary chemistry of life; molecular biology studies the complex interactions of systems of biological molecules; cellular biology examines the basic building block of all life, the cell; physiology examines the physical and chemical functions of the tissues, organs, and organ systems of an organism; and ecology examines how various organisms interact and associate with their environment.[18]

Cell Biology

Cell biology (formerly cytology, from the Greek kytos, "contain") is a scientific discipline that studies cells – their physiological properties, their structure, the organelles they contain, interactions with their environment, their life cycle, division and death.

> This is done both on a microscopic and molecular level. Cell biology research encompasses both the great diversity of single-celled organisms like bacteria and protozoa, as well as the many specialized cells in multicellular organisms such as humans.

Knowing the components of cells and how cells work is fundamental to all biological sciences.

> Appreciating the similarities and differences between cell types is particularly important to the fields of cell and molecular biology as well as to biomedical fields such as cancer research and developmental biology. These fundamental similarities and differences provide a unifying theme, sometimes allowing the principles learned from studying one cell type to be extrapolated and generalized to other cell types. Therefore, research in cell biology is closely related to genetics, biochemistry, molecular biology, immunology, and developmental biology.

Each type of protein is usually sent to a particular part of the cell.

> An important part of cell biology is the investigation of molecular mechanisms by which proteins are moved to different places inside cells or secreted from cells.

Processes – Movement of Proteins

Most proteins are synthesized by ribosomes in the rough endoplasmic reticulum.

> Ribosomes contain the nucleic acid RNA, which assembles and joins amino acids to make proteins. They can be found alone or in groups within the cytoplasm as well as on the RER.

This process is known as protein biosynthesis.

> Biosynthesis (also called biogenesis) is an enzyme-catalysed process in cells of living organisms by which substrates are converted to more complex products (also simply known as protein translation). Some proteins, such as

those to be incorporated in membranes (known as membrane proteins), are transported into the "rough" endoplasmic reticulum (ER) during synthesis. This process can be followed by transportation and processing in the Golgi apparatus.

The Golgi apparatus is a large organelle that processes proteins and prepares them for use both inside, and outside the cell.

The Golgi apparatus is somewhat like a post office. It receives items (proteins from the ER), packages and labels them, and then sends them onto their destinations (to different parts of the cell or to the cell membrane for transport out of the cell). From the Golgi, membrane proteins can move to the plasma membrane, to other sub-cellular compartments, or they can be secreted from the cell.

The ER and Golgi can be thought of as the "membrane protein synthesis compartment" and the "membrane protein processing compartment," respectively.

There is a semi-constant flux of proteins through these compartments. ER and Golgi-resident proteins associate with other proteins but remain in their respective compartments. Other proteins "flow" through the ER and Golgi to the plasma membrane. Motor proteins transport membrane protein-containing vesicles along cytoskeletal tracks to distant parts of cells such as axon terminals.

Some proteins that are made in the cytoplasm contain structural features that target them for transport into mitochondria or the nucleus.

Some mitochondrial proteins are made inside mitochondria and are coded for by mitochondrial DNA. In plants, chloroplasts also make some cell proteins.

Extracellular and cell surface proteins destined to be degraded can move back into intracellular compartments on being incorporated into endocytosed vesicles some of which fuse with lysosomes where the proteins are broken down to their individual amino acids. The degradation of some membrane proteins begins while still at the cell surface when they are separated by secretases. Proteins that function in the cytoplasm are often degraded by proteasomes.

Other cellular processes

Active and Passive transport - Movement of molecules into and out of cells.
Autophagy - The process whereby cells "eat" their own internal components or microbial invaders.
Adhesion - Holding together cells and tissues.
Reproduction - Made possible by the combination of sperm made in the testiculi (contained in some male cells' nuclei) and the egg made in the ovary (contained in the nucleus of a female cell). When the sperm breaks through the hard outer shell of the egg a new cell embryo is formed, which, in humans, grows to full size in 9

months.
Cell movement - Chemotaxis, Contraction, cilia and flagella.
Cell signalling - Regulation of cell behavior by signals from outside.
DNA repair and Cell death
Metabolism - Glycolysis, respiration, Photosynthesis
Transcription and mRNA splicing - gene expression.

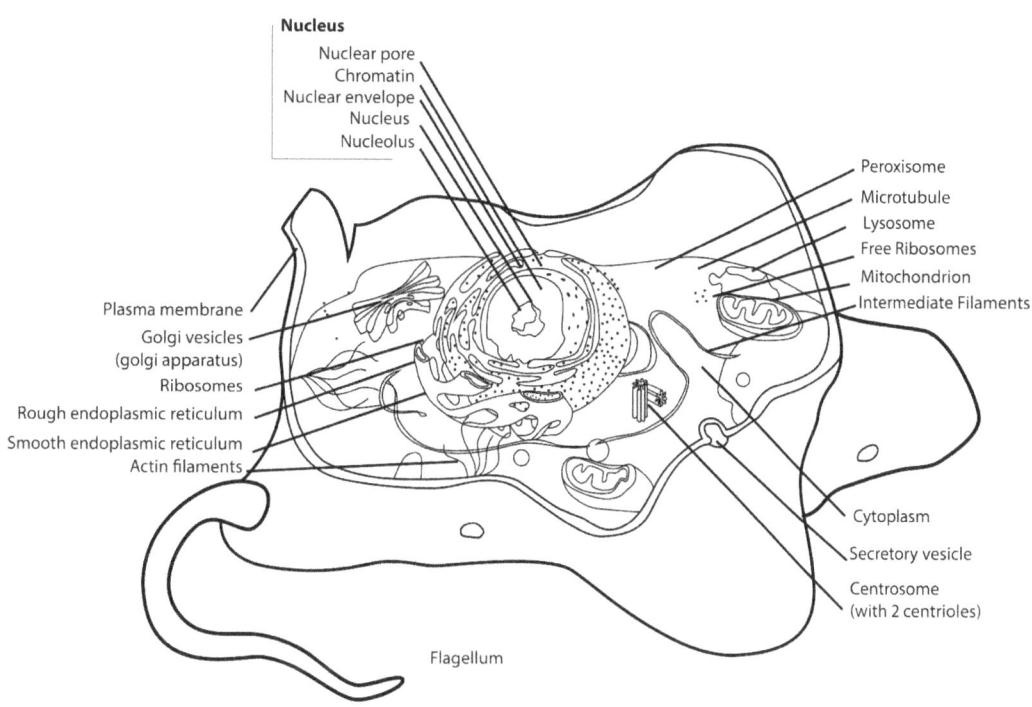

Internal cellular structures

Chloroplast - key organelle for photosynthesis (only found in plant cells)
Cilia - motile microtubule-containing structures of eukaryotes
Cytoplasm - contents of the main fluid-filled space inside cells
Cytoskeleton - protein filaments inside cells
Endoplasmic reticulum - major site of membrane protein synthesis
Flagella - motile structures of bacteria, archaea and eukaryotes
Golgi apparatus - site of protein glycosylation in the endomembrane system
Lipid bilayer - fundamental organizational structure of cell membranes
Lysosome - break down cellular waste products and debris into simple compounds (only found in animal cells)
Membrane lipid and protein barrier
Mitochondrion - major energy-producing organelle by releasing it as ATP
Nucleus - holds most of the DNA of eukaryotic cells and controls all cellular activities

Organelle - term used for major subcellular structures
Ribosome - RNA and protein complex required for protein synthesis in cells
Vesicle - small membrane-bounded spheres inside cells

Chromosomes, genes, proteins, RNA and DNA

The concepts of genes, chromosomes, proteins, RNA and DNA are all interrelated genetic terms. Chromosomes are made up of genes, the DNA contains the chromosomes and the RNA interprets and implements the information in the RNA. Here is a break down of each of them.

Proteins

Proteins are biological molecules that are made up of a chain or chains of amino acids. Proteins play many very vital roles in living organisms. Protein is essential for the performance of many bodily functions such as replicating DNA, transporting nutrients and molecules within the body, responding to stimuli, and acting as a catalyst for metabolic reactions within the living organism, among other things. There are different types of proteins and they play various roles. The difference in proteins would be determined by their unique arrangement or sequence of amino acids.

Genes

A gene is the molecular hereditary unity of an organism and a small part of the chromosome. It is the term used to describe a portion of RNA or DNA code that performs a particular function in the organism. Genes are essential to life because they specify the functions of all proteins and RNA chains. Genes contain the information to maintain and build the cells in the organism and contain genetic information that would be passed onto the offspring.

Genes hold the information for biological traits and functions some of which can clearly be seen and some of which are hidden. For example, the information contained in specific genes determines factors such as eye color, hair color, number of limbs, height and so on. Some traits such as blood type and the thousands of metabolic reactions and biochemical process that take place in the body to sustain life are defined unseen by the genes.

A gene is set of basic instruction embedded on a sequence of nucleic acids. The gene is a locatable region of the DNA genome sequence that corresponds with a unit of inheritance and associated with a particular body function or set of functions.

Chromosomes

The chromosome is a piece of the DNA containing several genes. The chromosome is an organized part of the DNA. It is a single piece of coiled DNA. The chromosome contains several genes, DNA-bound proteins, nucleotide sequences and regulatory elements. The DNA-bound proteins help to hold the DNA together and regulate its functions.

Since the chromosomes contain the genes, they contain almost all the genetic information of the organism. Chromosomes differ from one organism to another. The DNA molecule could be linear or circular. The chromosome can contain from 100,000 to over 3 million nucleotides in one long chain depending on the organism. Cells with defined nuclei (eukaryotic cells) usually have large linear shaped chromosomes. Cells without clearly defined nuclei (prokaryotic cells) usually have smaller sized circular chromosomes.

Chromosomes are essential in the process of cell division. In mitosis cell division, the chromosomes have to be replicated and then divided between the two resulting daughter cells. This ensures that the resulting two daughter cells are genetically identical to the original mother cell.

DNA

DNA or Deoxyribonucleic acid is an essential component of life. It has been described as the blueprint of a living organism. It contains vital genetic information and instructions that are required for the proper functioning and development of all types and forms of living organisms and even viruses. DNA, proteins and RNA are the three most important macro-molecules that are essential for any form of life.

The genetic information contained in the DNA is encoded as a sequence of nucleotides known as G, A, and C. With G being guanine, A adenine, T thymine and C cytosine. These nucleotides are arranged as DNA molecules in a double-stranded helix. The strands run in opposite directions and are thus anti-parallel. The DNA contains long structures known as chromosomes.

RNA

RNA or Ribonucleic acids are large biological molecules that perform the important roles of decoding, coding, regulating and expressing the genes and the information contained within them. RNA, DNA and proteins are three essential components for all form of life. The RNA is also composed of nucleotides, but unlike the DNA that is double stranded, the RNA is single stranded.

In organisms, some RNA components serve as messengers to convey genetic information to direct the synthesis or use of specific proteins for specific purposes. It can thus be said that RNA is essential for the proper carrying out of the information contained in the DNA genes. RNA plays important roles within the cell such as helping to catalyze biological reactions sense and communicate cellular signals and control gene expressions. RNA is also essential for protein synthesis.

Mitosis and Meiosis

Meiosis and mitosis are two types of cellular division and they play a very important role in cell reproduction and the maintenance of tissues.

The cell is the basic functional unit of living organisms. It is made up of a collection of organelles and other cell matter dispersed within the cell membrane. For new cells to form, existing cells divide through the process of meiosis or mitosis, depending on the type of cell and reason for division.

Mitosis refers to the division of a cell into two identical cells.

The original cell goes through a process of duplication of its genetic material and then equally divides its contents into two new daughter cells. The process of mitosis goes through several stages until the two cells segregate to form two distinct but genetically identical cells.

Mitosis cell division

During mitosis the cell divides its nucleus and then separates its organelles and chromosomes into two identical parts. The mother cell then divides into two genetically identical cells with equal parts of the cellular contents. The nuclei, cell membrane, organelles and cytoplasm of the cell would be shared between the two new cells.

Mitosis cell division is complex and fast. The process takes place in stages with each stage comprising of a set of activities that lead to the next set. The stages of mitosis are Prophase, Prometaphase, Metaphase, Anaphase and Telophase. Mitosis occurs in some unicellular organisms and within animal and human cells. Unicellular organisms use mitosis to reproduce their like and within animal and humans, mitosis is used to replace cells and repair tissues.

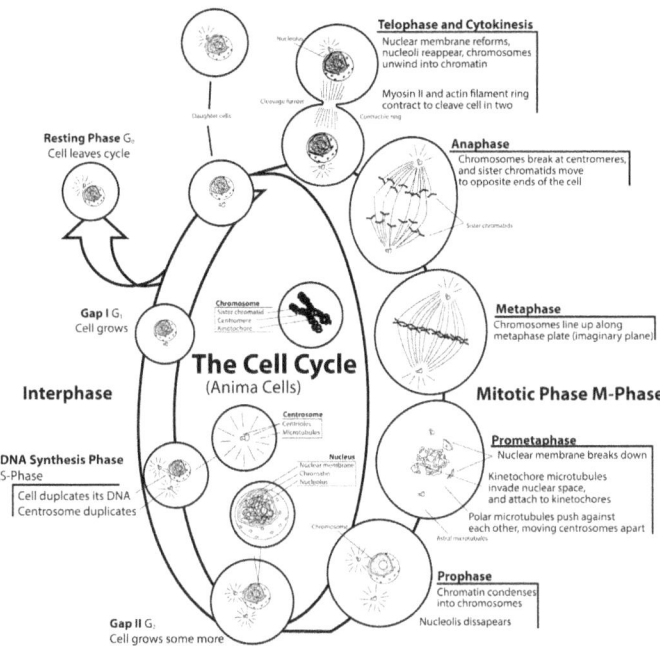

Meiosis

Meiosis occurs when one cell from the male and one from the female combine or fuse to form one diploid cell, which then splits to form four haploid cells.

The diploid cell contains copies of the chromosome and genetic information from both parents. The resulting four haploid cells will contain a copy of each chromosome.

Each chromosome in the four cells will contain a unique blend of the paternal and maternal genetic information, which makes it possible for the offspring to share some genetic resemblance to both parents while remaining genetically distinct from both of them. This nature of meiosis cell division is what accounts for the genetic diversity that is available today as each offspring DNA is a unique blend of its maternal and paternal genetic DNA.

Mitosis and meiosis have some similarities in that they are both types of cell division among living organisms.

There is however still some differences among them. For example, mitosis occurs within a cell with no interactions with other cells. The individual cell simply divides and produces two genetically identical cells. With meiosis, the process involves two cells from both the male and female in a form sexual reproduction. The resultant cells are four cells that are genetically different from their parents. The process of meiosis was discovered by Oscar Hertwig and Mitosis was discovered by Walther Flemming.

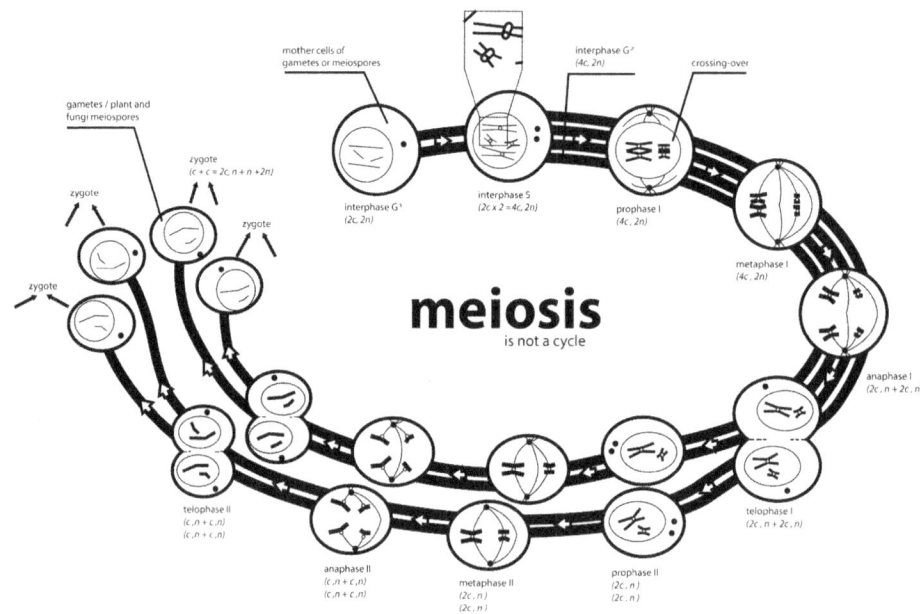

Heredity: Genes and Mutation

All of the genetic material that tells our cells what jobs they hold is stored in our DNA (deoxyribonucleic acid). When complex creatures such as humans reproduce, our DNA is copied and combined with our mate's DNA to create a new genetic sequence for our offspring.

> This information is stored in our genes and encoded in DNA base pairs through different combinations of the chemical groupings adenine and thymine (represented by A and T) and guanine and cytosine (represented by G and C). Each gene covers a small portion of our DNA and is responsible for creating the protein that section of DNA holds instructions for.

Genes contain two alleles, one from each of our parents. When we reproduce we will transfer one, and only one, of each allele to our children.

> Alleles can be either dominant or recessive, and by combining the pairs of alleles we get from our parents, we can determine what our genes say we should be like. This genetic description of ourselves is known as our genotype. Genotype is our exact genetic makeup, and it determines our physical

characteristics such as basic hair, eye and skin color. Related to the genotype is our phenotype, which describes the characteristics we display when our genes interact with the environment. For example, skin color is determined by a person's genotype, but the effect the sun has on skin—does the person tan, freckle, burn or even come away without any noticeable effect at all?—is an expression of phenotype.

Under normal circumstances people's genes will transfer directly from their parents following Mendel's Laws of Inheritance. Errors are common though.

DNA reproduction, however, is not necessarily a flawless process. Errors can develop either at random or due to outside influences such as radiation or chemicals in the environment. These errors, when related to heredity are called de novo mutations; they occur during embryonic development. Some mutations have no effect at all on the person's genetic makeup, but others can alter the way genes express themselves. Whether this is a good thing or not depends entirely on what genes are altered in what ways. Some mutations can cause children to be born sick or to have a higher susceptibility to disease by changing the types of proteins that their genes produce, or even by stopping certain proteins from being produced all together. Others, though, can be an improvement to the child's genetic structure. It is important to remember that the entire process of evolution is based on how random mutations throughout history have affected an individual's ability to interact with the environment.

Several notable examples of beneficial mutations stemming from natural selection can be seen in bubonic plague resistant European populations and malaria resistant African populations.

Both groups have genes built from specific alleles that create disease blocking proteins. (The CCR5 protein in people of European descent blocks the plague—and HIV sometimes—and the sickle cell protein in people of African descent blocks malaria.) These genes are widespread throughout their respective populations as a result of natural selection, which killed those who lived in these groups' ancestral regions but who did not possess the mutation. Had these diseases never existed, the mutations would have been considered neutral, providing no benefit yet causing no harm.

There are several ways that errors in DNA reproduction can cause mutations.

Chemicals can be inserted into, or deleted from base pairs, causing the chemical composition of the pairs to change and, thus, changing the alleles of the gene represented by those pairs. A portion of the DNA strand may also duplicate itself, or it may shift itself, causing the half of the base pair on one side of the DNA strand to link to the wrong half on the other side.

Heredity: Mendelian Inheritance

The father of genetics was a 19th century Austrian monk named Gregor Johann Mendel who became famous for his work crossbreeding peas in the garden of his monastery.

> Aside from his life as a monk, Mendel was a highly educated physicist, studying first at the University of Olomouc (in the modern day Czech Republic) and later at the University of Vienna.

Mendel's work with peas revolutionized the scientific understanding of heredity and yielded two important laws: the Law of Segregation and the Law of Independent Assortment. To better understand these laws, however, we first need to look at the work of another geneticist, Reginald Punnett.

> In 1900 while Punnett was doing his graduate work at the University of Cambridge in England, Gregor Mendel's work on genetics, which did not receive much attention during his lifetime, was being rediscovered. Punnett became an early follower of Mendelian genetics and developed the Punnett square as a means to organize the assortment of inherited alleles as Mendel described them. A Punnett square is simply a box with several squares drawn inside it and with the allele for a particular gene from each parent listed on either the top or the side. Each square shows a possible genotype (or set of alleles that define the gene) that can be inherited by the offspring of those parents. We will see Punnett squares as we explain Mendel's laws.

Law of Segregation

Mendel's Law of Segregation says that only half of the alleles of each parent's genes are transferred to their offspring, with the other half coming from the other parent.

Each gene contains two alleles. For instance a gene for trait 'A' could contain the alleles AA, Aa or aa, with

> The 'A' being the dominant form of the allele and 'a' being the recessive form. (Offspring with one or more dominant alleles exhibit the trait; offspring with only recessive forms do not.) The Law of Segregation says that one allele will come from one parent, and one will come from the other, and it is the parent's combined genetic makeup (rather than one parent's particular genotype) that will determine the genes of their offspring.

> Mendel also showed that the probability a certain trait would spread from parents to children was 3:1, if both parents had one dominant and one recessive form of the gene, also known has having heterozygous alleles. (Having two of the same alleles—AA or aa—is homozygous.)

Punnett squares

The Punnett square below represents the possible children born to two parents with Aa alleles expressing the 'A' gene.

	A	a
A	**AA**	**Aa**
a	**Aa**	aa

The three genes in bold, with at least one capital letter (AA, Aa and the other Aa), represent cases in which the presence of at least one dominant allele will cause the trait to manifest in the offspring. The remaining one (aa) represents the one case where the child does not manifest the trait even though both his or her parents do. (This could be the one brunette in a family of redheads, for instance.) Provided, both parents have one dominant and one recessive allele, the distribution will always be 3:1.

Law of Independent Assortment

Mendel's second law, the Law of Independent Assortment, shows that the alleles of multiple genes will mix independently of one another.

When two separate genotypes are tracked, the genes will produce 16 separate possible combinations spread out in a 9:3:3:1 ratio. This is also known as a dihybrid cross, while dealing with a single set of alleles is a monohybrid cross.

We can demonstrate this by assuming that we have a male and a female each with heterozygous alleles making them blond and tall. We can represent this with the genotypes BbTt in each. We should also assume that a 'bb' genotype would give someone brown hair and 'tt' would make them short. Since the Law of Independent Assortment says that each allele will mix independently, we end up with four combinations of genotype that each parent can pass on: BT, Bt, bT and bt. These can then be mapped in a slightly larger Punnett square that looks like this:

	BT	Bt	bT	bt
BT	**BBTT**	**BBTt**	**BbTT**	**BbTt**
Bt	**BBTt**	**BBtt**	**BbTt**	**Bbtt**
bT	**BbTT**	**BbTt**	bbTT	bbTt
bt	**BbTt**	**Bbtt**	bbTt	bbtt

This is the distribution of the tall, blond couple's possible children. Nine would also be tall and blond, three would be short and blond, three would be tall and brunette, and one would be short and brunette. This follows the 9:3:3:1 ratio set out by Mendel.

Classification

Classification

Taxonomic classification is the primary method of organizing the Earth's biology.
Taxonomy means,

>1. The classification of organisms in an ordered system that shows natural relationships.
>2. The science, laws, or principles of classification

>The earliest form of classification that bears any resemblance to the current system can be traced back to ancient Greece with Aristotle's organization of animals based on reproduction.

The classification into kingdoms (animal, mineral and vegetable) was developed by Carolus Linnaeus.

>The true father of modern taxonomical classification, however, is Carolus Linnaeus, who in the early 18th century developed a system of kingdoms that separated life into the categories animal, mineral and vegetable. Although Linnaeus's work lacked what would today be considered essential technologies (such as microscopes capable of imaging bacteria) and theories (such as evolution), much of his system has survived in modern classification.

Charles Darwin's theory of evolution was an important factor in taxonomic classification.

>With Charles Darwin's publication of On the Origin of Species in 1859 the evolutionary process became a major factor in taxonomic classification. For the first time biology could be classified by grouping the direct descendants of common ancestors rather than just grouping creatures with similar characteristics.

The main classifications are, domain, kingdom, phylum, class, order, family, genus and species.

>Today, most scientists accept a hierarchical structuring of biology that goes from general, or large, to specific: domain, kingdom, phylum, class, order, family, genus and species. (There are sometimes smaller subcategories such as superfamily, subfamily, tribe and subspecies listed, but these are the primary eight categories.) Domain is the newest of these and is split into three primary groups: Bacteria, Archaea and Eukarya.

>Each of these domains is split again with Bacteria splitting into the Kingdom Bacteria, Archaea splitting into the Kingdom Archaea and Eukarya splitting into the four kingdoms of Protista, Plantae, Fungi and finally our kingdom, Animalia. The Domain Eukarya splits so many times because eukaryotic

cells are highly complex, containing such important features as cell walls and nuclei. As a result of this complexity, eukaryotic cells have gone through a more diverse evolutionary process than prokaryotic cells such as bacteria and archaea, and thus Eukarya make up all complex life on Earth

Rank	Fruit fly	Human	Pea	*E. coli*
Domain	Eukarya	Eukarya	Eukarya	Bacteria
Kingdom	Animalia	Animalia	Plantae	Bacteria
Phylum or **Division**	Arthropoda	Chordata	Magnoliophyta	
Subphylum or subdivision	Hexapoda	Vertebrata		
Class	Insecta	Mammalia	Magnoliopsida	
Subclass	Pterygota	Theria	Rosidae	
Order	Diptera	Primates	Fabales	
Suborder	Brachycera		Fabineae	
Family	Drosophilidae	Hominidae	Fabaceae	
Subfamily	Drosophilinae	Homininae	Faboideae	
Genus	*Drosophila*	*Homo*	*Pisum*	*Escherichia*
Species	*D. melanogaster*	*H. sapiens*	*P. sativum*	*E. coli*

Each Kingdom has a huge number of organisms. Bacteria and Archaea (single celled organisms).

Within each of the kingdoms the number of creatures is far too many to list. It is estimated that there could be as many as 100 million different species on Earth, although nowhere near that many have been physically cataloged. Of these, the majority are Bacteria and Archaea.

Another Example - Homo Sapiens

Since there is no way to list all the different subdivisions of life on Earth here, we might as well focus on one specific animal: us, Homo sapiens. We are members of the Domain Eukarya, the Kingdom Animalia, the Phylum Chordata, the Class Mammalia, the Order Primates, the Family Hominidae, the Genus Homo, the Species Homo sapiens and finally the Subspecies Homo sapiens sapiens. This classification is able to demonstrate our exact biological position relative to life on Earth.

One important thing which a system like this tells us is that Homo, which is Latin for "human," is not actually our species, but our genus. This is an easy fact to forget since we are the only members of our genus not yet extinct. However, anthropologically speaking there have been many humans including Homo habilis, Homo erectus and Homo neanderthalensis.

Taxonomical classification is an evolutionary map

Furthermore, the taxonomical classification system can be seen as a map of evolution on the planet. Plants, animals and bacteria can be traced back to common ancestors and newly discovered species can be classified relative to their ancestors, descendants and cousins. The Genus Homo, for instance, is a direct offshoot of the Tribe Hominini. (A tribe is a subcategory of the category of family, which here, is Hominidae.) Another genus that falls under the Tribe Hominini is Pan, which houses the species Chimpanzee. This shows us that until relatively recently in the history of life, Homo sapiens and Chimpanzees were the same creature, and that Chimpanzees only split off just before Homo sapiens became fully human.

Chemistry

Chemistry is the science of matter, especially its chemical reactions, but also its composition, structure and properties. Chemistry is concerned with atoms and their interactions with other atoms, and particularly with the properties of chemical bonds.

Chemistry is sometimes called "the central science" because it connects physics with other natural sciences such as geology and biology. Chemistry is a branch of physical science but distinct from physics.

Traditional chemistry starts with the study of elementary particles, atoms, molecules, substances, metals, crystals and other aggregates of matter. In solid, liquid, and gas states, whether in isolation or combination. The interactions, reactions and transformations that are studied in chemistry are a result of interaction either between different chemical substances or between matter and energy.

A chemical reaction is a transformation of some substances into one or more different substances.

It can be symbolically depicted through a chemical equation. The number of atoms on the left and the right in the equation for a chemical transformation is most often equal. The nature of chemical reactions a substance may undergo and the energy changes that may accompany it, are constrained by certain basic rules, known as chemical laws.

Energy and entropy considerations are invariably important in almost all chemical studies.

Chemical substances are classified in terms of their structure, phase as well as their chemical compositions. They can be analyzed using the tools of chemical analysis, e.g. spectroscopy and chromatography. Scientists engaged in chemical research are known as chemists. Most chemists specialize in one or more sub-disciplines.

Basic Concepts in Chemistry

Atoms

Atoms are some of the basic building blocks of matter. Each atom is an element—an identifiable substance that cannot be further broken down into other identifiable substances.

There are just over 100 such elements, and each of them can combine with themselves and with other elements to create all the various molecules that exist in the universe. The poison gas chlorine and the explosive metal sodium, for instance, can combine at the atomic level to form sodium chloride, also known as salt.

For thousands of years atoms were thought to be the smallest thing possible. (The word "atom" comes from an ancient Greek word meaning "unbreakable.") However, experiments performed in the mid to late 19th century began to show the presence of small particles, electrons, in electric current. By the early 20th century, the electron was known to be a part of the atom that orbited a yet undefined atomic core. A few years later, in 1919, the proton was discovered and found to exist in the nuclei of all atoms.

The protons and neutrons inside an atomic nucleus are not fundamental particles. That is, they can be divided into still smaller pieces.

Protons and neutrons are known as hadrons, which is a class of particle made up of quarks. (Quarks are a fundamental particle.) There are two distinct types of hadrons, baryons and mesons, and both protons and neutrons are baryons, meaning they are both made up of a combination of three quarks. Besides, being hadrons, protons and neutrons are also known as nucleons because of their place within the nucleus. Protons have a mass of around 1.6726×10^{-27} kg and neutrons have a nearly identical mass of 1.6929×10^{-27} kg. Both particles have a ½ spin.

The number of protons inside an atomic nucleus determines what element the atom is.

An element with only one proton, for instance, is hydrogen. An element with two is helium. One with three is lithium, and so on. No element (except for hydrogen) can exist with only protons in its nucleus. Atoms need neutrons to bond the protons together using the strong force. In general atoms (again except for hydrogen) have an equal number of protons and neutrons in their nuclei.

Atoms with an uneven number of protons and neutrons are called isotopes.

Isotopes have all the same chemical properties as their evenly balanced counterparts, but their nuclei are not usually as stable and are more willing to react with other elements. (Two deuterium atoms, hydrogen isotopes with one proton and one neutron in their nucleus rather than only one proton, will fuse much more readily than two regular hydrogen atoms.)

Nearly all an atoms' mass is within its nucleus. Outside the nucleus there is a lot of empty space occupied only by a few, tiny electrons.

Electrons were once viewed as orbiting an atom like planets orbit the sun. We now know that this is wrong in several ways. For one, electrons do not really "orbit" in the sense we are used to. At the quantum level no particle is really a particle, but is actually both a particle and a wave simultaneously. Heisenberg's uncertainty principle looks at this odd truth about reality and says you cannot watch an electron orbit the nucleus as you would watch the Earth orbit the sun. Instead, you have to observe only one of the electron's physical characteristics at a time, either viewing it as a particle in a fixed position outside the nucleus or as a wave encircling the nucleus like a halo.

Additionally, planets orbiting their stars can orbit at any distance they want. In fact, every object in our solar system has an elliptical orbit, meaning that they all move in more oval rather than circular shapes, getting closer and farther from the sun at various points. Electrons cannot do this under any circumstances.

Atoms have what are known as electron shells, which are the levels that an electron is able to occupy.

Electrons cannot exist between these shells; instead they jump from one to the next instantaneously. Each electron shell can hold a different number of atoms. When a shell fills up, additional electrons fill the outer shells. The outermost shell of any atom is called the valence shell, and it is the electrons in this shell that interact with the electrons of other atoms. The important thing about the valence shell is that each electron shell has a specific number of electrons that it can hold, and it wants to hold that many.

When atoms join; their connecting valence electrons take up two valence shell spots, one on each atom.

This means that the fewer electrons an atom has in its valence shell, the more likely it is to interact with other atoms. Conversely, the more electrons it has, the less likely it is to interact.

Electrons can also momentarily jump from one electron shell to the next if they are hit with a burst of energy from a photon.

When photons hit atoms, the energy is briefly absorbed by the electrons, and this momentarily knocks them into higher "orbits." The particular "orbit" the electron is knocked into depends on the type of atom, and when the electron gives up its higher energy level it re-emits a photon at a slightly different wavelength than the one it absorbed, providing a characteristic signal of that atom and showing exactly what "orbit" the electron was knocked into.

This is the phenomenon responsible for spectral lines in light and is the reason we can tell what elements make up stars and planets just by looking at them.

> Unlike protons and neutrons, electrons are a fundamental particle. They are known as leptons.

> Electrons have a negative charge that is generally balanced out by the positive charge of their atom's protons.

Charged atoms, which have either gained or lost an electron for various reasons, are called ions.

> Ions, like isotopes, have the same properties that the regular element does; they simply have different tendencies towards reacting with other atoms. Electrons have a mass of $9.1094 \times 10\text{-}31$ kg and a $-½$ spin.

Element

The concept of chemical element is related to that of chemical substance. A chemical element is specifically a substance which has a single type of atom.

> A chemical element is characterized by the number of protons in the nuclei of its atoms. This number is known as the atomic number of the element. For example, all atoms with 6 protons in their nuclei are atoms of the chemical element carbon, and all atoms with 92 protons in their nuclei are atoms of the element uranium.

Compound

A compound is a substance with a particular ratio of atoms of particular chemical elements which determines its composition, and a particular organization which determines chemical properties.

> For example, water is a compound containing hydrogen and oxygen in the ratio of two to one, with the oxygen atom between the two hydrogen atoms, and an angle of $104.5°$ between them. Compounds are formed and interconverted by chemical reactions.

Substance

A chemical substance is a kind of matter with a definite composition and set of properties.

> Strictly speaking, a mixture of compounds, elements or compounds and elements is not a chemical substance, but it may be called a chemical. Most of the substances we encounter in our daily life are some kind of mixture; for example: air, alloys, biomass, etc.

Nomenclature of substances is a critical part of the language of chemistry. Generally it refers to a system for naming chemical compounds.

Earlier in the history of chemistry substances were given names by their discoverer, which often led to some confusion and difficulty. However, today the IUPAC system of chemical nomenclature allows chemists to specify by name specific compounds amongst the vast variety of possible chemicals.

The standard nomenclature of chemical substances is set by the International Union of Pure and Applied Chemistry (IUPAC). There are well-defined systems in place for naming chemical species. Organic compounds are named according to the organic nomenclature system. Inorganic compounds are named according to the inorganic nomenclature system. In addition the Chemical Abstracts Service has devised a method to index chemical substance. In this scheme each chemical substance is identifiable by a number known as CAS registry number.

Molecule

Molecules are two or more atoms joined through a chemical bond to form chemicals.

Molecules differ from atoms in that molecules can be further broken down into smaller pieces and into elements while atoms cannot. (This was actually the 18th century definition of an atom: a recognizable structure that can no longer be broken down into smaller bits.)

Atoms are joined into molecules in two main ways: through covalent bonds and through ionic bonds.

Covalent bonds are the primary type of chemical bond that forms molecules. They occur when atoms with only partially filled valence electron shells, an atom's outermost electron shell, come together to share electrons. Hydrogen atoms, for instance, each have only one electron, while their valence shell is capable of holding two. When two hydrogen atoms come together each share the other's electron, using it to occupy its valence shell's free space forming the H2 molecule: hydrogen gas.

Not all covalent bond's are the same.

Different atoms have different levels of positive charge coming from in their nuclei, and although, under normal circumstances, the negative charge of the atom's electrons balances that out (keeping the atom electrically neutral) the chemical bonding process has a way of exploiting this situation. If we look at the H2 molecule again, everyday experience tells us that it has a strong tendency to seek out and bond with oxygen (O) molecules forming H2O, or water. There are two main reasons for this. The first comes from the regular old covalent bonds that are already holding H2 together. If bonded to another atom, hydrogen gains the ability to form a new valence shell that can hold 6 electrons. Since oxygen is the only molecule naturally to have 6 electrons in its valence shell, it is the most eager to bond with hydrogen. However, oxygen also has 8 protons in its nucleus compared to the total of 2 in the H2 molecule. This means that as the atoms come closer and prepare to bond, the electrons from both atoms are pulled closer to the oxygen molecule and farther from the hydrogen. An atom's proclivity to pull electrons towards itself is called its electronegativity, which creates polar covalent bonds. Due to this connection, polar covalent bonds are the strongest molecular bond, which is why molecules like water are so prevalent in our solar system and, likely, throughout the galaxy.

One very interesting aspect of polar covalent bonds is the hydrogen bond.

When a hydrogen atom bonds with another electronegative atom, the newly created molecule develops an intense polar attraction to all other electronegative atoms. This attraction works almost like a magnet with one end of the molecule exhibiting a positive charge (due to the effects of the polar covalent bonds pulling all the electrons towards one end of the molecule) and the other end exhibiting a negative charge. This phenomena is responsible for, among other things, the way water molecules stick to one another so readily. This is why you can fill a glass of water to a millimeter or so above the rim before it spills.

Hydrogen bonds are also responsible for how hydrophilic and hydrophobic molecules react to being mixed with water.

Hydrophilic molecules are molecules like NaCl (salt) which exhibit their own strong charge for reasons we will discuss in a moment. The charged salt molecules mix eagerly with the charged water molecules due to the extra pull of the hydrogen bond. Conversely, hydrophobic molecules such as oil will not mix with water because they are neutrally charged and do not like charged molecules. This is the reason you have to shake up an oil based salad dressing each time you use it. The oil and the water never truly mix, and given only a short time they will separate.

A very different type of bond between atoms is called the ionic bond.

Ionic bonds only occur between ions, atoms that are either positively or negatively charged due to having an unequal number of protons and electrons. Ionic bonds always occur between metals and non-metals, such as the gas chlorinc (Cl) and the alkaline metal sodium (Na). In their normal states, neither of these elements are ions, but when they approach one another, the sodium gives the chlorine one of its electrons forming Cl- and Na+ ions, which subsequently become attracted to one another. Since no electrons are actually lost, the molecule still technically has a neutral charge; it is only the atoms that are charged.

In ionic bonds it is always the metal which gives its electron to the non-metal. Additionally, in a diluted or liquid form, molecules that are created like this will always conduct electricity. This is why salt water can make such a good conductor.

Ions and salts

An ion is a charged species, an atom or a molecule, that has lost or gained one or more electrons.

Positively charged cations (e.g. sodium cation Na+) and negatively charged anions (e.g. chloride Cl−) can form a crystalline lattice of neutral salts (e.g. sodium chloride NaCl). Examples of polyatomic ions that do not split during acid-base reactions are hydroxide (OH−) and phosphate (PO4 3−).

Ions in the gaseous phase are often known as plasma.

Acidity and basicity

A substance can often be classified as an acid or a base. There are several different theories which explain acid-base behavior. The simplest is Arrhenius theory.

The Arrhenius theory states than an acid is a substance that produces hydronium ions when it is dissolved in water, and a base is one that produces hydroxide ions when dissolved in water. According to Brønsted–Lowry acid-base theory, acids are substances that donate a positive hydrogen ion to another substance in a chemical reaction; by extension, a base is the substance which receives that hydrogen ion.

A third common theory is Lewis acid-base theory, which is based on the formation of new chemical bonds.

Lewis theory explains that an acid is a substance which is capable of accepting a pair of electrons from another substance during the process of bond formation, while a base is a substance which can provide a pair of electrons to form a new bond. According to concept from Lewis, the crucial things being exchanged are charges. There are several other ways in which a substance may be classified as an acid or a base, as is evident in the history of this concept

Acid strength is commonly measured by two methods. The most common is pH.

One measurement, based on the Arrhenius definition of acidity, is pH, which is a measurement of the hydronium ion concentration in a solution, as expressed on a negative logarithmic scale. Thus, solutions that have a low pH have a high hydronium ion concentration, and can be said to be more acidic. The other measurement, based on the Brønsted–Lowry definition, is the acid dissociation constant (Ka), which measure the relative ability of a substance to act as an acid under the Brønsted–Lowry definition of an acid. That is, substances with a higher Ka are more likely to donate hydrogen ions in chemical reactions than those with lower Ka values.

Phase

Besides the specific chemical properties that distinguish chemical classifications, chemicals can exist in several phases.

For the most part, the chemical classifications are independent of these bulk phase classifications; however, some more exotic phases are incompatible with certain chemical properties. A phase is a set of states of a chemical system that have similar bulk structural properties, over a range of conditions, such as pressure or temperature.

Physical properties, such as density and refractive index tend to fall within values characteristic of the phase. The phase of matter is defined by the phase transition, which is when energy put into, or taken out of the system goes into rearranging the structure of the system, instead of changing the bulk conditions.

Phase can be continuous.

Sometimes the distinction between phases can be continuous instead of having a discrete boundary, here the matter is considered to be in a supercritical state. When three states meet based on the conditions, it is known as a triple point and since this is invariant, it is a convenient way to define a set of conditions.

The most familiar examples of phases are solids, liquids, and gases. Many substances exhibit multiple solid phases. For example, there are three phases of solid iron (alpha, gamma, and delta) that vary based on temperature and pressure. A principal difference between solid phases is the crystal structure, or arrangement, of the atoms. Another phase commonly encountered in the study of chemistry is the aqueous phase, which is the state of substances dissolved in aqueous solution (that is, in water).

Less familiar phases include plasmas, Bose-Einstein condensates and fermionic condensates and the paramagnetic and ferromagnetic phases of magnetic materials. While most phases deal with three-dimensional systems, it is also possible to define analogs in two-dimensional systems, which has received attention for its relevance to systems in biology.

Redox

Redox is a concept related to the ability of atoms of various substances to lose or gain electrons.

Substances that can oxidize other substances are said to be oxidative and are known as oxidizing agents, oxidants or oxidizers. An oxidant removes electrons from another substance. Similarly, substances that can reduce other substances are said to be reductive and are known as reducing agents, reductants, or reducers.

A reductant transfers electrons to another substance, and is thus oxidized itself. And because it "donates" electrons it is also called an electron donor.

> Oxidation and reduction properly refer to a change in oxidation number—the actual transfer of electrons may never occur. Thus, oxidation is better defined as an increase in oxidation number, and reduction as a decrease in oxidation number.

Bonding

Electron atomic and molecular orbitals

Atoms sticking together in molecules or crystals are said to be bonded with one another.

> A chemical bond may be visualized as the multipole balance between the positive charges in the nuclei and the negative charges oscillating about them. More than simple attraction and repulsion, the energies and distributions characterize the availability of an electron to bond to another atom.

A chemical bond can be a covalent bond, an ionic bond, a hydrogen bond or just because of Van der Waals force.

> Each of these kinds of bond is ascribed to some potential. These potentials create the interactions which hold atoms together in molecules or crystals. In many simple compounds, Valence Bond Theory, the Valence Shell Electron Pair Repulsion model (VSEPR), and the concept of oxidation number explains molecular structure and composition.

Reaction

During chemical reactions, bonds between atoms break and form, resulting in different substances with different properties.

> In a blast furnace, iron oxide, a compound, reacts with carbon monoxide to form iron, a chemical element, and carbon dioxide.

> When a chemical substance is transformed as a result of its interaction with another or energy, a chemical reaction is said to have occurred. Chemical reaction is therefore a concept related to the 'reaction' of a substance when it comes in close contact with another, whether, as a mixture or a solution; exposure to some form of energy, or both. It results in some energy exchange between the constituents of the reaction as well with the system environment which may be designed vessels which are often laboratory glassware.

Chemical reactions can result in the formation or dissociation of molecules, that is, molecules breaking apart to form two or more smaller molecules, or rearrangement of atoms within, or across molecules.

> Chemical reactions usually involve the making or breaking of chemical bonds. Oxidation, reduction, dissociation, acid-base neutralization and molecular rearrangement are some of the commonly used kinds of chemical reactions.

A chemical reaction can be symbolically depicted through a chemical equation. While in a non-nuclear chemical reaction the number and kind of atoms on both sides of the equation are equal, for a nuclear reaction this holds true only for the nuclear particles viz. protons and neutrons.

The sequence of steps in which the reorganization of chemical bonds may be taking place during a chemical reaction is called its mechanism.

A chemical reaction can be envisioned to take place in several steps, each of which may have a different speed. Many reaction intermediates with variable stability can thus be envisaged during the course of a reaction. Reaction mechanisms are proposed to explain the kinetics and the relative product mix of a reaction. Many physical chemists specialize in exploring and proposing the mechanisms of various chemical reactions. Several empirical rules, like the Woodward-Hoffmann rules often come handy while proposing a mechanism for a chemical reaction.

Equilibrium

Although the concept of equilibrium is widely used across sciences, in the context of chemistry, it arises whenever several different states of the chemical composition are possible.

For example, in a mixture of several chemical compounds that can react with one another, when a substance can be present in more than one kind of phase.

A system of chemical substances at equilibrium even though having an unchanging composition is most often not static; molecules of the substances continue to react with one another thus giving rise to a dynamic equilibrium. Thus the concept describes the state in which the parameters such as chemical composition remain unchanged over time. Chemicals present in biological systems are invariably not at equilibrium; they are far from equilibrium.

The Periodic Table

The periodic table contains the known chemical elements displayed in a special tabular arrangement based on their electron configurations, atomic numbers and recurring chemical properties.

The first semblance of a periodic table was by Antoine Lavoisier in 1789. He published a list or table of the 33 chemical elements known since then. He grouped the elements into earths, non-metals, gases and metals. The next century after that discovery saw several chemists looking for a better classification method and this caused the periodic table as we have it today.

Structure of the Periodic Table

The standard periodic table is an 18 column by 7 rows table containing the main chemical elements. Beneath that is a smaller 15 column by 2 rows table. The periodic table can be broken into 4 rectangular blocks: the P block is by the right, S block is left, D block is at the middle and the F block is underneath that. The elements in the blocks are based on which sub-shell the last electron resides.

The chemical elements on the table are arranged in order of increasing atomic number, which refers to the number of protons of the element. The periodic table can be used to study the chemical behavior of chemical elements, which makes it a very important tool widely used in chemistry.

The periodic table contains only chemical elements. Mixtures, compounds or small atomic particles of elements are not included. Each element on the table has a unique atomic number, which represents the number of protons contained in the element's nucleus.

A new period or row begins when an element has a new electron shell with a first electron. Columns or groups are based on the configuration of electrons of the atom. Elements that have an equal number of atoms in a specific sub-shell are listed under the same column. For example, selenium and oxygen both have 4 electrons in their outermost sub shell and so are listed under the P column. Elements with similar properties are listed in the same group although some elements in the same period can also share similar properties too. Since the elements grouped together have related properties, one can easily predict the property of an element if the properties of the surrounding elements are already known.

Rows are Periods

The rows of the periodic table are called periods. Elements on a row have the same number of electron shells or atomic orbitals. Elements on the first row have just one atomic orbital, elements on the second row have 2, and so it goes until the elements on the seventh row have 7 electron shells or atomic orbitals.

Columns are Groups

Columns from up to down in the table are called groups. The columns in the D, P and S blocks are called groups. Elements within a group have equal number of electrons in their outermost electron shell or orbital. The electrons on the outer shell are called valence electrons and there are the electrons that combine with other elements in a chemical reaction.

The Periodic table contains natural and synthesized elements

The elements up to californium are natural existing elements (94) while the rest were laboratory synthesized. Till date, chemists are still working to produce elements beyond the present 118th element, ununoctium. 114 of the 118 elements on the table have been officially recognized by the International Union of Pure and Applied Chemistry (IUPAC). Elements listed on the table under 113, 115, 117 and 118 have been synthesized but are yet to officially recognized by the IUPAC and are only known by their systematic element names.

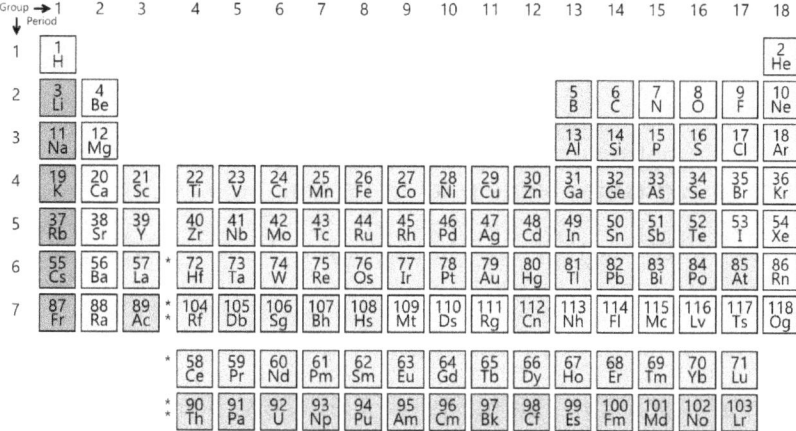

Chemistry and Energy

In the context of chemistry, energy is an attribute of a substance because of its atomic, molecular or total structure. Since a chemical transformation is accompanied with a change in one or more of these kinds of structure, it is invariably accompanied with an increase or decrease of energy of the substances involved.

> Some energy is transferred between the surroundings and the reactants of the reaction as heat or light; thus the products of a reaction may have more or less energy than the reactants.

Exergonic, Endergonic, Exothermic and Endothermic

> A reaction is said to be exergonic if the final state is lower on the energy scale than the initial state; for endergonic reactions the situation is the reverse. A reaction is said to be exothermic if the reaction releases heat to the surroundings; for endothermic reactions, the reaction absorbs heat from the surroundings.

Chemical reactions are invariably not possible unless the reactants surmount an energy barrier known as the activation energy.

> The speed of a chemical reaction (at given temperature T) is related to the activation energy E, by the Boltzmann's population factor e − E / kT - that is the probability of molecule to have energy greater than or equal to E at the given temperature T. This exponential dependence of a reaction rate on temperature is known as the Arrhenius equation. The activation energy necessary for a chemical reaction can be heat, light, electricity or mechanical force in the form of ultrasound.

How to Solve Molarity Questions

Molarity is also called, amount-of-substance concentration, amount concentration, substance concentration, or simply concentration.

The Molarity of a solution simply means the amount of moles contained in every liter of a solution. To better understand the concept of molarity of a solution it is necessary to first understand some related terms.

- A solute – is the substance that is being dissolved such as sugar or mercury.

- A solvent – refers to the liquid that the solute is being dissolved in.

- A solution – refers to the mixture of the solvent and the solute so that solution equals solvent plus solute.

The Molarity of the solution is thus a measurement of the molar concentration of the solute in the solution. The molarity of a solution is measured in moles of solute per liter of solution, or mol/liter. For example, if the molarity of a mercury solution is 1M, it simply means that there is 1 mole of sugar contained in every 1 liter of the solution.

The formula for molarity is = moles of solute/total liters of solution

Here is a typical question:

If 2 moles of salt is dissolved to form 1 liter of solution, calculate the molarity of the solution.

a. 1 M solution
b. 1.5 M solution
c. 2 M solution
d. 2.5 M solution

The formula for calculating molarity when the moles of the solute and liters of the solution are given is = moles of solute/ liters of solution.

Moles of Solute = 2 moles of sugar

Solution liters = 1 liters

The molarity of the solution = 2 moles of solvent/1 liters of solution = 2 M solution.

Basic Physics

Kinetic and Mechanical Energy

The kinetic energy of an object is the energy it possesses due to its motion.

>Kinetic energy is the work needed to accelerate a body of a given mass from rest to a stated velocity. Like all forms of energy, kinetic energy is measured in joules. Kinetic energy can be imparted to an object when an energy source is tapped to accelerate it. It also happens when one object with kinetic energy slams into another object and kinetic energy from the first object is transferred to the second.

>However it happens, imparting kinetic energy to an object causes it to accelerate. In this way movement is nothing more than an indication of the quantity of kinetic energy an object has. An object will hold onto its kinetic energy until it is able to transfer it to something else, which allows it to slow down again.

When an object has the same level of kinetic energy, it will move at a consistent velocity forever. This is Newton's first law of motion.

The transfer of kinetic energy from one object to another can occur in many ways.

>The transfer of kinetic energy can be as simple and mundane as a baseball flying through the air—interacting with all the various molecules of oxygen, carbon dioxide, nitrogen and all the other gasses that make up our atmosphere, and transferring its kinetic energy to them—speeding them up and slowing itself down in the process. Or it can be as chaotic as a speeding truck losing control on an icy road and slamming into a wall.

Different types of interactions between objects appear to be different but are in fact the same.

>The interaction between the baseball and the air and between the truck and the wall are only superficially different. One appears more chaotic than the other only because of the differences in mass between a baseball and a truck and the differences in "negative energy" possessed by free-floating air molecules compared to a solid wall. At its most basic, however, the same events are taking place in both examples. Molecules in both the wall and the air scatter when the kinetic energy that they receive causes them to move, and this produces heat and sound.

Kinetic energy can be calculated with the formula $KE = \frac{1}{2}mv^2$ where m is the mass of the object in kilograms, and v is its velocity in meters/second.

Kinetic energy increases by the square of an objects velocity.

One important aspect of kinetic energy that makes it so potentially destructive is that the kinetic energy a moving object carries, does not increase on pace with its velocity, but relative to the square of its velocity. If you double an object's velocity, you will quadruple the quantity of kinetic energy it possesses ($2^2=4$). If you quadruple the velocity, you increase the kinetic energy by sixteen times ($4^2=16$). This can lead to relatively small masses possessing very high kinetic energy levels when they are accelerated to only nominally high speeds. This is one reason why modern kinetic energy weapons (such as firearms) are able to cause large amounts of damage while being extremely compact.

Mechanical Energy

Mechanical energy is the ability of an object to do work.

When discussing energy it is important to take a moment to understand mechanical energy and how it relates to the objects it interacts with. Mechanical energy is not a separate type of energy in the way that potential energy and kinetic energy differ from one another.

Mechanical energy is the potential energy available to an object added to all of the kinetic energy available to it, providing a total energy output.

For instance, in our description of potential energy there is the example of a pole-vaulter hanging in mid air with her pole bent at a near right angle to the ground. The bend in the pole-vaulter's pole contains elastic potential energy, which will help her clear the bar. However, that is not the only source of energy the pole-vaulter is restricted to. For any one who has ever seen a track and field competition, you know that pole-vaulters take long, running starts before planting their poles in the ground. This imparts kinetic energy to the runners body, and it is that kinetic energy plus the pole's elastic potential energy that are added together in mid air to impart the total mechanical energy that drives the pole-vaulter high into the air and over the bar.

Potential Energy

There are two main types of potential energy: gravitational potential energy and elastic potential energy.

Potential energy is the potential an object has to act on other objects. As gravitational potential energy, the object is raised off the ground and is waiting for the force of gravity pulling at 9.8 m/s^2, to grab hold of it and pull it towards the Earth.

This type of energy is very common in everyday life. It describes everything from a book falling off its shelf to a child tripping on a crack in the sidewalk.

Because gravitational potential energy is so common, the equation describing it PEgrav=mass*g*height should not be hard to figure out since it contains only easily observable features of matter: an object's mass, the force of gravity (g), and the object's height off the ground when it started falling.

Note that the height does not have to be measured from the ground. Any point can be chosen—such as a table top or even a point in mid-air—if you are only concerned with the energy an object would have if it fell from the point it was currently at to the point you have chosen.

Gravitational Potential Energy Example

If we take the example of a 1kg weight positioned at a height of 1 meter above the surface of Earth (where the gravity is 9.8 m/s^2—try this on Mars and you will get a different result), we end with the equation PEgrav=1*9.8*1, which equals 9.8 joules of gravitational potential energy. A 1g weight positioned at the same height would be PEgrav=.001*9.8*1 or .0098J of potential energy, while a 1kg weight positioned a kilometer up would equal PEgrav=1*9.8*1000 or 9800J of potential energy.

From this equation you may have picked up on the fact that the height an object is raised to is directly proportional to the quantity of gravitational potential energy it has. Take a 1kg object and raise it to 5m, and you get 49J of potential energy. Double that to 10m, and you get 98J. Triple it to 15m and you will get 147J—three times the original 49J.

Elastic Potential Energy

Elastic potential energy occurs when an object is stretched or compressed out of its normal "resting" shape. The quantity of energy that will be released when it finally returns to rest is the quantity of elastic potential energy it has while stretched or compressed.

A common example of elastic potential energy is when an archer draws back the string of his bow. The farther back the bowstring is pulled, the more it will stretch. The more it stretches the more potential energy it will have waiting to send into the arrow.

Elastic potential energy of an object can be determined using Hooke's law of elasticity. Hooke's law states that F=-kx where F is the force the material will exert as it returns to its resting state measured in Newtons, x is the quantity of displacement the material undergoes measured in meters, and k is the spring constant and is measured in Newtons/meter.

To determine the potential energy of an elastic or springy material you use the equation PE=½kx^2. According to this equation, an object such as a spring with a spring constant of 5N/m that is stretched 3 meters past its resting point would have a potential energy of 22.5J. That is, ½*5*3^2 = 2.5*9 = 22.5J.

Remember that elastic potential energy affects much more than just what you would consider elastic or springy material such as rubber bands, bungee cords and springs. There is elastic potential energy in a pole-vaulter's pole at the point where she is in the air and hanging onto a pole that is bent nearly sideways. In the next instant, her forward momentum will be boosted by the conversion of her pole's potential energy into kinetic energy, pushing her over the bar. Similarly, when a hockey player shoots the puck, he drags his stick along the ice as it moves forward, bending the shaft backwards slightly. This adds extra force to the puck as the stick snaps forward back into its normal resting position.

Energy: Work and Power

In the simplest terms, energy is the ability to do work.

Energy allows objects and people to affect the physical world and displace (or move) other objects or people.

Work in the physics sense is a very specific concept.

It is measured in joules, which are 1 Newton of force that displaces something by 1 meter. (J=Nm) As the mass of the object being displaced varies, the quantity of work in joules required to move it a meter will vary too.

To determine the quantity of work being done, you can use the equation W=F*d*cosΘ.

This defines work as the force applied, multiplied by the distance the object was displaced, multiplied by the cosine of Θ (Theta).

The force is measured in Newtons. Distance is measured in meters. The tricky part of this equation is determining the cosine of Θ. Θ represents the difference in angle between the vector (or direction) the force is acting in and the vector the displacement is occurring. That means that there are really only three possible values for Θ.

If the force is pushing or pulling in one direction, and the object being displaced is moving in that same direction, then there is no difference in angle between the vectors and Θ=0°. This is the sort of force you get when a child pulls her sled across a snowy field. The direction the child is pulling and the direction the sled is traveling are the same. Since cos0=1 and the quantity of work is determined simply by multiplying the force and the displacement.

You should note that the angle of the vectors is determined by their relationship to one another and not to some ideal flat surface. That is, if the child is pulling her sled up a steep hill rather than across a field, the angle of Θ is still going to be 0° since the force she exerts on the sled and the sled itself are still traveling in the same direction.

The second possibility is when the force vector acts in the opposite direction of the object's displacement. This gives you what is called "negative work" because the energy is working to hinder the object from moving rather than to help it. In this instance $\Theta=180°$ since the vector in which the force is acting and the vector in which the object is moving are opposite. This force is most commonly observed when dealing with friction. It is the reason that hockey pucks and soccer balls will not travel forever; the force of friction exerted by the ice and by the grass is acting in the opposite direction.

The final difference in vectors is when the force being exerted on an object is at a right angle to its displacement. Here, $\Theta=90°$. You can picture this as a server carrying a tray of drinks over to your table, and it provides for some odd conclusions. Since the force we are talking about is the force the server to hold the tray vertically, but the displacement vector of the tray is horizontally across the room, we find that the force the server exerts, does no work at all. It is not responsible for moving the tray horizontally towards your table.

This is represented mathematically with the fact that the $\cos 90=0$, meaning that the original equation $W=F*d*\cos\Theta$ would be $W=F*d*0$. Without adding any other information in, it is already obvious that work is going to equal zero joules.

A different way to imagine this is to think of cargo in the back of a truck.

It took work to load the cargo up onto the truck from the ground (the force vector and the displacement vector were both pointing in the same direction), but once the cargo was loaded, no additional work was required to keep it there. The truck could drive from one end of the country to the other, but zero joules of work would be exerted keeping the cargo in place in the back of the truck.

When you add a unit of time to your calculations of work, you get a new classification: power.

Power is the rate at which work is done. The equation that measures power is power=work/time. In this equation work is measured in joules, time is measured in seconds and power is measured in watts.
Since, as we noted above, one joule is the same as one Newton multiplied by one meter, this equation can also be written as power=(force*displacement)/time where force is measured in Newtons and displacement is measured in meters. However, this opens further possibilities. Since the math does not care whether we first multiply force with displacement before dividing the whole thing by time, or whether we divide displacement by time and then multiply the answer by force, we find the equation can also be written as power=force(displacement/time).
Given that displacement is measured in meters and the time in seconds, what we are really saying here is that power equals the quantity of force

applied to an object multiplied by that object's velocity (m/s).
Thus we get two equations describing power: power=work/time and power=force*velocity.

By definition, power has an inverse relationship with time; the less time that it takes for the work to be done, the more power is being applied. Power also has a direct relationship with force and velocity. Increase either the quantity of force being applied to an object, or the speed at which it is traveling, and you have increased the power.

Defining Force and Newton's Three Laws

In physics force is the term given to anything that has the power to act on an object, causing its displacement in one direction or another.

Forces are a somewhat abstract concept, and it took thousands of years to identify accurately and describe them. It was not until the 17th century when a man named Isaac Newton began to describe accurately the basic physical forces and show how they acted on matter.

Force is measured using the unit Newton (N). One Newton can be defined with the formula $1N=1kg(1m/s^2)$. In other words, if you accelerate a kilogram of matter by one meter per second per second, you have exerted one Newton of force on it.

Newton developed three laws to explain the interactions of matter he observed. The first is often known as the "Law of Inertia."

It states that an object at rest will stay at rest, and an object in motion will stay in motion, unless a force acts on it to change its state. This means that if you fire a spaceship out into the vacuum of space, and keep it clear from planets and stars that will apply force to it, the ship will keep going at the same speed forever.

This tendency to stay moving or stay at rest is known as inertia. Inertia is directly related to an object's mass; the more mass an object has, the more inertia it will have and the harder to speed up or slow it down. This is implied by the equation defining one Newton of force, but it is also obvious in everyday life. You have to exert more force to push a box of books across the floor than you would to push a box of clothes the same size. The box of books has more mass, so it has more inertia. Similarly, a baseball player can easily catch and stop a baseball thrown at over 100km/hr. If you were to ask that same player to stop a truck traveling at 100km/hr, you would get much less pleasant results.

One important thing to remember about force is that it is a vector quantity, meaning that it points in a specific direction.

> Set a one kilogram object down on a table and you will have the force of gravity pulling it down at one Newton, and the force of all the atoms in the table pushing it up at one Newton. This is said to be a state of equilibrium, and it causes no change to the object's velocity. However, if the table had been poorly built and was only capable of pushing up at .75 Newtons, the object would pull through, snapping the table at its weakest points, and fall until it found something that was capable of applying the needed force to hold it up against gravity.

> As such, an object can only be at rest if it has no forces acting on it, or if it has equal and opposite forces acting on it keeping it at equilibrium. If an unopposed force acts on an object, it will move.

Newton's second law describes with what happens when you have the sort of unbalanced forces that we just described.

> It explains the movement of objects through the equation $F=ma$, where F is the force in Newtons, m is the object's mass in kilograms, and a is the object's acceleration in meters per second per second (m/s^2).

> Just like with Newton's first law, this equation shows that mass is very important when it comes to using a force to move objects. The larger the mass, the more force you will need to accelerate or decelerate it to the same velocity.

Newton's third law states simply that for every action there is an equal and opposite reaction.

> This means that if I pound my hand down on my desk right now, my desk will also be hitting up at my hand with the exact same force. This may sound strange, but it is the reason that pounding your hand on your desk can damage your desk and hurt your hand at the same time. It is also the reason that baseball bats can snap while imparting force onto the ball, and why a moving car hitting stationary wall will damage both.

Force: Friction

Friction is the force that resists the motion of objects relative to other objects.

> When two surfaces move relative to each other, the force of friction is what slows them down. Friction applies to all matter, whether it is a book sliding down a slanting shelf, a soccer ball rolling on the ground or a baseball flying though the air. Friction is a constant opposing force that keeps things from traveling forever.

Several laws describe how friction works.

Amontons' first law of friction says that, "The force of friction is directly proportional to the applied load." His second law of friction says that, "The force of friction is independent of the apparent area of contact." Similarly, Coulomb's law of friction states that, "Kinetic friction is independent of the sliding velocity."

The two main types of Friction are static friction and kinetic friction.

Static friction is what you get when one stationary object is stacked on top of another stationary object, such as a book resting on a table. The static friction between the book and the table determines how much sticking power there is between them, and at what angle you would have to tilt the table before the force of gravity overpowers the force of friction and starts the book sliding.

To figure out the maximum quantity of static friction possible before the book starts sliding, you use the formula $f_s = \mu_s F_n$ where f_s is the total quantity of static friction(pronounced "mu") is the coefficient of static friction and F_n is the "normal force," the force being exerted perpendicularly through the surface into the object resting on it, keeping the object from breaking through the surface.

Another way to examine static friction is to calculate the angle the table will have to reach before the book will start sliding.

This is also known as the angle of repose, and it can be calculated using the formula $\tan\theta = \mu_s$ where θ (pronounced "theta") is the angle of repose and μ_s is the coefficient of static friction.

Aside from determining the angles books will slide off tables, calculating static friction allows tire manufacturers to determine how "grippy" their treads are. If there were no friction, the wheel would not be a functional tool because it would not push itself against the road while moving. The higher the coefficient of friction between the tire and the road, the more grip the tire has.

Kinetic friction is like the inverse of static friction.

It is the force that causes moving objects to slow down. Kinetic friction applies to two surfaces moving in respect to one another such as the bottom of a snowboard and the snowy ground. It can be calculated using the same basic formula used to calculate static friction: $f_k = \mu_k F_n$ with the only differences being the sub-k marks replacing the sub-s marks of the previous equation, signifying kinetic friction.

As kinetic friction slows an object, the object's kinetic energy is transformed into heat.

Fundamental Forces: Electromagnetism

Electromagnetism is one of the four fundamental forces. It is far more common than gravity, but only if you know where to look.

> Electromagnetism is responsible for nearly all interactions in which gravity plays no part. It is what holds negatively charged electrons in orbit around the positively charged protons in the nucleus of an atom. It is also the force that joins atoms to create molecules.

It is also electromagnetism that is responsible for the fact that matter—which is made up of atoms and at the subatomic level is mostly empty space—feels solid.

> When you sit down in your chair, it is the electromagnetic attraction between the chair's atoms and between your body's atoms that keep you from falling through the chair and, conversely, that keep the chair from passing through you.

Electromagnetic force acts through a field.

> This sort of field can occur as a result of positively or negatively charged atoms (ions), atoms which have either, greater or fewer electrons than protons, causing their overall charge to be unbalanced. Magnetic fields can also be created by applying electric current to conductive material (such as wire) with a conductive core (such as a nail).

Electric current is nothing more than a steady flow of electrons, and by turning on the current you send electrons through the core.

> This aligns all the atoms in the metal so that they are parallel with each other, and this creates a magnetic field. When you turn the electric current off, the electrons stop flowing, and the atoms, no longer forced by the current to line up, cease to be magnetic.

All electromagnetic fields have a positive and a negative pole.

> Even the Earth's magnetic field, which is caused by the convective forces in the planet's core, sends electrons out of its negative pole (in the geographic North Pole) and reaccepts them at its positive pole (in the geographic South Pole in Antarctica). The Earth's magnetic field, like all magnetic fields, is able to affect charged particles.

Magnetic fields move in one direction around a magnet.

> This direction is always the same relative to the flow of current from negative to positive poles, and it is easy to test the direction of the field using the "right hand rule." Close your fist and make a "thumbs up" sign with your right hand. The positive pole is represented by the tip of your thumb, the negative by the other end of your hand, and the direction of the magnetic field by where your closed fingers are. Thus, if you point your thumb at

yourself, your magnet has current coming out its negative pole pointed towards you and looping back around to the positive pole pointed away from you, and the field is pointed counter-clockwise, which here is to your left.

The effects of a magnetic field do not go on forever but follow the inverse square law.

The farther you move from a magnetic field, the less its force will affect you. By moving x times away from a magnetic field, you feel $1/x^2$ times less magnetism.

Closely related to the electromagnetic field is electromagnetic radiation.

This radiation can take many forms, the most familiar of which being light, radio waves that carry radio and broadcast television, microwaves that cook our food, x-rays that can image the insides or our bodies, and gamma rays that come down from space and would have killed us all long ago if it were not for the Earth's magnetic field interacting with them.

Electromagnetic radiation is created, according to James Clerk Maxwell, by the oscillations of electromagnetic fields, which create electromagnetic waves.

The wave's frequency (or how energetic it is) determines what part of the electromagnetic spectrum it occupies—whether it is a gamma ray, a blue light or a radio signal. Electromagnetic radiation is the same thing as light, with what we are used to as visible light being a range of specific frequencies within the electromagnetic spectrum, so all electromagnetic radiation moves at the speed of light.

At the quantum level, the electromagnetic force has a transfer particle moving back and forth between charged atoms, attracting and repelling them. The electromagnetic transfer particle is the photon.

Fundamental Forces: Gravity

Gravity may be the most commonly, consciously experienced force.

We can see its effects everyday when books fall off shelves, when stray baseballs arc downwards and crash through windows and when Australians time and again fail to fall off the bottom of the world and out into space. Gravity is also largely responsible for the structure of the universe. Without it, stars would not ignite and begin fusion reactions, planets would not condense out of dust and metal and most matter would have no attraction to other matter in any way. Without gravity, life would not exist.

It may seem strange to learn that gravity is the weakest of all forces given that it holds the entire galaxy together.

> Still, even with the gravitational mass of the entire planet pulling on an object such as a ball—causing it to sit motionless on the floor rather than float aimlessly off into space—a toddler could easily pick it up and run off with it, and there would be nothing the planet could do about it. Match that with the force an electromagnet exerts on metal; there is no comparison.

The idea of gravity as a force was first formulated by Isaac Newton in the late 17th century.

> Newton's ideas were further elaborated on in the early 20th century by Albert Einstein, who described gravity as the effect of mass warping the fabric of space-time. This process is often portrayed as a large ball creating a divot in a flat sheet of space-time. The divot curves space-time and can catch objects that would otherwise be traveling in straight lines and redirect or even capture them.

On Earth gravity pulls objects towards the center of the planet at $9.8m/s^2$.

> The squared rate of time shows that gravity is by its nature a force causing acceleration. Every second, the force of gravity increases the speed of an object by an additional $9.8m/s$, provided nothing able to resist the force gets in its way.

In Einstein's view of the universe, gravity moved in waves, which traveled through space at the speed of light.

> As a result, he demonstrated that the force of gravity would take time to reach the object it was acting on. If, for instance, the sun were suddenly to vanish from the solar system, it would take eight minutes for the Earth to go flying off into space—the same quantity of time it would take for us to stop seeing the sun's light.

Another way to view gravity is through a series of transfer particles that interact with matter and draw it closer together.

> Transfer particles come into play in quantum mechanics, and they replace gravity waves as the method of spreading the force through the universe. (Actually, replace is not the right word, as quantum mechanics shows that particles and waves are really the same thing, simply looked at from different perspectives.) In quantum mechanics gravity's transfer particle is called a graviton, and it moves at the speed of light.

The farther you move from a gravitational mass, the less its force will affect you.

> The drop in the gravitational force is governed by what is known as the inverse square law, which says the attraction of any object drops relative

to the square of the distance you move from it. If you are floating over the surface of the planet and then move x times away from it, you will feel $1/x^2$ times less gravity. So if you move 10 times farther away from where you were, you will feel 1/100 the force gravity.

Fundamental Forces: Strong and Weak Nuclear Forces

The strong and weak nuclear forces are fundamental forces, but they were discovered much later than electromagnetism and gravity primarily because they only interact with matter at a subatomic level.

Strong nuclear force is the strongest of the four fundamental forces.

> Strong nuclear force is 100 times stronger than the next strongest force, electromagnetism, and 1036 times the strength of the weakest force, gravity. That said, for the thousands of years people have been studying physics, it never occurred to anyone to even look for the strong force. That is because, despite the strong force's strength, it has such a limited range that it only interacts with matter across the distance of an atom's nucleus. In fact, its range is only about 10-15 meters, so small that the nuclei of the largest atoms—those filled with the highest number of protons and neutrons—are only just barely small enough for the strong force to keep working, making the nuclei of those atoms unstable.

The strong force was not discovered until the 1930s when scientists discovered the neutron.

> Until that time atomic nuclei were thought to consist of a collection of protons and electrons grouped together in such a way that kept them mutually attracted to each other. With the discovery of the neutron, however, a new force was needed to hold positively charged protons together with uncharged neutrons.

Strong Nuclear force interacts with Quarks.

> The strong force actually does not interact directly with the protons and neutrons but with the fundamental particle that makes up protons and neutrons, quarks. Quarks come in three different color groupings: red, green and blue. (Quarks are not actually these colors; red, green and blue are just familiar names given to bits of matter that are utterly outside our experience as humans, to make them easier to comprehend.) The different colors of quarks combine to create protons and neutrons. Within each proton and neutron, the strong force holds the quarks together. That, in turn, bleeds out into the rest of the nucleus in a residual effect, holding the protons and neutrons together as well.

> Like the other fundamental forces, the strong force is mediated at the

quantum level using a transfer particle known as a gluon. However, unlike the transfer particles for gravity and electromagnetism (gravitons and photons, respectively), gluons have mass. It is the gluon's mass that limits the area where it can spread the strong force to only within the nucleus.

Weak nuclear force causes a type of radioactive decay.

The other fundamental force operating inside the nucleus is the weak force. The weak force causes a specific type of radioactive decay called beta decay, so named because it causes the decaying atom to emit a beta particle, which can be either an electron or a positron (a form of anti-mater also known as an anti-electron), as a byproduct of changing into a different element.

Several things happen at once during beta decay, and we should look at each one individually. We saw while looking at the strong force that an atom's protons and neutrons are made up of smaller, fundamental particles called quarks, and it is the quarks that actually interact with the strong force. As it turns out, quarks are the only particle that interacts with all four fundamental forces, which means that inside the nucleus they are interacting with the weak force as well.

Besides three different colors: red, blue and green, Quarks can be divided into six different flavors: up, down, charm, strange, top and bottom.

Before we get to how the weak force interacts with quarks, there is something else you should understand them. We mentioned above that quarks come in three different colors: red, blue and green. However, they also can be divided into six different flavors: up, down, charm, strange, top and bottom. (This makes 18 different possible combinations of quark, each with a color and a flavor.) Of these flavors only up and down quarks are stable enough to form protons and neutrons.

The weak force switches up quarks to down quarks, and down quarks to up quarks.

This is the only thing the weak force does, but it has several effects. First since quarks join to produce protons and neutrons (two up quarks and one down quark make a proton, while two down and one up quark make a neutron), the sudden change of one type of quark to another changes that combination. β− decay is beta decay where change of quarks causes a neutron to become a proton. This also causes the atom to emit an electron and a electron antineutrino. β + decay is the opposite, where a proton changes to a neutron and the atom emits a positron and an electron neutrino.

In both cases the decaying atom changes into a different kind of atom. In general, beta decay takes place in unstable isotopes (atoms that have a different number of protons and neutrons) and stabilizes the nucleus by equalizing the ratio of these particles. For instance, beta decay will turn the unstable plutonium 15 into far more stable strontium 16.

States of Matter

Matter on Earth can exist in three main states or phases: solid, liquid and gas. There is also a fourth phase, plasma, that occurs when matter is superheated.

> The primary difference between the different phases of matter is the behavior of molecules relative to the temperature the matter is exposed to. The lower the temperature, the closer together and more locked together the molecules are. The higher the temperature, the farther apart the molecules are and the more they move relative to one another.

Solid

Solid matter exists in a state where its molecules are locked together in a rigid structure preventing them from moving and, as a result, solid matter is held together in a specific shape.

> There are two primary types of solids, each defined by the structures in which their molecules are held. When the molecules in solid matter maintain a uniform organization, they form a polycrystalline structure. This is how molecules in metal, ice and salt are organized. Polycrystalline structure are generally a result of the molecules' ionic properties. Water molecules, for instance, are formed in such a way that there are distinct ends, one with two hydrogen atoms and one with a single oxygen atom. The structure of the atoms within a water molecule means these ends are charged, giving it what amounts to poles and causing water molecules to join only in specific patterns. Under a microscope polycrystalline solids are generally described as resembling lattice work or a chain link fence, with the same pattern of molecules from one end to the other.
>
> When molecule's electromagnetic properties do not incline them to form into particular structures, they glob together in whatever patterns they can. This produces amorphous solids, most notably foams, glass and many types of plastic. Amorphous solids have no regular pattern throughout their structure and, as a result, are poor conductors of heat and electricity.

Liquid

When solids are heated past a certain point, the electromagnetic bonds holding their molecules together loosen, and the molecules are able to move more freely.

> While the temperatures required for this to happen can vary widely, the particular physical qualities of a liquid are always the same. Liquids are considered to be fluids, which differ from solids primarily in their ability to take the shape of any container they are held in. This is the result of a less intense electromagnetic connection between the molecules than there

is in solids; however, there is still enough of that liquid still want to stay all in the same place. This is why liquids still maintain a low density that is nearly identical to their densities in solid form, and why they will maintain a constant volume rather than just drift off the way gasses do.

Liquids also have a property known as viscosity, which describes their willingness to flow over and away from themselves. Liquids such as water and honey have constant viscosity and are known as Newtonian fluids. Non-Newtonian fluids, such as a goopy mixture of water and cornstarch can change their viscosities.

Gas

The third state of matter that is commonly found on Earth is gas. Gasses are formed when matter is heated beyond its liquid state so that the electromagnetic bonds holding its molecules together are severed almost completely.

Gasses are also considered fluids and like liquids have no definite shape. However, unlike liquids they lack a definite volume and have an extremely low density compared to their solid forms.

Since gasses lack both a shape and a volume, they will expand to fill any container they are placed in. Left unbounded they will expand forever. Conversely, gasses are perfectly happy to compress together in an enclosed space. (However, the more molecules of a gas that are enclosed in a space together, the higher the gas's pressure—the force exerted by the molecules on the container's surface—will be.) One interesting thing about this expansion and compression is that it will always be homogeneous, meaning that as a gas expands to fill a container, there will never be pockets of higher density of molecules in some areas with a lower density of molecules in others. The molecules will expand to fill the container equally.

Plasma

Plasma is the next step up from a gas; it is when a gas's molecules become super heated to the point where the molecular bonds themselves break down and the atoms begin shedding their electrons.

Although plasma is rarely found on Earth, it is the most common state of matter throughout the universe. (It is the primary state of matter in stars, for instance.) Plasma has some unique characteristics, not the least of which is that it is ionized, or electrically charged. In many ways plasma acts like a gas. It lacks any definite shape or volume, and it will homogeneously fill any container. But it can also be manipulated by electromagnetic fields, which alters its shape or contain it. Plasma is a super-heated, magnetically charged gas.

Oxidation and Reduction

Oxidation is a chemical reaction involving the loss of electrons or the increase of the oxidation state of an element by an atom, molecule or ion.

Reduction is the opposite side of the chemical reaction that involves the gain of an electron, or the decrease in the oxidation state of an element by an ion, molecule or atom.

Originally, the word oxidation was used to refer only to the reaction of an element with oxygen to produce an oxide.

> Oxygen was the first recognized oxidizing agent and thus the name oxidation. The use of the word oxidation later expanded to include reaction with any element or substances that accomplish parallel chemical reactions as that produced by oxygen. Today, oxidation is used to refer to all processes and reactions that involve a loss of electrons or an increase in the oxidation state.

The word reduction was originally used to refer to all chemical reactions that involved the loss of weight of a metallic ore or metal oxide by heating.

> When a metal oxide is heated to extract the metal, oxygen is lost as a gas and the overall weight decreases. In time, it was discovered that the metallic ore or element being reduced actually gained some electrons. Today, the chemical application of the term reduction has been enlarged to include all processes and reactions that involve the gain of electrons or the decrease in the oxidation state.

Redox is a word coined from reduction and oxidation. Redox, or oxidation and reduction reactions comprise chemical reactions where the oxidation state of the atoms involved have been changed.

> Redox could occur in as simple a chemical process as the oxidation process where carbon is oxidized to produce carbon dioxide (CO_2) or the use of hydrogen in the reduction of carbon to produce methane (CH_4). Redox could also occur in relatively complex reactions such as the complex process of oxidizing glucose inside the human body.
>
> Redox reactions are primarily associated with the production of oxides with the interaction with oxygen and other such like oxidation substances. However, redox reactions would also include the transfer of electrons during the reaction process.
>
> One peculiar characteristic of redox or oxidation and reduction reactions is that they occur as a matched set. You can thus not have an oxidation reaction, without having a corresponding reduction reaction. This is the reason why an oxidation or reduction reaction on its own is known as a half reaction. Together both form the complete reaction because they cannot

occur on their own. One side of the reaction loses electrons while the other side gains electrons during the reaction.

In is very important to note that while the loss or gain of electrons usually happens in most oxidation and reduction reactions, chemical reactions where electrons are not gained or lost can still be called oxidation and reduction reactions.

The definition of oxidation and reduction reactions could thus be more accurately defined as; Oxidation is the increase in the oxidation state, and Reduction is the decrease of the oxidation state even though electrons may not always be transferred.

The transfer of electrons would usually result in the change of oxidation state, but several reactions qualify to be termed as oxidation or reduction reactions even though no electrons where transferred. A good example of these would be reactions involving chemical covalent bonds.

Speed, Acceleration and Force Problems

Acceleration

In physics, acceleration is the rate at which the velocity of a body changes with time. For example, an object such as a car that starts from a full stop, then travels in a straight line at increasing speed, is accelerating in the direction of travel. If the car changes direction at constant speed, there is strictly speaking an acceleration, although not described as such; passengers in the car will experience a force pushing them back into their seats in linear acceleration, and a sideways force on changing direction. If the speed of the car decreases, or decelerates, mathematically it is acceleration in the opposite direction. [8]

The formula for acceleration = $A = (V_f - V_0)/t$ and is measured in meters per second^2.

Here is a typical question:

A car starts from standing top and in 10 seconds is travelling 20/meters per second. What is the acceleration?

    a. 0.5 m/sec^2
    b. 1.5 m/sec^2
    c. 1 m/sec^2
    d. 2 m/sec^2

The formula for acceleration = $A = (V_f - V_0)/t$
so $A = (20 \text{ m/sec} - 0 \text{ m/sec})/10 \text{ sec} = 2 \text{ m/sec}^2$

Speed

Speed is the rate of change of an objects position, or,
speed = (total distance traveled)/(total time taken).

Here is a typical question:

A rocket travels 3000 meters in 5 seconds. How fast is it travelling?

    a. 100 m/sec
    b. 200 m/sec
    c. 500 m/sec
    d. 600 m/sec

Speed = (total distance traveled)/(total time taken)
3000/5 = 600 meters per second.

Force

An everyday definition of Force is the push or pull. The more scientific definition of Force is any influence that causes an object to change its movement or direction. Force is measured in Newtons, (usually N) named after Sir Isaac Newton, and his formulation of the Second Law of motion, F = ma, where F = force, m = mass and a = acceleration.

$1 N = 1 kg \, m/s^2$.

Therefore,

Force = Mass times Acceleration Measured in Newtons.
Acceleration is the change in speed over time.
Speed is the change in position over time.

Here is a typical question:

How much force is needed to accelerate a car that weights 500 kg to 10 m/s²?

    a. 20,000 N
    b. 30,000 N
    c. 40,000 N
    d. 50,000 N

Force = Mass times Acceleration Measured in Newtons.
F = 500 X 10 = 50,000 N

Momentum

Momentum is the sum of the mass of an object and its velocity. This means that momentum measures the force produced by an object's mass and velocity.

For example, a very heavy object moving fast has a large momentum—it takes a large and prolonged force to get a very heavy object up to this speed, and it takes a large and prolonged force to bring it to a stop afterwards. If the object were lighter, or moving more slowly, then it would have less momentum, and it would be easier (i.e. require less force) to bring it to a stop.

The formula for calculating momentum is =
Momentum = mass x velocity
Or
P = MV
Where P = momentum, V = velocity and M = mass

Based on the above definition, clearly the momentum of a car and a bicycle both travelling at 20 m/s will not be the same, because although the velocity of the two objects are the same, their mass is different. The car would have greater momentum, due to its larger mass.

Note:

The SI unit for velocity = m/s
SI unit for Mass = kg
So therefore momentum = kg x m/s and the SI unit for momentum is kg x m/s

Momentum must always have a direction and so the final answer must reflect the direction of the momentum or velocity.

Here is a typical question:

What is the momentum of a log weighing 700 kg that is rolling down a hill at 4.6 m/s?

    a. 3220 kg x m/s down the hill
    b. 3320 kg x m/s
    c. 3320 down hill
    d. 3320 M

Answer: A

P = MV
P = 700 X 4.6
P = 3220 kg x m/s down the hill.

Practice Test Questions Set 1

The questions below are not the same as you will find on the CAE[c] - that would be too easy! And nobody knows what the questions will be and they change all the time. Below are general questions that cover the same subject areas as the CAE[c]. So, while the format and exact wording of the questions may differ slightly, and change from year to year, if you can answer the questions below, you will have no problem with the CAE[c].

For the best results, take these practice test questions as if it were the real exam. Set aside time when you will not be disturbed, and a location that is quiet and free of distractions. Read the instructions carefully, read each question carefully, and answer to the best of your ability.
Use the bubble answer sheets provided. When you have completed the practice questions, check your answer against the Answer Key and read the explanation provided.

Do not attempt more than one set of practice test questions in one day. After completing the first practice test, wait two or three days before attempting the second set of questions.

Social Studies

1. A B C D
2. A B C D
3. A B C D
4. A B C D
5. A B C D
6. A B C D
7. A B C D
8. A B C D
9. A B C D
10. A B C D
11. A B C D
12. A B C D
13. A B C D
14. A B C D
15. A B C D
16. A B C D
17. A B C D
18. A B C D
19. A B C D
20. A B C D
21. A B C D
22. A B C D
23. A B C D
24. A B C D
25. A B C D
26. A B C D
27. A B C D
28. A B C D
29. A B C D
30. A B C D
31. A B C D
32. A B C D
33. A B C D
34. A B C D
35. A B C D
36. A B C D
37. A B C D
38. A B C D
39. A B C D
40. A B C D
41. A B C D
42. A B C D
43. A B C D
44. A B C D
45. A B C D
46. A B C D
47. A B C D
48. A B C D
49. A B C D
50. A B C D

Language Arts - Reading

1. Ⓐ Ⓑ Ⓒ Ⓓ
2. Ⓐ Ⓑ Ⓒ Ⓓ
3. Ⓐ Ⓑ Ⓒ Ⓓ
4. Ⓐ Ⓑ Ⓒ Ⓓ
5. Ⓐ Ⓑ Ⓒ Ⓓ
6. Ⓐ Ⓑ Ⓒ Ⓓ
7. Ⓐ Ⓑ Ⓒ Ⓓ
8. Ⓐ Ⓑ Ⓒ Ⓓ
9. Ⓐ Ⓑ Ⓒ Ⓓ
10. Ⓐ Ⓑ Ⓒ Ⓓ
11. Ⓐ Ⓑ Ⓒ Ⓓ
12. Ⓐ Ⓑ Ⓒ Ⓓ
13. Ⓐ Ⓑ Ⓒ Ⓓ
14. Ⓐ Ⓑ Ⓒ Ⓓ
15. Ⓐ Ⓑ Ⓒ Ⓓ
16. Ⓐ Ⓑ Ⓒ Ⓓ
17. Ⓐ Ⓑ Ⓒ Ⓓ
18. Ⓐ Ⓑ Ⓒ Ⓓ
19. Ⓐ Ⓑ Ⓒ Ⓓ
20. Ⓐ Ⓑ Ⓒ Ⓓ
21. Ⓐ Ⓑ Ⓒ Ⓓ
22. Ⓐ Ⓑ Ⓒ Ⓓ
23. Ⓐ Ⓑ Ⓒ Ⓓ
24. Ⓐ Ⓑ Ⓒ Ⓓ
25. Ⓐ Ⓑ Ⓒ Ⓓ
26. Ⓐ Ⓑ Ⓒ Ⓓ
27. Ⓐ Ⓑ Ⓒ Ⓓ
28. Ⓐ Ⓑ Ⓒ Ⓓ
29. Ⓐ Ⓑ Ⓒ Ⓓ
30. Ⓐ Ⓑ Ⓒ Ⓓ
31. Ⓐ Ⓑ Ⓒ Ⓓ
32. Ⓐ Ⓑ Ⓒ Ⓓ
33. Ⓐ Ⓑ Ⓒ Ⓓ
34. Ⓐ Ⓑ Ⓒ Ⓓ
35. Ⓐ Ⓑ Ⓒ Ⓓ
36. Ⓐ Ⓑ Ⓒ Ⓓ
37. Ⓐ Ⓑ Ⓒ Ⓓ
38. Ⓐ Ⓑ Ⓒ Ⓓ
39. Ⓐ Ⓑ Ⓒ Ⓓ
40. Ⓐ Ⓑ Ⓒ Ⓓ

Mathematics Parts I and II

Practice Test Questions 1

1. Ⓐ B Ⓒ D
2. Ⓐ Ⓑ Ⓒ Ⓓ
3. Ⓐ Ⓑ Ⓒ Ⓓ
4. Ⓐ Ⓑ Ⓒ Ⓓ
5. Ⓐ Ⓑ Ⓒ Ⓓ
6. Ⓐ Ⓑ Ⓒ Ⓓ
7. Ⓐ Ⓑ Ⓒ Ⓓ
8. Ⓐ Ⓑ Ⓒ Ⓓ
9. Ⓐ Ⓑ Ⓒ Ⓓ
10. Ⓐ Ⓑ Ⓒ Ⓓ
11. Ⓐ Ⓑ Ⓒ Ⓓ
12. Ⓐ Ⓑ Ⓒ Ⓓ
13. Ⓐ Ⓑ Ⓒ Ⓓ
14. Ⓐ Ⓑ Ⓒ Ⓓ
15. Ⓐ Ⓑ Ⓒ Ⓓ
16. Ⓐ Ⓑ Ⓒ Ⓓ
17. Ⓐ Ⓑ Ⓒ Ⓓ
18. Ⓐ Ⓑ Ⓒ Ⓓ
19. Ⓐ Ⓑ Ⓒ Ⓓ
20. Ⓐ Ⓑ Ⓒ Ⓓ
21. Ⓐ Ⓑ Ⓒ Ⓓ
22. Ⓐ Ⓑ Ⓒ Ⓓ
23. Ⓐ Ⓑ Ⓒ Ⓓ
24. Ⓐ Ⓑ Ⓒ Ⓓ
25. Ⓐ Ⓑ Ⓒ Ⓓ
26. Ⓐ Ⓑ Ⓒ Ⓓ
27. Ⓐ Ⓑ Ⓒ Ⓓ
28. Ⓐ Ⓑ Ⓒ Ⓓ
29. Ⓐ Ⓑ Ⓒ Ⓓ
30. Ⓐ Ⓑ Ⓒ Ⓓ
31. Ⓐ Ⓑ Ⓒ Ⓓ
32. Ⓐ Ⓑ Ⓒ Ⓓ
33. Ⓐ Ⓑ Ⓒ Ⓓ
34. Ⓐ Ⓑ Ⓒ Ⓓ
35. Ⓐ Ⓑ Ⓒ Ⓓ
36. Ⓐ Ⓑ Ⓒ Ⓓ
37. Ⓐ Ⓑ Ⓒ Ⓓ
38. Ⓐ Ⓑ Ⓒ Ⓓ
39. Ⓐ Ⓑ Ⓒ Ⓓ
40. Ⓐ Ⓑ Ⓒ Ⓓ
41. Ⓐ Ⓑ Ⓒ Ⓓ
42. Ⓐ Ⓑ Ⓒ Ⓓ
43. Ⓐ Ⓑ Ⓒ Ⓓ
44. Ⓐ Ⓑ Ⓒ Ⓓ
45. Ⓐ Ⓑ Ⓒ Ⓓ
46. Ⓐ Ⓑ Ⓒ Ⓓ
47. Ⓐ Ⓑ Ⓒ Ⓓ
48. Ⓐ Ⓑ Ⓒ Ⓓ
49. Ⓐ Ⓑ Ⓒ Ⓓ
50. Ⓐ Ⓑ Ⓒ Ⓓ

Language Arts - Writing

1. A B C D
2. A B C D
3. A B C D
4. A B C D
5. A B C D
6. A B C D
7. A B C D
8. A B C D
9. A B C D
10. A B C D
11. A B C D
12. A B C D
13. A B C D
14. A B C D
15. A B C D
16. A B C D
17. A B C D

18. A B C D
19. A B C D
20. A B C D
21. A B C D
22. A B C D
23. A B C D
24. A B C D
25. A B C D
26. A B C D
27. A B C D
28. A B C D
29. A B C D
30. A B C D
31. A B C D
32. A B C D
33. A B C D
34. A B C D

35. A B C D
36. A B C D
37. A B C D
38. A B C D
39. A B C D
40. A B C D
41. A B C D
42. A B C D
43. A B C D
44. A B C D
45. A B C D
46. A B C D
47. A B C D
48. A B C D
49. A B C D
50. A B C D

Science

1. A B C D
2. A B C D
3. A B C D
4. A B C D
5. A B C D
6. A B C D
7. A B C D
8. A B C D
9. A B C D
10. A B C D
11. A B C D
12. A B C D
13. A B C D
14. A B C D
15. A B C D
16. A B C D
17. A B C D
18. A B C D
19. A B C D
20. A B C D
21. A B C D
22. A B C D
23. A B C D
24. A B C D
25. A B C D
26. A B C D
27. A B C D
28. A B C D
29. A B C D
30. A B C D
31. A B C D
32. A B C D
33. A B C D
34. A B C D
35. A B C D
36. A B C D
37. A B C D
38. A B C D
39. A B C D
40. A B C D
41. A B C D
42. A B C D
43. A B C D
44. A B C D
45. A B C D
46. A B C D
47. A B C D
48. A B C D
49. A B C D
50. A B C D

Part 1 - Social Studies

1. Who are the descendants of 17th and 18th century French settlers?

   a. The Québécois

   b. The Acadians

   c. The Ontarians

   d. A and B

2. Early in Canadian history, what happened when different tribes came into contact with each other?

   a. Increase in conflict

   b. Growing resources

   c. Declining resources

   d. Growing communities

3. Who were the first Europeans to land on Canadian shores?

   a. The Aboriginals

   b. The Vikings

   c. The seafarers

   d. European Explorers

4. Where did the Vikings land?

   a. Labrador and Newfoundland

   b. Greenland and Newfoundland

   c. Labrador and Greenland

   d. None of the above

5. What are the first European settlements now called?

   a. Quebec City

   b. Maine and Quebec City

   c. Nova Scotia and Quebec City

   d. Maine and Nova Scotia

6. What year was the fortress at Quebec City established?

    a. 1806

    b. 1680

    c. 1608

    d. 1860

7. Who did King Charles II give exclusive trading rights to?

    a. Hudson's Bay Trading Company

    b. Trading companies in Montreal

    c. Trading companies on the East coast

    d. Trading companies owned by the English

8. What year was the Battle of the Plains of Abraham?

    a. 1759

    b. 1750

    c. 1859

    d. 1810

9. What are the present day names for Upper and Lower Canada?

    a. Montreal and Halifax

    b. Quebec and Halifax

    c. Ontario and Quebec

    d. Ontario and Montreal

10. Which group of people made Upper Canada their home?

    a. English-speaking Protestant Loyalists

    b. The Black Loyalists

    c. The English speaking Catholics

    d. French-speaking Catholics

11. How was Canada officially given its name?

    a. The elected representatives

    b. The Constitutional Act

    c. The people of Canada

    d. The various religious groups

12. What year was the first representative assembly elected ?

   a. 1578
   b. 1758
   c. 1785
   d. 1587

Passage 1 - The Renaissance

Questions 13 - 14 refer to the following passage

The period between 14th and 17th century is regarded in European history as being the cultural bridge that links modern history with the Middle Ages. What started in Italy as a cultural movement in the late part of the medieval period, spread across Europe and sparked the era known as the Early Modern Age.

The Renaissance came with its own adopted version of humanism that was derived from a rediscovery or re-acceptance of Greek philosophy, like "Man is the measure of all things" (Protagoras). This wave of thinking was reflected in architecture, science, art, literature and politics. The recycled method of making concrete and the use of perspective in oil painting are early examples of this era. The creation of metal movable type did help in spreading ideas of the later part of the 15th century, but the changes of the Renaissance era were not felt uniformly across Europe.

The Renaissance as a cultural movement included innovating of vernacular and Latin literature. Starting with the reawakened style of classical source based learning, in the 14th century, credited to Petrarch; the development of several rendering techniques like linear perspective to capture a more realistic reality in art and painting; and the broad but gradual reforms in education. The Renaissance contribution in politics included the development of conventions and customs of diplomacy. In science, it promoted an increased dependence on inductive reasoning and observation. The Renaissance did see significant advancements in several intellectual, political and social pursuits. However, the period is best known for its contributions to the development of by polymaths like Michelangelo and Leonardo da Vinci that inspired the phrase "Renaissance man."

13. Based on context which of the following would be the best definition for a "polymath?"

   a. Someone skilled in math and science
   b. Someone skilled in several different pursuits, including art and science
   c. Someone who has multiple college degrees
   d. Someone with an eidetic memory

14. The text above claims that the impacts of the Renaissance "were not felt uniformly across Europe." Which of the following is the likeliest reason for the difference between locations?

    a. Distance from Italy where the Renaissance started

    b. Differences in cultural and religious beliefs

    c. Distance inland, away from ocean trade routes

    d. All of the above.

Passage 2 - The Renaissance II

Questions 15 - 16 refer to the following passage

Florence, Italy was the birth place of the Renaissance in the 14th century. Several explanations have been put forward to explain the characteristics and origins of the period based on different factors such as the political structure of Florence at the time; it's civic and social peculiarities, the behavior of the dominant family (the Medici) in Florence, and the influx of Greek tests and scholars after the Ottoman Turks conquered Constantinople. Other major cities where the Renaissance also flourished include city-states in northern Italy like Genoa, Bologna, Venice, Milan and eventually Rome with the emergence of the Renaissance Papacy.

The history of the Renaissance period is long and indeed complex. Some historians have debated among themselves the significance of Renaissance as a historical delineation and even as a term. These set of historians do not support the glorification of the Renaissance period during the 19th century or the celebration of individual heroes of the period as "Renaissance men." Erwin Panofsky, an art historian made an observation of the resistance of some historians to the "Renaissance" concept.

15. Which of the following is the most likely reason that the Renaissance started in Italy?

    a. Italy is centrally located in Europe

    b. Italy was a central trade hub which increased the spread of ideas

    c. Italy was the most advanced civilization at the time

    d. Italy was the wealthiest Nation at the time

16. Opinion or Fact: The Renaissance was an important period in World History

    a. Opinion

    b. Fact

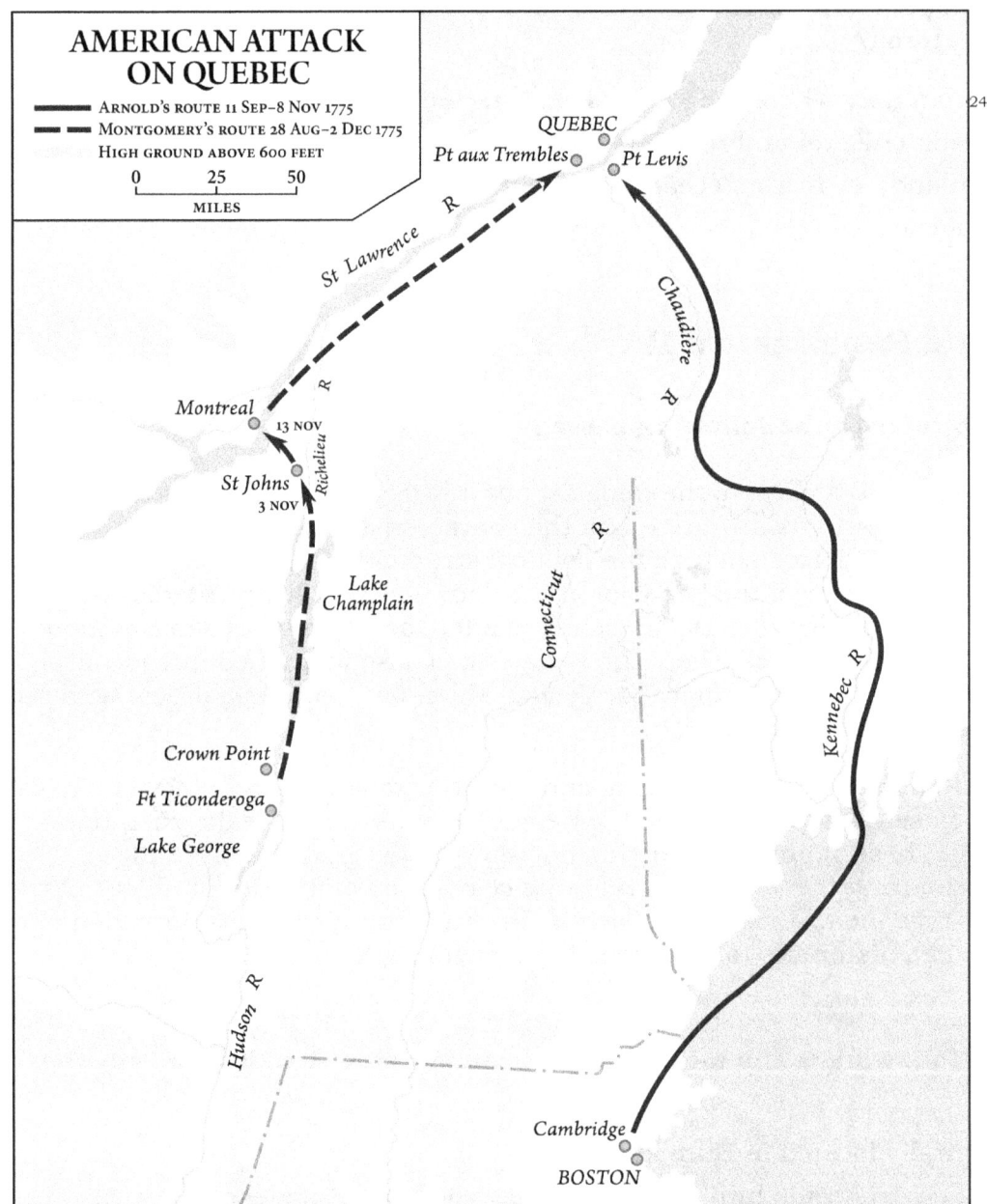

Question 17 refer to the above map

17. Based on the map above, was the American attack on Québec likely a success or a failure?

    a. Success. The troops were able to travel along the waterways which would be easier than a direct over land route. Arnold's forces had just successfully taken Montreal which would mean no reinforcements for the British. The British would be surprised by another winter attack.

    b. Failure. The troops were not traveling on boats though they were along the waterways. Arnold's forces were tired and depleted after a fight at Montreal. The Canadian winter meant illness and starvation further weakened troops.

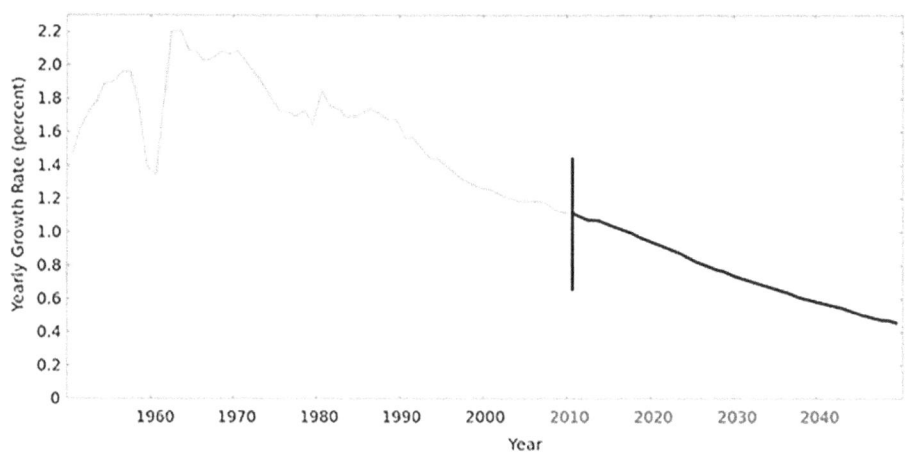

Questions 18 - 19 refer to the above graph

18. The change from grey to black on the graph indicates which of the following

a. The grey indicates periods of high change where the black indicates periods of stability

b. The grey indicates periods before 2000 while the black indicates periods after 2000

c. The grey indicates periods of time that have recorded data while the black are predictions of the future

d. The change from grey to black is arbitrary

19. Opinion or Fact: The yearly growth rate percent will continue to decrease every year until 2040.

a. Opinion

b. Fact

Passage 3 - Geography

Questions 20 - 21 refer to the following passage

Geography can be broadly divided into two main sub-fields, which are physical geography and human geography. Human geography deals with the built environment, focusing on how man creates, views, influence and manage space. Physical geography focuses on the natural environment. This part of geography studies how organisms, soil, climate, landforms and water interact and produce. A third field of geography, environmental geography, has been developed from the difference between these two approaches. Environmental geography combines human and physical geography and examines the interactions between humans and the environment.

20. Based on the passage above which of the fields of geography would be interested in studying the impact of a beaver dam on a river?

   a. Physical Geography

   b. Human Geography

   c. Environmental Geography

   d. None of the above

21. Based on the passage above, which field of geography would study the impact of a man-made dam on a river?

   a. Physical Geography

   b. Human Geography

   c. Environmental Geography

   d. None of the above

Passage 4 - Related Fields to Geography

Questions 22 - 23 refer to the following passage

The application of geography can be seen in spatial planning, regional planning and urban planning. They all use the geographical approach to determine whether to develop or not develop, and how to develop land to meet desired criteria such is beauty, economic opportunities, safety, the promotion and preservation of natural heritage, and many others. Planning of cities, rural communities and towns can thus be considered as applied geography.

22. Based on the text above, which of the types of planning would be most interested in the number of towns drawing on a fresh water lake.

   a. Spatial planning

   b. Regional Planning

   c. Urban Planning

   d. Rural Planning

23. The applied geographical approach would not study which of the following

   a. Local species of flora to plant in a designed city park

   b. Access to fresh water sources

   c. The impact of a solar farm on the economic and aesthetic health of a town

   d. The applied geographical approach would study each of these.

Passage 5 - Canadian Government

Questions 24 - 27 refer to the following passage

Canada holds the traditional values of a constitutional monarchy, in which the Head of State is the Sovereign (King or Queen). The current Sovereign is Queen Elizabeth II. This individual rules according the Canada's Constitution, which is the document outlining the rule of law. The Sovereign's role varies, but generally Her Majesty is a symbol of Canadian heritage and a reflection of Canada's rich history.

A distinction must be made between the Sovereign, who is the head of state, and the Prime Minister, who is the head of government. Canada's Governor General serves as the Sovereign's representative, and his or her term is usually limited to five years. Lieutenant Governors serve as Sovereign representatives in each of the ten provinces.

24. Which of the following countries has a government most like the Canadian Government

    a. The United States

    b. Great Britain

    c. France

    d. Mexico

25. Based on the passage above, is Queen Elizabeth II involved in the day-to-day running of the Canadian Government:

    a. Yes, she is an absolute monarch with complete control of the government

    b. Yes, she instructs the Prime Minister on her desires for the government

    c. No, she is represented through Canada's Governor General

    d. No, she has no ability to influence government

26. Based on the passage above, what is the hierarchy of the Canadian Government?

    a. The Queen, The Prime Minister, The Governor General, The Lieutenant Governors

    b. The Queen, The Governor General, The Prime Minister, The Lieutenant Governor

    c. The Prime Minister, The Governor General, The Lieutenant Governors

    d. The Governor General, The Prime Minister, The Lieutenant Governors

27. Opinion or Fact: The Prime Minister is the most powerful person in the Canadian Government.

    a. Opinion

    b. Fact

Passage 6 - Canadian Government
Questions 28 - 31 refer to the following passage

Just as the government is divided into three levels, so too is the Parliament. These three parts are the Sovereign (King or Queen), the Senate, and the House of Commons. The Prime Minister, the figurehead of government, selects Cabinet ministers and is tasked with the general operations and procedures of the government. The House of Commons represents the people and is made up of elected members of Parliament. Senators, who may serve until the age of 75, are chosen by the Governor General, who is counseled by the Prime Minister. For any bill to become a law, it must be accepted by both the House of Commons and the Senate, while also receiving royal assent from the Governor General.

The government of Canada, like all democracies, is based on the will of the people. It is therefore important for everyone of voting age to participate, in order that every voice may be heard.

28. Based on the text, how does a bill become a law in Canada?

a. A bill goes through the House of Commons and The Senate. Then the Bill is signed into a Law by the Prime Minister

b. A bill goes through the House of Commons and The Senate. Then the Bill is signed into a Law by the Governor General

c. A bill goes through the House of Commons and The Senate. Then the Bill is signed into a Law by the Governor General unless the Prime Minister opposes it.

d. A bill goes through the House of Commons and The Senate. Then the Bill is signed into a Law by the Prime Minister unless the Governor General opposes it.

29. The Prime Minister selects:

a. Cabinet Ministers

b. Senators

c. The Governor General

d. None of the above

30. The Canadian People vote for:

a. The House of Commons
b. The Senators
c. The Cabinet Ministers
d. None of the Above

31. The Canadian Government has two branches, The Executive Branch and The Legislative Branch. Which branch is the Prime Minister a part of?

a. The Executive Branch
b. The Legislative Branch
c. Both Branches
d. Neither Branch

Questions 32 refers to the above photograph

32. The purpose of the above photograph is to show:

a. The impact that trains had on travel
b. The cultural diversity of Canada
c. The plight of new immigrants to Canada
d. The technological advancement of Canadian transportation

Questions 33 refers to the above painting

33. The image above is a famous painting by artist Benjamin West. It's titled The Death of General Wolfe. Based on the image above, which of the following is not true:

    a. General Wolfe was an American General

    b. General Wolfe died in North America

    c. General Wolfe was well liked and respected by his soldiers

    d. General Wolfe died as the result of a battle War of 1812 - 1

34. What was the significance of the British North America Act of 1867?

    a. It granted Canada complete independence from Britain.

    b. It established Canada as a federal dominion within the British Empire.

    c. It abolished the monarchy in Canada.

    d. It created the United Nations.

35. Which of the following is NOT a right protected by the Canadian Charter of Rights and Freedoms?

    a. Freedom of expression

    b. The right to a fair trial

    c. The right to bear arms

    d. Equality rights

36. The Quiet Revolution in Quebec during the 1960s primarily involved which of the following?

   a. A movement to separate Quebec from Canada

   b. A period of rapid economic and social change, emphasizing secularism and modernization

   c. A peaceful transition of power from the British monarchy to French leaders

   d. A conflict between French and English-speaking Canadians

37. Which of the following best describes the significance of the 1982 Constitution Act?

   a. It granted Canada the right to amend its own Constitution without British approval.

   b. It removed the British monarch as Canada's head of state.

   c. It abolished the Senate in Canada.

   d. It marked the end of the French-English divide in Canadian politics.

Passage 7 - Microeconomics 2

Questions 38 - 39 refer to the following passage

There are different market structures. Perfectly competitive markets are characterized by many sellers and buyers. In this market structure, no individual participant is big enough to determine price as the goods sold are homogenous in nature. Every participant is thus a "price taker" since they cannot set or influence product prices. In real life situations, markets usually experience conditions relating to imperfect conditions.

Forms of markets would include duopoly (only two sellers), monopoly (only one seller), oligopoly (few sellers), monopolistic competition (many sellers of differentiated goods), monopsony (only one buyer) and oligopsony (few buyers). Imperfect competition differs from perfect competition, because in imperfect competition the market power is distributed unequally. Under imperfect competition, firms or sellers can afford to be "price makers," meaning that since they can influence prices with the large share of market power that they possess. [4]

38. Which of the following is a better market for consumers?

   a. A perfectly competitive market

   b. A duopoly

   c. An oligopoly

   d. A monopoly

39. Which of the following gives the sellers the most control over product price?

    a. A perfectly competitive market

    b. A duopoly

    c. An oligopoly

    d. A monopoly

Passage 8 - Microeconomics 3

Questions 40 - 41 refer to the following passage

Microeconomics is only concerned with analyzing individual markets based on the assumption that what happens in a particular market has no effect on any other markets. This assumption helps the micro-economist simplify the economic system under study. This form of analysis is called partial-equilibrium analysis (demand and supply). This style of analysis aggregates or sums up the total activity in just one market. General-equilibrium theory is the study of different markets and the activities within the markets. General-equilibrium theory aggregates or sums up total activity across all the various markets. This theory studies the changes that occur in the markets and how they interact towards equilibrium. [4]

40. The New York Central Stock Exchange would be best analyzed using:

    a. Partial-Equilibrium Analysis because the NYCSE is just one market

    b. Partial-Equilibrium Analysis because only American businesses and investors can invest in the NYCSE

    c. General-Equilibrium Theory because the NYCSE is very large and complex

    d. General-Equilibrium Theory because the NYCSE is impacted by other markets and stock exchanges around the world.

41. Based on the text's characterization of Microeconomics, which of the following is probably true:

    a. Micro: Complex

    b. Micro: Easily Understandable

    c. Micro: Small

    d. Micro: Large

Passage 9 - Firms

Questions 42 - 43 refer to the following passage

People do not always trade on markets directly. Most times, on the side of supply, they produce and work through firms. Popular types of firms would include partnerships, trusts and corporations. Ronald Coase is quoted as saying that people would begin to produce and organize their work in firms when the costs of trading through firms becomes lower that the cost of trading directly on the market. Firms are better able to combine capital and labor to achieve better economies of scale (as long as average cost declines when the number of units produced increases) than individuals trading directly on the market. [4]

42. Based on the passage above, which of the following is not true:

   a. Most sellers trade on the market as firms

   b. Trading through firms costs less per individual than trading individually would

   c. Average cost per product usually increases when the number of products created increases

   d. All of the above are true

43. According to the passage above, which of the following is not a reason why suppliers work though firms?

   a. Firms bring sellers together, meaning that there is less competition

   b. Large firms are more trustworthy than small businesses

   c. Firms decrease cost per unit made

   d. Firms come in a variety of different types and styles to best suit the individual business

Passage 12 - Firms II

Questions 44 - 45 refer to the following passage

Perfectly competitive markets are characterized by many producers where, none can individually exert any significant influence on price. Industrial organizations study the demand and supply interactions in such markets to understand the strategy of those firms who lack significant influence over price. It analyzes the structure of perfectly competitive markets and their interactions. Other common markets also understudied apart from perfect competition include various forms of monopoly, oligopoly and monopolistic completion. [4]

44. Which of the following is the best definition of an oligopoly marketplace?

   a. A market where all suppliers/sellers have equal influence on price

   b. A market where there are many suppliers/sellers of a product, but those products differ in small ways and are therefore not exact substitutes

   c. A market where there are very few supplier/sellers

   d. A market where there is one supplier/seller

45. Which of the following is the best definition of a monopolistic completion marketplace?

   a. A market where all suppliers/sellers have equal influence on price

   b. A market where there are many suppliers/sellers of a product, but those products differ in small ways and are therefore not exact substitutes

   c. A market where there are very few supplier/sellers

   d. A market where there is one supplier/seller

Passage 13 - Market Failure

Questions 46 - 47 refer to the following passage

"Market failure" is a term used to encompass different problems that may hamper the use of regular economic assumptions. Economists have different ways to categorize market failures, however, some categories are popular.

Incomplete markets and information asymmetries can lead to economic inefficiency. Efficiency can be improved through legal, regulatory and market remedies. [4]

46. Incomplete markets exist when there are not enough people producing products to meet demand. Based on your understanding of supply and demand, which of the following should happen when there is an incomplete market

   a. Demand increases which makes the product more expensive

   b. Demand increases which makes the produce less expensive

   c. Demand decreases which makes the product more expensive

   d. Demand decreases which makes the product less expensive.

47. Which of the following is the most likely definition for information asymmetries?

   a. The inefficiency created when one side of a transaction has different information than the other side of the transaction

   b. The inefficiency created when the two sides of a transaction have difficulty communicating desired results of a transaction

   c. The inefficiency create when the two sides of a desired transaction don't know who they're trading with

   d. The inefficiency created when one side of a transaction hides their identity from the other side of the transaction

Passage 14 - Early Peoples

Questions 48 - 50 refer to the following passage

The Aboriginals, the first settlers of Canada, are divided into three distinct groups of people: Indigenous or First Nations, Inuit, and Métis. Indigenous refers to all non-Inuit, non-Métis people groups. Often called First Nations, a term coined in the 1970s, the First Nations occupied many of the land reserves throughout Canada and has a large urban population. The term "indian" is no longer used; "First Nations" is the preferred term.

The Inuit, or "the people" in the Inuktitut language, are spread throughout the arctic regions of Canada. Their vast knowledge of nature and the environment has allowed them to thrive in the coldest regions of Canada. Almost three quarters of Inuit in Canada live in Inuit Nunangat. Inuit Nunangat stretches from Labrador to the Northwest Territories and comprises four regions: Nunatsiavut, Nunavik, Nunavut and the Inuvialuit region. The Inuit make up roughly 4% of the native population.

The Métis, a unique population of Aboriginal and European descent, make up about 30% of the native population. Most Métis once spoke, and many still speak, Metis French, or a mixed language, Michif. Most the Métis occupy the Prairie provinces of Canada.

48. What are three unique groups of first settlers?

    a. Aboriginals, French and English

    b. Aboriginals, Inuits and Metis

    c. First Nations, Inuit, and Métis.

    d. Inuits, French and Métis.

49. What term was used to refer to non-Inuit, non-Métis peoples?

    a. The English

    b. The French

    c. Aboriginals

    d. First Nations

50. Which group makes up about 5% of the Native population?

    a. Inuits and Métis.

    b. First Nations

    c. Métis

    d. Inuit

Language Arts - Reading

Passage 1 - Tarzan of the Apes

Edgar Rice Burroughs

Questions 1 - 2 refer to the following passage

Almost silently the ape-man sped on in the track of Terkoz and his prey, but the sound of his approach reached the ears of the fleeing beast and spurred it on to greater speed.

Three miles were covered before Tarzan overtook them, and then Terkoz, seeing that further flight was futile, dropped to the ground in a small open glade, that he might turn and fight for his prize or be free to escape unhampered if he saw that the pursuer was more than a match for him.

He still grasped Jane in one great arm as Tarzan bounded like a leopard into the arena which nature had provided for this primeval-like battle.

When Terkoz saw that it was Tarzan who pursued him, he jumped to the conclusion that this was Tarzan's woman, since they were of the same kind--white and hairless--and so he rejoiced at this opportunity for double revenge upon his hated enemy.

To Jane the strange apparition of this god-like man was as wine to sick nerves.

From the description which Clayton and her father and Mr. Philander had given her, she knew that it must be the same wonderful creature who had saved them, and she saw in him only a protector and a friend.

But as Terkoz pushed her roughly aside to meet Tarzan's charge, and she saw the great proportions of the ape and the mighty muscles and the fierce fangs, her heart quailed. How could any vanquish such a mighty antagonist?

Like two charging bulls they came together, and like two wolves sought each other's throat. Against the long canines of the ape was pitted the thin blade of the man's knife.

1. Based on the author's description of Terkoz, he is most probably which of the following?

    a. A lion
    b. A poacher
    c. A white man
    d. An ape

2. Apes, leopards, wolves and bulls: the author describes Tarzan through animal imagery to suggest:

   a. That Tarzan has the power to shape-shift
   b. That Tarzan has grown up among many animals
   c. That Tarzan is uncivilized
   d. That Tarzan straddles the worlds of man and nature

Passage 2 - Not That it Matters

A. A. Milne

Questions 3 - 7 refer to the following passage

Sometimes when the printer is waiting for an article which really should have been sent to him the day before, I sit at my desk and wonder if there is any possible subject in the whole world upon which I can possibly find anything to say. On one such occasion I left it to Fate, which decided, by means of a dictionary opened at random, that I should deliver myself of a few thoughts about goldfish. (You will find this article later on in the book.) But to-day I do not need to bother about a subject. To-day I am without a care. Nothing less has happened than that I have a new nib in my pen.

In the ordinary way, when Shakespeare writes a tragedy, or Mr. Blank gives you one of his charming little essays, a certain amount of thought goes on before pen is put to paper. One cannot write "Scene I. An Open Place. Thunder and Lightning. Enter Three Witches," or "As I look up from my window, the nodding daffodils beckon to me to take the morning," one cannot give of one's best in this way on the spur of the moment. At least, others cannot.

But when I have a new nib in my pen, then I can go straight from my breakfast to the blotting-paper, and a new sheet of foolscap fills itself magically with a stream of blue-black words. When poets and idiots talk of the pleasure of writing, they mean the pleasure of giving a piece of their minds to the public; with an old nib a tedious business. They do not mean (as I do) the pleasure of the artist in seeing beautifully shaped "k's" and sinuous "s's" grow beneath his steel. Anybody else writing this article might wonder "Will my readers like it?" I only tell myself "How the compositors will love it!"

But perhaps they will not love it. Maybe I am a little above their heads. I remember on one First of January receiving an anonymous postcard wishing me a happy New Year, and suggesting that I should give the compositors a happy New Year also by writing more generously. In those days I got a thousand words upon one sheet 8 in. by 5 in. I adopted the suggestion, but it was a wrench; as it would be for a painter of miniatures forced to spend the rest of his life painting the Town Council of Boffington in the manner of Herkomer. My canvases are bigger now, but they are still impressionistic. "Pretty, but what is it?"

remains the obvious comment; one steps back a pace and saws the air with the hand; "You see it better from here, my love," one says to one's wife. But if there be one compositor not carried away by the mad rush of life, who in a leisurely hour (the luncheon one, for instance) looks at the beautiful words with the eye of an artist, not of a wage-earner, he, I think, will be satisfied; he will be as glad as I am of my new nib. Does it matter, then, what you who see only the printed word think of it?

A woman, who had studied what she called the science of calligraphy, once offered to tell my character from my handwriting. I prepared a special sample for her; it was full of sentences like "To be good is to be happy," "Faith is the lode-star of life," "We should always be kind to animals," and so on.

I wanted her to do her best. She gave the morning to it, and told me at lunch that I was "synthetic." Probably you think that the compositor has failed me here and printed "synthetic" when I wrote "sympathetic." In just this way I misunderstood my calligraphist at first, and I looked as sympathetic as I could.

However, she repeated "synthetic," so that there could be no mistake. I begged her to tell me more, for I had thought that every letter would reveal a secret, but all she would add was "and not analytic." I went about for the rest of the day saying proudly to myself "I am synthetic! I am synthetic! I am synthetic!" and then I would add regretfully, "Alas, I am not analytic!" I had no idea what it meant.

3. The most accurate description of the author's view on other writers is:

    a. They are more ordinary than he

    b. They devote more thought to their work before they get down to writing

    c. If they happen to be poets, they are idiots

    d. Other writers are comparatively more spontaneous

4. By "writing more generously," the anonymous postcard is advising the author to:

    a. Clean up his writing

    b. Promote positive messages

    c. Make his letters larger

    d. A & C

5. "My canvases are bigger now, but they are still impressionistic." This comment qualifies which of the following?

    a. The author's subject matter: he is writing on more general topics

    b. The visual appearance of the author's writing, which he is attempting to enlarge

    c. The author's perception of his imagined audience, which he is beginning to integrate more

    d. The notion that the author, his style changed, wonders what kind of impression his writing will have

6. According to the author, compositors (those who set type to print text) will appreciate his work under what condition?

    a. When they look for artistry, rather than for work to be completed

    b. Only when they are on their lunch breaks

    c. When they are sane and see with clear eyes

    d. Only if they are calligraphers

7. The most probable reason the calligrapher labels the author "synthetic" is:

    a. She suspects that the author uses machinery, such as a typewriter, to write

    b. She meant to call him "sympathetic"

    c. The author is too focused on appearances

    d. He synthesizes (brings together) different ideas in his writing

Passage 2 - The Voyages of Dr. Dolittle

Hugh Lofting

Questions 8 - 11 refer to the following passage

TWO days after that we had all in readiness for our departure. On this voyage Jip begged so hard to be taken that the Doctor finally gave in and said he could come. Polynesia and Chee-Chee were the only other animals to go with us. Dab-Dab was left in charge of the house and the animal family we were to leave behind.

Of course, as is always the way, at the last moment we kept remembering things we had forgotten; and when we finally closed the house up and went down the steps to the road, we were all burdened with armfuls of odd packages.

Halfway to the river, the Doctor suddenly remembered that he had left the stock-pot boiling on the kitchen-fire. However, we saw a blackbird flying by who nested in our garden, and the Doctor asked her to go back for us and tell Dab-Dab about it.

Down at the river-wall we found a great crowd waiting to see us off. Standing right near the gang-plank were my mother and father. I hoped that they would not make a scene, or burst into tears or anything like that. But as a matter of fact they behaved quite well—for parents. My mother said something about being sure not to get my feet wet; and my father just smiled a crooked sort of smile, patted me on the back and wished me luck. Good-byes are awfully uncomfortable things and I was glad when it was over and we passed on to the ship.

We were a little surprised not to see Matthew Mugg among the crowd. We had felt sure that he would be there; and the Doctor had intended to give him some extra instructions about the food for the animals we had left at the house.

At last, after much pulling and tugging, we got the anchor up and undid a lot of mooring-ropes. Then the _Curlew_ began to move gently down the river with the out-running tide, while the people on the wall cheered and waved their handkerchiefs.

We bumped into one or two other boats getting out into the stream; and at one sharp bend in the river we got stuck on a mud bank for a few minutes. But though the people on the shore seemed to get very excited at these things, the Doctor did not appear to be disturbed by them in the least.

"These little accidents will happen in the most carefully regulated voyages," he said as he leaned over the side and fished for his boots which had got stuck in the mud while we were pushing off. "Sailing is much easier when you get out into the open sea. There aren't so many silly things to bump into."

8. Readers can best infer that Jip is:

   a. Spiteful

   b. Insecure

   c. A parrot

   d. Some kind of animal

9. The size and energy of the crowd indicates:

   a. The Doctor secretly enjoys his celebrity status

   b. The voyagers are leaving for a very long time

   c. A & B

   d. None of the above

10. For which of the following is there the least evidence?

   a. Doctor Doolittle is capable of speaking to animals

   b. Doctor Doolittle tends not to let life's little upsets affect him greatly

   c. A rocky start to getting out the river bodes ill for the voyage to come

   d. Matthew Mugg is not an animal

11. The Doctor's point about accidents happening "in the most carefully regulated voyages" is most similar to which of the following?

   a. A good plan has many contingencies

   b. It is pointless to cry over spilt milk

   c. It is impossible to account for everything

   d. One bad thing leads to another

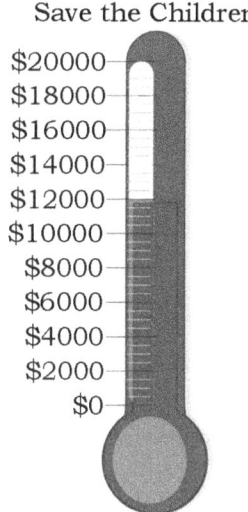

Questions 12 - 13 refer to the following graphic. Consider the graphic above.

The Save the Children fund has a fund-raising goal of $20,000. Approximately how much of their goal have they achieved?

    a. 3/5
    b. 3/4
    c. 1/2
    d. 1/3

13. Consider the graphic above. The Save the Children fund has a fund-raising goal of $16,000. About how much of their goal have they achieved?

    a. 3/5
    b. 3/4
    c. 1/2
    d. 1/3

Passage 3 - Lowest Price Guarantee

Get it for less. Guaranteed!

Questions 14 - 16 refer to the following passage.

ABC Electric will beat any advertised price by 10% of the difference.

1) If you find a lower advertised price, we will beat it by 10% of the difference.

2) If you find a lower advertised price within 30 days* of your purchase we will beat it by 10% of the difference.

3) If our own price is reduced within 30 days* of your purchase, bring in your receipt and we will refund the difference.

*14 days for computers, monitors, printers, laptops, tablets, cellular & wireless devices, home security products, projectors, camcorders, digital cameras, radar detectors, portable DVD players, DJ and pro-audio equipment, and air conditioners.

14. I bought a radar detector 15 days ago and saw an ad for the same model only cheaper. Can I get 10% of the difference refunded?

   a. Yes. Since it is less than 30 days, you can get 10% of the difference refunded.

   b. No. Since it is more than 14 days, you cannot get 10% of the difference refunded.

   c. It depends on the cashier.

   d. Yes. You can get the difference refunded.

15. I bought a flat-screen TV for $500 10 days ago and found an advertisement for the same TV, at another store, on sale for $400. How much will ABC refund under this guarantee?

   a. $100
   b. $110
   c. $10
   d. $400

16. What is the purpose of this passage?

   a. To inform
   b. To educate
   c. To persuade
   d. To entertain

Passage 4 - Songs Of Innocence and Songs of Experience
William Blake

Questions 17 - 20 refer to the following passage

The Echoing Green

The sun does arise,
And make happy the skies;
The merry bells ring
To welcome the Spring;
The skylark and thrush,
The birds of the bush,
Sing louder around
To the bells' cheerful sound;
While our sports shall be seen
On the echoing green.

Old John, with white hair,
Does laugh away care,
Sitting under the oak,
Among the old folk.
They laugh at our play,
And soon they all say,
'Such, such were the joys
When we all—girls and boys—
In our youth-time were seen
On the echoing green.'

Till the little ones, weary,
No more can be merry:
The sun does descend,
And our sports have an end.
Round the laps of their mothers
Many sisters and brothers,
Like birds in their nest,
Are ready for rest,
And sport no more seen
On the darkening green.

17. Which of the following choices best represents the symbolic significance of the echoing green?

    a. A sports field

    b. Life, always to be extinguished at the end

    c. The highs and lows of old age

    d. Cycling seasons and life experiences

18. The voice's tone in this poem is most probably:

- a. Celebratory
- b. Wistful
- c. Unsure
- d. Doting

19. Which pair of motifs are most central to this poem?

- a. Birds and the color green
- b. "Blood is thicker than water," and "The young know too little, the old too much"
- c. Age and Spring
- d. Echoes and the sun

20. What effect of the rhyme scheme is reasonable to infer?

- a. That the poem was intended to be sung
- b. That life's many moments will be revisited and happen anew
- c. That darkness is inevitable
- d. That the poem is intended for children

Passage 5 - The Daffodils

William Wordsworth

Questions 21 - 24 refer to the following passage.

I wandered lonely as a cloud
That floats on high o'er vales and hills,
When all at once I saw a crowd,
A host, of golden daffodils;
Beside the lake, beneath the trees,
Fluttering and dancing in the breeze.

Continuous as the stars that shine
And twinkle on the Milky Way,
They stretched in never-ending line
Along the margin of a bay:
Ten thousand saw I at a glance,
Tossing their heads in sprightly dance.

The waves beside them danced, but they
Out-did the sparkling waves in glee:
A Poet could not but be gay,
In such a jocund company:

I gazed--and gazed--but little thought
What wealth the show to me had brought:

For oft, when on my couch I lie
In vacant or in pensive mood,
They flash upon that inward eye
Which is the bliss of solitude;
And then my heart with pleasure fills,
And dances with the daffodils.

21. Is the author of this poem a lover of nature?

    a. Yes

    b. No

    c. Uncertain. There isn't enough information

22. What is the general mood of this poem?

    a. Sad

    b. Thoughtful

    c. Happy

    d. Excited

23. What does sprightly mean?

    a. Growing very fast

    b. Sad and melancholy

    c. Weak and slow

    d. Happy and full of life

24. What is jocund company?

    a. Sad

    b. Happy

    c. Joyful

    d. Boring

Passage 6 - Where art Thou, my Beloved Son,

William Wordsworth

Questions 25 - 29 refer to the following passage.

    Where art thou, worse to me than dead?
    Oh find me, prosperous or undone!
    Or, if the grave be now thy bed,
    Why am I ignorant of the same
    That I may rest; and neither blame
    Nor sorrow may attend thy name?

II   Seven years, alas! to have received
    No tidings of an only child;
    To have despaired, have hoped, believed,
    And been for evermore beguiled; [1]
    Sometimes with thoughts of very bliss!
    I catch at them, and then I miss;
    Was ever darkness like to this?

III   He was among the prime in worth,
    An object beauteous to behold;
    Well born, well bred; I sent him forth
    Ingenuous, innocent, and bold:
    If things ensued that wanted grace,
    As hath been said, they were not base;
    And never blush was on my face.

IV   Ah! little doth the young-one dream,
    When full of play and childish cares,
    What power is in [2] his wildest scream,
    Heard by his mother unawares!
    He knows it not, he cannot guess:
    Years to a mother bring distress;
    But do not make her love the less.

V   Neglect me! no, I suffered long
    From that ill thought; and, being blind,
    Said, "Pride shall help me in my wrong:
    Kind mother have I been, as kind
    As ever breathed:" and that is true;
    I've wet my path with tears like dew,
    Weeping for him when no one knew.

VI   My Son, if thou be humbled, poor,
    Hopeless of honour and of gain,
    Oh! do not dread thy mother's door;

      Think not of me with grief and pain:
      I now can see with better eyes;
      And worldly grandeur I despise,
      And fortune with her gifts and lies.

VII   Alas! the fowls of heaven have wings,
      And blasts of heaven will aid their flight;
      They mount--how short a voyage brings
      The wanderers back to their delight!
      Chains tie us down by land and sea;
      And wishes, vain as mine, may be
      All that is left to comfort thee.

VIII   Perhaps some dungeon hears thee groan,
      Maimed, mangled by inhuman men;
      Or thou upon a desert thrown
      Inheritest the lion's den;
      Or hast been summoned to the deep,
      Thou, thou and all thy mates, to keep
      An incommunicable sleep.

IX   I look for ghosts; but none will force
      Their way to me: 'tis falsely said
      That there was ever intercourse
      Between [3] the living and the dead;
      For, surely, then I should have sight
      Of him I wait for day and night,
      With love and longings infinite.

X   My apprehensions come in crowds;
      I dread the rustling of the grass;
      The very shadows of the clouds
      Have power to shake me as they pass:
      I question things and do not find
      One that will answer to my mind;
      And all the world appears unkind.

XI   Beyond participation lie
      My troubles, and beyond relief:
      If any chance to heave a sigh,
      They pity me, and not my grief.
      Then come to me, my Son, or send
      Some tidings that my woes may end;
      I have no other earthly friend!

25. What is the mother's main concern?

    a. The death of her son

    b. Profound regret for her overbearing nature

    c. Her son's refusal to speak to her

    d. Not knowing what has happened to her son

26. It is possible to infer of the son in this poem that:

    a. He is certainly dead

    b. He is a businessman who was led astray

    c. He is a dashing lad whose behavior was perhaps questionable

    d. He suffers from night-terrors

27. The meaning of the final three lines in the seventh stanza, "Chains tie us down by land and sea /And wishes, vain as mine, may be all that is left to comfort thee" is most perceptively described by which choice?

    a. Unable to search for her lost son, prayers are all the mother has left to offer him

    b. This is an illusion to imprisonment — the mother cannot find her son because she has accepted responsibility for his crimes

    c. The mother can provide no comfort to her son

    d. A religious reference: God has determined to shackle the mother to her past life

28. The best word to describe the tone of this poem is:

    a. Woeful

    b. Demure

    c. Dissatisfied

    d. Furtive

29. What is the main idea of the third stanza ("He was among... And never blush was on my face.")?

    a. The mother here is subtly bragging about the riches with which she endowed her son's upbringing, though he ultimately abused these

    b. The main idea is that the son beguiled his mother, pretending to be charming and innocent when in fact he was nefarious.

    c. The main idea is to establish the mother's paramount opinion of her son

    d. Here the mother discloses that it was her fault that she let her beautiful son go, though she would never admit to this

Passage 7 - On the High Road

Antov Checkov

Questions 30 - 32 refer to the following passage.

SAVVA. Don't talk, kind man!

MERIK. Quiet, old wolf! You're a savage race! Herods! Sellers of your souls! [To TIHON] Come here, take off my boots! Look sharp now!

TIHON. Eh, he's let himself go I [Laughs] Awful, isn't it.

MERIK. Go on, do as you're told! Quick now! [Pause] Do you hear me, or don't you? Am I talking to you or the wall? [Stands up]

TIHON. Well... give over.

MERIK. I want you, you fleecer, to take the boots off me, a poor tramp.

TIHON. Well, well... don't get excited. Here have a glass.... Have a drink, now!

MERIK. People, what do I want? Do I want him to stand me vodka, or to take off my boots? Didn't I say it properly? [To TIHON] Didn't you hear me rightly? I'll wait a moment, perhaps you'll hear me then.

[There is excitement among the pilgrims and tramps, who half-raise themselves to look at TIHON and MERIK. They wait in silence.]

TIHON. The devil brought you here! [Comes out from behind the bar] What a gentleman! Come on now. [Takes off MERIK'S boots] You child of Cain...

MERIK. That's right. Put them side by side.... Like that... you can go now!

TIHON. [Returns to the bar-counter] You're too fond of being clever. You do it again and I'll turn you out of the inn! Yes! [To BORTSOV, who is approaching] You, again?

BORTSOV. Look here, suppose I give you something made of gold.... I will give it to you.

TIHON. What are you shaking for? Talk sense!

BORTSOV. It may be mean and wicked on my part, but what am I to do? I'm doing this wicked thing, not reckoning on what's to come.... If I was tried for it, they'd let me off. Take it, only on condition that you return it later, when I come back from town. I give it to you in front of these witnesses. You will be my witnesses! [Takes a gold medallion out from the breast of his coat] Here it is.... I ought to take the portrait out, but I've nowhere to put it; I'm wet all over.... Well, take the portrait, too! Only mind this... don't let your fingers touch that face.... Please... I was rude to you, my dear fellow, I was a fool, but forgive me and... don't touch it with your fingers.... Don't look at that face with your eyes. [Gives TIHON the medallion.]

TIHON. [Examining it] Stolen property.... All right, then, drink.... [Pours out vodka] Confound you.

BORTSOV. Only don't you touch it... with your fingers. [Drinks slowly, with feverish pauses.]

TIHON. [Opens the medallion] Hm... a lady!... Where did you get hold of this?

30. Which option best describes Tihon's attitude toward Merik?

    a. Antagonistic

    b. Frustrated

    c. Playful

    d. Tolerant

31. What is the likeliest reason Bortsov gives Tihon his medallion?

    a. It is to pay his due for staying at Tihon's inn

    b. It belonged first to Tihon, and so is now being returned

    c. Bortsov entrusts its safe-keeping to Tihon while he, Bortsov, goes to commit a crime

    d. Bortsov intends to compensate Tihon for a prior act of foolishness

32. By the end of this passage, what can readers infer about Tihon's personality/character?

    a. He is his own man — compliant to others requests, he is nonetheless hard-pressed not to do what he wants

    b. He is spiteful, and dislikes running the inn, where he is always at the whims of others

    c. He indulges too much in drink, and presumably needs alcohol to function.

    d. He finds being around others tiresome

Passage 8 - A Doll's House

Henrik Ibsen

Questions 33 - 36 refer to the following passage.

ACT I

SCENE - A room furnished comfortably and tastefully, but not extravagantly. At the back, a door to the right leads to the entrance-hall, another to the left leads to Helmer's study. Between the doors stands a piano. In the middle of the left-hand wall is a door, and beyond it a window. Near the window are a round table, arm-chairs and a small sofa. In the right-hand wall, at the farther end, another door; and on the same side, nearer the footlights, a stove, two easy chairs and a rocking-chair; between the stove and the door, a small table. Engravings on the walls; a cabinet with china and other small objects; a small book-case with well-bound books. The floors are carpeted, and a fire burns in the stove. It is winter.

A bell rings in the hall; shortly afterwards the door is heard to open. Enter NORA, humming a tune and in high spirits. She is in outdoor dress and carries a number of parcels; these she lays on the table to the right. She leaves the outer door open after her, and through it is seen a PORTER who is carrying a Christmas Tree and a basket, which he gives to the MAID who has opened the door.)

NORA. Hide the Christmas Tree carefully, Helen. Be sure the children do not see it until this evening, when it is dressed. (To the PORTER, taking out her purse.) How much?

PORTER. Sixpence.

NORA. There is a shilling. No, keep the change. (The PORTER thanks her, and goes out. NORA shuts the door. She is laughing to herself, as she takes off her hat and coat. She takes a packet of macaroons from her pocket and eats one or two; then goes cautiously to her husband's door and listens.) Yes, he is in. (Still humming, she goes to the table on the right.)

HELMER (calls out from his room). Is that my little lark twittering out there?

NORA (busy opening some of the parcels). Yes, it is!

HELMER. Is it my little squirrel bustling about?

NORA. Yes!

33. What word best describes the mood of this scene?

   a. Seasonal

   b. Festive

   c. Happy

   d. Welcoming

34. The reader can infer that the main idea of this scene is to:

   a. Introduce the setting of the play

   b. Suggest the dynamic between Nora and Mr. Helmer

   c. Allude to the chid-like excitement for Christmas

   d. Foreshadow misfortune

35. Which of the following does not contribute to Nora's characterization?

   a. Paying the porter generously

   b. Giving instructions for the Christmas tree to Helen

   c. Mr. Helmer's pet-names for his wife

   d. Laying her parcels on the table

36. The description of the Helmers' home tells the reader that:

   a. They are not very rich

   b. They are a progressive family

   c. They are Christian

   d. They are a well-educated, upper-middle class family

The Civil War

Questions 37 - 40 refer to the following passage.

The Civil War began on April 12, 1861. The first shots of the Civil War were fired in Fort Sumter, South Carolina. Even though more American lives were lost in the Civil War than in any other war, not one person died on that first day. The war began because eleven Southern states seceded from the Union and tried to start their own government, The Confederate States of America.

Why did the states secede? The issue of slavery was a primary cause of the Civil War. The eleven southern states relied heavily on their slaves to foster their farming and plantation lifestyles. The northern states, many of whom had already abolished slavery, did not feel that the southern states should have slaves. The north wanted to free all the slaves and President Lincoln's goal was to both end slavery and preserve the Union. He had Congress declare war on the Confederacy on April 14, 1862. For four long, blood soaked years, the North and South fought.

From 1861 to mid 1863, it seemed as if the South would win this war. However, on July 1, 1863, an epic three day battle was waged on a field in Gettysburg, Pennsylvania. Gettysburg is remembered for being one of the bloodiest battles in American history. At the end of the three days, the North turned the tide of the war in their favor. The North then went onto dominate the South for the remainder of the war. A famous episode is General Sherman's "March to The Sea," where he famously led the Union Army through Georgia and the Carolinas, burning and destroying everything in their path.

In 1865, the Union army invaded and captured the Confederate capital of Richmond Virginia. Robert E. Lee, leader of the Confederacy surrendered to General Ulysses S. Grant, leader of the Union forces, on April 9, 1865. The Civil War was over and the Union was preserved.

37. What does secede mean?

    a. To break away from

    b. To accomplish

    c. To join

    d. To lose

38. Which of the following statements summarizes a FACT from the passage?

    a. Congress declared war and then the Battle of Fort Sumter began.

    b. Congress declared war after shots were fired at Fort Sumter.

    c. President Lincoln was pro slavery

    d. President Lincoln was at Fort Sumter with Congress

39. Which event finally led the Confederacy to surrender?

    a. The battle of Gettysburg

    b. The battle of Bull Run

    c. The invasion of the confederate capital of Richmond

    d. Sherman's March to the Sea

40. What does the word abolish as used in this passage mean?

    a. To ban

    b. To polish

    c. To support

    d. To destroy

Mathematics - Parts I and II

1. Brad has agreed to buy everyone a Coke. Each drink costs $1.89, and there are 5 friends. Estimate Brad's cost.

    a. $7
    b. $8
    c. $10
    d. $12

2. $c = 4$, $n = 5$ and $x = 3$. Then $2cnx/2n =$?

    a. 12
    b. 50
    c. 8
    d. 21

3. What fraction of $1500 is $75?

    a. 1/14
    b. 3/5
    c. 7/10
    d. 1/20

4. Estimate 16 x 230.

    a. 31,000
    b. 301,000
    c. 3,100
    d. 3,000,000

5. Below is the attendance for a class of 45.

Day	Number of Absent Students
Monday	5
Tuesday	9
Wednesday	4
Thursday	10
Friday	6

What is the average attendance for the week?

   a. 88%

   b. 85%

   c. 81%

   d. 77%

6. John purchased a jacket at a 7% discount. He had a membership which gave him an additional 2% discount on the discounted price. If he paid $425, what is the retail price of the jacket?

   a. $460

   b. $466

   c. $466

   d. $472

7. 40% of a number is equal to 90. What is the half of the number?

   a. 18

   b. 112.5

   c. 225

   d. 120

8. 1/4 + 3/10 =

   a. 9/10

   b. 11/20

   c. 7/15

   d. 3/40

9. A map uses a scale of 1:2,000   How much distance on the ground is 5.2 inches on the map if the scale is in inches?

   a. 100,400

   b. 10,500

   c. 10,400

   d. 1,400

10. A shop sells a piece of industrial equipment for $545. If 15% of the cost was added to the price as value-added tax, what is the actual cost of the equipment?

    a. $490.40

    b. $473.91

    c. $505.00

    d. $503.15

11. What is 0.27 + 0.33 expressed as a fraction?

    a. 3/6

    b. 4/7

    c. 3/5

    d. 2/7

12. 5 men have to share a load weighing 10 kg 550 g equally among themselves. How much weight will each man have to carry?

    a. 900 g

    b. 1.5 kg

    c. 3 kg

    d. 2 kg 110 g

13. A square lawn has an area of 62,500 square meters. What is the cost of building fence around it at a rate of $5.5 per meter?

    a. $4,000

    b. $5,500

    c. $4,500

    d. $5,000

14. A mother is 7 times older than her child. In 25 years, her age will be double that of her child. How old is the mother now?

    a. 35

    b. 33

    c. 30

    d. 25

15. If a discount of 20% is given for a desk and Mark saves $45, how much did he pay for the desk?

a. $225
b. $160
c. $180
d. $210

16. In a grade 8 exam, students are asked to divide a number by 3/2, but a student mistakenly multiplied the number by 3/2 and the answer is 5 more than the required one. What was the number?

a. 4
b. 5
c. 6
d. 8

17. Divide 243 by 3^3

a. 243
b. 11
c. 9
d. 27

18. Solve the following equation 4(y + 6) = 3y + 30

a. y = 20
b. y = 6
c. y = 30/7
d. y = 30

19. Divide $x^2 - y^2$ by x - y.

a. x - y
b. x + y
c. xy
d. y - x

20. Solve for x if, $10^2 \times 100^2 = 1000^x$

    a. x = 2
    b. x = 3
    c. x = -2
    d. x = 0

21. Given polynomials $A = -2x^4 + x^2 - 3x$, $B = x^4 - x^3 + 5$ and $C = x^4 + 2x^3 + 4x + 5$, find $A + B - C$.

    a. $x^3 + x^2 + x + 10$
    b. $-3x^3 + x^2 - 7x + 10$
    c. $-2x^4 - 3x^3 + x^2 - 7x$
    d. $-3x^4 + x^3 + 2 - 7x$

22. Solve the inequality: $(x - 6)^2 \geq x^2 + 12$

    a. $[2, +\infty)$
    b. $(2, +\infty)$
    c. $(-\infty, 2]$
    d. $(12, +\infty)$

23. Divide $x^3 - 3x^2 + 3x - 1$ by $x - 1$.

    a. $x^2 - 1$
    b. $x^2 + 1$
    c. $x^2 - 2x + 1$
    d. $x^2 + 2x + 1$

24. Express 9 x 9 x 9 in exponential form and standard form.

    a. $9^3 = 719$
    b. $9^3 = 629$
    c. $9^3 = 729$
    d. $10^3 = 729$

25. Using the factoring method, solve the quadratic equation: $x^2 - 5x - 6 = 0$

    a. -6 and 1
    b. -1 and 6
    c. 1 and 6
    d. -6 and -1

26. Divide 0.524 by 10^3

   a. 0.0524
   b. 0.000524
   c. 0.00524
   d. 524

27. Factor the polynomial $x^3y^3 - x^2y^8$.

   a. $x^2y^3(x - y^5)$
   b. $x^3y^3(1 - y^5)$
   c. $x^2y^2(x - y^6)$
   d. $xy^3(x - y^5)$

28. Find the solution for the following linear equation: $5x/2 = (3x + 24)/6$.

   a. -1
   b. 0
   c. 1
   d. 2

29. $3^2 \times 3^5$

   a. 3^{17}
   b. 3^5
   c. 4^8
   d. 3^7

30. Solve the system, if a is some real number:

$ax + y = 1$
$x + ay = 1$

   a. (1, a)
   b. (1/a + 1, 1)
   c. (1/(a + 1), 1/(a + 1))
   d. (a, 1/a + 1)

31. Solve $3^8 \div 3^5$

   a. 3^3
   b. 3^5
   c. 3^6

d. 3^4

32. Solve the linear equation: 3(x + 2) - 2(1 - x) = 4x + 5

   a. -1
   b. 0
   c. 1
   d. 2

33. Simplify the following expression: $3x^a + 6a^x - x^a + (-5a^x) - 2x^a$

   a. $a^x + x^a$
   b. $a^x - x^a$
   c. a^x
   d. x^a

34. Add polynomials $-3x^2 + 2x + 6$ and $-x^2 - x - 1$.

   a. $-2x^2 + x + 5$
   b. $-4x^2 + x + 5$
   c. $-2x^2 + 3x + 5$
   d. $-4x^2 + 3x + 5$

35. 10^4 is not equal to which of the following?

   a. 100,000
   b. 10 x 10 x 10 x 10
   c. $10^2 \times 10^2$
   d. 10,000

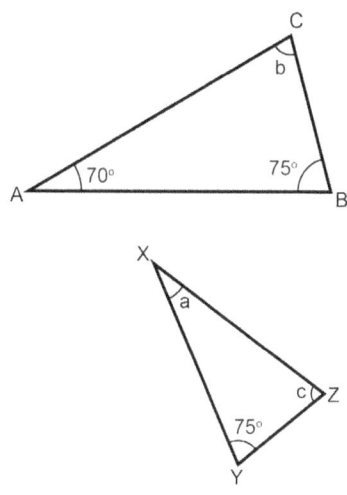

36. What are the respective values of a, b & c if both triangles are similar?

   a. 70°, 70°, 35°
   b. 70°, 35°, 70°
   c. 35°, 35°, 35°
   d. 70°, 75°, 35°

37. Consider 2 triangles, ABC and A'B'C', where:

   BC = B'C'
   AC = A'C'
   RA = RA'

   Are these 2 triangles congruent?

   a. Yes
   b. No
   c. Not enough information

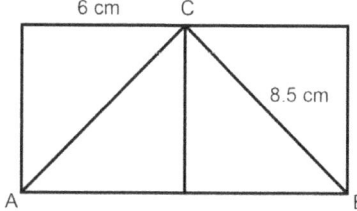

Note: Figure not drawn to scale

38. Assuming the 2 quadrangles are identical rectangles, what is the perimeter of △ABC in the above shape?

    a. 25.5 cm

    b. 27 cm

    c. 30 cm

    d. 29 cm

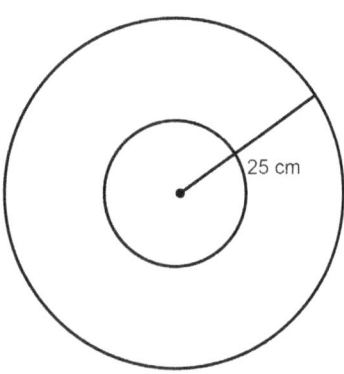

Note: figure not drawn to scale

39. What is the distance traveled by the wheel above, when it makes 175 revolutions?

    a. 87.5 π m

    b. 875 π m

    c. 8.75 π m

    d. 8750 π m

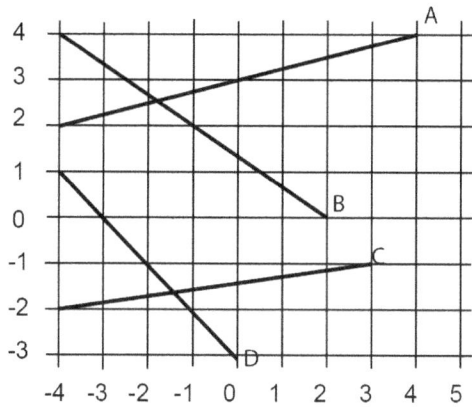

40. Which of the lines above represents the equation 2y − x = 4?

    a. A
    b. B
    c. C
    d. D

41. Find the sides of a right triangle whose sides are consecutive numbers.

    a. 1, 2, 3
    b. 2, 3, 4
    c. 3, 4, 5
    d. 4, 5, 6

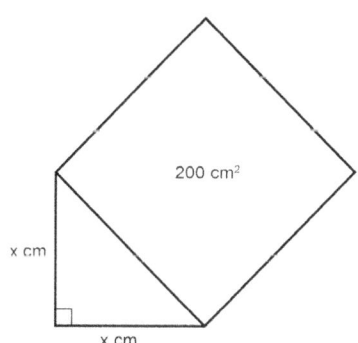

Note: figure not drawn to scale

42. Assuming the quadrangle is square, what is the length of the sides in the triangle above?

    a. 10
    b. 20
    c. 100
    d. 40

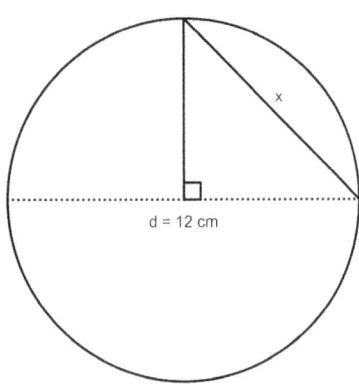

Note: figure not drawn to scale

43. Calculate the length of side x.

    a. 6.46
    b. 8.48
    c. 3.6
    d. 6.4

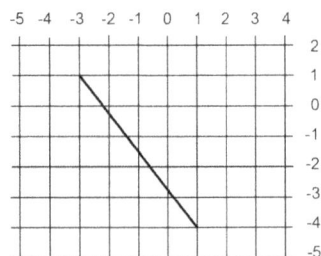

44. What is the slope of the line shown above?

    a. 5/4
    b. -4/5
    c. -5/4
    d. -4/5

45. The inner angles of a triangle are given as x + 20, 3x − 10 and 8x + 50. Find the difference between the smallest and the largest angles.

    a. 65

    b. 75

    c. 110

    d. 150

46. How many different ways can a reader choose 3 books out of 4, ignoring the order of selection?

    a. 3

    b. 4

    c. 9

    d. 12

47. Smith and Simon are playing a card game. Smith will win if a card drawn from a deck of 52 is either a 7 or a diamond, and Simon will win if the drawn card is an even number. Which statement is more likely to be correct?

    a. Simon will win more games.

    b. Smith will win more games.

    c. They have same winning probability.

    d. A decision cannot be made from the provided data.

48. In a museum, there are 250 visitors. An interviewer asks 50 people the number of days they visit museums per year as shown below.

# of days museum visited per year	# of visitors interviewed
5	12
3	18
12	8
20	2
4	10

Based on the data, what is the most reasonable estimate for the number of visitors who visit museums 20 days in a year?

    a. 2

    b. 8

    c. 10

    d. 12

49. There are six people planning to sit on a bench. Three of them want to sit side-by-side. How many possible seating arrangements are there?

a. 96

b. 120

c. 144

d. 720

50. In an exhibition area, there are 100 bulbs and 9 of them are damaged. 12 bulbs are chosen randomly. What is the probability to choose exactly 3 damaged bulbs? Round your answer to the nearest hundredths.

a. 0.03

b. 0.08

c. 0.11

d. 0.18

Language Arts - Writing

Curiosity's Mission

Questions 1 - 4 refer to the following passage

Mankind's thirst for knowledge about ourselves and the universe has always been insatiable, making curiosity a driving force for human advances through history. [1] Not only that, human curiosity and creativity have created countless works of fiction that speculate about future discoveries. [2]

Our neighboring planet Mars, for example, has long led scientists and writers to generate stories about living on the Red Planet. [3] Serious endeavors in science and technology are motivated by our never-ending questions. [4] So far, NASA has carried out several exploratory missions to Mars and the rover robot Curiosity is the latest and most sophisticated. [5]

Curiosity was launched in late November 2011 from Cape Canaveral Air Force Station in Florida. [6] It successfully landed on Mars on August 6, 2012 searching for evidence of life. [7] The car sized robot, weighing about a ton, is equipped with all the technical capacities to carry out its mission to explore our neighbor for biological, geological and geochemical traces of life. [8] It will also test the Martian soil and surface to collect data about its planetary evolution and surface radiation. [9]

Curiosity has been engineered with cutting-edge technologies worth over 2.5 billion US dollars. [10] The most incredible component of the rover is the on-board science lab. [11] Apart from that, it consists of a communications system that allows transmission of commands to the rover from the control centre at NASA, enabling direct control of the robot's activities on the surface of the Red Planet. [12] The Curiosity rover has a number of mounted cameras which assists navigation, as well as capturing images from the Martian surface and transmitting them back to Earth. [13]

1. How would you re-write sentence 1?

a. No changes

b. Mankind's thirst for knowledge has always been insatiable, making curiosity a driving factor for human advances through history.

c. Mankind's thirst for knowledge is insatiable, making curiosity a driving factor for human advances through history.

d. Humankind's thirst for knowledge is insatiable, making curiosity a driving force in advances throughout history.

2. Which sentence in the third paragraph is least relevant to the main idea of the third paragraph?

a. 6

b. 8

c. 9

d. 10

3. Which of the following changes would focus attention on the main idea of the last paragraph?

a. To achieve its goals, Curiosity has been engineered with cutting-edge technologies worth over 2.5 billion US dollars.

b. Because a lot of funding was available for this project, Curiosity has been engineered with cutting-edge technologies worth over 2.5 billion US dollars.

c. As there is no guarantee that it will succeed in its mission, Curiosity has been engineered with cutting-edge technologies worth over 2.5 billion US dollars.

d. NASA's scientific data is so reliable that, being assured of no risk of failure in the mission, Curiosity has been engineered with cutting-edge technologies worth over 2.5 billion US dollars.

4. Which of the following is/are needed in sentence 5?

a. So far, "NASA" has carried out several exploration missions to Mars and the rover robot Curiosity is the latest and most sophisticated of all.

b. So far, NASA has carried out several exploratory missions to Mars and the rover robot Curiosity is the latest and most sophisticated of all.

c. So far, NASA has carried out several exploration missions to Mars and the rover robot -Curiosity- is the latest and most sophisticated of all.

d. So far, NASA has carried out several exploratory missions to Mars and the rover robot "Curiosity" is the latest and most sophisticated of all.

Green Energy from Olive Oil

Questions 5 - 8 refer to the following passage

The debate over developing sustainable energy sources have been very active in the past two decades. [1] With continued concern over global climate change, environmentalists are urging governments for lowering their dependence on fossil fuels in order for ensuring reduced carbon emission into the atmosphere. [2] Consequently, governments worldwide are turning their attention to the search for non-emissive sources of energy. [3] Renewable substitutes under extensive research are solar power, wind, geothermal energy and harnessing energy from ocean waves. [4]

While the search for environment friendly energy sources is already under way, developing these alternatives at a reasonable cost is a major challenge. [5] No cost-effective replacement for fossil fuels has yet been found. [6] However, recent years have seen remarkable progress in the field of solar energy. [7] Ted Sargent, a Professor at University of Toronto, Canada, has discovered that olive oil has the capacity to capture solar radiation and emit electrons resulting in an electric current. [8] This is a major discovery in the solar power generation industry as it offers a cheap source of harnessing the Sun's energy. [9]

Oleic acid, the main ingredient of olive oil, absorbs infrared radiation is the major component of the Sun's radiation reaching the Earth. [10] The discovery is significant because so far, no attempt has been made to use the abundant infrared radiation we receive throughout the year. [11] Capturing this heat wave radiation, along with the photons that are present in sunlight, increases the efficiency of the solar cells that are already being manufactured commercially. [12] And to make it possible, Professor Sargent has developed a new kind of solar cell called "quantum dots," tiny cells made from gels of tin, bismuth, lead, sulphur and selenium mixed with extra pure olive oil. [13] The resulting ink-like crystal absorbs both photons and infrared radiation and has the capacity to transmit electrons and produce a current. [14]

This new method of capturing the Sun's energy is considered a breakthrough in the solar power industry as it offers cheaper alternatives to the existing use of silicon crystals which are costly to manufacture. [15] And although the invention is yet to prove its efficiency, a lot of funding has already been dedicated to further research. [16]

5. What sentence from the passage is an example of a sentence fragment?

    a. 6
    b. 10
    c. 11
    d. 13

6. Which of the following sentences should be deleted to reduce redundancy?

   a. 5
   b. 6
   c. 9
   d. 15

7. Which of the following changes are needed in sentence 10?

   a. Oleic acid, the main ingredient of olive oil, absorbs infrared radiation is the major component of the Sun's radiation reaching the Earth.

   b. Oleic acid, the main ingredient of olive oil, absorbs infrared radiation, which is the major component of the Sun's radiation reaching the Earth.

   c. Oleic acid, the main ingredient of olive oil absorbs infrared radiation that is the major component of the Sun's radiation reaching the Earth.

   d. Oleic acid, the main ingredient of olive oil, absorbs infrared radiation what is the major component of the Sun's radiation reaching the Earth.

8. Which of the following changes are needed in sentence 2?

   a. With continued concern over global climate change, environmentalists are urging governments to lowering their dependence on fossil fuels to ensuring reduced carbon emission into the atmosphere.

   b. With continued concern over global climate change, environmentalists are urging governments lower their dependence on fossil fuels in order for ensuring reduced carbon emission into the atmosphere.

   c. With continued concern over global climate change, environmentalists are urging governments to lower their dependence on fossil fuels in order for ensuring reduced carbon emission into the atmosphere.

   d. With continued concern over global climate change, environmentalists are urging governments to lower their dependence on fossil fuels to ensure reduced carbon emission into the atmosphere.

Hunting Lost Cities from Space

Questions 9 - 12 refer to the following passage

Satellite imaging has become widespread with improvements in telecommunication over the past two decades. [1] Communication satellites in orbit around the Earth have enabled large-scale mapping of the planet's surface which has become freely available thanks to technology giants like Google. [2] Satellite mapping has opened up new possibilities in diverse fields of science and technology. [3]

The key feature of the new tool, according to Professor Sarah Parcak, who discovered many cities, temples and pyramids covered under sands and sediment; is that it offers a wider perspective in size and scale of the location under study. [4] Along with the visual information that the satellite images provide, numerous details about the sites can be obtained from infrared (IR) and gravitational field images. [5] This information, coupled with conventional on-site procedures, are vital for archeology. [6]

IR data collected from satellite imaging provide clues about the activities of humans living in the contemporary times of their civilizations- including their agriculture, vegetation, structures, habitation roads and much more. [7] This type of information is derived from IR imagery which detects IR radiation present in sunlight as it is reflected by the Earth. [8] Different points in a civilization reflect IR radiation in different proportions, revealing the contrast between different areas and provide detailed insight about the causes of these differing heat signatures. [9]

9. Which of the following changes in sentence 6 would focus attention on the main idea of the second paragraph?

a. These information, along with a supply of some heavy machinery, will help the excavation of every archeological site accomplished within a short period of time.

b. This information, coupled with conventional on-site procedures, help archaeologists plan their excavation carefully and efficiently.

c. Such details are valuable records of ancient history and are essential assets of any civilization.

d. Such details, unfortunately, are available to archeological firms who are willing to invest a lot of money on putting satellites into orbit.

10. Which of the following sentences should be modified to reduce redundancy?

a. 7
b. 8
c. 9
d. 10

11. Which of the following sentences, if inserted after sentence 3, would best illustrate the main idea of the passage?

a. The application has inspired archaeologists to use it for searching for the traces of ancient civilizations and other anthropological dynamics.

b. The new technology will be very useful for excavation of archeological sites.

c. The application is a breakthrough for archeology and anthropology since it will allows us to zoom into the distant past to look for lost civilizations.

d. The concept has many positive aspects in the field of archeological science and excavation.

12. Which of the following change(s) is/are needed to sentence 4?

a. The key feature of the new tool- according to Professor Sarah Parcak, who discovered many cities, temples and pyramids covered under sands and sediment- is that it offers a wider perspective in size and scale of the location under study.

b. The key feature of the new tool- according to Professor Sarah Parcak- who discovered many cities, temples and pyramids covered under sands and sediment, is that it offers a wider perspective in size and scale of the location under study.

c. The key feature of the new tool according to Professor Sarah Parcak- who discovered many cities, temples and pyramids covered under sands and sediment- is that it offers a wider perspective in size and scale of the location under study.

d. The key feature of the new tool, according to Professor Sarah Parcak- who discovered many cities, temples and pyramids covered under sands and sediment is that it offers a wider perspective in size and scale of the location under study.

Malala's Dream

Questions 13 - 16 refer to the following passage

Every child wants to attend school where they can interact, communicate with others and learn the art of life; discover themselves, socialize, have fun and make friends. [1] When they reach adolescence, children start framing their identity by making choices for their future career. [2] It was not so different with Malala Yousafzawi, who was an exemplary student and a responsible daughter since early childhood. [3] She always wanted to be a doctor, and upon entering her secondary school, started to work toward her dream. [4]

However, for girls in such a conservative society, where women's rights have little or no value, achieving such a lofty goal is pretty much impossible, not to mention the many other challenges of living in an unstable country like Pakistan. [5] Add to that an extreme conservative mentality that interferes in anyone's life whose world views do not match theirs. [6]

Malala's dreams were encountered with the obstacles that were also crushing the aspirations of millions of other young girls like her. [7] But unlike others who feared suppression and defamation, Malala stood up for her rights and looked to overcome the challenges facing her. [8] And while doing so, advanced the struggles of all girls like her with similar ambitions. [9] Persuaded by her father, who is a professional educator, she decided to give up her ambition of becoming a doctor and work for the education and establishment of girls in Mingora, a suburban town in Swat District. [10] In doing so, she had to sacrifice her own dreams, believing that at least millions other dreams will be fulfilled at the expense of just one. [1]1

Malala become a professional educator- campaigning for education for girls, side-by-side with her charismatic father who sponsored schools in the district where they live. [12] In the process, she somehow managed to uphold the courage to address the issues facing education for girls and proposed solutions for them. [13] Her sense of leadership soon made her popular among the local girls, and their parents, who supported her in fulfilling the educational rights of girls. [14] At the same time, however, Malala became the target of extremists. [15] She was shot in the head in an assassination attempt while she was returning home from school. [16]

13. Which sentence is not consistent with the author's purpose?

  a. 9
  b. 11
  c. 12
  d. 13

14. Which of the following changes in sentence 10 would focus attention on the main idea of the second paragraph?

  a. Persuaded by her father, who is a professional educator, she sufficed in bearing a mediocre aim of becoming a simple schoolteacher and work for the education and establishment of girls in her locality, Mingora, a suburban town in Swat District.

  b. Instructed by her father, who is a professional educator, she decided to give up her ambition of becoming a doctor and work for the education and establishment of girls in her locality, Mingora, a suburban town in Swat District.

  c. Inspired by her father, who is a professional educator himself, she decided to work for the education and establishment of girls in her locality, Mingora, a suburban town in Swat District.

  d. Contrary to her father, who is a professional educator, she persisted in becoming a doctor and vetoed to leave her father if he turned out to be an obstacle.

15. Which of the following sentences, if inserted before sentence 11, would best illustrate the main idea of the passage?

  a. She wishes to become a politician and aims to serve the women and girls of her community and establish their fundamental rights.

  b. She aims to become the President of Pakistan and remove all the obstacles facing women and girls by one command.

  c. She set her new ambition to be a lawyer and sue the people who oppose girls' education under human rights jurisdiction.

  d. She wishes to set her own network of women community and tackle the people who refuse their education rights with guerilla warfare and violence.

16. Which of the following changes are needed in sentence 7?

a. Malala's dreams were countered with the obstacles that were also crushing the aspirations of millions of other young girls like her.

b. Malala's dreams were met with the obstacles that were also destroying the aspirations of millions of other young girls like her.

c. Malala's dreams encountered the same obstacles that were also crushing the aspirations of millions of other young girls like her.

d. Malala's dreams were confronted with the obstacles that were also shattering the aspirations of millions of other young girls like her.

Scam City Istanbul

Questions 17 - 20 refer to the following passage

I have been doing this for twenty five years! [1] This is my job; to make profit for the pub I work for and for myself. [2] I know foreigners here are looking for company; so why not make some bucks out of from it! [3] They are tourists and they are willing to spend their money on good company and quality time. [4] So, what I offer is my time. [5] And I earn a commission from the pub. [6]

Of course, you need to track the right tourist right from the beginning and it is easy for me to know who is new to the city, or at least who is new to this Istiklal Avenue. [7] I know this city like the back of my hand. [8] It is our city. [9] It is easy to tell who is a newcomer and where he stays. [10] We even know their hotel room. [11] I am not the only one making a living from this job. [12] I have two hundred fifty colleagues in this avenue- all equipped with the latest tracking systems. [13]

All we have to do is to wait for them to come out of their private-premises and once they are onto the streets we are non-stop after them. [14] We watch where they go and what they do. [15] What they buy and what they eat until we get to meet them in the evening. [16] That is when we make our income. [17] A single drink does the trick. [18]

We are all known to the bartender, so when we enter the bar with our customer he knows which drink to offer me and which to offer my client. [19] This way, we do not get drunk. [20] My job is to talk my client into having at least half his drink. [21] And that is what I am good at. [22] I know it is false company, but I do it with perfection. [23] I offer him conversation and company, ask if he needs anything, wants anything and stuff like that - and make him consume his drink. [24] The rest is up to the waiter. [25] The waiter politely presents the astronomical bill that has nothing to do with me. [26] After all, to him, I am just another guy like him looking to have a good drink at a bar in Istanbul! [27]

17. Which sentence from the passage is an example of a sentence fragment?

   a. 12
   b. 14
   c. 16
   d. 22

18. Which of the following change(s) is/are needed in sentence 14?

   a. All we have to do is to wait for them to come out of their private premises and once they are onto the streets we are non-stop after them.
   b. All we have to do is to wait for them to come out of their private-premises and once they are onto the streets we are nonstop after them.
   c. All we have to do is to wait for them to come out of their private premises and once they are onto the streets we are nonstop after them.
   d. No change is necessary.

19. Which of the following sentences, if inserted before sentence 27, would best illustrate the main idea of the passage?

   a. It is the waiter and the bill that strikes him like a thunderbolt, not me!
   b. It is the waiter and the bill that outrages him, not me!
   c. It is the waiter that strikes him with the bill, not me!
   d. It is the waiter who robs him and takes away all his money, not me!

20. Which of the following sentences contains non-standard usage?

   a. 3
   b. 4
   c. 12
   d. 13

The Future of Augmented Reality

Questions 21 - 24 refer to the following passage

In just a few years, Facebook has became popular worldwide, bringing with it other social media sites like Twitter. [1] Telecommunications has entered its third generation, and with unprecedented marketing from companies around the world, smart phones have become a 'must-have' accessory for everyone in the developed world. [2] In 2010, Information Technology experienced a renaissance called "the Apps Revolution"- a phenomena that is generating applications for every computing device imaginable, in every available language. [3] This has solicited application developers to explore more avant-garde concepts that offer the capacity to be integrated into their applications. [4] Developers integrated augmented reality into their applications and created applications like

MapLens, SiteLens, Layar and the AR game ARhrrrr! [5]

These applications are only a few demonstrations of the true potential of augmented reality. [6] They are, in fact, just the "tip of the iceberg" to developer firms like Layar, who are getting ready to release APPs that do real-time underwater exploration. [7] And more and more APP developers are joining this race chasing after the huge profits available in this new industry. [8]

Since science and technology are interrelated, advances in one field directly affect the other. [9] For example; progress in visual elements technology lead to development of programs with more visual elements that required faster processors to run. [10] So, hardware must be upgraded to keep up with the new generation software. [11] This, in turn, results in more investment being allocated to material sciences to create new materials to engineer and manufacture faster processor chips. [12]

Knowledge in the field is rapidly expanding, leading rival multinationals to invest in new fields of science and create applications similar to Layar, Google Glass, Junaio and many others. [13]

21. Which of the following change(s) to sentence 5 would focus attention on the main idea of the first paragraph?

a. Developers incorporated augmented reality with their applications and created applications like MapLens, SiteLens, Layar and the AR game ARhrrrr!

b. Augmented reality has turned out to be one such idea that soon was incorporated into applications like MapLens, SiteLens, Layar and the AR game ARhrrrr!

c. Augmented reality offered intense opportunity to developers in this regard.

d. Augmented reality started to fuel the blooming apps industry.

22. Which of the following sentences, if inserted after sentence 8, would best illustrate the main idea of the passage?

a. The "Application Revolution" definitely has a bright future for scientists.

b. Augmented reality, therefore, bears the challenge of inseminating many unknown dimensions and poses the threat of drowning underwater.

c. The so-called "Apps Revolution," therefore, is likely to be one of the driving factors orchestrating the rapid advancements in the AR sector and thus has the capability to shape its future.

d. Application Revolution certainly contains the energy of youth that will change the world with the blessings in augmented reality.

23. Which of the following changes are needed in sentence 4?

a. This has lead application developers to explore more avant-garde concepts that offer the capacity to be integrated into their applications.

b. This has tempted application developers to explore more avant-garde concepts that offer the possibility to be integrated into their applications.

c. This has caused application developers to explore more avant-garde concepts that offer the potential to be integrated into their applications.

d. This aftermath caused application developers to explore more avant-garde concepts that offer the capacity to be integrated into their applications.

24. Which of the following change(s) is/are needed in sentence 12?

a. This, in turn, resulted in more investment being allocated to material sciences to create new materials for engineering and manufacturing faster processor chips.

b. This, in turn, resulted in more investment to be allocated for material sciences to create new materials for engineering and manufacturing faster processor chips.

c. This, in turn, resulted in more investment to be allocated to material sciences in order for creating new materials to engineer and manufacture faster processor chips.

d. This, in turn, resulted in more investment to be allocated to material sciences in order for creating new materials for engineering and manufacturing faster processor chips.

The Legend of Alexandre Pato

Questions 25 - 28 refer to the following passage

Although well-known among his fans for the "duck dance" he performs after scoring, Alexandre Rodrigues da Silva has earned the name "Pato" for his ducky skills with the ball he uses to out-class his opponent in the field. [1] Already a promising talent in his early teens, Pato came into the limelight at the 2006 Club World Cup after becoming the youngest player, at 17 years and 102 days, to score a goal in a FIFA organized event- a feat previously held for decades by his legendary compatriot Pele. [2]

Alexandre started his soccer career at the age of 16 in the Brazilian club Sports Club, Internacional, from Rio Grande do Sul, and soon established himself as the main striker (forward). [3] Not only that; being the youngest recruit and the point of focus of his team fans, he led Internacional to their first title in the Recopa Sudamericana with his goals in the 2005-06 Season. [4]

At the age of only 17, Pato was transferred to the Italian giant AC Milan, and after a year, became the team's top scorer, with 18 goals in the 2008-09 Season. [5] The same year, he made his first international appearance and triumphed over Pele, once again by scoring the fastest goal in an international debut by a Brazilian. [6] The following season, Pato won the 2009 Series A Young Player of the Year award. [7] Still a teenager, he became the talk of Europe alongside the likes of Cristiano Ronaldo, Lionel Messi and Kaka. [8]

With brilliant performances, and an even a brighter future ahead, he suffered a serious hamstring injury in the 2010-11 Season. 9 A torn ligament kept him away from the field for a long time. [10] Despite this, he made one or two appearances, helping the much weakened Italian side hold their ground in the Italian Series A after the transfer of his countryman Kaka to the Spanish team, Real Madrid. [11]

Pato made a comeback from the injuries that disabled him in the 2011-12 Season, scoring the fifth fastest goal in any Champions' League encounter within 24 seconds of play against the Spanish powerhouse Barcelona. [12] However, his misfortunes seemed to stick, and he had to quit the season with another ligament injury. [13] Making a second return to San Siro in the following August, the young and valiant striker continued his glittering performance inspite of regular injuries in the 2012-13 Season. [14]

Lately, though, concerns over his future have surfaced due to his insistence on playing with un-recovered injuries which has lead Milan authorities to transfer him to a club where the load is lighter. [15] Pato was thereafter transferred back to Brazil to the Corinthians- one of the leading clubs in South America, full of contemporary and emerging stars like Carlos Tevez, Julio Cesar and Renato Augusto. [16]

With a lighter load in a home club where he is surrounded by native faces, Alexandre is expected to recover from his troubling injuries quickly. [17] After his long-awaited return, his fans will certainly look forward to his "duck-dance." [18]

25. Which of the following changes to sentence 7 would focus attention on the main idea of the second paragraph?

    a. The following season, Pato accomplished what he was yearning for throughout his life by winning the 2009 Series A Young Player of the Year award.

    b. The following season, Pato conquered Europe by winning the 2009 Series A Young Player of the Year award.

    c. The following season, Pato won the 2009 Series A Young Player of the Year award and proved his worth.

    d. The following season, Pato accomplished his first European ambition by winning the 2009 Series A Young Player of the Year award.

26. Which of the following sentences should be adjusted to reduce redundancy?

    a. 9

    b. 12

    c. 13

    d. 14

27. Which of the following change(s) is/are needed in sentence 1?

a. He is well known among his fans for the "duck dance" he performs after scoring, but Alexandre Rodrigues da Silva has earned the name "Pato" for his ducky skills with the ball that he uses to outclass his opponent in the field.

b. Although well-known among his fans for the "duck-dance" he performs after scoring, Alexandre Rodrigues da Silva has earned the name "Pato" for his ducky skills with the ball that he uses to outclass his opponent in the field.

c. He is well known among his fans for the "duck-dance" he performs after scoring, but Alexandre Rodrigues da Silva has earned the name "Pato" for his ducky skills with the ball that he uses to out-class his opponent in the field.

d. He is well-known among his fans for the duck-dance he performs after scoring, but Alexandre Rodrigues da Silva has earned the name "Pato" for his ducky skills with the ball that he uses to out-class his opponent in the field.

28. Which of the following change(s) is/are needed in sentence 14?

a. Making a second return to San Siro in the following August, the young and valiant striker continued his glittering performance in-spite regular injuries in the 2012-13 Season.

b. Making a second return to San Siro in the following August, the young and valiant striker continued his glittering performance in spite of regular injuries in the 2012-13 Season.

c. Making a second return to San Siro in the following August, the young and valiant striker continued his glittering performance in spite of regular injuries in the 2012-13 Season.

d. Making a second return to San Siro in the following August, the young and valiant striker continued his glittering performance in-spite of regular injuries in the 2012-13 Season.

Spring in Bengali

Questions 29 - 32 refer to the following passage

The days get warmer and the cool nights shorter. [1] There is dryness in the air and a drowsiness that suggests an afternoon nap. [2] Spring in the Bengali calendar, from the middle of February to the middle of April, are the months of Phalgoon and Chaitra. [3]

In the early days of spring, the trees, bereft of the leaves, look gaunt and ungainly. [4] But soon there are green shoots and the trees are covered with luxurious greenery. [5] Spring may witness the arrival of season's first rain and a nor'wester. [6]

The mango trees that start to spread flowers at the end of winter, are covered in spring. [7] Sapodia, curd fruit that have already arrived in late winter ripen in spring: and so is jujube. [8] Star fruit, whose season is from April to October, starts arriving in spring. [9] Rose apple also arrives in April. [10] Farmers grow sweet potato and peanuts in sandy soil in the spring. [11] Ironically, watermelon and jackfruit and litchis arrive no earlier than the middle of April! [12]

The dry season continues; the lakes, ponds and rivers dry up further. [13] Shing (stinging catfish), climbing perch, African catfish, and other smaller fish are easy to catch. [14] Some lakes and water ponds that dry up in the summer and turn into festival venues for children who race to scoop up the fish with bamboo baskets. [15]

29. Which sentence in the second paragraph is least relevant to the main idea of the second paragraph?

   a. 5

   b. 6

   c. 8

   d. 9

30. Which of the following changes to sentence 12 would focus attention on the main idea of the third paragraph?

   a. Ironically, watermelon and jackfruit and litchis arrive earlier than the middle of April!

   b. Interestingly, watermelon and jackfruit and litchis arrive no earlier than the middle of April!

   c. Surprisingly, even watermelon, jackfruit and litchis arrive by the middle of April!

   d. Unfortunately, watermelon and jackfruit and litchis arrive no earlier than the middle of April!

31. Which sentence is not consistent with the author's purpose?

   a. 12

   b. 16

   c. 13

   d. 14

32. Which of the following are needed in sentence 8?

   a. Sapodia and curd fruit that have already arrived in late winter ripen in spring: and does the jujube.

   b. Sapodia, curd fruit that have already arrived in late winter ripen in spring, and does the jujube.

   c. Sapodia and curd fruit that have already arrived in late winter ripen in spring- and so does the jujube.

   d. Sapodia, curd fruit that have already arrived in late winter ripen in spring; and so does the jujube.

What's in Curry Spice?

Questions 33 - 36 refer to the following passage

Its fragrance is distinct, yet many find the aroma in curry to be tasteless or even repugnant. [1] Still, many love any food cooked with this magical curry powder. [2] It has been an integral part of cuisine all over the world since ancient times and it is a common component of Ayurveda, the Indian traditional medicine. [3]

Curcumin, an extract from root turmeric, has been under extensive investigation in recent years due its remarkable healing abilities. [4] Turmeric, thought to have healing effects and health benefits for millennia, is a regular ingredient in spicy Indian diets. [5] Scientists claim that curcumin assists in killing cancerous cells and also prevents their expansion into neighboring healthy cells. [6] This natural compound has also been observed to reduce chemo-resistant cells which cannot be treated with existing techniques. [7] These results indicate that it will be a useful compound that will help in treating diseases like esophageal cancer. [8]

Curcumin also may prevent the death of brain cells after a stroke. [9] It does that by interfering in some of the reaction pathways which triggers the deactivation of normal cell functioning, helping brain cells remaining resistant to the aftermath of stroke in the hours following their experience. [10] This discovery has lead scientists to develop new treatments for dementia with compounds derived from the compound, due to its ability to help regenerate dying brain cells in dementia patients. [11]

The anti-oxidant property of curcumin is responsible for preventing further damage to living cells as well as acting as an intermediary in repairing existing damaged cells. [12] Repair and healing of the cell regeneration process by curcumin opens up new possibilities for treating arthritis as damaged bone cells are repaired by this powerful anti-oxidant molecule. [13] This will assist in the remedy and prevention of many bone diseases. [14]

33. Which sentence in the second paragraph is least relevant to the main idea of the second paragraph?

    a. 4
    b. 5
    c. 6
    d. 7

34. Which of the following sentences should be deleted to reduce redundancy?

    a. 4
    b. 6
    c. 7
    d. 8

35. Which of the following sentences, if inserted after sentence 3, would best illustrate the main idea of the passage?

a. Ayurveda is considered to possess magical powers that offer remedy for all kinds of pain.

b. The curry spice derived from powdered turmeric has proved itself to be useful in treating many diseases like cancer, arthritis and dementia.

c. Although curry powder is not consumed by many in America, as the following paragraphs point out, people should start adding the spice to their food from now on.

d. Curry spice is also mentioned ancient books for its amazing ability to cure uncommon diseases.

36. Which of the following changes are needed to sentence 10?

a. It does that by interfering in some of the reaction pathways which triggers the deactivation of normal cell functioning, helping brain cells remain resistant to the aftermath of stroke in the hours following their experience.

b. It does that by interfering in some of the reaction pathways which triggers the deactivation of normal cell functioning, helping brain cells to remain resistant to the aftermath of stroke in the hours following their experience.

c. It does this by interfering in some of the reaction pathways that trigger the deactivation of normal cell functioning, helping brain cells to remain resistant to the aftermath of stroke in the hours following their experience.

d. It does that by interfering in some of the reaction pathways that trigger the deactivation of normal cell functioning, helping brain cells to remain resistant to the aftermath of stroke in the hours following its experience.

Directions: Select the best choice to replace the underlined portion of the sentence.

37. If Joe had told me the truth, I wouldn't have been so angry.

a. No change is necessary

b. If Joe would have told me the truth, I wouldn't have been so angry.

c. I wouldn't have been so angry if Joe would have told the truth.

d. If Joe would have telled me the truth, I wouldn't have been so angry.

38. Although you may <u>not see nobody in the dark, it does not mean that not nobody</u> is there.

    a. Although you may not see nobody in the dark, it does not mean that nobody is there.

    b. Although you may not see anyone in the dark, it does not mean that not nobody is there.

    c. Although you may not see anyone in the dark, it does not mean that anyone is there.

    d. No change is necessary.

39. The Ford Motor Company was named for Henry Ford, <u>whom</u> had founded the company.

    a. The Ford Motor Company was named for Henry Ford, which had founded the company.

    b. The Ford Motor Company was named for Henry Ford, who founded the company.

    c. The Ford Motor Company was named for Henry Ford, whose had founded the company.

    d. No change is necessary.

40. Thomas Edison <u>will had been known</u> as the greatest inventor since he invented the light bulb, television, motion pictures, and phonograph.

    a. Thomas Edison has always been known as the greatest inventor since he invented the light bulb, television, motion pictures, and phonograph.

    b. Thomas Edison was always been known as the greatest inventor since he invented the light bulb, television, motion pictures, and phonograph.

    c. Thomas Edison must have had been always known as the greatest inventor since he invented the light bulb, television, motion pictures, and phonograph.

    d. No change is necessary.

41. The weatherman on Channel 6 said that this has been <u>the hottest summer</u> on record.

    a. The weatherman on Channel 6 said that this has been the most hotter summer on record

    b. The weatherman on Channel 6 said that this has been the most hottest summer on record

    c. The weatherman on Channel 6 said that this has been the hotter summer on record

    d. No change is necessary.

42. Although Joe is tall for his age, his brother Elliot is <u>the tallest of the two</u>.

   a. Although Joe is tall for his age, his brother Elliot is more tallest of the two.
   b. Although Joe is tall for his age, his brother Elliot is the tall the two.
   c. Although Joe is tall for his age, his brother Elliot is the taller of the two.
   d. No change is necessary

43. When KISS came to town, all the tickets <u>was sold out</u> before I could buy one.

   a. When KISS came to town, all the tickets will be sold out before I could buy one.
   b. When KISS came to town, all the tickets had been sold out before I could buy one.
   c. When KISS came to town, all the tickets were being sold out before I could buy one.
   d. No change is necessary.

44. The rules of most sports <u>has been</u> more complicated than we often realize.

   a. The rules of most sports are more complicated than we often realize.
   b. The rules of most sports is more complicated than we often realize.
   c. The rules of most sports was more complicated than we often realize.
   d. No change is necessary.

45. Neither of the Wright Brothers <u>had any doubts</u> that they would be successful with their flying machine.

   a. Neither of the Wright Brothers have any doubts that they would be successful with their flying machine.
   b. Neither of the Wright Brothers has any doubts that they would be successful with their flying machine.
   c. Neither of the Wright Brothers had any doubts that they would be successful with their flying machine.
   d. No change is necessary.

46. The Titanic <u>has already sunk</u> mere days into its maiden voyage.

   a. The Titanic will already sunk mere days into its maiden voyage.
   b. The Titanic already sank mere days into its maiden voyage.
   c. The Titanic sank mere days into its maiden voyage.
   d. No change is necessary.

47. To make chicken <u>soup; you</u> must first buy a chicken.

    a. To make chicken soup you must first buy a chicken.
    b. To make chicken soup you must first, buy a chicken.
    c. To make chicken soup, you must first buy a chicken.
    d. None of the choices are correct.

48. To travel around <u>the globe you have</u> to drive 25,000 miles.

    a. To travel around the globe, you have to drive 25000 miles.
    b. To travel around the globe, you have to drive, 25000 miles.
    c. None of the choices are correct.
    d. To travel around the globe, you have to drive 25,000 miles.

49. The dog loved chasing <u>bones; but never ate them:</u> it was running that he enjoyed.

    a. The dog loved chasing bones, but never ate them; it was running that he enjoyed.
    b. The dog loved chasing bones; but never ate them, it was running that he enjoyed.
    c. The dog loved chasing bones, but never ate them, it was running that he enjoyed.
    d. None of the choices are correct.

50. He had not paid the <u>rent, therefore,</u> the landlord changed the locks.

    a. None of the choices are correct.
    b. He had not paid the rent; therefore, the landlord changed the locks.
    c. He had not paid the rent, therefore; the landlord changed the locks.
    d. He had not paid the rent therefore, the landlord changed the locks.

Science

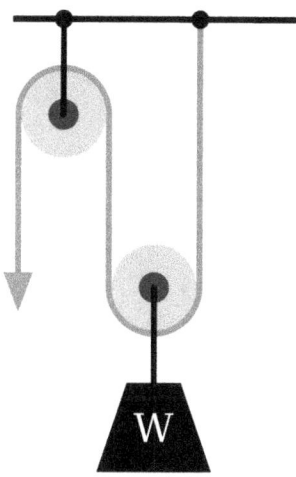

1. Consider the pulley arrangement above. If the weight is 100 pounds, how much force is required to lift it?

    a. 20 pounds

    b. 33 pounds

    c. 50 pounds

    d. 75 pounds

Population Dynamics - Beneficial Mutations

Questions 2 - 5 refer to the following passage and graph

Frequently mutations that cause changes in protein sequences can be harmful to an organism. However, on occasion, in a given environment, some mutations can have a positive effect, for example, it may allow a mutant organism to withstand particular environmental stresses better than wild-type organisms, or reproduce more quickly. In these cases, a mutation will tend to become more common in a population through natural selection.

In an experiment, random mutations were introduced into a vesicular stomatitis virus by site-directed mutagenesis, and the fitness of each mutant was compared with the ancestral type, the processed results can be seen below. A fitness of zero, less than one, one, more than one, respectively, indicates that mutations are lethal, deleterious, neutral, and advantageous.

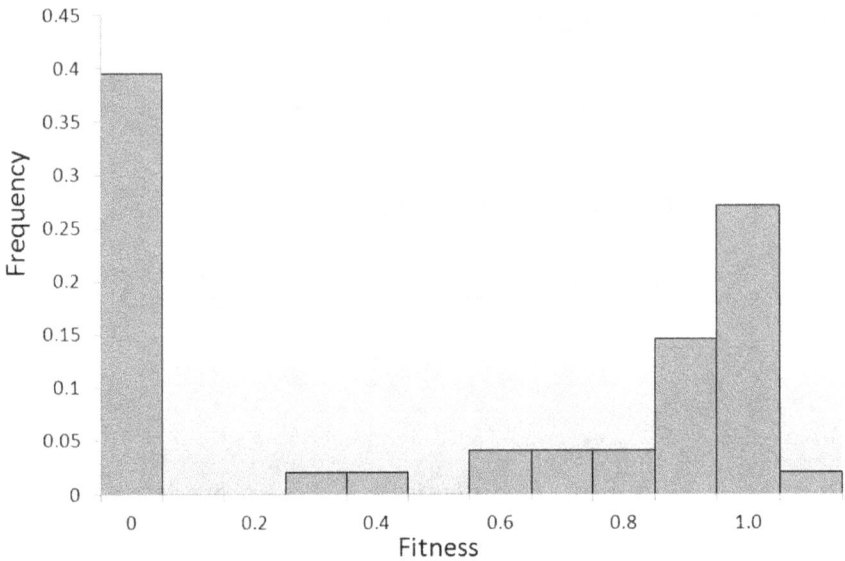

2. Which level of fitness is most frequent in the virus after introduction?

   a. Lethal
   b. Deleterious
   c. Neutral
   d. Advantageous

3. What is the total frequency of individuals with deleterious fitness?

   a. 2.8
   b. 0.33
   c. 0.4
   d. 5

4. Comment on the frequency of the mutation in the population, if it was left for several generations.

   a. The mutation will become more common in the population
   b. The mutation will become less common in the population
   c. The mutation will remain static in the population
   d. This mutation will cause the population to become extinct

5. Which of the following statements is true regarding this example of natural selection:

   a. Natural selection determines which trait (mutant or ancestral) will survive.

   b. Natural selection acts on the genotype of the virus

   c. Natural selection will determine the environment the virus is in.

   d. None of these

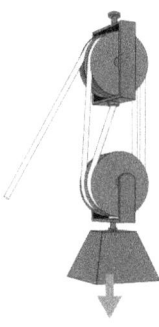

6. Consider the pulley arrangement above. If the weight is 200 pounds, how much force must be exerted downward on the rope?

   a. 200 pounds

   b. 100 pounds

   c. 50 pounds

   d. 25 pounds

7. Up-and-down or back-and-forth motion is called:

   a. Rotary motion

   b. Reciprocating motion

   c. Agitation motion

   d. Harmonic motion

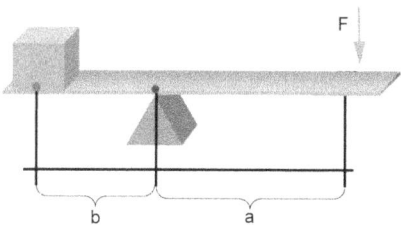

8. Consider the illustration above and the corresponding data:
Weight = W = 80 pounds
Distance from fulcrum to Weight = b = 10 feet
Distance from fulcrum to point where force is applied = a = 20 feet
How much force (F) must be applied to lift the weight?

  a. 80
  b. 40
  c. 20
  d. 10

9. A motorcycle travelling 90 mph accelerates to pass a truck. Five seconds later the motorcycle is going 120 mph. Calculate the motorcycles' acceleration.

  a. 6 mph/second^2
  b. 10 mph/second^2
  c. 15 mph/second^2
  d. 20 mph/second^2

The Global Human Population

Questions 10 - 14 refer to the following passage

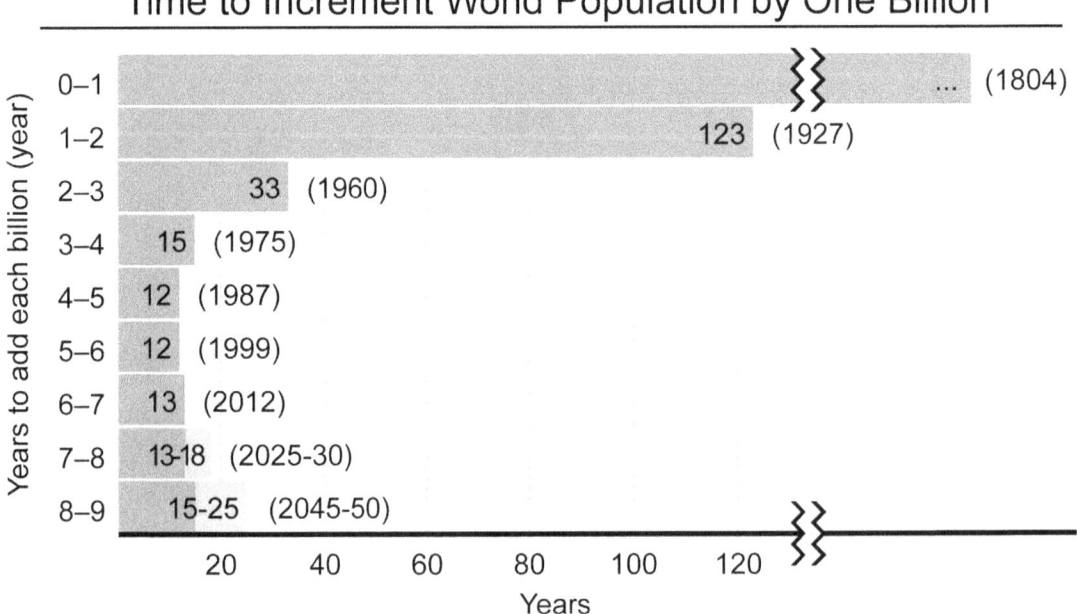

Globally, the human population growth amounts to approximately 75 million, or 1.1% per year. The last 100 years have seen a massive fourfold increase in the population, due to medical advances, lower mortality rates, and an increase in agricultural productivity made possible by the Green Revolution. Developed nations have seen a decline in their growth rates in recent decades; this can be attributed to their high standards of living. Japan's population began decreasing in 2005; it now has the highest standard of living in the world. Some countries are currently experiencing a decline in their population, especially in Eastern Europe. Low fertility rates, high death rates, and emigration are thought to be the main reasons for this decline. Population growth is also slowing in Southern Africa, due to the high number of AIDS-related deaths.

10. How much has the global population grown by from 1800 until 2012?

   a. 7 billion
   b. 13 billion
   c. 6 billion
   d. 1 billion

11. Around which year can we expect the global population to pass 8 billion?

   a. 2025
   b. 2030
   c. 2045
   d. 2050

12. For a population to continue to grow:

   a. Birth rates must exceed mortality rates
   b. Birth rates must be equal to mortality rates
   c. Birth rates must be less than mortality rates
   d. Birth rates must exceed morbidity rates

13. In some countries such as those in Eastern Europe, the population is in decline, which of the following factors would not be an explanation for this?

   a. Low fertility
   b. High death rates
   c. Emigration
   d. More advanced technology

14. What influence has the green revolution had on human population growth rates?

   a. It has increased the yield of crops
   b. It has lowered mortality rates
   c. It has reduced food costs
   d. All of the above

15. A _____ is a unit of inherited material, encoded by a strand of DNA and transcribed by RNA.

   a. Allele

   b. Phenotype

   c. Gene

   d. Genotype

16. A runner can sprint 6 meters per second. How far will she travel in 2 minutes?

   a. 600 meters

   b. 720 meters

   c. 760 meters

   d. 800 meters

17. Which of these is not an area studied in cell biology?

   a. Cells physiological properties

   b. Cell structure

   c. Cell life cycle

   d. Cellular scientists' biographies

18. How many elements are represented on the modern periodic table?

   a. 122 elements

   b. 99 elements

   c. 102 elements

   d. 118 elements

19. Three cars are travelling down an even road at a velocity of 110 m/s, calculate the car with the highest momentum if they are all moving at the same speed, but the first car weighs 2500 kg, second car weighs 2650 kg and third car weighs 2009 kg?

   a. First car

   b. Second car

   d. Third car

   d. All have same momentum

20. Starting with the weakest, arrange the fundamental forces of nature in order of strength.

   a. Gravity, Weak Nuclear Force, Electromagnetic Force, Strong Nuclear Force
   b. Weak Nuclear Force, Gravity, Electromagnetic Force, Strong Nuclear Force
   c. Strong Nuclear Force, Weak Nuclear Force, Electromagnetic Force, Gravity
   d. Gravity, Strong Nuclear Force, Weak Nuclear Force, Electromagnetic Force

Water Consumption

Questions 21 - 24 refer to the following passage.

The amount of water consumed by an individual can vary greatly, depending on the condition of the subject, the amount of physical exercise, and the environmental temperature and humidity the individual is in. For example, people in hotter climates require a much greater water intake than those in cooler climates.

The US reference daily intake (RDI) for water is 3.7 liters per day (l/day) for human males older than 18, and 2.7 l/day for human females older than 18. This value includes water contained in food, beverages, as well as drinking water. The misconception that everyone should drink two liters (68 ounces, or about eight 8-oz glasses) of water per day is wide-spread. However, various reviews of scientific literature on the topic performed in 2002 and 2008 could not find any reliable scientific evidence supporting this recommendation. When considering daily water intake, an individual's thirst provides a better guide for how much water they require rather than a specific, fixed number. Another, more flexible guideline is that a healthy person should urinate four times per day, and the urine should be a light yellow color.

A constant supply of water is necessary to replenish the fluids lost through normal physiological activities, such as respiration, perspiration, and urination. Furthermore, water does not necessarily need to be consumed as a liquid to contribute to one's daily intake. For instance, food provides 0.5 to 1 l/day, while the metabolism of protein, fat, and carbohydrates produces another 0.25 to 0.4 l/day. This means that 2 to 3 l/day of water for men and 1 to 2 l/day of water for women should be consumed as fluid to meet the Recommended Daily Intake (RDI).

21. Which of the following is not a factor that should influence an individual's daily water intake?

   a. The temperature of the environment
   b. The amount of physical activity
   c. The number of times a person urinates
   d. Whether the individual is male or female

22. According to the article above, how much water should an individual 18 years or older drink each day?

   a. 0.5-1 liters per day

   b. 1-3 liters per day

   c. 2.7 – 3.7 liters per day

   d. 0.25 -0.4 liters per day

23. What is the best indicator of the amount of water you should drink each day?

   a. Levels of thirst

   b. The recommended daily intake

   c. The reference daily intake

   d. The color of your urine

24. Which of the following is an opinion, rather than a fact:

   a. People in hotter climates drink more than people in cooler climates

   b. The body uses water for many processes

   c. Humans should drink eight glasses of water every day

   d. Food contains some of your daily water intake

25. What are electrons?

   a. Subatomic particles that carry a negative charge

   b. Subatomic particles that carry a positive charge

   c. Subatomic particles that carry both a negative and positive charge

   d. None of the above

26. Describe the periodic table.

   a. The periodic table is a tabular display of the chemical compounds organized on the basis of their atomic numbers, electron configurations, and recurring chemical properties.

   b. The periodic table is a tabular display of the chemical elements, organized on the basis of their atomic numbers, electron configurations, and recurring chemical properties.

   c. The periodic table is a tabular display of the chemical subatomic particles, organized on the basis of their atomic numbers, electron configurations, and recurring chemical properties.

   d. None of the above.

27. Describe bacteria.

a. Prokaryotic microorganisms that are usually just a few micrometres long.
b. A single-celled organism.
c. A virus.
d. Three or more molecules clumped together.

28. What is the difference, of any, between kinetic energy and potential energy?

a. Kinetic energy is the energy of a body that results from heat while potential energy is the energy possessed by an object that is chilled.
b. Kinetic energy is the energy of a body that results from motion while potential energy is the energy possessed by an object by virtue of its position or state, e.g., as in a compressed spring.
c. There is no difference between kinetic and potential energy; all energy is the same.
d. Potential energy is the energy of a body that results from motion while kinetic energy is the energy possessed by an object by virtue of its position or state, e.g., as in a compressed spring.

29. A rocket releases a satellite into orbit around Earth. The satellite travels at 2000 m/s in 25 seconds. What is the acceleration?

a. 60 m/sec^2
b. 80 m/sec^2
c. 100 m/sec^2
d. 120 m/sec^2

30. Name the four states in which matter exists.

a. Concrete, liquid, gas, and plasma
b. Solid, fluid, gas, and plasma
c. Solid, , vapor, and plasma
d. Solid, liquid, gas, and plasma

The Water Cycle

Questions 31 - 35 refer to the following passage

The water cycle, or hydrologic cycle, describes how water circulates between the earth's oceans, atmosphere, and land. As water goes through its cycle, it can be a solid (ice), a liquid (water), or a gas (water vapor). The processes involved the water cycle are depicted in the diagram below:

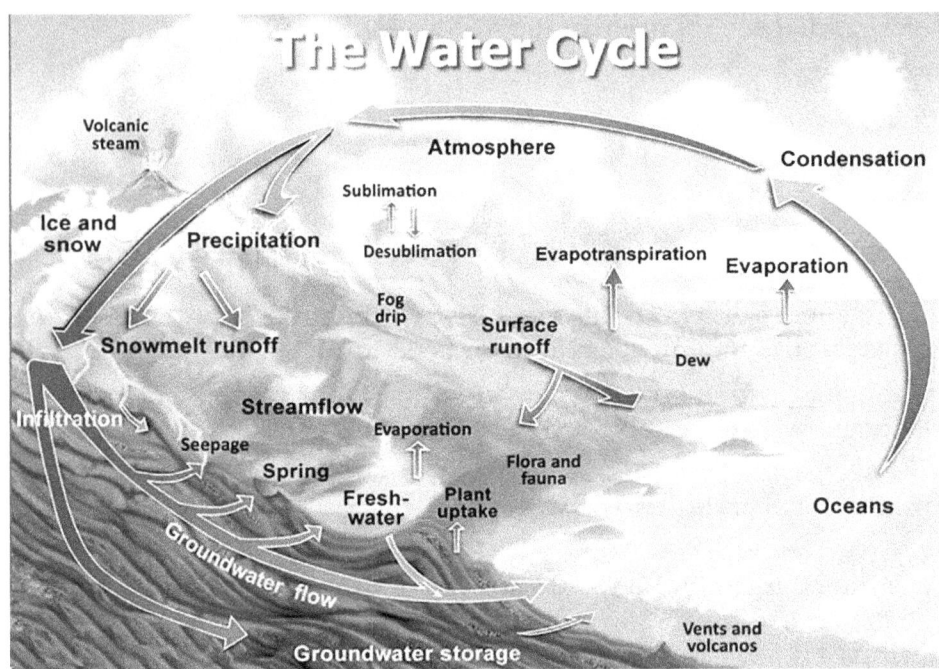

31. Which of the following would result in a decrease in the volume?

   a. Precipitation
   b. Evaporation
   c. Surface runoff
   d. Infiltration

32. The sun is said to drive the water cycle. Which of the following statements is the best reason for this?

   a. It heats water in oceans and seas, increasing evaporation rates
   b. It causes the ice and snow to melt increasing runoff
   c. It causes precipitation or rain
   d. It causes transpiration (removal of water) from plants

33. Which process or factor allows water to be turned directly from vapor into ice and snow?

   a. Snow melt runoff
   b. Precipitation
   c. Desublimation
   d. Evaporation

34. Which processes causes the environment to cool down.

   a. Evaporation and sublimation
   b. Precipitation and sublimation
   c. Evaporation and condensation
   d. precipitation and condensation

35. The water cycle leads to temperature changes in the environment. Which of the following reasons is the best explanation for this?

   a. When water takes energy (e.g., evaporation), the environment becomes cooler
   b. When water releases energy (e.g., condensation) the environment becomes warmer.
   c. When water releases energy, the environment becomes cooler, when the water gains energy the environment becomes warmer.
   d. A and B are both correct

Question 36 refers to the following diagram.

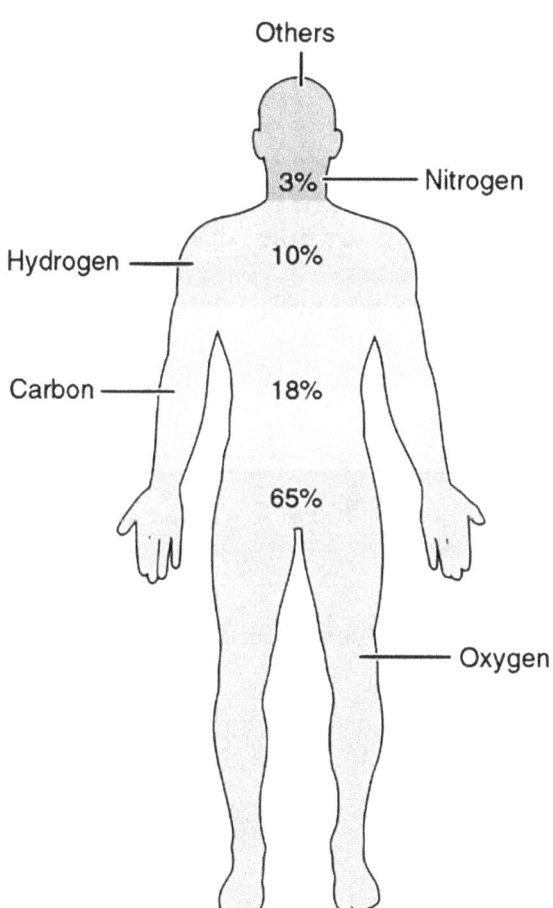

Elements of human body

36. Which element does the human body contain most of by mass?

   a. Oxygen
   b. Carbon
   c. Hydrogen
   d. Nitrogen

37. In a 70 kg person, what would be the approximate mass (kg) of hydrogen?

   a. 0.7 kg
   b. 7 kg
   c. 10 kg
   d. 700 kg

38. Which essential element in the human body is needed to build proteins such as DNA?

   a. Oxygen
   b. Hydrogen
   c. Carbon
   d. Nitrogen

39. The adult human body is approximately 53% water, yet the diagram above suggests that the hydrogen and oxygen contribute to 75% of our body composition. Which of the following would be the best explanation for this?

   a. Because our lungs are always taking in more oxygen than the body can use.
   b. Because oxygen and hydrogen are heavier separately than when they join together to form water
   c. Not all hydrogen and oxygen atoms in the human body are bonded together as water.
   d. None of these

40. What is the force per unit area exerted against a surface by the weight of air above that surface in the Earth's atmosphere?

   a. Gravitational force
   b. Atmospheric pressure
   c. Barometric density
   d. Aneroid pressure

Practice Test Questions 1

41. Describe kinetic energy.

   a. Kinetic energy is the energy an object possesses due to its mass.
   b. Kinetic energy is the energy an object possesses due to its motion.
   c. Kinetic energy is the energy an object possesses due to its chemical properties.
   d. Kinetic energy is the stored energy an object possesses.

42. How do atoms of different elements combine to form chemical mixtures?

   a. Atoms of different elements combine in simple whole-number ratios to form chemical compounds.
   b. Atoms of different components combine in simple fractional ratios to form chemical compounds.
   c. Atoms of the same element combine in simple whole-number ratios to form chemical compounds.
   d. Atoms of different elements combine in simple whole-number ratios to form chemical mixtures.

43. Find the momentum of a round stone weighing 12.05 kg rolling down a hill at 8 m/s.

   a. 95 kg m/sec down the hill.
   b. 96.4 kg m/sec down the hill.
   c. 100 kg m/sec down the hill.
   d. 90 kg m/sec down the hill.

44. Which of the following statements about non-metals are false?

   a. A non-metal is a substance that conducts heat and electricity poorly.
   b. Most known chemical elements are non-metals.
   c. A non-metal is brittle or waxy or gaseous.
   d. None of the statements are false.

45. The number of protons in the nucleus of an atom is the

   a. Atomic mass.
   b. Atomic weight.
   c. Atomic number.
   d. None of the above.

46. The molarity of an aqueous solution of CaCl is defined as the

a. moles of CaCl per milliliter of solution

b. grams of CaCl per liter of water

c. grams of CaCl per milliliter of solution

d. moles of CaCl per liter of solution

47. An electron is:

a. A tiny particle with a negative charge.

b. A tiny particle with a positive charge.

c. A tiny particle with a negative charge that orbits a nucleus.

d. A tiny particle with a positive charge that orbits an atom.

48. Newton's laws of motion consist of three physical laws that form the basis for classical mechanics. Which of the following is/are not included in these laws?

a. Unless acted on by a force, a body at rest stays at rest.

b. Unless acted on by a force, a body in motion will change direction and gradually slow until it eventually stops.

c. To every action, there is an equal and opposite reaction.

d. A body acted on by a force will accelerate in the same direction as the force at a magnitude that is directly proportional to the force.

49. A car starts from a full top and in 20 seconds is travelling 10/m per second. What is the acceleration?

a. 0.5 m/sec^2

b. 0.24 m/sec^2

c. 1 m/sec^2

d. 1.5 m/sec^2

50. The space station travels 1000 meters in 5 seconds. How fast is it travelling?

a. 100 meters/second

b. 200 meters/second

c. 50 meters/second

d. 500 meters/second

Answer Key

Social Studies

1. D
The Acadians (and the Québécois), are descendents of the early French settlers of Canada.

2. A
As they sought more and more resources for growing populations, war also became common as tribes came into contact.

3. B
Vikings were the first Europeans to land on Canadian shores.

4. A
Vikings first landed in Labrador and Newfoundland.

5. B
The first European settlements were established on what is now the Maine New Brunswick border.

6. C
In 1608 Champlain established a fortress in what is now Québec City.

7. A
King Charles the II of England gave the Hudson's Bay Trading Company exclusive trading rights in 1670.

8. A
The Battle of the Plains of Abraham at Québec city was fought in 1759.

44. B
The British passed the Quebec Act in 1774 to accommodate the majority French population in Quebec.

9. C
Upper Canada is present-day Ontario and Lower Canada is present-day Quebec.

10. D
French-speaking Catholics made their home in Upper Canada.

11. B
The Constitutional Act of 1791 formalized the name Canada.

12. B
1758 saw the first representative assembly elected in Halifax, Nova Scotia.

13. B
Polymaths have a wide range of skills and interests, usually in the fine arts, humanities and sciences.

Choice A is incorrect. Polymaths are not, despite the name, focused solely on math and science.
Choice C is incorrect. A person can hold numerous degrees and not be a polymath, although, most polymaths do hold several degrees.
Choice D is incorrect. Someone with an eidetic or "photographic" memory may become a polymath, but not all polymaths must have an eidetic memory.

14. D
All the answers are correct.

15. B
Italy was a central trade hub. The text mentions people traveling to and from the city to emphasize this influx of new cultures and ideas.
Choice A is incorrect. Italy is not a centrally located country.
Choice C is incorrect. Italy was advanced, but not as advanced as other cultures. This is demonstrated in text when the author mentions Constantinople.
Choice D is incorrect. Italy as a central trade hub was certainly wealthy, but this did not play a large role in starting the Renaissance.

16. B
Choice A is incorrect. The Renaissance is certainly an important time period, leading to several new techniques and revivals of old techniques. What critics are unsure of is the Renaissances' scale of importance and whether the Renaissance matters as much as other factors. Still it is an important period and therefore the correct answer is choice B.

17. B
While the troops are following the water ways, they are marching and not traveling by boat. The Key indicates that Arnold's forces had to march almost 150 miles in 21 days after they took Montreal. The winters are harsh and would have caused several problems for marching troops.

18. C
The black lines clearly indicate time periods some distance into the future which means that they are predictions.
Choice A is incorrect. There are periods on the grey side of the map that demonstrate stability, such as the gradual decrease from 1990-2000.
Choice B is incorrect because the grey lines continue after the year 2000.
Choice D is incorrect. Maps do not color code arbitrarily.

19. A
While it's likely that the percentage of yearly growth rate will continue to decrease into the future at this point it's only a prediction and therefore opinion, not fact.

20. A
Physical geography focuses on the natural environment according to the text and therefore would be interested in the impact of a natural species on its environment
Choice B is incorrect. Human geography is focused on the impact of humans on the creation of built environment.
Choice C is incorrect. Environmental geography considers the impact that humans have on an environment.

21. C
According to the text, environmental geography is the study of humans impacting a natural environment
Choice A is incorrect. Physical geography does not study human-built structures.
Choice B is incorrect. While human geography deals with man-made structures it does not consider the impact of the structures have on a natural environment

22. B
Regional planning considers the allocation of resources over a territory, which would include concerns over access to a fresh water lake.
Choice A is incorrect. Spatial planning deals with the distribution of people and would be more interested in analyzing the impact a park might have on local businesses.
Choice C is incorrect. Urban planning is focused on the development of urban spaces.
Choice D is incorrect. Rural planning is never mentioned in the text and serves as a distractor.

23. D
Each of the examples are things that the three different applied geographical approaches mentioned in text would be interested in examining.

24. B
Great Britain is also a constitutional monarchy.
Choice A is incorrect because the United States has a Constitution, but is not a monarchy.
Choice C is incorrect because France has a Prime Minister it is no longer a monarchy.
Choice D is incorrect because like the United States, Mexico has an elected President.

25. C
The Queen is represented through Canada's Governor General.
Choice A is incorrect because the Queen is a figurehead not an absolute monarch.
Choice B is incorrect because the Queen does not directly instruct the Prime Minister.
Choice D is incorrect because the Queen, while mainly a figurehead, does influence the government through the Governor General.

26. C
The Prime Minister is at the head of the government. The Governor General serves under him as The Queen's representative.
Choice A is incorrect because the Queen is not part of Canada's government. She is instead the head of state.
Choice B is incorrect because the Queen is not part of Canada's government. She's instead the head of state.
Choice D is incorrect because the Governor General assists the Prime Minister, who is the head of the government

27. B
Fact. While the Queen is Head of State, the Prime Minister is the head of the government and therefore holds the most power.

28. B
The Governor General signs bills into law.
Choice A is incorrect because the Prime Minister does not sign bills into law.
Choice C is incorrect because the Prime Minister does not play a role in lawmaking.
Choice D is incorrect because the Prime Minister does not sign laws.

29. A
The Prime Minister chooses his own cabinet members.
Choice B is incorrect because the Prime Minister does not select Senators. The Governor General is in charge of the selection of Senators though the Prime Minister can counsel the Governor General.
Choice C is incorrect because the Prime Minister does not choose the Governor General.

30. A
The Canadian people vote for the members of the House of Commons. Choice B is incorrect because the Senators are selected by the Governor General. Choice C is incorrect because the Prime Minister selects his own cabinet members

31. A
The Prime Minister is the head of the executive branch.
Choice B is incorrect because the Governor General is head of the legislative branch.

32. C
The image shows new immigrants possessing only what they can carry with them. The image is meant to help the audience understand the plight that new immigrants might face due to poverty and cultural barriers.
Choice A is incorrect because trains did open more of Canada to because, there is a better answer.
Choice B is incorrect because Canada is a very culturally diverse nation, there is a better answer.
Choice D is incorrect because trains were a technological advancement, but are not the focus of the image.

33. A
This image is from the French and First Nations War, known in England as the Seven Years War. Wolfe, dressed in the infamous "Redcoat" of a British soldier is not an American General, but a British General.
Choice B is incorrect because Wolfe did indeed die in North America as evidenced by the Native American at the bottom left.
Choice C is incorrect because Wolfe was well liked and respected, as evidenced by the soldiers surrounding and comforting him in the moment of his death. The Christ-like imagery also showed that he was probably respected by the painter as well.
Choice D is incorrect because the painting very clearly depicts a battlefield. West even paints a rifle at Wolfe's feet to drive home this point.

34. B
The British North America Act of 1867 established Canada as a federal dominion within the British Empire.

35. C
The Canadian Charter of Rights and Freedoms guarantees fundamental freedoms like freedom of expression, the right to a fair trial, and equality rights. However, unlike the U.S. Constitution, it does not guarantee the right to bear arms.

36. B
The Quiet Revolution was a period in Quebec characterized by the modernization of

the province, including the secularization of institutions (especially education) and the expansion of the welfare state. It marked a shift away from the influence of the Catholic Church.

37. A
The Constitution Act of 1982, which included the Canadian Charter of Rights and Freedoms, patriated the Canadian Constitution, meaning that Canada could amend its own Constitution without needing approval from the British Parliament. It did not remove the British monarch as head of state.

38. A
A market where there is a lot of competition means that prices are reduced to attract buyers.
Choice B is incorrect because while a duopoly would be better for buyers than a monopoly, it would not be as biased towards sellers as a perfectly competitive market
Choice C is incorrect because while an oligopoly would be better for buyers than a monopoly, it would not be as biased towards sellers as a perfectly competitive market
Choice B is incorrect because a monopoly is the worst market for buyers because the monopoly has no competition to drive down prices. This is why there is Anti-Trust legislation in most countries to prevent monopolies from forming.

39. D
A monopoly gives the seller the most power.
Choice A is incorrect because A perfectly competitive market is biased towards buyers, not sellers.
Choice B is incorrect because while a duopoly would be better for sellers than a more competitive market, it would still lower prices through competition.
Choice C is incorrect because an oligopoly is biased towards buyers, not sellers.

40. D
General Equilibrium theory should be used because it's impossible to consider the NYCSE without also having to consider the impacts of markets around the world.
Choice A is incorrect because the NYCSE has a scope of focus that is huge and encompasses several different markets
Choice B is incorrect because foreign investors and businesses can trade on the NYCSE
Choice C is incorrect because large size and high complexity markets can also happen under partial equilibrium analysis

41. C
Based on the text's characterization of Microeconomics, micro means small.

42. C
Cost per unit usually decreases when the units produced increases.
Choice A is incorrect and stated directly in the passage: "Most times, on the side of supply, they produce and work through firms."
Choice B is incorrect and stated directly in the passage: "…when the costs of trading through firms becomes lower that the cost of trading directly on the market"

43. B
While larger firms might be more trustworthy, this answer is not mentioned in the text.

Choice A is incorrect because firms do unite sellers decreasing competition and increasing prices.
Choice C is incorrect because firms utilize best practices to decrease cost per unit.
Choice D is incorrect as the passage mentions several different styles of firm.

44. C
This question is asking for the definition of an oligopoly market.
Choices A, B, and D are for a perfect competition market, monopolistic completion market, and monopoly market respectively.

45. B
This question is asking for the definition of a monopolistic completion market. Choices A, C, and D are for a perfect competition market, oligopoly market, and monopoly market respectively.

46. A
When supply cannot meet demand, demand increases and causes prices to increase
Choice B is incorrect because when demand increases, suppliers can sell their product at a higher market value
Choice C is incorrect because when supply decreases, demand increases.
Choice D is incorrect because when supply decreases, demand increases.

47. A
This question asks for students to identify the correct definition for information asymmetries.

48. C
The first settlers of Canada, the Aboriginals, included three groups: First Nations, Inuit, and Métis.

49. D
First Nations is the modern term for "indian."

Aboriginal is an all-encompassing term that includes Inuit, First Nations, and Métis.

50. D
The Inuit make up roughly 5% of the native population.

Language Arts - Reading

1. D
Choice D is the only possibility. The author refers to Terkoz as a beast, and twice describes him as an ape.

2. D
Animal imagery is used to qualify Tarzan's strength, appearance, and behavior. Simultaneously, Tarzan's humanity is not forgotten: Terkoz identifies Tarzan's pale skin and hairlessness, and the greatness of Terkoz's teeth (natural) are contrasted with the thinness or weakness of Tarzan's knife (man-made). Animal imagery weaves in Tarzan's humanity un-manlike characteristics. He is both a man and not a man, an animal, yet not fully animal. There is no indication that Tarzan actually becomes the animals he resembles: choice A is incorrect. Choice B is probably true, but in this passage no inference can be made about Tarzan's past or childhood. Choice C is a weak answer, as the animal imagery qualifies Tarzan's prowess, rather than his lack of civilization.

3. B
The author mentions that for authors such as Shakespeare or "Mr. Blank" (i.e. any given writer), "a certain amount of thought goes on before pen is put to paper." This does not hold for the essay's author, who maintains that, with a new nib (a part of an old-fashioned pen, which holds and dispenses small quantities of ink), he can get immediately to work. Choice A is a purposeful misreading of the first sentence of the second paragraph. Choice C likewise misconstrues the author's words. In fact, the author feels something of the opposite of choice D is true.

4. C
Choice A misses the mark — the author asserts throughout that his writing, while difficult to see, is of exceptional quality and therefore neatness. Choice B is irrelevant. As choice A is incorrect, so must be choice D. Choice C is correct (and therefore choice E is not a viable choice). The reader's comprehension that the author used to get one thousand words on standard 8.5 by 11 inch paper (which typically accommodates only a few hundred reasonably sized typed words at most) will help them determine that the author's script must be exceptionally small. Writing larger would be generous insofar as allowing his publishers to actually read what he has written.

5. B
The author remains on the topic of the size of his script. This line is his acknowledgment that while he has increased the size a little, his writing may still appear more like an impression of writing, rather than as legible script. Choices A is false, the author has not mentioned his style of writing nor the content he approaches. Choice C is irrelevant. D may seem likely, as the following sentences imagine a response to his writing. Again, though, he has not changed his style, and the comment makes no inquiry as to what others will think.

6. A
The author specifies that when they look "with the eye of an artist" they will appreciate his work. Choice B merely suggests a time during which they might look at his work with such an eye, but not how they will do so. Choices C and D are unsupported and untenable.

7. C
As the author points out that he does not know what the calligrapher means by "synthetic," readers, too, may have trouble finding the answer. Choice B can be eliminated, since the author specifies that the calligrapher did intend to say "synthetic." There is no evidence for, nor mention of, machinery, nor the process of synthesis, so choices A and D can be eliminated. While the author hopes that his writing, interpreted by the calligrapher, will suggest he is full of secrets (e.g. complex), the label "synthetic" is not directed at dismissing this perception — i.e. to suggest that one is synthetic does not mean they have no secrets. Choice C is thus the only possible choice, and can be further rationalized as the calligrapher adds that the author is "not analytic." The reader should understand that the author's writing has been described with a heavy focus on appearances, given more to the quality of the look than the content of the writing. The author himself admits he writes without really planning, and is so uninspired in terms of what to write he will even choose a random topic from a dictionary. Consequently, his writing is synthetic (e.g. insincere, fabricated, not genuine).

8. D
While it is clear Jip wants to be brought along, there is scant evidence for choice B, and none for choice A. The reader will narrow their choices down to choices C and D — C being too specific and without proof, the reader must choose choice D.

9. B
Looking closely, choice E makes a general statement about the habits of crowds relative to Dr. Doolittle, which the reader has no way to ascertain. Choice D is therefore incorrect. It ought to be clear to the reader, based on the emotions of the crowd — the waving and cheering, for instance — as well as the amount of luggage mentioned earlier in the passage, that there is something special about this voyage. Choice B therefore is the best fit, as there is no way to know the Doctor's feelings about his apparent celebrity.

10. C
This question asks the reader to find the most unsupported choice. The first paragraph has Doolittle give instructions to a crow, so choice A can be eliminated. Evidence of choice B is found where the Doctor, without appearing disturbed, un sticks the boat from the mud. Choice D may appear debatable, but the reader will infer that since Doctor Doolittle wanted to instruct Matthew in the feeding of the animals, moreover Matthew has a family name, "Mugg," which no animal in the passage possesses, Matthew ergo is not an animal himself. Thus, the reader will choose choice C, which has no evidence; Doolittle in fact mentions that the voyage will be easier once the open sea is reached.

11. C
Choice C rephrases the Doctor's words most closely, where a "regulated" voyage can be understood as one in which every possible event is accounted. The reader can eliminate Choices B and D, which are irrelevant. Choices A mentions planning, yet choice A is incorrect because the Doctor does not suggest it is necessary to have alternatives.

12. A
The Save the Children's fund has raised $12,000 out of $20,000, or 12/20. Simplifying, $12/20 = 3/5$

13. B
The Save the Children's fund has raised $12,000 out of $16,000, or 12/16. Simplifying, 12/16 = 3/4.

14. B
The time limit for radar detectors is 14 days. Since you made the purchase 15 days ago, you do not qualify for the guarantee.

15. B
Since you made the purchase 10 days ago, you are covered by the guarantee. Since it is an advertised price at a different store, ABC Electric will "beat" the price by 10% of the difference, which is,

500 – 400 = 100 – difference in price

100 X 10% = $10 – 10% of the difference

The advertised lower price is $400. ABC will beat this price by 10% so they will refund $100 + 10 = $110.

16. C
The purpose of this passage is to persuade.

17. D
Choice A is clearly wrong as this is the literal significance of the echoing green. Choice B flies in the face of the "echoing" quality of the poem, that day becomes night, which again becomes day, or that the old return to their youth by reliving it through the next generations of children. The poem is not exclusively focused on old age; choice C does not account for the central role of children and youth. E is irrelevant, the poem makes no claim about the echoing green achieving some transcendent status. Choice D is thus the correct choice, reflecting both the attention to natural imagery and the human lifespan.

18. A
To make the correct choice, choice A, the reader is best informed by the first two stanzas, which are replete with brightness, song, merriment, play, laughter, and joy. While the elderly do reminisce on youth, they "laugh away care" — choice B is therefore an inappropriate choice. Choices C and E have no proof. Choice D, though promising, is incorrect. It is hard to make a case for "Doting," foremost because the poem is not romantic in nature, nor does the voice seem to confer especial care, concern, or affect on his various subjects.

19. C
The reader is reminded that a motif is a dominant feature that appears persistently throughout a literary work. Though some support could be given for green as a motif, birds appear as subjects and not as a motif, making choice A ultimately impractical. Readers of literature will comprehend that choice B contains two themes, not motifs, and hence can be discarded. Choice D suffers a similar fate to choice A: the echo is surely a motif while the sun surely is not — readers may infer that the sun is connects well to the poem's content, enabling seasons and days to come and go (and come again). While true, the sun's role is not considered in these terms, and indeed the sun is only

mentioned once. The poem's celebration of life is framed in terms of age, the young and the old, the inevitable passing of life and its return anew. Spring is the very season when life returns, i.e. when new life is born, when things become alive, and can be understood as the echoing green itself.

20. B
Choice B is the best choice, as each stanza echoes at the end the "seen, green" rhyme. In this way, each stanza features a return, just as the poem reflects the cycle of life. Choices A and D are impossible to prove and can be discounted. Choice C is possible, given the poem concludes with "On the darkening green." Inevitable darkness only accounts for half of the poem's message, however, and the reader should infer that lightness, too, is inevitable.

21. A
The author is enjoying the daffodils very much and so we can infer that he is a lover of nature.

22. C
The mood of this poem is happy. From the last line,

And then my heart with pleasure fills,
And dances with the daffodils.

23. D
Sprightly means happy and full of life. From the lines before and after sprightly, we can see it means happy.

Ten thousand saw I at a glance,
Tossing their heads in sprightly dance.

The waves beside them danced, but they
Out-did the sparkling waves in glee:

24. C
Joyful is the best answer. Happy is a possible answer, but joyful is better. Jocund means jovial, exuberant, light-hearted; merry and in high spirits. From the poem,

Ten thousand saw I at a glance,
Tossing their heads in sprightly dance.

The waves beside them danced, but they
Out-did the sparkling waves in glee:

25. D
While the mother worries her son may be dead, the bulk of the poem describes her various interpretations as to what may have happened to him since he left — death or otherwise. Choice A can be dismissed, and choice D is the best choice. Choice B is irrelevant. Choices C appears in the poem, but do not accurately portray the mother's main concerns.

26. C
Evidence for choices A, B, and D is scant or circumstantial.

27. A
The chains represent the mother's inability to search for her son — e.g. unlike angels, she cannot simply fly where she will. Wishes, or prayers, for her son's safety and safe return, are clearly all the mother has left to give, hence, "All that is left to comfort thee." Choice B is wrong: chains here do not refer to penitentiary, and there is no evidence of crimes or taking responsibility therefor. Choice C is irrelevant, as the comfort provided here, is figurative. Choice D is untenable, there is no suggestion, direct or otherwise, of divine interference.

28. A
Choices B and D can be immediately rejected. Choice C comes close in accuracy, but does not capture the mother's intense sorrow. Choice A is the best choice.

29. C
The good breeding and relative comfort is indicated ("Well born, well bred; I sent him forth"), yet there is no evidence of abuse on the son's part. Choice A is inaccurate. Like A, choice B is inaccurate as there is no evidence that the son is not what he claimed (or was claimed) to be. There is no account of the son's deceit. Choice C is the best choice. The mother praises his qualities, and dismisses potentially negative rumors about him. Choices D is a fanciful answer and read too much into the lines without proof.

30. D
Choices A and B are close, but slightly misconstrued. Tihon obviously does not relish taking Merik's boots off, yet he is not openly hostile, and does not appear especially perturbed by Merik's demands and insults. Tihon does have some fun at Merik's expense, but his attitude cannot be said to be purely playful — choice C is incorrect.

31. C
The key here is Bortsov's admission: "I'm doing this wicked thing, not reckoning on what's to come..." In other words, Bortsov is about to embark on criminal activity, and in the case of unforeseen consequences, such as a trial, he would like Tihon to safe-keep his possession. Choice C is therefore the best answer. Bortsov does effect an apology for his treatment of Tihon, but neither choices A nor D are satisfied by further evidence in the text. Choice B is unsubstantiated.

32. A
Choice B through E have no evidence, while, considering choice A, the reader is aware that Tihon in one instance refused at first to take off Merik's boots, and in another disregarded completely Bortsov's instructions not to open the medallion and look at the portrait. There is no evidence he does this malicious, or is spurred on by vodka or social weariness. All but choice A can be rejected.

33. B
The setting is clearly near Christmas, as indicated by the parcels and Christmas tree. Nora enters in high spirits, humming, and generously overpays the porter. In this context, and choice A is too vague. Choice C is a good choice, but does not reflect the holiday spirit evoked in the above-mentioned details. Choice D is unclear and imprecise. B, therefore, makes the best choice.

34. A
Choice D is unprovable. Choice C is plausible, save that the reader has no reason to believe Nora's excitement is specifically child-like. The reader will observe the amount of detail in the scene notes, the design of the space and arrangement of furniture and decoration and so on. Under these circumstances, while a case could be made for Choice B, A provides the best choice, especially given the significance conferred to the Christmas setting.

35. D
Laying parcels on the table indicates very little of Nora's character. Choice A supports her generosity, while Choice B describes her thoughtfulness relative to her children. Choice C's pet-names establishing the loving relationship, and it may be noteworthy that birds and squirrels tend to be high energy animals.

36. D
The opposite of choice A is true — they clearly have means. Choices B and C are impossible to confirm. In the extensive notes of the finery and furniture of the Helmers' home, fitted out even with a book-case and a piano.

37. A
Secede means to break away from because the 11 states wanted to leave the United States and form their own country.

Choice B is incorrect because the states were not accomplishing anything. Choice C is incorrect because the states were trying to leave the USA not join it. Choice D is incorrect because the states seceded before they lost the war.

38. B
Look at the dates in the passage. The shots were fired on April 12 and Congress declared war on April 14.

Choice C is incorrect because the passage states that Lincoln was against slavery. Choice D is incorrect because it never mentions who was or was not at Fort Sumter.

39. C
The passage states that Lee surrendered to Grant after the capture of the capital of the Confederacy, which is Richmond.

Choice A is incorrect because the war continued for 2 years after Gettysburg. Choice B is incorrect because that battle is not mentioned in the passage. Choice D is incorrect because the capture of the capital occurred after the march to the sea.

40. A
When the passage said that the North had abolished slavery, it implies that slaves were no longer allowed in the North. In essence slavery was banned.

Choice B makes no sense relative to the context of the passage. Choice C is incorrect because we know the North was fighting against slavery, not for it. Choice D is incorrect because slavery is not a tangible thing that can be destroyed. It is a practice that had to be outlawed or banned.

Mathematics - Parts I & II

1. C
If there are 5 friends and each drink costs $1.89, we can round up to $2 per drink and estimate the total cost at, 5 X $2 = $10.
The actual, cost is 5 X $1.89 = $9.45.

2. A
2cnx = 2(4 x 5 x 3) =, 2 x 60/2 x 5 =, 120/10 = 12

3. D
75/1500 = 15/300 = 3/60 = 1/20

4. C
16 X 230 is about 3,100. The actual number is 3680.

5. B

Day	Number of Absent Students	Number of Present Students	% Attendance
Monday	5	40	88.88%
Tuesday	9	36	80.00%
Wednesday	4	41	91.11%
Thursday	10	35	77.77%
Friday	6	39	86.66%

To find the average or mean, sum the series and divide by the number of items.
88.88 + 80.00 + 91.11 + 77.77 + 86.66/5
424.42/5 = 84.88
Round up to 85%.

Percentage attendance will be 85%

6. C
Let the original price be 100x.

At the rate of 7% discount, the discount will be 100x * 7/100 = 7x. So, the discounted price will be = 100x - 7x = 93x.

Over this price, at the rate of 2% additional discount, the discount will be 93x * 2/100 = 1.86x. So, the additionally discounted price will be = 93x - 1.86x = 91.14x.

This is the amount which John has paid for the jacket:

91.14x = 425

x = 425 / 91.14 = 4.6631

The jacket costs 100x. So, 100x = 100 * 4.6631 = $466.31.

When rounded to the nearest whole number, this is equal to $466.

7. B
40/100 X = 90
40X = (90 * 100) = 9000
x = 9000/40 = 900/4 = 225
Half of 225 = 112.5

8. B
First, see if you can eliminate any choices. 1/4 + 1/3 is going to equal about 1/2.

Choice A, 9/10, is very close to 1, so it can be eliminated.
Choices B and C are very close to 1/2 so they should be considered. Choice D is less than half and very close to zero, so it can be eliminated.

Looking at the denominators, choice C has denominator of 15, and choice B has denominator of 20. Right away, notice that 20 is common multiple of 4 and 10, and 15 is not.

9. C
1 inch on map = 2,000 inches on ground. So, 5.2 inches on map = 5.2 * 2,000 = 10,400 inches on ground.

10. B
Actual cost = X, therefore, 545 = x + 0.15x, 545 = 1x + 0.15x, 545 = 1.15x, x = 545/1.15 = 473.9

11. C
0.27 + 0.33 = 0.60 and 0.60 = 60/100 = 3/5

12. D
First, we need to convert all units to grams. Since 1000 g = 1 kg:

10 kg 550 g = 10 * 1000 g + 550 g = 10,000 g + 550 g = 10,550 g.

10,550 g is shared between 5 men. So each man will have to carry 10,550/5 = 2,110 g

2,110 g = 2,000 g + 110 g = 2 kg 110 g

13. B
As the lawn is square, the length of one side will be the square root of the area. $\sqrt{62,500}$ = 250 meters. So, the perimeter is 4 times the length of one side:

250 * 4 = 1000 meters.

Since each meter costs $5.5, the total cost of the fence will be 1000 * 5.5 = $5,500.

14. A
The easiest way to solve age problems is to use a table:

	Mother	Child
Now	7x	x
25 years later	7x + 25	x + 25

Now, mother is 7 times older than her child. So, if we say that the child is x years old, mother is 7x years old. In 25 years, 25 will be added to their ages. We are told that in 25 years, mother's age will double her child's age. So,

7x + 25 = 2(x + 25) ... by solving this equation, we reach x that is the child's age:

7x + 25 = 2x + 50

7x - 2x = 50 - 25

5x = 25

x = 5

Mother is 7x years old: 7x = 7 * 5 = 35

15. C
By the given information in the question, we understand that the discounted part is the saved amount. If we say that the original price of the desk is 100x; by 20% discount rate, 20x will be the discounted part:

20x = 45

We know that Mark paid 20% less than the original price. So, he paid 100x - 20x = 80x. We are asked to find 80x. With a simple direct proportion, we can find the result:

20x = 45

80x = ?

By cross multiplication, we find the result:

? = 80x * 45 / 20x = 4 * 45 = $180

16. C
Let the number be x.

x/(3/2) is the required result.

x * (3/2) is the operation the student does mistakenly. We are told that the multiplication result is 5 more than the division result that is the required one:

x * (3/2) = x/(3/2) + 5 ... by solving this equation, we find x.

3x/2 = 2x/3 + 5

3x/2 - 2x/3 = 5 ... by equating the denominators to 6:

9x/6 - 4x/6 = 5

(9x - 4x)/6 = 5

5x/6 = 5

5x = 30

x = 6

17. C
243/(3 x 3 x 3) = 243/27 = 9

18. B
4y + 24 = 3y + 30, = 4y – 3y + 24 = 30, = y + 24 = 30, = y = 30 – 24, = y = 6

19. B
$(x^2 - y^2) / (x - y) = x + y$

$\underline{-(x^2 - xy)}$
$\quad\quad xy - y^2$

$\underline{-(xy - y^2)}$
$\quad\quad 0$

20. A
10 x 10 x 100 x 100 = 1000^x, = 100 x 10,000 = 1000^x, = 1,000,000 = 1000^x = x = 2

21. C
We are asked to find A + B - C. By paying attention to the sign distribution; we write the polynomials and operate:

A + B - C = $(-2x^4 + x^2 - 3x) + (x^4 - x^3 + 5) - (x^4 + 2x^3 + 4x + 5)$

= $-2x^4 + x^2 - 3x + x^4 - x^3 + 5 - x^4 - 2x^3 - 4x - 5$

= $-2x^4 + x^4 - x^4 - x^3 - 2x^3 + x^2 - 3x - 4x + 5 - 5$ ... similar terms written together to ease summing/substituting.

= $-2x^4 - 3x^3 + x^2 - 7x$

22. C
To find the solution for the inequality, we need to simplify it first:

$(x - 6)^2 \geq x^2 + 12$ ... we can write the open form of the left side:

$x^2 - 12x + 36 \geq x^2 + 12$ ... x^2 terms on both sides cancel:

-12x + 36 ≥ 12 ... Now, we aim to have x alone on one side. So, we subtract 36 from both sides:

-12x + 36 - 36 ≥ 12 - 36

-12x ≥ -24 ... We divide both sides by -12. This means that the inequality will change its direction:

x ≤ 2 ... x can be 2 or a smaller value.

This result is shown by (-∞, 2].

23. C
$(x^3 - 3x^2 + 3x - 1) / (x - 1) = x^2 - 2x + 1$
$\underline{-(x^3 - x^2)}$
$\quad\quad -2x^2 + 3x - 1$

$$\underline{-(-2x^2 + 2x)}$$
$$x - 1$$
$$\underline{-(x - 1)}$$
$$0$$

24. C
Exponential form is 9^3 and standard from is 729

25. B
$x^2 - 5x - 6 = 0$

We try to separate the middle term -5x to find common factors with x^2 and -6 separately:

$x^2 - 6x + x - 6 = 0$ ... Here, we see that x is a common factor for x^2 and -6x:

$x(x - 6) + x - 6 = 0$ ... Here, we have x times x - 6 and 1 time x - 6 summed up. This means that we have x + 1 times x - 6:

$(x + 1)(x - 6) = 0$ ... This is true when either or both expressions in the parenthesis are equal to zero:

$x + 1 = 0$ ... $x = -1$

$x - 6 = 0$ ... $x = 6$

-1 and 6 are the solutions for this quadratic equation.

26. B
0.524/ (10 * 10 * 10) = 0.524/1000 ... This means that we need to carry the decimal point 3 decimals left from the point it is now:

= 0.0.0.0.524 = 0.000524

The correct answer is (b).

27. A
We need to find the greatest common divisor of the two terms to factor the expression. We should remember that if the bases of exponent numbers are the same, the multiplication of two terms is found by summing the powers and writing on the same base. Similarly; when dividing, the power of the divisor is subtracted from the power of the divided.

Both x^3y^3 and x^2y^8 contain x^2 and y^3. So;

$x^3y^3 - x^2y^8 = x * x^2y^3 - y^5 * x^2y^3$ ... We can carry x^2y^3 out as the factor:

$= x^2y^3(x - y^5)$

28. D
Our aim to collect the 'knowns' on one side and the unknowns (x terms) on the other side:

$5x/2 = (3x + 24)/6$ ... First, we can simplify the denominators of both sides by 2:

$5x = (3x + 24)/3$ ... Now, Cross multiply:

15x = 3x + 24

15x - 3x = 24

12x = 24

x = 24/12 = 2

29. D
When multiplying exponents with the same base, add the exponents. $3^2 \times 3^5 = 3^{2+5} = 3^7$

30. C
Solving the system means finding x and y. Since we also have a in the system, we will find x and y depending on a.

We can obtain y by using the equation ax + y = 1:

y = 1 - ax ... Then, we can insert this value into the second equation:

x + a(1 - ax) = 1

x + a - a²x = 1

x - a²x = 1 - a

x(1 - a²) = 1 - a ... We need to obtain x alone:

x = (1 - a)/(1 - a²) ... Here, 1 - a² = (1 - a)(1 + a) is used:

x = (1 - a)/((1 - a)(1 + a)) ... Simplifying by (1 - a):

x = 1/(a + 1) ... Now we know the value of x. By using either of the equations, we can find the value of y. Let us use y = 1 - ax:

y = 1 - a * 1/(a + 1)

y = 1 - a/(a + 1) ... By writing on the same denominator:

y = ((a + 1) - a)/(a + 1)

y = (a + 1 - a)/(a + 1) ... a and -a cancel:

y = 1/(a + 1) ... x and y are found to be equal.

The solution of the system is (1/(a + 1), 1/(a + 1))

31. A
To divide exponents with the same base, subtract the exponents. $3^{8-5} = 3^3$

32. C
To solve the linear equation, we operate the 'knowns' and unknowns within each other and try to obtain x term (which is the unknown) alone on one side of the equation:

3(x + 2) - 2(1 - x) = 4x + 5 ... We remove the parenthesis by distributing the factors:

3x + 6 - 2 + 2x = 4x + 5

5x + 4 = 4x + 5

5x - 4x = 5 - 4

x = 1

33. C
$3x^a + 6a^x - x^a + (-5a^x) - 2x^a = 3x^a + 6a^x - x^a - 5a^x - 2x^a = a^x$

34. B
By paying attention to the sign distribution; we write the polynomials and operate:
$(-3x^2 + 2x + 6) + (-x^2 - x - 1)$

$= -3x^2 + 2x + 6 - x^2 - x - 1$

$= -3x^2 - x^2 + 2x - x + 6 - 1$ ... similar terms written together to ease summing/substituting.

$= -4x^2 + x + 5$

35. A
10^4 is not equal to 100,000
$10^4 = 10 \times 10 \times 10 \times 10 = 10^2 \times 10^2 = 10,000$

36. D
Comparing angles on similar triangles, a, b and c will be 70°, 75°, 35°

37. A
Yes the triangles are congruent.

38. D
Perimeter of triangle ABC is asked.
Perimeter of a triangle = sum of the three sides.

Here, Perimeter of ΔABC = |AC| + |CB| + |AB|.

Since the triangle is located in the middle of two adjacent and identical rectangles, we find the side lengths using these rectangles:

|AB| = 6 + 6 = 12 cm

|CB| = 8.5 cm

|AC| = |CB| = 8.5 cm

Perimeter = |AC| + |CB| + |AB| = 8.5 + 8.5 + 12 = 29 cm

39. A
The wheel travels 2πr distance when it makes one revolution. Here, r stands for the radius. The radius is given as 25 cm in the figure. So,
2πr = 2π * 25 = 50π cm is the distance traveled in one revolution.

In 175 revolutions: 175 * 50π = 8750π cm is traveled.

We are asked to find the distance in meter.

1 m = 100 cm So;

8750π cm = 8750π / 100 = 87.5π m

40. A

If a line represents an equation, all points on that line should satisfy the equation. Meaning that all (x, y) pairs present on the line should be able to verify that 2y - x is equal to 4. We can find out the correct line by trying a (x, y) point existing on each line. It is easier to choose points on the intersection of the grid lines:

Let us try the point (4, 4) on line A:

2 * 4 - 4 = 4

8 - 4 = 4

4 = 4 ... this is a correct result, so the equation for line A is 2y - x = 4.

Let us try other points to check the other lines:

Point (-1, 2) on line B:

2 * 2 - (-1) = 4

4 + 1 = 4

5 = 4 ... this is a wrong result, so the equation for line B is not 2y - x = 4.

Point (3, -1) on line C:

2 * (-1) - 3 = 4

-2 - 3 = 4

-5 = 4 ... this is a wrong result, so the equation for line C is not 2y - x = 4.

Point (-2, -1) on line D:

2 * (-1) - (-2) = 4

-2 + 2 = 4

0 = 4 ... this is a wrong result, so the equation for line D is not 2y - x = 4.

41. C

In a right angle, Pythagorean Theorem is applicable:
$a^2 + b^2 = c^2$ ... Here, a and b represent the adjacent and opposite sides, c represents the hypotenuse. Hypotenuse is larger than the other two sides.

In this question, we need to try each answer choice by applying $a^2 + b^2 = c^2$ to see if it is satisfied; by inserting the largest number into c:

a. 1, 2, 3:

$1^2 + 2^2 = 3^2$

1 + 4 = 9

5 = 9 ... This is not correct, so answer choice does not represent a right angle whose sides are consecutive numbers.

b. 2, 3, 4:

$2^2 + 3^2 = 4^2$

$4 + 9 = 16$

13 = 16 ... This is not correct, so this answer choice does not represent a right angle whose sides are consecutive numbers.

c. 3, 4, 5:

$3^2 + 4^2 = 5^2$

$9 + 16 = 25$

25 = 25 ... This is correct, 3, 4, 5 are also consecutive numbers; so this answer choice represents a right angle whose sides are consecutive numbers.

d. 4, 5, 6:

$4^2 + 5^2 = 6^2$

$16 + 25 = 36$

41 = 36 ... This is not correct, so this answer choice does not represent a right angle whose sides are consecutive numbers.

42. A
If we call one side of the square "a," the area of the square will be a^2.

We know that $a^2 = 200$ cm^2.

On the other hand; there is an isosceles right triangle. Using the Pythagorean Theorem:

(Hypotenuse)^2 = (Perpendicular)^2 + (Base)^2
$h^2 = a^2 + b^2$

Given: $h^2 = 200$, $a = b = x$
Then, $x^2 + x^2 = 200$, $2x^2 = 200$, $x^2 = 100$
$x = 10$

43. B
In the question, we have a right triangle formed inside the circle. We are asked to find the length of the hypotenuse of this triangle. We can find the other two sides of the triangle by using circle properties:

The diameter of the circle is equal to 12 cm. The legs of the right triangle are the radii of the circle; so they are 6 cm long.

Using the Pythagorean Theorem:

(Hypotenuse)^2 = (Perpendicular)^2 + (Base)^2
$h^2 = a^2 + b^2$

Given: d (diameter)= 12 & r (radius) = a = b = 6

$h^2 = a^2 + b^2$
$h^2 = 6^2 + 6^2$, $h^2 = 36 + 36$
$h^2 = 72$
$h = \sqrt{72}$
$h = 8.48$

44. C
Slope (m) = $\dfrac{\text{change in y}}{\text{change in x}}$

$(x_1, y_1) = (-3, 1)$ & $(x_2, y_2) = (1, -4)$
Slope = $[-4 - 1]/[1-(-3)] = -5/4$

45. C
The inner angles of a triangle sum up to 180^0. Let us sum three expressions given for the inner angles equating to 180^0 and then find x:

$(x + 20) + (3x – 10) + (8x + 50) = 180$
$x + 3x + 8x + 20 – 10 + 50 = 180$
$12x + 60 = 180$
$12x = 120$
$x = 10$

Without calculation, it is obvious that 8x + 50 is the largest angle, but we cannot know which of the remaining two expressions gives the smallest value; so, let us calculate each:
$x + 20 = 10 + 20 = 30$
$3x – 10 = 30 – 10 = 20$
$8x + 50 = 80 + 50 = 130$

The largest angle is 130^0 and the smallest is 20^0. Their difference is simply $130 – 20 = 110^0$.

46. B
Ignoring the order means this is a combination problem, not permutation. The reader will choose 3 books out of 4. So,

C(4, 3) = 4! / (3! * (4 - 3)!) = 4! / (3! * 1!) = 4

There are 4 different ways.

Ignoring the order means this is a combination problem, not permutation. The reader will choose 3 books out of 4. So,

C(4, 3) = 4! / (3! * (4 - 3)!) = 4! / (3! * 1!) = 4

There are 4 different ways.

47. B
There are 52 cards. Smith has 16 cards in which he can win. Therefore, his winning probability in a single game will be 16/52. Simon has 20 cards in which he can win, so his probability of winning in a single draw is 20/52.

48. C

First, let us find the sample proportion. The sample is the interviewed visitors who visit museums 20 days in a year. 2 people interviewed mention that they visit museums 20 days in a year.

Sample proportion:
2 / (12 + 18 + 8 + 2 + 10) = 2 / 50

The population size is 250.

The estimated number is found by:
population size * sample proportion:

= 250 * 2 / 50 = 10 visitors

49. C
When solving this type of question, drawing a picture makes it easier to visualize the calculations. Here, there are six people but three of them do not want to sit separately. Then, we can accept these three people (always sitting together) as one person.

Now, there are 4 people to sit on the bench. 4 people can line up in 4! different ways. Don't to forget that three people that are accepted as 1 can sit in 3! different ways without getting separated. We need to multiply the two factorials to find all possibilities:

6 people can sit in 4! * 3! = 24 * 6 = 144 different ways.

50. B
Notice that 3 out of 9 damaged bulbs should be chosen to have exactly 3 damaged bulbs. Since 3 bulbs are chosen, we have (12 - 3 = 9) 9 bulbs to choose further, within the safe bulbs. These 9 bulbs should be chosen from 100 - 9 damaged = 93 safe bulbs. These two cases are multiplied as follows:

C(9, 3) * C(93, 9)

The overall number of possible ways of choosing 12 bulbs out of 100 bulbs is found by:

C(100, 12)

The probability is:
(C(9, 3) * C(93, 9)) / C(100, 12) = ((9! / (6! * 3!)) * (93! / (84! * 9!))) / (100! / (88! * 12!))

= ((9 * 8 * 7 * 6!) / (6! * 3!)) * ((93 * 92 * 91 * ... * 84!) / (84! * 9!)) * ((88! * 12!) / (100 * 99 * 98 * ... * 88!))

= 84 * ((12 * 11 * 10 * 9!) / 9!) * ((93 * 92 * 91 * ... * 85) / (100 * 99 * 98 * ... * 89))
= (84 * 12 * 11 * 10) * (88 * 87 * 86 * 85) / (100 * 99 * 98 * 97 * 96 * 95 * 94) = (11 * 29 * 43 * 17) / (5 * 7 * 97 * 47 * 19)

= 0.076916... or, 0.08

Language Arts - Writing

1. D

Suggested revision of sentence 1, "Humankind's thirst for knowledge is insatiable, making curiosity a driving force for advances throughout history."

Use the gender neutral "humankind. Replace the past perfect "has always been" with the present tense to make a simpler and more direct sentence. "Though history" is incorrect. Use "throughout" when referring to a time period. Replace the preposition "for" with "in."

2. A

Sentence 6 is the least relevant. "Curiosity was launched in late November 2011 from Cape Canaveral Air Force Station in Florida."

The third paragraph talks about the objectives of the rover. All sentences other than sentence 7 mention the objectives. This sentence, however, informs about when the spacecraft was launched.

3. A

Sentence 10 is least relevant to the main idea of the third paragraph. The following changes are suggested, "<u>To achieve its goals</u>, Curiosity has been engineered with cutting-edge technologies worth a budgetary expense exceeding 2.5 billion US dollars."

Clearly, the last paragraph talks about how Curiosity has been engineered to accomplish its objectives. The previous paragraph addressing the objectives of the rover, addition of the phrase "To achieve its goals," in choice A, acts as a transition sentence between the paragraphs.

4. D

The changes needed to sentence 5 are, "So far, NASA has carried out several exploratory missions to Mars and the rover robot "Curiosity" is the latest and most sophisticated of all."

"Curiosity" is the name of a spacecraft that was assigned the particular name because of its association of its mission to satisfy our curiosity about the planet Mars. In this respect, the name bears a special meaning and emphasis, which must be reflected in representing it using the quotation mark.

Use of the adjective "exploratory" to describe the missions is correct.

Choice D offers these changes.

5. C

Sentence 11 is a fragment. "The discovery is significant because so far, no attempt has been made to use the abundant infrared radiation we receive throughout the year."

The fragment contains a subordinate clause derived from the complete thought "The discovery is significant because so far no attempt has been made to make use of the infra-red radiation that we receive in an abundant supply throughout the year." It also contains the subject of the main clause, "The discovery," but does not have any verbal phrase for the main clause. Since the main clause remains incomplete, the thought is expressed in part. Therefore, it is a sentence fragment.

6. C
Sentence 9 can be deleted to reduce redundancy. "This is a major discovery in the solar power generation industry as it offers a cheap source of harnessing the Sun's energy."

Sentence 9 contributes to double redundancy; that is, it repeats two separate ideas. Along with repeating the cost-effective characteristic of the new discovery, it also reiterates the fact that it is a major discovery, both of which are unnecessary. It also interferes in the paragraph transition which can be established between sentence 8 and 10 if it is removed.

7. B
Suggested corrections to sentence 10, "Oleic acid, the main ingredient of olive oil, absorbs infra-red radiation, which is the major component of the Sun's radiation reaching the Earth."

The sentence is missing the subordinate conjunction "which" or "that" necessary to construct the subordinate clause, with a comma before "which." Choices B and C suggest these changes, but since choice C contains a punctuation error, only B is has the valid answer.

8. D
Suggested changes to sentence 2, "With continued concern over global climate change, environmentalists are urging governments to lower their dependence on fossil fuels to ensure reduced carbon emission into the atmosphere."

This sentence contains inappropriate use of gerunds and infinitives. To-infinitives are preferred when the continuous form of a main verb is used right before or after them. Here,, "urging" should be followed by the to-infinitive of "lower." Further across the sentence, the linking phrase "to," has only one acceptable form; itself. Therefore, the verb which is linked to must contain the infinitive form. The gerund form must be discarded. The only valid choice is D.

9. B
Suggested changes to sentence 6 are, "This information, coupled with conventional on-site procedures, help archaeologists plan their excavation carefully and efficiently."

The second paragraph points out the significance of satellite imaging for archeological studies. The original sentence only makes a general claim. Choice A contradicts excavation principles by adding "along with a supply of heavy machinery" which would destroy the site. Choice B, more appropriately, adds the aspects of archcological excavation that are going to be boosted by the technology. Choices C and D offer very little relevance to satellite imaging and the dimensions of excavation that are going to be affected.

10. C
Sentence 9 can be re-written, "Different points in a civilization reflect IR radiation differently, provide detailed insight about the causes of these differing heat signatures."

This is a shorter and more concise sentence which eliminates some details.

11. A
The following sentence, inserted after sentence 3, would best illustrate the main idea, "The application has inspired archaeologists to use it for searching for the traces of ancient civilizations and other anthropological dynamics."

Choice A points out the significance of the application with some details that are addressed in the subsequent paragraphs. All other choices are either too general or less relevant to the main idea of the passage.

12. A
Suggested changes to sentence 4 are, "The key feature of the new tool- according to Professor Sarah Parcak, who discovered many cities, temples and pyramids covered under sands and sediment- is that it offers a wider perspective in size and scale of the location."

The changes in this sentence are related to punctuation. The original sentence contains a semicolon before a verbal phrase which is not justifiable with its standard use. The sentence can be modified using parenthetic dashes since using parenthetic commas makes the sentence very complicated as the sentence contains several clauses and a list.

13. D
Sentence 13 is not consistent with the author's purpose.
"In the process, she somehow managed to uphold the courage to address the issues facing education for girls and proposed solutions for them."

This sentence, ironically contrasts the character of the passage, and in a way belittles Malala's efforts to address the issues facing girls education, particularly with the words "somehow," "managed" and "uphold." This is, to a great extent, inconsistent with the author's appreciation of Malala.

14. C
Suggested changes to sentence 10 to focus attention on the main idea are, "Inspired by her father, who is an professional educator himself, she decided to work for the education and establishment of girls in her locality, Mingora, a suburban town in Swat District."

The second paragraph discusses the challenges facing Malala and young girls like her. It fine-tunes the reason why Malala had to change her ambition even though she is a talented and successful student; showing that she actually did not give up on her ambition, but rather sacrificed it for materializing others'. In this sense, her father was a role model from whom she could receive inspiration only; not persuasion, instruction or contradiction- for making up her mind to be an professional educator like him. Therefore, choices A, B and D are not relevant. Choice C focuses on the main idea.

15. A
The following sentence, if inserted before sentence 11, would illustrate the main idea, "She wishes to become a politician and aims to serve the women and girls of her community and establish their fundamental rights."

This sentence is interwoven with everything that the passage says about Malala. This also points to the title of the passage and makes the reader ponder with implicit questions like "how is her new dream associated with her first ambition of becoming a doctor?" The answers to such questions are already given in the passage; that her dream is a sacrifice at the same time.

16. C
Suggested changes to sentence 7 are, "Malala's dreams encountered the same obstacles that were also crushing the aspirations of millions of other young girls like her."

The changes needed are related to usage. "Were encountered with the obstacles," can be replaced with "encountered the same obstacles."

17. C
Sentence 16 is a fragment. "What they buy and what they eat until we get to meet them in the evening."

The fragment is an independent clause, not a main clause, starting with the relative pronoun "what." It does not present a complete thought, and is therefore a fragment.

18. C
Changes to sentence 14, "All we have to do is to wait for them to come out of their private premises and once they are onto the streets we are nonstop after them."

The existing sentence contains two compound modifiers that do not need the compounding. The word "private" is an adjective that describes the plural noun "premises" and therefore can exist as per the rules of parts of speech. Hyphenation is not necessary and makes no sense. Also the adverb "nonstop" does not need a hyphen since "non," here,, is no longer considered as a prefix to the little word "stop." Therefore, the hyphens in both cases are unnecessary. Choice C has both words without hyphens.

19. A
The following sentence, to be inserted before sentence 27, best illustrates the main idea of the passage. "It is the waiter and the bill that strikes him like a thunderbolt, not me!"

The main idea in this passage has to be deduced from the narration of the scammer. It provides hints about the way these networkers earn money by deceiving tourists coming to Istanbul to have a drink with them. In the end they trap them into paying huge amount for a single drink. In exchange, they receive commission from the bar. All these facts presented in the passage are reflected in the single sentence, choice A.

20. A
Sentence 3 contains non-standard usage. "I know foreigners here are looking for a good company; so why not make some bucks out of from it!"

The non-standard usage is apparent in the expression "out of from" which is intended to mean "from." Also, "out of" by itself could be used. This may be acceptable in a written piece (though strictly incorrect) for stylistic reasons as the speaker is not a native-speaker of English.

21. B
Suggested changes to sentence 5 are, "Augmented reality has turned out to be one such idea that soon was incorporated into applications like MapLens, SiteLens, Layar and the AR game ARhrrrr!"
Choice B best contributes to the cohesion of the paragraph by addressing the subordinate clause "more avant-garde concepts…" and making it the subject of the next sen-

tence. Other choices do not make augmented reality their subject as a "concept" so that they focus the main idea of the paragraph.

22. C
This sentence, inserted after sentence 8, best illustrates the main idea, "The so-called "Apps Revolution," therefore, is likely to be one of the driving factors orchestrating the rapid advancements in the AR sector and thus has the capability to shape its future."

The passage discusses a phenomenon that has the potential to determine the future of augmented reality. Choice C delicately reflects this generalization with the use of the arguments developed throughout the passage, making proper link to separate arguments with the sentence connector "therefore." Other choices either do not represent the arguments in the passage, or fail to make connections with them.

23. B
Suggested changes to sentence 4, "This has tempted application developers to explore more avant-garde concepts that offer the possibility to be integrated into their applications."

Vocabulary usage is questionable in this sentence. The word "solicit" is used when someone is inclined to something negative like something against the law, here it is used in the context of something innovative and that has the potential to serve humanity. Also, "capacity" is not something that is "offered" and the noun is not used best in descriptive phrases that involve the passive form. Therefore, they must be replaced. Considering all combinations that are offered in the choices, B has the right set of appropriate vocabulary.

24. A
Suggested changes to sentence 12, "This, in turn, resulted in more investment being allocated to material sciences to create new materials for engineering and manufacturing faster processor chips."

This sentence is too wordy and the phrase, "to be allocated to." is awkward. This can be replaced with "being allocated to" for a much smoother, shorter sentence.

25. D
Suggested changes to sentence 7 to focus attention on the main idea in paragraph 2, "The following season, Pato accomplished his first European ambition by winning the 2009 Series A Young Player of the Year award."

The second paragraph discusses Pato's achievements in Europe. Choice D expresses and relates them to his ambition more appropriately than the other choices.

26. B
Sentence 12 contains a redundant phrase. "Pato made a comeback from the injuries that disabled him in the 2011-12 Season, scoring the fifth fastest goal in any Champions' League encounter within 24 seconds of play against the Spanish powerhouse Barcelona."

The phrase, "injuries that disabled him" is redundant.

27. B
The changes to sentence 1 are, "Although well-known among his fans for the "duck-dance" he performs after scoring, Alexandre Rodrigues da Silva has earned the name "Pato" for his ducky skills with the ball that he uses to outclass his opponent in the field."

The changes needed in the first sentence are related to the use of punctuation. The correct form of "well known" is with a hyphen. "Duck dance," refers to the special dance resembling those of ducks therefore it must be inside quotation mark to emphasize its special meaning. In addition, it must be hyphenated since the noun turns out to be a compound modifier of the original noun "dance." Also, the extended verb "outclass" has been inappropriately hyphenated. All these changes are carried out in choice B only.

28. B
Suggested changes to sentence 14, "Making a second return to San Siro in the following August, the young and valiant striker continued his glittering performance in spite of regular injuries in the 2012-13 Season."

The use of the linking phrase "in spite of" has been compromised in this sentence. The sentence uses "inspite." The correct suggestion is made in choice B, and all other suggestions like "inspite of," "in-spite" and "in-spite of" has no basis in grammar.

29. B
Sentence 6 is the least relevant to the main idea of the second paragraph. "Spring may witness the arrival of season's first rain and of a nor'wester."

All other sentences in the paragraph talk about the trees. Sentence 6 talks about the arrival of rain and thunderstorms.

30. C
Suggested changes to sentence 12 to focus attention on the main idea of the third paragraph are, "Surprisingly, even watermelon, jackfruit and litchis arrive by the middle of April!"

The third paragraph discusses the availability of various fruits in spring. Apart from sentence 12, all the sentences do it cohesively. Sentence 12 is somewhat inconsistent with the main idea of the paragraph. It is possible to make it more relevant to the paragraph and add more cohesion between sentences by adjusting it to the form suggested in choice C. Addition of "even" coupled with changing the sentence from negative to affirmative brings the focus of the paragraph to this sentence. Other choices fail to do this as the negative tone of the language used remains intact in the suggested changes.

31. A
Sentence 15 is not consistent with the author's purpose. "Some lakes and water ponds that dry up in the summer and turn into festival venues for children who race to scoop up the fish with bamboo baskets."

Sentence 15 talks about summer and is the only sentence to do so. This is not consistent with the author's purpose, to describe spring in Bengali.

32. C
Suggested changes to sentence 8 are, "Sapodia and curd fruit that have already arrived in late winter ripen in spring- and does the jujube."
The mistakes in the sentence are related to punctuation. The original sentence uses a comma after "sapodia" that must not be used when the list of nouns is only two. Instead,

it must be replaced by "and." Also, the original sentence uses a colon after an independent clause which is not in conformity with its accepted usage. Using a dash after the clause to express the thought after it is more appropriate. So, choice C is correct whereas choices B and D are discarded because they retain the comma after "sapodia" while choice A is not considered correct for having the colon.

33. B
Sentence 5 is the least relevant to the main idea of paragraph 2. "Turmeric, thought to have healing effects and health benefits for millennia, is a regular ingredient in spicy Indian diets.

The second paragraph discusses the role of curcumin as a compound that helps in the treatment of cancer. All the sentences, except sentence 5 in the paragraph, talk about this issue. Sentence 5- describing it as a regular ingredient of Indian diets- is, therefore, the least relevant sentence.

34. D
Sentence 8 can be deleted to reduce redundancy "These results indicate that it will be a useful compound that will help in treating diseases like esophageal cancer."

Sentences 4, 6 and 7 (choices A, B and C respectively) discusses the various aspects involved in the role of curcumin as a compound assisting cancer therapy and they are conceptually interlinked as well as effectively contributing to the cohesion of the paragraph. However, choice D unnecessarily generalizes all the roles played by curcumin that are expressed in the previous sentences.

35. B
The following sentence can be inserted after sentence 3 to illustrate the main idea of the passage, "The curry spice derived from powdered turmeric has proved itself to be useful in treating many diseases like cancer, arthritis and dementia."

The passage lacks a connecting sentence that bridges the introductory passage with the developing paragraphs following. In this respect, only choice B offers a missing link that is relevant to the scientific observations presented in the subsequent paragraphs.

36. D
Suggested changes to sentence 10 are, "It does this by interfering in some of the reaction pathways that trigger the deactivation of normal cell functioning, helping brain cells to remain resistant to the aftermath of stroke in the hours following its experience."

There are four grammar mistakes in the sentence, "It does that by interfering in some of the reaction pathways which triggers the deactivation of normal cell functioning, helping brain cells remaining resistant to the aftermath of stroke in the hours following their experience."

- "that" should "this."
- "triggers" has been used for the plural "pathways" which should be replace by its plural verb.
- The gerund "remaining" has been used after "helping" which should be replaced by its to-infinitive counterpart "to remain."
- "experience" here refers to the occurrence of the stroke, not the experience by the cells and therefore must be assigned to the "stroke" itself. So, "they" must be replaced by "its."

37. A
The third conditional is used for talking about an unreal situation (that did not happen) in the past. For example, "If I had studied harder, [if clause] I would have passed the exam [main clause]. Which is the same as, "I failed the exam, because I didn't study hard enough."

38. C
Double negative sentence. In double negative sentences, one negative is replaced with "any."

39. B
The sentence refers to a person, so "who" is the only correct choice.

40. A
The sentence requires the past perfect "has always been known." Furthermore, this is the only grammatically correct choice.

41. B
The superlative, "hottest," is used when expressing a temperature greater than that of anything to which it is being compared.

42. C
When comparing two items, use "the taller." When comparing more than two items, use "the tallest."

43. B
The past perfect form is used to describe an event that occurred in the past, and prior to another event.

44. A
The subject is "rules" so the present tense plural form, "are," is used to agree with "realize."

45. C
The simple past tense, "had," is correct because it refers to completed action in the past.

46. C
The simple past tense, "sank," is correct because it refers to completed action in the past.

47. C
Comma separate phrases.

48. D
The comma separates clauses and numbers are separated with a comma. The correct sentence is,
'To travel around the globe, you have to drive 25,000 miles.

49. A
The dog loved chasing bones, but never ate them; it was running that he enjoyed.

50. B
The semicolon links independent clauses with a conjunction (therefore).

Science

1. B
Notice the weight is attached to one end of the rope *and* to one pulley. The force required to lift a 100 pound weight with this arrangement is 100/3 = 33.

2. A
The greatest frequency in the population is a fitness of 0, which is considered lethal.

3. B
(0.3 x0.02) + (0.4 x 0.02) + (0.6 x 0.05) + (0.7 x 0.05) + (0.8 x 0.05) + (0.9 x 0.15)

= 0.325 (0.33 rounded)

4. B
For a mutation to become widespread in a population it needs to be inherited by the offspring, alleles that are lethal or deleterious are not passed on in most cases, as the carrier often does not reach reproductive maturity. Therefore we can expect the mutation to become less common, making choice B is correct.

5. A
The interactions between individuals and their environment (i.e., the trait) are what determines whether their genetic information will be passed on or not. Here, the individuals who are wild type would have a higher level of fitness and therefore be more likely to reproduce (or for viruses, replicate) and pass on their non-mutant genotype.

6. C
50 pounds of force much be exerted downward on the rope to lift the 200 pound weight. Since there are 4 pulleys, each will take 1/4 of the load. 200/4 = 50 pounds.

7. B
Up-and-down or back-and-forth motion is called reciprocal motion.

8. B
To solve for F, Weight X b (distance from fulcrum to weight) = Force X a (distance from fulcrum to point where force is applied)
80 X 10 = F X 20
800/20 = F
F =40

9. A
The formula for acceleration = A = $(V_f - V_0)/t$
so A = (120 -90)/5 sec = 6 mph/second^2

10. C
The population was around 1 billion in 1804 and was around 7 billion in 2012. Therefore, the answer is 6 billion.

11. B
Choice A is incorrect as the population may reach 8 billion in 2025, but it is not predicted to pass 8 billion. The point when the population is expected to pass 8 billion is choice B.

12. A
For a population to grow, there must be more births (i.e., people entering the population) than deaths (leaving the population). Choice B is incorrect as this would result in no growth. Choice C is incorrect as this would lead to a declining population. Choice D is incorrect as morbidity refers to the number of people with disease, these people are still living. Therefore, they do not take away from the population numbers.

13. D
Low fertility (conception rates), high death rates and emigration (people leaving) all cause a population to decline, more advanced technology allows people to survive a lot longer than they would have in previous decades. Therefore choice D is the correct answer.

14. B
The green revolution refers to advances in agriculture, regarding yield, use of chemicals such as herbicides and pesticides, etc. However, only choice B relates to human population growth rates.

15. C
A gene is a unit of inherited material, encoded by a strand of DNA and transcribed by RNA.

16. B
Speed = (total distance traveled)/(total time taken)
6 = x/120   (convert minutes to seconds)
6 * 120 = x
X = 720 meters

17. D
Cellular scientists' biographies are not studied in cell biology. The physiological properties of cells, cell structure and the life cycle of a cell are all valid topics of study within the field of cell biology.

18. D
The periodic table contains 118 elements.

19. C
Momentum is a product of velocity and mass. If they are all traveling at the same speed, the car that weighs the most would have the highest momentum.

20. A
Starting with the weakest, the fundamental forces of nature in order of strength are, Gravity, Weak nuclear force, Electromagnetic force, Strong nuclear force.
Note: Although gravitational force is the weakest of the four, it acts over great distances. Electromagnetic force is of order 10^{39} times stronger than gravity.

21. C
This is the result of water intake, rather than a determining factor. Choice A is incorrect because higher temperatures mean an individual will sweat more and therefore require more water to replenish their supply. Choice B is incorrect because it increases the rate of sweating. Choice D is incorrect as men usually have a higher water requirement than women.

22. B
Choice B is correct as it excludes the amount taken from food, metabolism and is appropriate for both males and females. Choice A is incorrect as this is the amount of water that comes from food. Choice C is incorrect as this is the US reference daily intake and does not reflect the water in foods and other beverages. Choice D is incorrect as this is the amount that is made as a result of our bodies metabolizing our food.

23. A
Choice A is the best answer as it directly relates to the individual's situation rather than, recommendations designed to meet the requirements of most people as in Choices B and C. Choice D is also incorrect as urine color can be influenced by a variety of foods, medications and health issues.

24. C
There is no scientific evidence which states that we should drink this much water each day.

25. A
Electrons are subatomic particles that carry a negative charge.

26. B
The periodic table is a tabular display of the chemical elements, organized on the basis of their atomic numbers, electron configurations, and recurring chemical properties.

27. A
Bacteria are prokaryotic microorganisms that are usually just a few micrometers long.

28. B
Kinetic energy is the energy of a body that results from motion while potential energy is the energy possessed by an object by virtue of its position or state, e.g., as in a compressed spring.

29. B
The formula for acceleration = $A = (V_f - V_0)/t$
so $A = (2000 - 0)/25$ sec $= 80$ m/sec^2

30. D
The four states in which matter exists are solid, liquid, gas, and plasma.
The state of matter is determined by the strength of the bonds between the atoms that make up matter.

31. B
Precipitation or rain, surface runoff, and infiltration increase the volume of water. Therefore choices A, C, and D are incorrect. B is correct as evaporation from the sun turns the water into vapor, thus removing water from the ocean/sea.

32. A
The earth is mostly water (approximately 70%) therefore the capacity for evaporation from water bodies is huge. While choices B, and D are also correct, their contribution to moving the water from a liquid to a vapor is much smaller than that which comes from evaporation. Choice C (precipitation) is the opposite process causing vapor to turn into a liquid.

33. C
The snow is heated by the sun to the extent that it skips the liquid state and becomes a vapor. Choice A is incorrect because snow melt is where snow and ice (solid) turns into water (liquid). Choice B is incorrect because this is water vapor turning into a liquid (snow and ice are solid). Choice D is incorrect as evaporation is the change from a liquid to a vapor.

34. A
Choice A is the best answer as these both require energy to be removed from the environment (i.e., these processes require heat input) to change the state of the water from liquid to vapor (evaporation) and from solid to vapor (sublimation). Choice B is partially correct (sublimation), however precipitation requires the opposite heat exchange to occur (i.e., heat output) when water vapor in the clouds turns into a liquid, it results in the environment warming up. Choice C is also partially correct. However, condensation occurs when a vapor turns into a liquid and also causes heat to be released into the environment. Choice D both require energy to be released and are therefore incorrect.

35. D
Both choices A and B are the two parts of the same process. Therefore choice D is the best answer. The water cycle involves an exchange of heat energy, as is seen in any change of state, this means it moves in both directions. To turn from a liquid to a vapor requires energy input. This energy comes from the environment in the form of heat, so the environment is losing heat. Releasing energy from water is the same as giving the heat to the environment, therefore the temperature increases. C is incorrect as it has the heat exchange around the wrong way.

36. A
The body contains 65% oxygen according to the diagram

37. B
10% of 70kg = 7kg

38. D
Proteins contain amino acids (amine meaning nitrogen)

39. C
Choice C is correct because there are many other chemicals in our bodies which also require hydrogen and oxygen, for instance, hydrogen bonds join DNA, carbon dioxide that we exhale contains CO2 (O being oxygen)

40. B
Atmospheric pressure is the force per unit area exerted against a surface by the weight of air above that surface in the Earth's atmosphere.

41. B
Kinetic energy is the energy an object possesses due to its motion.

42. A
Atoms of different elements combine in simple whole-number ratios to form chemical compounds.

43. B
Formula - P= kg x m/s
= 12.05kg x 8m/s
= 96.4 kg x m/s down the hill.
Note that the final answer has the proper SI unit of momentum (kg x m/s) after it and it also mentions the direction of the movement.

44. D
All of the statements are true.

   a. A non-metal is a substance that conducts heat and electricity poorly.

   b. Most known chemical elements are non-metals.

   c. A non-metal is brittle or waxy or gaseous.

45. C
In chemistry, the number of protons in the nucleus of an atom is known as the atomic number, which determines the chemical element to which the atom belongs.

46. D
The molarity of an aqueous solution of CaCl is defined as the moles of CaCl per liter of solution.

47. C
An electron is a tiny particle with a negative charge that orbits a nucleus.

48. B
Unless acted on by a force, a body in motion will change direction and gradually slow until it eventually stops.

This answer is related to Newton's 1st law of motion, which states that, unless acted on by a force, a body at rest stays at rest, and a moving body continues moving at the same speed in a straight line.

49. A
The formula for acceleration = $A = (V_f - V_0)/t$
so $A = (10 \text{ m/sec} - 0 \text{ m/sec})/20 \text{ sec} = 0.5 \text{ m/sec}^2$

50. B
Speed = (total distance traveled)/(total time taken)
1000/5 = 200 meters per second

Analyzing your practice tests

Go through your answers carefully. For each wrong answer, refer to the explanations, and work through the questions step-by-step.

What kind of question are you getting wrong? (e.g. reading comprehension, science, algebra, basic math etc.)

Look for patterns in your incorrect answers. What is it *exactly* that you are doing wrong or don't understand.

What types of questions do you have the most difficulty with? Refer to the tutorials and try to understand the reasoning that gives the correct answer.

Refer back to chapter one and re-do your study schedule

Practice Test Questions Set 2

The questions below are not the same as you will find on the CAE^C - that would be too easy! And nobody knows what the questions will be and they change all the time. Below are general questions that cover the same subject areas as the CAE^C. So, while the format and exact wording of the questions may differ slightly, and change from year to year, if you can answer the questions below, you will have no problem with the CAE^C.

For the best results, take these Practice Test Questions as if it were the real exam. Set aside time when you will not be disturbed, and a location that is quiet and free of distractions. Read the instructions carefully, read each question carefully, and answer to the best of your ability.
Use the bubble answer sheets provided. When you have completed the Practice Questions, check your answer against the Answer Key and read the explanation provided.

Do not attempt more than one set of practice test questions in one day. After completing the first practice test, wait two or three days before attempting the second set of questions.

Social Studies

1. A B C D
2. A B C D
3. A B C D
4. A B C D
5. A B C D
6. A B C D
7. A B C D
8. A B C D
9. A B C D
10. A B C D
11. A B C D
12. A B C D
13. A B C D
14. A B C D
15. A B C D
16. A B C D
17. A B C D
18. A B C D
19. A B C D
20. A B C D
21. A B C D
22. A B C D
23. A B C D
24. A B C D
25. A B C D
26. A B C D
27. A B C D
28. A B C D
29. A B C D
30. A B C D
31. A B C D
32. A B C D
33. A B C D
34. A B C D
35. A B C D
36. A B C D
37. A B C D
38. A B C D
39. A B C D
40. A B C D
41. A B C D
42. A B C D
43. A B C D
44. A B C D
45. A B C D
46. A B C D
47. A B C D
48. A B C D
49. A B C D
50. A B C D

Language Arts - Reading

1. A B C D
2. A B C D
3. A B C D
4. A B C D
5. A B C D
6. A B C D
7. A B C D
8. A B C D
9. A B C D
10. A B C D
11. A B C D
12. A B C D
13. A B C D
14. A B C D
15. A B C D
16. A B C D
17. A B C D

18. A B C D
19. A B C D
20. A B C D
21. A B C D
22. A B C D
23. A B C D
24. A B C D
25. A B C D
26. A B C D
27. A B C D
28. A B C D
29. A B C D
30. A B C D
31. A B C D
32. A B C D
33. A B C D
34. A B C D

35. A B C D
36. A B C D
37. A B C D
38. A B C D
39. A B C D
40. A B C D

Mathematics Parts I and II

1. A B C D
2. A B C D
3. A B C D
4. A B C D
5. A B C D
6. A B C D
7. A B C D
8. A B C D
9. A B C D
10. A B C D
11. A B C D
12. A B C D
13. A B C D
14. A B C D
15. A B C D
16. A B C D
17. A B C D
18. A B C D
19. A B C D
20. A B C D
21. A B C D
22. A B C D
23. A B C D
24. A B C D
25. A B C D
26. A B C D
27. A B C D
28. A B C D
29. A B C D
30. A B C D
31. A B C D
32. A B C D
33. A B C D
34. A B C D
35. A B C D
36. A B C D
37. A B C D
38. A B C D
39. A B C D
40. A B C D
41. A B C D
42. A B C D
43. A B C D
44. A B C D
45. A B C D
46. A B C D
47. A B C D
48. A B C D
49. A B C D
50. A B C D

Language Arts - Writing

1. A B C D
2. A B C D
3. A B C D
4. A B C D
5. A B C D
6. A B C D
7. A B C D
8. A B C D
9. A B C D
10. A B C D
11. A B C D
12. A B C D
13. A B C D
14. A B C D
15. A B C D
16. A B C D
17. A B C D
18. A B C D
19. A B C D
20. A B C D
21. A B C D
22. A B C D
23. A B C D
24. A B C D
25. A B C D
26. A B C D
27. A B C D
28. A B C D
29. A B C D
30. A B C D
31. A B C D
32. A B C D
33. A B C D
34. A B C D
35. A B C D
36. A B C D
37. A B C D
38. A B C D
39. A B C D
40. A B C D
41. A B C D
42. A B C D
43. A B C D
44. A B C D
45. A B C D
46. A B C D
47. A B C D
48. A B C D
49. A B C D
50. A B C D

Language Arts - Writing

Science

1. A B C D
2. A B C D
3. A B C D
4. A B C D
5. A B C D
6. A B C D
7. A B C D
8. A B C D
9. A B C D
10. A B C D
11. A B C D
12. A B C D
13. A B C D
14. A B C D
15. A B C D
16. A B C D
17. A B C D
18. A B C D
19. A B C D
20. A B C D
21. A B C D
22. A B C D
23. A B C D
24. A B C D
25. A B C D
26. A B C D
27. A B C D
28. A B C D
29. A B C D
30. A B C D
31. A B C D
32. A B C D
33. A B C D
34. A B C D
35. A B C D
36. A B C D
37. A B C D
38. A B C D
39. A B C D
40. A B C D
41. A B C D
42. A B C D
43. A B C D
44. A B C D
45. A B C D
46. A B C D
47. A B C D
48. A B C D
49. A B C D
50. A B C D

Part I - Social Studies

1. In which year did the British Parliament pass the British North America Act?

   a. 1876

   b. 1867

   c. 1786

   d. 1768

2. Who was the first Prime Minister of Canada?

   a. Sir John Alexander Macdonald

   b. Sir Louis-Hippolyte La Fontaine

   c. Robert Baldwin

   d. Joseph Howe

3. Who was the leader of the Aboriginals who fought Canada?

   a. Joseph Howe

   b. Lord Durham

   c. Louis Riel

   d. Robert Baldwin

4. What was one of the major developments of the late 19th century in Canada?

   a. Joining the East and West by railroad

   b. Construction of bridges

   c. Granting voting rights

   d. Constitution of the Police force

5. What was the colony at Quebec City renamed as?

   a. The Quebec Province

   b. The Province of Quebec City

   c. The Province of Quebec

   d. The Quebec City Province

6. What is the name of the holiday celebrated for veterans who fought in World War I?

   a. Remembrance Day

   b. Canada Day

   c. Veteran's Day

   d. Dominion Day

7. What type of government does Canada have?

   a. Parliamentary Democracy

   b. Democratic Parliament

   c. House of Commons

   d. Federalism

8. What are the three branches of parliament?

   a. The Sovereign, Congress and Senate

   b. The Senate, Prime Minister and House of Commons

   c. The House of Commons, Senate and Sovereign

   d. President, Senate and House of Commons

Question 9 refers to the above cartoon.

9. Published in 1774, what is the historical context for this political cartoon?

   a. This cartoon depicts Great Britain taking territory form the Native Americans to create the American Colonies

   b. This cartoon depicts the Intolerable Acts being forced on the American people

   c. This cartoon depicts the violence and torture that captured revolutionaries suffered during the American revolution

   d. This cartoon depicts Anti-American sentiment in Britain after the war.

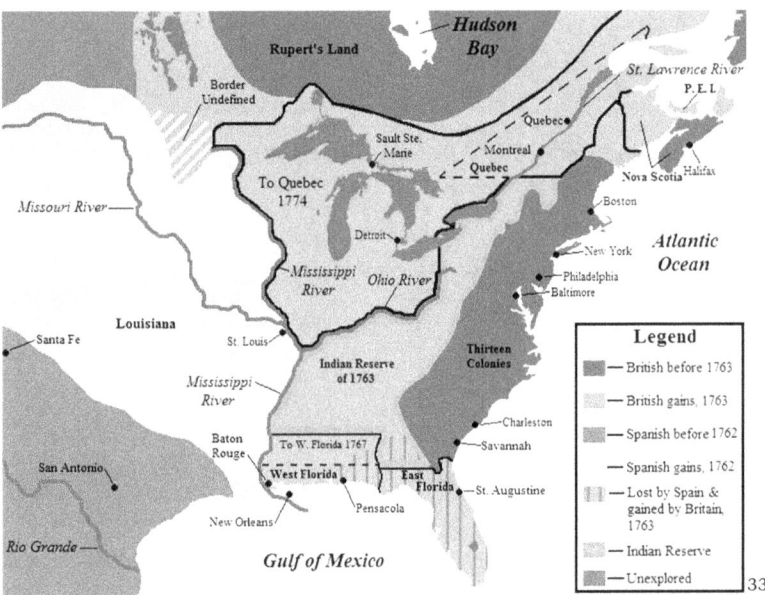

Question 10 refers to the map above.

10. Based on the map above, which country was more aggressive in creating American colonies in the 1760s?

   a. Britain

   b. France

   c. Spain

   d. None of the above

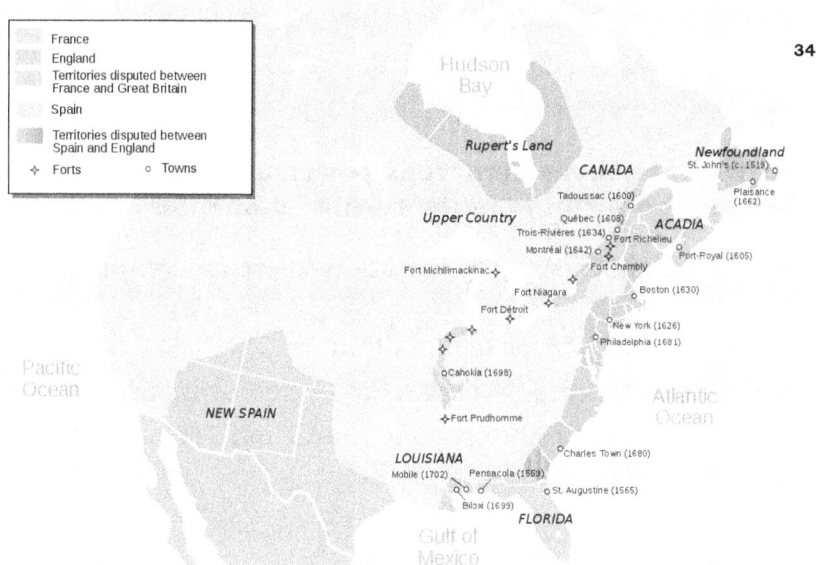

Question 11 refers to the map above.

11. Based on the map above, which European power had the most well developed territory

- a. Great Britain
- b. France
- c. Spain
- d. None of the above

New Economic Geography

Questions 11 - 13 refer to the following passage.

With the rise of the New Economy, economic inequalities are increasing spatially. The New Economy, generally characterized by globalization, increasing use of information and communications technology, growth of knowledge goods, and feminization, has enabled economic geographers to study social and spatial divisions caused by the arising New Economy, including the emerging digital divide.

The new economic geographies consist of primarily service-based sectors of the economy that use innovative technology, such as industries where people rely on computers and the internet. Within these is a switch from manufacturing-based economies to the digital economy. In these sectors, competition makes technological changes robust. These high technology sectors rely heavily on interpersonal relationships and trust, as developing things like software is very different from other kinds of industrial manufacturing—it requires intense levels of cooperation between many different people, as well as the use of tacit knowledge. As a result of cooperation becoming a necessity, there is a clustering in the high-tech new economy of many firms.

12. Opinion or Fact: The digital divide leads to an increase in economic inequality.

   a. Opinion

   b. Fact

13. Based on the passage above, why are there numerous powerful high tech companies when there are only a few powerful manufacturing companies?

   a. High Tech companies rely on one another for cooperation to create complex software

   b. High tech companies rely on one another for competition

   c. High Tech companies haven't been around as long as manufacturing companies

   d. Manufacturing companies are more difficult to create than High Tech companies.

Environmental Issues

Questions 14 - 15 refer to the following passage.

Environmental issues are harmful trouble effects of human activity on the biophysical environment. Environmental protection is a practice of protecting the natural environment on individual, organizational or governmental levels, for the benefit of both the environment and humans. Environmentalism, a social and environmental movement, addresses environmental issues through advocacy, education and activism.

The carbon dioxide equivalent of greenhouse gases (GHG) in the atmosphere has already exceeded 400 parts per million (NOAA) (with total "long-term" GHG exceeding 455 parts per million). (Intergovernmental Panel on Climate Change Report) This level is considered a tipping point. "The amount of greenhouse gas in the atmosphere is already above the threshold that can potentially cause dangerous climate change. We are already at risk of many areas of pollution...It's not next year or next decade, it's now." Report from the UN Office for the Coordination of Humanitarian Affairs (OCHA)

"Climate disasters are on the rise. Around 70 percent of disasters are now climate related – up from around 50 percent from two decades ago.

These disasters take a heavier human toll and come with a higher price tag. In the last decade, 2.4 billion people were affected by climate related disasters, compared to 1.7 billion in the previous decade. The cost of responding to disasters has risen tenfold between 1992 and 2008. Destructive sudden heavy rains, intense tropical storms, repeated flooding and droughts are likely to increase, as will the vulnerability of local communities in the absence of strong concerted action." "Climate change is not just a distant future threat. It is the main driver behind rising humanitarian needs and we are seeing its impact. The number of people affected and the damages inflicted by extreme weather has been unprecedented."

Environment destruction caused by humans is a global problem, and this is a problem that is on going every day. By year 2050, the global human population is expected to grow by 2 billion people, thereby reaching a level of 9.6 billion people (Living Blue Planet 24). The human effects on Earth can be seen in many different ways. A main one is the temperature rise, and according to the report "Our Changing Climate," the global warming that has been going on for the past 50 years is primarily due to human activities (Walsh, et al. 20). Since 1895, the U.S. average temperature has increased from 1.3 °F to 1.9 °F, with most of the increase taken place since around year 1970.

14. Opinion or Fact: Humans have caused harm to the climate, causing it to change in dangerous ways

   a. Opinion

   b. Fact

15. Based on the article above, which of the following is not a climate related disaster?

   a. Floods

   b. Droughts

   c. Earthquakes

   d. Wild Fires

16. What was the start of the Great Depression?

   a. Prohibition

   b. The stock market collapse of 1929

   c. Germany defaulting on its loans to the United States after World War I

   d. The Dust Bowl

17. What caused the Great Depression?

   a. Excessive borrowing

   b. Restricting the amount of money in the economy

   c. People not spending money

   d. All of the above

Related Fields to Geography

Questions 18 - 19 refer to the following passage.

During the 1950s, Walter Isard and his regional science movement, worked to develop a more analytic and quantitative base to geographical questions, contrasting the traditional descriptive tendencies of geographical approaches. Regional sciences includes the body of knowledge where a fundamental role is played by the spatial dimension. Examples of regional science would include human geography, resource management, regional economics, population distribution, environmental quality, transport and communication, urban and regional planning, location theory and landscape ecology.

18. Which of the following best summarizes the passage above?

    a. Before the 1950s geographical approaches primarily used descriptive language. Regional scientists wanted to continue this tradition.

    b. Before the 1950s geographical approaches primarily used descriptive language. Regional scientists wanted to use analytic language instead.

    c. Before the 1950s geographical approaches primarily used analytic language. Regional scientists wanted to continue this tradition.

    d. Before the 1950s geographical approaches primarily used analytic language. Regional scientists wanted to use descriptive language instead.

19. Which of the following would not interest regional scientists?

    a. A map that displays population density

    b. A map that displays areas for potential resource extraction.

    c. A map that displays the phone lines for a town.

    d. A regional scientist would be interested in all of the above.

William Morris Davis - Passage 4

Questions 20 - 21 refer to the following passage.

Another major event in the late nineteenth and early twentieth centuries will give a major boost to development of geography and will take place in the United States. It is the work of the famous geographer William Morris Davis who not only made important contributions to the establishment of discipline in his country, but revolutionized the field to develop geographical cycle theory which he proposed as a paradigm for geography in general, although in actually served as a paradigm for physical geography.

His theory explained that mountains and other landforms are shaped by the influence of several factors in the geographical cycle. He explained that the cycle begins with the lifting of the relief by geological processes (faults, volcanism, tectonic upheaval, etc.). Geographical factors such as rivers and runoff begins to create the V-shaped valleys between the mountains (the stage called "youth"). During this first stage, the terrain is steeper and more irregular. Over time, the currents can carve wider valleys ("maturity") and then start to wind, towering hills only ("senescence"). Finally, everything comes to what is a plain flat plain at the lowest elevation possible (called "baseline") This plain was called by Davis' "peneplain" meaning "almost plain" Then the rejuvenation occurs and there is another mountain lift and the cycle continues. Although Davis's theory is not entirely accurate, it was absolutely revolutionary and unique in its time and helped to modernize and create geography subfield of geomorphology. Its implications prompted a myriad of research in various branches of physical geography. In the case of the Paleogeography this theory provided a model for understanding the evolution of the landscape.

For hydrology, glaciology, and climatology as a boost investigated as studying geographic factors shape the landscape and affect the cycle. The bulk of the work of William Morris Davis led to the development of a new branch of physical geography: Geomorphology whose contents until then did not differ from the rest of geography. Shortly after this branch would present a major development. Some of his disciples made significant contributions to various branches of physical geography such as Curtis Marbut and his invaluable legacy for Pedology, Mark Jefferson, Isaiah Bowman, among others.

20. Based on the passage above, which of the following is the best definition for geomorphology?

   a. The study of the ways in which water shaped the surface of the earth.
   b. The study of the earth's surface and how it is changed.
   c. The study of the ways in which volcanos and earthquakes shaped the surface of the earth
   d. The study of the flat areas of the earth's surface.

21. Which of the following sections of Davis's theory were incorrect.

   a. Rejuvenation - mountains are created by tectonic plates, earthquakes, volcanoes, ect.
   b. Youth - Rivers and rain runoff carve valleys
   c. Maturity - Valleys are widened into canyons by continued use.
   d. Baseline - Everything flattens again until there's no more mountains.

Canadian Government - The Provincial Government

Questions 22 - 25 refer to the following passage.

The Provincial level (from the Latin provincia, meaning under Roman rule: from pro, to be in favour of something, and vincere, to conquer) and the territorial level (from the Latin terra, meaning land).

At the Provincial level, Members of the Legislative Assembly (MLAs) are elected.

An individual, known as the Premier, serves the role of Prime Minister in each province or territory. In the three territories, the Commissioner, a representative of the federal government, also plays an important role in the legislature.

Depending on the province or territory, these individuals may be called members of one of the following:

Legislative Assembly (MLA)
National Assembly (MNA)
Provincial Parliament (MPP)
House of Assembly (MHA)

The 10 provinces and 3 territories share some responsibilities with the Federal government, such as, immigration, agriculture, and the environment.

Examples of Provincial responsibilities include, education, health care, natural resources, highways as well as property and civil rights.

22. Based on the text, are provinces and territories the same thing?

    a. Yes, they just have different names because of when they joined Canada

    b. Yes, they just have different names because of their different sizes

    c. No, the 10 provinces make up the 3 Canadian Territories

    d. No, the 10 provinces and 3 Territories have different governments

23. Which of the following is a responsibility held by the Provinces/Territories?

    a. Maintaining the Canadian Boarder

    b. Maintaining Roads

    c. Environment Regulation

    d. None of the Above

24. Which of the following is a shared responsibility held by the Provinces/Territories and the Federal Government?

    a. Educating the Public

    b. Providing Health Care

    c. Regulating Immigration

    d. None of the Above

25. Which of the following has more power?

    a. Legislative Assembly (MLA)

    b. National Assembly (MNA)

    c. Provincial Parliament (MPP)

    d. They're all equal

Canadian Government - Federal Elections

Questions 26 - 28 refer to the following passage.

Federal elections in Canada are held every four years on the third Monday in October. It is, however, possible for the Prime Minister to call an earlier election. There are 308 1electoral districts in Canada, each represented by a Member of Parliament (MP), elected by the resident of each electoral district to the House of Commons.

An individual who runs for office is called a candidate. There can be many candidates in each election, but these individuals must be over the age of 18. The candidate who receives the most votes becomes the representative for that electoral district.

26. There are 338 electoral districts in Canada, according to the text. There are 10 Provinces and 3 Territories. How are these districts most likely distributed?

   a. By size. Each district is the same number of square miles.
   b. By population. Each district has a similar number of people.
   c. By wealth. Wealthier areas get more votes.
   d. By royal decree. Each district is drawn by The Queen.

27. Candidates are elected based on

   a. A popular vote
   b. A majority vote
   c. An electoral college vote
   d. A popular vote with the consent of the Prime Minister

28. What is it called when the Prime Minister calls for an earlier election?

   a. A Snap Election
   b. A Re-election
   c. A Recall Election
   d. There is no name for this type of election

Canadian Government

Questions 29 - 31 refer to the following passage.

With the support of the Members of Parliament, the Prime Minister runs the government along with his or her party. This individual must, however, maintain a vote of confidence by the MPs, or the Prime Minister will be defeated and a new election is called.

The Prime Minister is responsible for selecting Cabinet ministers, who run each department of the federal government. Working together with the Prime Minister, these ministers make laws, manage budgets, and make other major decisions.

Those who are not members of the party in power are called opposition parties. These parties are important because they provide different viewpoints on critical issues, which helps the government solve problems in a way that serves the majority. There are three major parties in Canada: The Conservative Party, the New Democratic Party, and the Liberal Party.

29. What is the purpose of having a Prime Minister maintain a vote of confidence?

   a. It forces the Prime Minister to consider the public's opinion
   b. It makes the Prime Minister more likely to work with the opposition parties
   c. It encourages the Prime Minister to be open and transparent
   d. All of the above are true.

30. Opinion or Fact: The opposition parties do not play an important role in government

   a. Opinion
   b. Fact

31. What is the length of time for the Prime Minister's term without a vote of no confidence?

   a. 4 years, like the MPs
   b. 5 years, like the Governor General
   c. 10 years, for two Governor Generals
   d. There is no limit

Questions 32 - 33 refer to the photograph above

Practice Test Questions 2   373

32. When was the photograph above most likely taken?

   a. 1920s

   b. 1940s

   c. 1960s

   d. 1980s

33. The purpose of the photograph is to show:

   a. The aftermath of a fire protesting the WWI prohibition on alcohol

   b. The aftermath of German firebombing during WWII

   c. The aftermath of a fire and the success of modern fire fighting

   d. The aftermath of a riot during the Great Depression

Question 34 refers to the painting above.

34. This painting, by Frances Anne Hopkins is meant to capture the realities of life for early Canadian colonists. Here early colonists travel on a voyage to collect goods for sale. Which item did early colonists trade in?

   a. Timber for shipbuilding

   b. Tobacco

   c. Animal Furs

   d. Gold

Confederation I

Questions 35 - 36 refer to the passage below.

The Seventy-Two Resolutions from the 1864 Quebec Conference and Charlottetown Conference laid out the framework for uniting British colonies in North America into a federation. They had been adopted by most of the provinces of Canada and became the basis for the London Conference of 1866, which led to the formation of the Dominion of Canada on July 1, 1867. The term dominion was chosen to show Canada's status as a self-governing colony of the British Empire, the first time it was used about a country. With the coming into force of the British North America Act (enacted by the British Parliament), the Province of Canada, New Brunswick, and Nova Scotia became a federated kingdom in its own right. (According to J. McCullough, use of the phrase "Dominion of Canada ... was gradually phased out" during the "late 1940's, 50's, and early 60's" with the growth of "post-colonial Canadian nationalism."

35. Which of the following is the best example of a federation?

    a. The European Union

    b. The United States

    c. The Peoples Republic of China

    d. All of the above are Federations

36. Is Canada still a dominion of Great Britain?

    a. Yes, Canada still recognizes the monarch's control of the government as an absolute monarchy

    b. Yes, Canada still recognizes the monarch as Head of State as part of their Constitutional Monarchy

    c. No, Canada has a Constitution making the monarchy obsolete.

    d. No, Canada is a fully independent nation.

Confederation - Passage 2

Questions 37 - 38 refer to the passage below.

Federation emerged from multiple impulses: the British wanted Canada to defend itself; the Maritimes needed railroad connections, which were promised in 1867; British-Canadian nationalism sought to unite the lands into one country, dominated by the English language and British culture; many French-Canadians saw an opportunity to exert political control within a new largely French-speaking Quebec and fears of possible U.S. expansion northward. On a political level, there was a desire for the expansion of responsible government and elimination of the legislative deadlock between Upper and Lower Canada, and their replacement with provincial legislatures in a federation. This was especially pushed by the liberal Reform movement of Upper Canada and the French-Canadian Parti rouge in Lower Canada who favored a decentralized union in comparison to the Upper Canadian Conservative party and to some degree the French-Canadian Parti bleu, which favored a centralized union.

37. Federalism is the belief in a strong central government. Anti-Federalism is the belief in a strong provincial government. Based on the passage above which of the following supported a Federalist government

   a. Liberal Reform Movement of Upper Canada
   b. The French Canadian Parti Rouge in Lower Canada
   c. The Upper Canadian Conservative Party
   d. A & B

38. Which of the following was not a concern that led to the Canadian Federation

   a. Fear of American expansion
   b. Fear of Native American expansion
   c. Increased Nationalism
   d. Desire for a faster government

Market Failure 2

Questions 39 - 40 refer to the passage below.

Extreme economies of scale can lead to natural monopoly. Competition failure of an extreme case as a restraint on producers can result in the overlapping concepts of "practical" and "technical" monopoly.

39. A pharmaceutical business creates a new treatment for cancer. They patent their treatment, which restricts anyone from creating generic versions of their product for seven years. What type of monopoly do they have?

   a. A practical monopoly
   b. A technical monopoly
   c. A geographical monopoly
   d. This is not an example of a monopoly

40. An electricity company funds the construction of a new power grid in a small town. They use their own grid for free and are therefore able to charge their customers a lower rate. What type of monopoly does this lead to?

   a. A practical monopoly
   b. A technical monopoly
   c. A geographical monopoly
   d. This is not an example of a monopoly

Market Failure 3

Questions 41 - 42 refer to the passage below.

Public goods are those goods under supplied in a regular market. The major defining features of public goods is that people can consume them without paying and several people can consume the goods same time.

Externalities happen when there are significant social benefits or costs from consumption or production not reflected in prices at the market. As an example, education may lead to positive externalities such as less crime and an increase in skilled labor, while air pollution may lead to negative externality. Governments usually use taxes or other methods to restrict the production and sale of goods with negative externality. They subsidize or use other methods to promote goods that have positive externalities. Governments use this strategy to correct the distortions in prices caused by externalities. Demand and supply theory at the elementary stage is able to predict equilibrium but cannot account for adjustment speed due to equilibrium changes cause by shifts in demand or supply. [4]

41. Which of the following is a public good?

    a. Movie Theatres
    b. Mass Transit
    c. Grocery Stores
    d. Public Broadcasting

42. Which of the following is a negative externality of public roads?

    a. Taxes
    b. Toll Roads
    c. Air Pollution
    d. Traffic

The Business Cycle 1

Questions 43 - 44 refer to the passage and chart below.

The economics of an economy undergoing depression was the impetus for the creation of a separate discipline of study known as "macroeconomics." During the 1930s Great Depression era, John Maynard Keynes published a book titled The General Theory of Employment, Interest and Money. The book outlined the major theories of what became known as Keynesian economics. Keynes argued that aggregate demand during periods of economic downturns may be insufficient resulting in high levels of unemployment and inefficiency. [4]

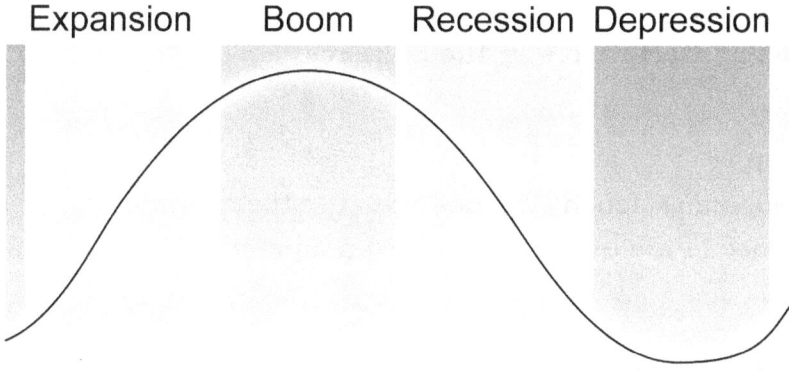

43. Based on the image above, how would economists characterize the United States housing market collapse (2007-2009)?

a. Expansion
b. Boom
c. Recession
d. Depression

44. Which of the following best explains Keynesian economics, based on the definition from the text: "...aggregate demand during periods of economic downturns may be insufficient resulting in high levels of unemployment and inefficiency?"

a. Demand decreases during periods of economic instability. This results in decreasing supply and less needed workers

b. Demand decreases during periods of economic instability. This results in increasing supply and less needed workers.

c. Demand increases during periods of economic instability. This results in decreasing supply that workers cannot afford, leading to a search for new jobs

d. Demand increases during periods of economic instability. This results in increasing supply that workers cannot afford, leading to a search for new jobs

The Business Cycle 2

Questions 43 - 44 refer to the passage and chart below.

Keynes advocated that the public sector should take active steps to formulate policies to respond to economic downturns. Such active policies can include fiscal policies by governments or monetary policies by central banks to stabilize output during the business cycle. A fundamental conclusion to be drawn from Keynesian economics is thus that, in some circumstances, there exists no effective automatic mechanism to move employment and output to full levels. The most influential interpretation of the General Theory is the IS/LM model developed by John Hicks. [4]

45. In 2009, President Obama passed the American Recovery and Reinvestment Act in response to the US Housing Market Collapse. Based on the text above, would Keynes approve of Obama's interference in the market?

a. Yes, Keynes would approve

b. No, Keynes would not approve

c. Keynes would claim that Obama's actions did not influence the outcome

d. There is not enough evidence in the text to determine an answer

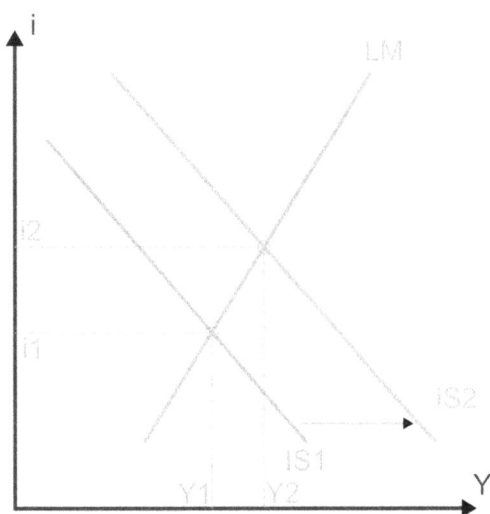

46. Above is a model of the IS/LM model mentioned in the text. Which of the following is true?

a. Higher interest rates (i) lead to an increase in the GDP (y)

b. Higher interest rates (i) lead to a decrease in the GDP (y)

c. Both are true

d. Neither are true

47. Which of the following is an accurate depiction of the graph above?

a. As Price increases, Quantity increases

b. As Price increases, Quantity decreases

c. As Price incrcases, Demand decreases

d. As Price increases, supply increases

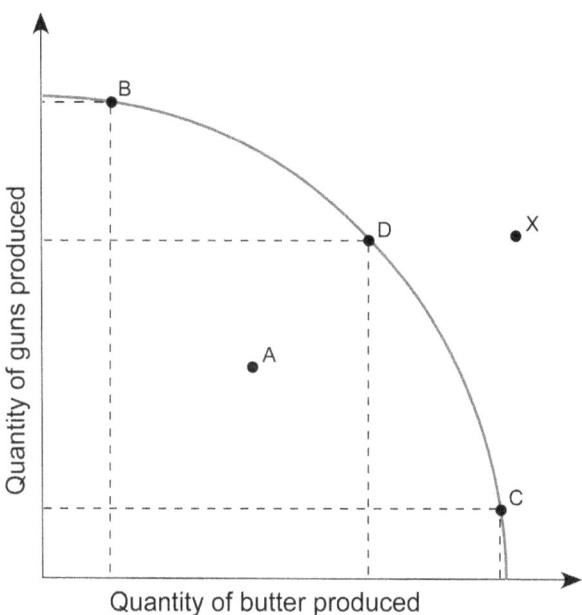

48. Above is the famous "Guns and Butter Curve" used to teach the idea of opportunity cost. Based on the graph, which of the following is the best explanation for opportunity cost?

a. As production of one product increases, so does production of the other, indicating a healthy economy

b. As production of one product increases, the other product is unaffected because they exist in different markets, thus investors should diversify their investments.

c. As production of one product increases, production of the other decreases due to production limits.

d. None of the above are true.

49. The federal government can print more money to stimulate the economy, but what does this lead to?

a. Deflation

b. Stagflation

c. Inflation

d. Stagnation

50. Classical economics holds that over time, economic problems will be corrected by the

   a. Policies of the government
   b. Invisible hand of the market
   c. People
   d. Raising of taxes

Reading

Passage 1 - Tarzan of the Apes

Edgar Rice Burroughs

Questions 1 - 2 refer to the following passage

Almost silently the ape-man sped on in the track of Terkoz and his prey, but the sound of his approach reached the ears of the fleeing beast and spurred it on to greater speed.

Three miles were covered before Tarzan overtook them, and then Terkoz, seeing that further flight was futile, dropped to the ground in a small open glade, that he might turn and fight for his prize or be free to escape unhampered if he saw that the pursuer was more than a match for him.

He still grasped Jane in one great arm as Tarzan bounded like a leopard into the arena which nature had provided for this primeval-like battle.

When Terkoz saw that it was Tarzan who pursued him, he jumped to the conclusion that this was Tarzan's woman, since they were of the same kind--white and hairless--and so he rejoiced at this opportunity for double revenge upon his hated enemy.

To Jane the strange apparition of this god-like man was as wine to sick nerves.

From the description which Clayton and her father and Mr. Philander had given her, she knew that it must be the same wonderful creature who had saved them, and she saw in him only a protector and a friend.

But as Terkoz pushed her roughly aside to meet Tarzan's charge, and she saw the great proportions of the ape and the mighty muscles and the fierce fangs, her heart quailed. How could any vanquish such a mighty antagonist?

Like two charging bulls they came together, and like two wolves sought each other's throat. Against the long canines of the ape was pitted the thin blade of the man's knife.

1. Based on the author's description of Terkoz, he is most probably which of the following?

    a. A lion

    b. A poacher

    c. A white man

    d. An ape

2. Apes, leopards, wolves and bulls: the author describes Tarzan through animal imagery to suggest:

    a. That Tarzan has the power to shape-shift.

    b. That Tarzan has grown up among many animals.

    c. That Tarzan is uncivilized.

    d. That Tarzan straddles the worlds of man and nature.

Passage 2 - The Voyages of Dr. Dolittle

Hugh Lofting

Questions 3 - 5 refer to the following passage

Stealthily creeping up the sands till she could get behind the cover of some bushes before she took to her wings, Polynesia went off in the direction of the town; while I remained alone upon the shore fascinatedly watching this unbelievable monster wallowing in the shallow sea.

It moved very little. From time to time it lifted its head out of the water showing its enormously long neck and horns. Occasionally it would try and draw itself up, the way a snail does when he goes to move, but almost at once it would sink down again as if exhausted. It seemed to me to act as though it were hurt underneath; but the lower part of it, which was below the level of the water, I could not see.

I was still absorbed in watching the great beast when Polynesia returned with the Doctor. They approached so silently and so cautiously that I neither saw nor heard them coming till I found them crouching beside me on the sand.

One sight of the snail changed the Doctor completely. His eyes just sparkled with delight. I had not seen him so thrilled and happy since the time we caught the Jabizri beetle when we first landed on the island.

3. Readers can attribute the Doctor's happiness at seeing the "snail" to:

   a. The fact that it reminds him of the Jabizri beetle

   b. The Doctor's penchant for terrible beasts

   c. The innate beauty of the "snail."

   d. His fascination with strange and interesting creatures

4. For the narrator, the most fascinating thing about the beast is:

   a. Its neck and horns

   b. Its resemblance to a snail

   c. The Doctor's reaction to it

   d. Its strangeness

5. What is the most appropriate inference to make about the setting?

   a. The setting is the near future or age-old past, and is a time when mega-fauna roam the Earth once more

   b. The setting is much the same as Jurassic Park, a theme park where impossible creatures now live

   c. It is a tropical jungle, vividly abound with life of every kind

   d. Land, surrounded by water

Passage 3 - A Man of Means

P. G. Wodehouse and C. H. Bovill

Questions 6 - 10 refer to the following passage

When the Coppins wanted anything, they asked for it; and it seemed to Roland that they wanted pretty nearly everything. If Mr. Coppin had reached his present age without the assistance of a gold watch, he might surely have struggled along to the end on gun-metal. In any case, a man of his years should have been thinking of higher things than mere gauds and trinkets. A like criticism applied to Mrs. Coppin's demand for a silk petticoat, which struck Roland as simply indecent. Frank and Percy took theirs mostly in specie. It was Muriel who struck the worst blow by insisting on a hired motor-car.

Roland hated motor-cars, especially when they were driven by Albert Potter, as this one was. Albert, that strong, silent man, had but one way of expressing his emotions, namely to open the throttle and shave the paint off trolley-cars. Disappointed love was giving Albert a good deal of discomfort at this time, and he found it made him feel better to go round corners on two wheels. As Muriel sat next to him on these expeditions, Roland squashing into the tonneau with Frank and Percy, his torments were subtle. He was not given a chance to forget, and the only way in which he could obtain a momentary diminution of the agony was to increase the speed to sixty miles an hour.

It was in this fashion that they journeyed to the neighboring town of Lexingham to see M. Etienne Feriaud perform his feat of looping the loop in his aeroplane.

It was Brother Frank's idea that they should make up a party to go and see M. Feriaud. Frank's was one of those generous, unspoiled natures which never grow _blasé_ at the sight of a fellow human taking a sporting chance at hara-kiri. He was a well-known figure at every wild animal exhibition within a radius of fifty miles, and M. Feriaud drew him like a magnet.

6. From Roland's point of view, the Coppins:

    a. Frequently buy things they do not need.

    b. Have outdated tastes in fineries.

    c. Live above their means.

    d. Are exclusively driven by material wants.

7. Which of the following choices best describes the narrators' tone in this passage?

    a. Humorous

    b. Sarcastic

    c. Dour

    d. Hopeful

8. It is reasonable to guess that Albert Potter's "subtle torments" include:

    a. His overly occupied motor-car.

    b. Chauffeuring his unrequited love and her partner.

    c. Expressing emotions by driving dangerously.

    d. Roland's displeasure at motor-cars.

9. The authors portray Frank as:

    a. Malicious

    b. Childish

    c. Excitable

    d. Suicidal

10. The central point of this passage is to:

    a. Establish the antagonism between Albert and Roland.

    b. Change the setting from the Coppins' home to Lexingham.

    c. Describe Roland's consternation with the Coppins.

    d. Build the action, which will peak in the following section.

Passage 4 - Old Mother West Wind

Thornton W. Burgess

Questions 11 - 13 refer to the following passage

"In those days all the Frogs had tails, long handsome tails of which they were very, very proud indeed," continued Grandfather Frog. "The King of all the Frogs was twice as big as any other Frog, and his tail was three times as long. He was very proud, oh, very proud indeed of his long tail. He used to sit and admire it until he thought that there never had been and never could be another such tail. He used to wave it back and forth in the water, and every time he waved it all the other Frogs would cry 'Ah!' and 'Oh!' Every day the King grew more vain. He did nothing at all but eat and sleep and admire his tail.

"Now all the other Frogs did just as the King did, so pretty soon none of the Frogs were doing anything but sitting about eating, sleeping and admiring their own tails and the King's.

"Now you all know that people who do nothing worth while in this world are of no use and there is little room for them. So when Mother Nature saw how useless had become the Frog tribe she called the King Frog before her and she said:

"'Because you can think of nothing but your beautiful tail it shall be taken away from you. Because you do nothing but eat and sleep your mouth shall become wide like a door, and your eyes shall start forth from your head. You shall become bow-legged and ugly to look at, and all the world shall laugh at you.'

"The King Frog looked at his beautiful tail and already it seemed to have grown shorter. He looked again and it was shorter still. Every time he looked his tail had grown shorter and smaller. By and by when he looked there was nothing left but a little stub which he couldn't even wriggle. Then even that disappeared, his eyes popped out of his head and his mouth grew bigger and bigger."

Old Grandfather Frog stopped and looked sadly at a foolish green fly coming his way. "Chug-arum," said Grandfather Frog, opening his mouth very wide and hopping up in the air. When he sat down again on his big lily pad the green fly was nowhere to be seen. Grandfather Frog smacked his lips and continued:

"And from that day to this every Frog has started life with a big tail, and as he has grown bigger and bigger his tail has grown smaller and smaller, until finally it disappears, and then he remembers how foolish and useless it is to be vain of what nature has given us. And that is how I came to lose my tail," finished Grandfather Frog.

11. It is implied that the eagle's head is white because:

a. He possesses angelic qualities

b. This represents Mother Nature "crowning" him King of Birds

c. He is the biggest and strongest of all birds

d. He is as old as King Bear

12. What can be reasonably inferred from the story's conclusion, about the rulership of animals?

a. Tradition is less important than innovation

b. Peter Rabbit is now more educated about the laws of the animal kingdom

c. Birds of a feather flock together

d. Might makes right

13. Sammy Jay's telling of the story of King Eagle suggests that:

a. Peter Rabbit is, in fact, jealous of the ability to fly.

b. Mother Nature may make significant decisions on a whim.

c. There is some doubt as to why the eagle is the King of Birds.

d. Stories are necessary to resolve disputes.

Passage 5 - Mother West Wind 'How' Stories

Thornton W. Burgess

How Old King Eagle Won His White Head

Questions 14 - 16 refer to the following passage

Peter Rabbit sat on the edge of the dear Old Briar-patch, staring up into the sky with his head tipped back until it made his neck ache. Way, way up in the sky was a black speck sailing across the snowy white face of a cloud. It didn't seem possible that it could be alive way up there. But it was. Peter knew that it was, and he knew who it was. It was King Eagle. By and by it disappeared over towards the Great Mountain. Peter rubbed the back of his neck, which ached because he had tipped his head back so long. Then he gave a little sigh.

"I wonder what it seems like to be able to fly like that," said he out loud, a way he sometimes has.

"Are you envious?" asked a voice so close to him that Peter jumped. There was Sammy Jay sitting in a little tree just over his head.

"No!" snapped Peter, for it made him a wee bit cross to be so startled.

"No, I'm not envious, Sammy Jay. I'm not envious of any bird. The ground is good enough for me. I was just wondering, that's all."

"Have you ever seen King Eagle close to?" asked Sammy.

"Once," replied Peter. "Once he came down to the Green Meadows and sat in that lone tree over there, and I was squatting in a bunch of grass quite near and could see him very plainly. He is big and fierce-looking, but he looks his name, every inch a king. I've wondered a good many times since how it happens that he has a white head."

"Because," replied Sammy, "he is just what he looks to be,--king of the birds,--and that white head is the sign of his royalty given his great-great-ever-so-great-grandfather by Old Mother Nature, way back in the beginning of things."

Peter's eyes sparkled. "Tell me about it, Sammy," he begged. "Tell me about it, and I won't quarrel with you any more."

"All right, Peter. I'll tell you the story, because it will do you good to hear it. I supposed everybody knew it. All birds do. That is why we all look up to King Eagle," replied Sammy.

"Way back in the beginning of things, old King Bear ruled in the Green Forest, as you know. That is, he ruled the animals and all the little people who lived on the ground, but he didn't rule the birds. You see the birds were not willing to be ruled over by an animal. They wanted one of their own kind. So they refused to have old King Bear as their king and went to Old Mother Nature to ask her to appoint a king of the air. Now Mr. Eagle was one of the biggest and strongest and most respected of all the birds of the air. There were some, like Mr. Goose and Mr. Swan, who were bigger, but they spent most of their time on the water or the earth, and they had no great claws or hooked beak to command respect as did Mr. Eagle. So Old Mother Nature made Mr. Eagle king of the air, and as was quite right and proper, all the birds hastened to pay him homage.

14. It is implied that the eagle's head is white because:

    a. He possesses angelic qualities

    b. This represents Mother Nature "crowning" him King of Birds

    c. He is the biggest and strongest of all birds

    d. He is as old as King Bear

15. What can be reasonably inferred from the story's conclusion, about the rulership of animals?

    a. Tradition is less important than innovation

    b. Peter Rabbit is now more educated about the laws of the animal kingdom

    c. Birds of a feather flock together

    d. Might makes right

16. Sammy Jay's telling of the story of King Eagle suggests that:

    a. Peter Rabbit is, in fact, jealous of the ability to fly.

    b. Mother Nature may make significant decisions on a whim.

    c. There is some doubt as to why the eagle is the King of Birds.

    d. Different animal species do not share their traditional stories.

Passage 6 - Date Squares

Questions 17 - 20 refer to the following recipe.

Ingredients

1 1/2 cups rolled oats
1 1/2 cups sifted pastry flour
1/4 teaspoon salt
3/4 teaspoon baking soda
1 cup packed brown sugar
3/4 cup butter, softened

3/4 pound pitted dates, diced
1 cup water
1/3 cup packed brown sugar
1 teaspoon lemon juice

Directions

Preheat oven to 350 degrees F (175 degrees C).

In a large bowl, combine oats, pastry flour, salt, 1 cup brown sugar, and baking soda. Mix in the butter until crumbly. Press half of the mixture into the bottom of a 9-inch square baking pan.

In a small saucepan over medium heat, combine the dates, water, and 1/3 cup brown sugar. Bring to a boil, and cook for 3 minutes, stirring every 30 seconds. Stir in lemon juice, and remove from heat. Spread the filling over the base, and pat the remaining crumb mixture on top.

Bake for 20 to 25 minutes in preheated oven, or until top is lightly toasted. Cool before cutting into squares.

17. What is a preheated oven?

    a. A special type of oven

    b. An oven that is heated to temperature

    c. An oven that is not heated to temperature

    d. An oven that has not been turned on

18. How many times will the mixture of dates, water and brown sugar need to be stirred?

    a. 2 times

    b. 4 times

    c. 6 times

    d. 8 times

    e. None of the above

19. What does pat mean?

    a. Gently tap

    b. Press hard

    c. Spread evenly

    d. None of the above

20. How much brown sugar does this recipe require?

    a. 1 cup

    b. 1 1/3 cups

    c. 2 cups

    d. 2 1/3 cups

Passage 7 - Excursions and Poems

The Writings of Henry David Thoreau, Volume V (of 20)

Henry David Thoreau

Questions 21 - 24 refer to the following recipe.

The river swelleth more and more,
Like some sweet influence stealing o'er
The passive town; and for a while
Each tussock makes a tiny isle,
Where, on some friendly Ararat,
Resteth the weary water-rat.

No ripple shows Musketaquid,
Her very current e'en is hid,
As deepest souls do calmest rest
When thoughts are swelling in the breast,
And she that in the summer's drought
Doth make a rippling and a rout,
Sleeps from Nahshawtuck to the Cliff,
Unruffled by a single skiff.

But by a thousand distant hills
The louder roar a thousand rills,
And many a spring which now is dumb,
And many a stream with smothered hum,
Doth swifter well and faster glide,
Though buried deep beneath the tide.
Our village shows a rural Venice,
Its broad lagoons where yonder fen is;
As lovely as the Bay of Naples
Yon placid cove amid the maples;
And in my neighbor's field of corn
I recognize the Golden Horn.

Here Nature taught from year to year,
When only red men came to hear,--
Methinks 't was in this school of art
Venice and Naples learned their part;
But still their mistress, to my mind,
Her young disciples leaves behind.

21. The voice's main purpose in this poem is to communicate that:

   a. Nature is a cruel mistress

   b. Parts of the United States bear uncanny resemblance to Italy

   c. What is striking about the scenery is how well the old architecture blends in with the greenery

   d. The voice's rural hometown rivals any Naples or Venice (places in Italy)

22. The overall mood of the poem is:

   a. Affectionate

   b. Dismissive

   c. Jealous

   d. Passive

23. "But still their mistress, to my mind/Her young disciples leave behind." What is the most probable message of these final lines?

   a. Americans have chosen a path that eschews traditional aboriginal wisdom

   b. The classical ideal of beauty takes its cues from Nature, and contemporary artists forget this fact

   c. Countryside travelers tend to be hot-headed, and thus lose their way

   d. The voice of the poem here reveals that Nature-as-mistress analogizes a wayward love affair, which those involved inevitably let drop

24. Which choice best fits the role/purpose of the Musketaquid? Note: The Musketaquid was a boat constructed by Thoreau.

    a. In light of the poem's religious references, e.g. to Ararat, the Musketaquid signifies the journey of self-discovering and embracing Christian beliefs

    b. There is no significance to the Musketaquid: it was included in the poem because the poet was proud of building it

    c. The Musketaquid serves to "transport" the reader through the lush countryside of the poem's setting.

    d. Featuring a boat in the poem helps the voice allude to Venice, a city known for its romantic aquatic setting

Passage 8 - Thunderstorms

Questions 25 - 28 refer to the following passage.

Warm air is less dense than cool air, so warm air rises within cooler air like a hot air balloon or warm water in an ocean current. Clouds form as warm air carrying moisture rises. As the warm air rises, it cools. The moist water vapor begins to condense as the temperature cools. This releases energy that keeps the air warmer than its surroundings. The result is that it continues to rise. If enough instability is present in the atmosphere, this process will continue long enough for cumulonimbus clouds to form. These clouds support lightning and thunder. All thunderstorms, regardless of type, go through three stages: the cumulus stage, the mature stage, and the dissipation stage. Depending on the conditions in the atmosphere, these three stages can take anywhere from 20 minutes to several hours.[33]

25. This passage tells us:

    a. Warm air is denser than cool air

    b. All thunderstorms will go through three stages.

    c. Thunderstorms may occur without clouds present.

    d. The stages of a thunderstorm conclude within just a few minutes.

26. When warm air rises through colder air, it results in:

    a. Evaporation

    b. Humidity

    c. Clear skies

    d. Condensation

27. What is the correct order?

a. Warm air rises, cools as it gets higher, water condenses, warms the air, and the air rises more.

b. Warm air rises, warms up more as it get higher, water condenses, warms the air, and the air rises more.

c. Warm air rises, cools as it gets higher, water condenses, cools the air, and the air rises more.

d. None of the above.

28. Cumulonimbus clouds are forming now. What must be true?

a. The process of warm air rising and water condensing hasn't started.
b. The process of warm air rising and water condensing is just starting now.
c. The process of warm air rising and water condensing has being going on for some time.
d. None of the above.

Passage 9 - On The High Road

Antov Checkov

A Dramatic Study

Questions 29 - 32 refer to the following passage.

Characters

    Tihon Evstigneyev, The Proprietor Of A Inn On The Main Road
    Semyon Sergeyevitch Bortsov, A Ruined Landowner
    Maria Egorovna, His Wife
    Savva, An Aged Pilgrim
    Nazarovna And Efimovna, Women Pilgrims
    Fedya, A Labourer
    Egor Merik, A Tramp
    Kusma, A Driver
    Postman
    Bortsov's Wife's Coachman
    Pilgrims, Cattle-Dealers, Etc.

The action takes place in one of the provinces of Southern Russia

[The scene is laid in TIHON'S bar. On the right is the bar-counter and shelves with bottles. At the back is a door leading out of the house. Over it, on the outside, hangs a dirty red lantern. The floor and the forms, which stand against the wall, are closely occupied by pilgrims and passers-by. Many of them, for lack of space, are sleeping as they sit. It is late at night. As the curtain rises thunder is heard, and lightning is seen through the door.]

[TIHON is behind the counter. FEDYA is half-lying in a heap on one of the forms, and is quietly playing on a concertina. Next to him is BORTSOV, wearing a shabby summer overcoat. SAVVA, NAZAROVNA, and EFIMOVNA are stretched out on the floor by the benches.]

EFIMOVNA. [To NAZAROVNA] Give the old man a nudge dear! Can't get any answer out of him.

NAZAROVNA. [Lifting the corner of a cloth covering of SAVVA'S face] Are you alive or are you dead, you holy man?

SAVVA. Why should I be dead? I'm alive, mother! [Raises himself on his elbow] Cover up my feet, there's a saint! That's it. A bit more on the right one. That's it, mother. God be good to us.

NAZAROVNA. [Wrapping up SAVVA'S feet] Sleep, little father.

SAVVA. What sleep can I have? If only I had the patience to endure this pain, mother; sleep's quite another matter. A sinner doesn't deserve to be given rest. What's that noise, pilgrim-woman?

NAZAROVNA. God is sending a storm. The wind is wailing, and the rain is pouring down, pouring down. All down the roof and into the windows like dried peas. Do you hear? The windows of heaven are opened... [Thunder] Holy, holy, holy...

29. Which choice best describes the main purpose of this scene?

   a. The scene is meant to draw out the tensions between religious and socialist values — a conflict typical of Soviet era Russia, the setting of the play

   b. The scene depicts the suffering and misfortune of a hodge-podge of characters brought together by the storm

   c. The scene is intended to characterize the pilgrims as pariahs and misfits

   d. In the main, the scene establishes the struggle between the willful downtrodden and their vengeful god

30. It can be inferred from this scene that Savva is:

   a. Dying

   b. Nazirovna and Efimovna's father

   c. Delusional

   d. Reconciled to his suffering

31. Savva's pain is most likely attributable to which of the following?

   a. Sin, or the punishment of God
   b. Tihon, who bears him ill will
   c. An accident in the storm
   d. His travels

32. What kind of mood is established in this first scene?

   a. Cruel and hopeless
   b. Decreasing
   c. Gloomy
   d. Holy
   e. Confused

Passage 10 - Trifles

Susan Glaspell

Questions 33 - 37 refer to the following passage.

Characters

George Henderson (County Attorney)
Henry Peters (Sheriff)
Lewis Hale, A Neighboring Farmer
Mrs Peters
Mrs Hale

SCENE: _The kitchen is the now abandoned farmhouse of_ JOHN WRIGHT, _a gloomy kitchen, and left without having been put in order--unwashed pans under the sink, a loaf of bread outside the bread-box, a dish-towel on the table--other signs of incompleted work. At the rear the outer door opens and the_ SHERIFF _comes in followed by the_ COUNTY ATTORNEY and HALE. The SHERIFF and HALE are men in middle life, the COUNTY ATTORNEY is a young man; all are much bundled up and go at once to the stove. They are followed by the two women--the SHERIFF's wife first; she is a slight wiry woman, a thin nervous face. MRS HALE is larger and would ordinarily be called more comfortable looking, but she is disturbed now and looks fearfully about as she enters. The women have come in slowly, and stand close together near the door.

COUNTY ATTORNEY: (rubbing his hands) This feels good. Come up to the fire, ladies.

MRS PETERS: (after taking a step forward) I'm not -- cold.

SHERIFF: (unbuttoning his overcoat and stepping away from the stove as if to mark the beginning of official business) Now, Mr Hale, before we move things about, you explain to Mr Henderson just what you saw when you came here yesterday morning.

COUNTY ATTORNEY: By the way, has anything been moved? Are things just as you left them yesterday?

SHERIFF: (looking about) It's just the same. When it dropped below zero last night I thought I'd better send Frank out this morning to make a fire for us--no use getting pneumonia with a big case on, but I told him not to touch anything except the stove--and you know Frank.
COUNTY ATTORNEY: Somebody should have been left here yesterday.

SHERIFF: Oh--yesterday. When I had to send Frank to Morris Center for that man who went crazy--I want you to know I had my hands full yesterday. I knew you could get back from Omaha by today and as long as I went over everything here myself

COUNTY ATTORNEY: Well, Mr Hale, tell just what happened when you came here yesterday morning.

HALE: Harry and I had started to town with a load of potatoes. We came along the road from my place and as I got here I said, I'm going to see if I can't get John Wright to go in with me on a party telephone.' I spoke to Wright about it once before and he put me off, saying folks talked too much anyway, and all he asked was peace and quiet--I guess you know about how much he talked himself; but I thought maybe if I went to the house and talked about it before his wife, though I said to Harry that I didn't know as what his wife wanted made much difference to John

COUNTY ATTORNEY: Let's talk about that later, Mr Hale. I do want to talk about that, but tell now just what happened when you got to the house.

HALE: I didn't hear or see anything; I knocked at the door, and still it was all quiet inside. I knew they must be up, it was past eight o'clock. So I knocked again, and I thought I heard somebody say, 'Come in.' I wasn't sure, I'm not sure yet, but I opened the door--this door (indicating the door by which the two women are still standing) and there in that rocker--(pointing to it) sat Mrs Wright.

(They all look at the rocker.)

COUNTY ATTORNEY: What--was she doing?

HALE: She was rockin' back and forth. She had her apron in her hand and was kind of--pleating it.

COUNTY ATTORNEY: And how did she--look?

HALE: Well, she looked queer.

COUNTY ATTORNEY: How do you mean--queer?

HALE: Well, as if she didn't know what she was going to do next. And kind of done up.

33. The Sheriff and County Attorney are visiting the Wrights' kitchen for what purpose?

a. To investigate a murder

b. To take Hale's account of events at the Wright household

c. To check in on the women

d. To compare facts

34. The relationship between the Sheriff and County Attorney is best described as:

a. Competitive

b. Caring

c. Each is critical of the other

d. Professional

35. What can be inferred from Hale's statement to the Sheriff and Attorney?

a. Wright was going to invest with his neighbors in a telephone

b. Mrs. Wright is the killer

c. Hale's views on sexual orientation are conservative

d. The rural setting of the scene

36. The description of Mrs. Wright as "kind of done up" implies:

a. Mrs. Wright was well-dressed on the night of her husband's death

b. Mrs. Wright was attempting to hide her guilt

c. Mrs. Wright was extremely tired out when Hale found her

d. Mrs. Wright looked clean

37. What evidence do we have that something is wrong with the kitchen?

a. A murder took place there

b. The reaction of the Sheriff and Mr. Hale's wives

c. Signs of incomplete work

d. Its location: it is in an abandoned farmhouse

Passage 11 - What is Mardi Gras?

Questions 38 – 40 refer to the following passage.

Mardi Gras is fast becoming one of the South's most famous and most celebrated holidays. The word Mardi Gras comes from the French and the literal translation is "Fat Tuesday." The holiday has also been called Shrove Tuesday, due to its associations with Lent. The purpose of Mardi Gras is to celebrate and enjoy before the Lenten season of fasting and repentance begins.

What originated by the French Explorers in New Orleans, Louisiana in the 17th century is now celebrated all over the world. Panama, Italy, Belgium and Brazil all host large scale Mardi Gras celebrations, and many smaller cities and towns celebrate this fun loving Tuesday as well. Usually held in February or early March, Mardi Gras is a day of extravagance, a day for people to eat, drink and be merry, to wear costumes, masks and to dance to jazz music.

The French explorers on the Mississippi River would be in shock today if they saw the opulence of the parades and floats that grace the New Orleans streets during Mardi Gras these days. Parades in New Orleans are divided by organizations. These are more commonly known as Krewes.

Being a member of a Krewe is quite a task because Krewes are responsible for overseeing the parades. Each Krewe's parade is ruled by a Mardi Gras "King and Queen." The role of the King and Queen is to "bestow" gifts on their adoring fans as the floats ride along the street. They throw doubloons, which is fake money and usually colored green, purple and gold, which are the colors of Mardi Gras. Beads in those color shades are also thrown and cups are thrown as well. Beads are by far the most popular souvenir of any Mardi Gras parade, with each spectator attempting to gather as many as possible.

38. The purpose of Mardi Gras is to

    a. Repent for a month.

    b. Celebrate in extravagant ways.

    c. Be a member of a Krewe.

    d. Explore the Mississippi.

39. From reading the passage we can infer that "Kings and Queens"

    a. Have to be members of a Krewe.

    b. Have to be French.

    c. Have to know how to speak French.

    d. Have to give away their own money.

40. Which group of people began to hold Mardi Gras celebrations?

   a. Settlers from Italy

   b. Members of Krewes

   c. French explorers

   d. Belgium explorers

Mathematics

1. A map uses a scale of 1:100,000. How much distance on the ground is 3 inches on the map if the scale is in inches?

   a. 13 inches

   b. 300,000 inches

   c. 30,000 inches

   d. 333.999 inches

2. Divide 9.60 by 3.2.

   a. 2.50

   b. 3

   c. 2.3

   d. 6.4

3. Which one of the following is greater than a third?

   a. 84/231

   b. 6/35

   c. 3/22

   d. b and c

4. Which of the following numbers is the largest?

   a. 1

   b. $\sqrt{2}$

   c. 3/2

   d. 4/3

5. Driver B drove his car 20 km/h faster than the driver A, and driver B traveled 480 km 2 hours before driver A. What was the speed of driver A?

   a. 70
   b. 80
   c. 60
   d. 90

6. If a train travels at 72 kilometers per hour, how far will it travel in 12 seconds?

   a. 200 meters
   b. 220 meters
   c. 240 meters
   d. 260 meters

7. Tony bought 15 dozen eggs for $80. 16 eggs were broken during loading and unloading. He sold the remaining eggs for $0.54 each. What is his percent profit?

   a. 11%
   b. 11.2%
   c. 11.5%
   d. 12%

8. In a class of 83 students, 72 are present. What percent of students are absent?

   a. 12%
   b. 13%
   c. 14%
   d. 15%

9. In a local election at polling station A, 945 voters cast their vote out of 1270 registered voters. At polling station B, 860 cast their vote out of 1050 registered voters and at station C, 1210 cast their vote out of 1440 registered voters. What was the total turnout including all three polling stations?

   a. 70%
   b. 74%
   c. 76%
   d. 80%

10. Estimate 5205 ÷ 25

    a. 108
    b. 308
    c. 208
    d. 408

11. 7/15 − 3/10 =

    a. 1/6
    b. 4/5
    c. 1/7
    d. 1 1/3

12. Susan wants to buy a leather jacket that costs $545.00 and is on sale for 10% off. What is the approximate cost?

    a. $525
    b. $450
    c. $475
    d. $500

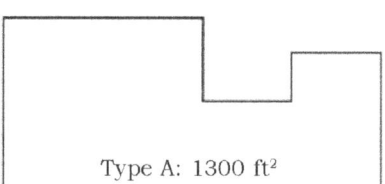

Type A: 1300 ft²

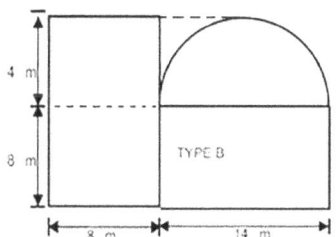

TYPE B
4 m
8 m
8 m
14 m

13. The price of houses in a certain subdivision is based on the total area. Susan is watching her budget and wants to choose the house with the lowest area. Which house type, A (1300 ft²) or B, should she choose if she would like the house with the lowest price?
(1cm² = 4.0ft² & π = 22/7)

    a. Type B is smaller 140 ft²

    b. Type A is smaller

    c. Type B is smaller at 855 ft²

    d. Type B is larger

14. Estimate 2009 x 108.

    a. 110,000

    b. 2,0000

    c. 21,000

    d. 210,000

15. Simplify 0.12 + 1 2/5 – 1 3/5

    a. 1 1/25

    b. 3 3/25

    c. 1 2/5

    d. 2 3/5

16. Using the quadratic formula, solve the quadratic equation: $0.9x^2 + 1.8x - 2.7 = 0$

    a. 1 and 3

    b. -3 and 1

    c. -3 and -1

    d. -1 and 3

17. Subtract polynomial $5x^3 + x^2 + x + 5$ from $4x^3 - 2x^2 - 10$.

    a. $-x^3 - 3x^2 - x - 15$

    b. $9x^3 - 3x^2 - x - 15$

    c. $-x^3 - x^2 + x - 5$

    d. $9x^3 - x^2 + x + 5$

Practice Test Questions 2

18. Find x and y from the following system of equations:

$(4x + 5y)/3 = ((x - 3y)/2) + 4$
$(3x + y)/2 = ((2x + 7y)/3) - 1$

    a. (1, 3)

    b. (2, 1)

    c. (1, 1)

    d. (0, 1)

19. Using the factoring method, solve the quadratic equation: $x^2 + 12x - 13 = 0$

    a. -13 and 1

    b. -13 and -1

    c. 1 and 13

    d. -1 and 13

20. Using the quadratic formula, solve the quadratic equation: $((x^2 + 4x + 4) + (x^2 - 4x + 4)) / (x^2 - 4) = 0$.

    a. It has infinite numbers of solutions

    b. 0 and 1

    c. It has no solutions

    d. 0

21. Turn the following expression into a simple polynomial:

$5(3x^2 - 2) - x^2(2 - 3x)$

    a. $3x^3 + 17x^2 - 10$

    b. $3x^3 + 13x^2 + 10$

    c. $-3x^3 - 13x^2 - 10$

    d. $3x^3 + 13x^2 - 10$

22. Solve $(x^3 + 2)(x^2 - x) - x^5$.

    a. $2x^5 - x^4 + 2x^2 - 2x$

    b. $-x^4 + 2x^2 - 2x$

    c. $-x^4 - 2x^2 - 2x$

    d. $-x^4 + 2x^2 + 2x$

23. 9ab² + 8ab² =

  a. ab²
  b. 17ab²
  c. 17
  d. 17a²b²

24. Factor the polynomial x² - 7x - 30.

  a. (x + 15)(x - 2)
  b. (x + 10)(x - 3)
  c. (x - 10)(x + 3)
  d. (x - 15)(x + 2)

25. Turn the following expression into a simple polynomial: 1 - x(1 - x(1 - x))

  a. x³ + x² - x + 1
  b. -x³ - x² + x + 1
  c. -x³ + x² - x + 1
  d. x³ + x² - x - 1

26. 7(2y + 8) + 1 – 4(y + 5) =

  a. 10y + 36
  b. 10y + 77
  c. 18y + 37
  d. 10y + 37

27. Richard gives 's' amount of salary to each of his 'n' employees weekly. If he has 'x' amount of money then how many days he can employ these 'n' employees.

  a. sx/7n
  b. 7x/nx
  c. nx/7s
  d. 7x/ns

28. Factor the polynomial x² - 3x - 4.

  a. (x + 1)(x - 4)
  b. (x - 1)(x + 4)
  c. (x - 1)(x - 4)
  d. (x + 1)(x + 4)

29. Solve the inequality: (2x + 1)/(2x - 1) < 1.

    a. (-2, + ∞)

    b. (1, + ∞)

    c. (-∞, -2)

    d. (-∞, 1/2)

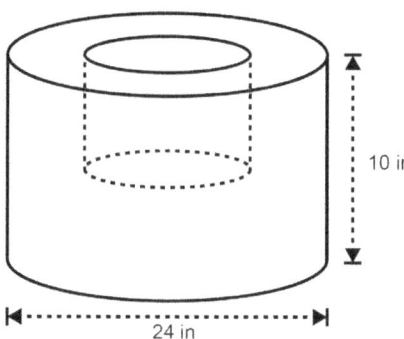

Note: Figure not drawn to scale

30. What is the volume of the above solid made by a hollow cylinder that is half the size (in all dimensions) of the larger cylinder?

    a. 1440 π in³

    b. 1260 π in³

    c. 1040 π in³

    d. 960 π in³

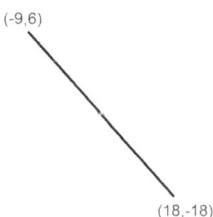

31. What is the slope of the line above?

    a. -8/9

    b. 9/8

    c. -9/8

    d. 8/9

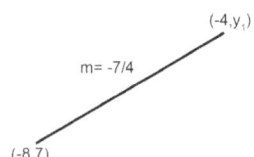

32. With the data given above, what is the value of y_1?

   a. 0
   b. -7
   c. 7
   d. 8

33. The area of a rectangle is 20 cm². If one side increases by 1 cm and other by 2 cm, the area of the new rectangle is 35 cm². Find the sides of the original rectangle.

   a. (4,8)
   b. (4,5)
   c. (2.5,8)
   d. b and c

34. Find the solution for the following linear equation:
$1/(4x - 2) = 5/6$

   a. 0.2
   b. 0.4
   c. 0.6
   d. 0.8

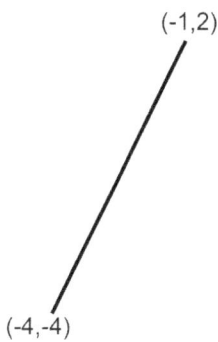

35. What is the slope of the line above?

a. 1
b. 2
c. 3
d. -2

36. How much water can be stored in a cylindrical container 5 meters in diameter and 12 meters high?

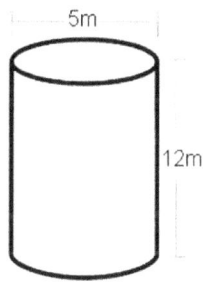

a. 235.65 m³
b. 223.65 m³
c. 240.65 m³
d. 252.65 m³

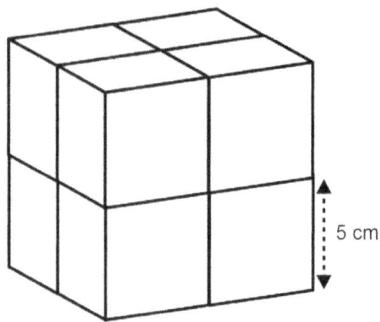

Note: Figure not drawn to scale

37. Assuming the figure above has cubes, what is the volume?

    a. 125 cm³
    b. 875 cm³
    c. 1000 cm³
    d. 500 cm³

38. Solve

x √5 - y = √5
x - y √5 = 5

    a. (0, -√5)
    b. (0, √5)
    c. (-√5, 0)
    d. (√5, 0)

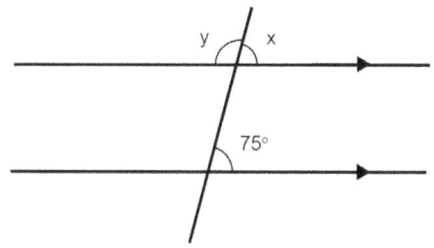

39. What is the value of the angle y?

   a. 25°
   b. 15°
   c. 30°
   d. 105°

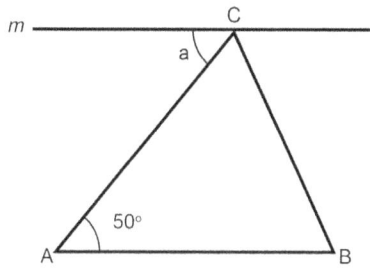

40. If the line *m* is parallel to the side AB of △ABC, what is angle *a*?

   a. 130°
   b. 25°
   c. 65°
   d. 50°

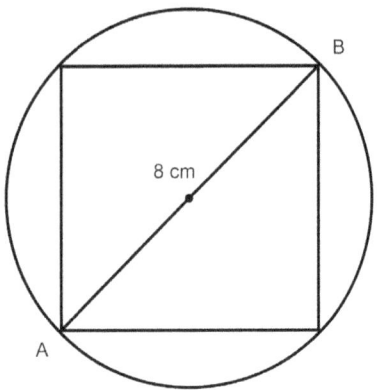

Note: figure not drawn to scale

41. What is area of the circle above?

    a. 4 π cm²
    b. 12 π cm²
    c. 10 π cm²
    d. 16 π cm²

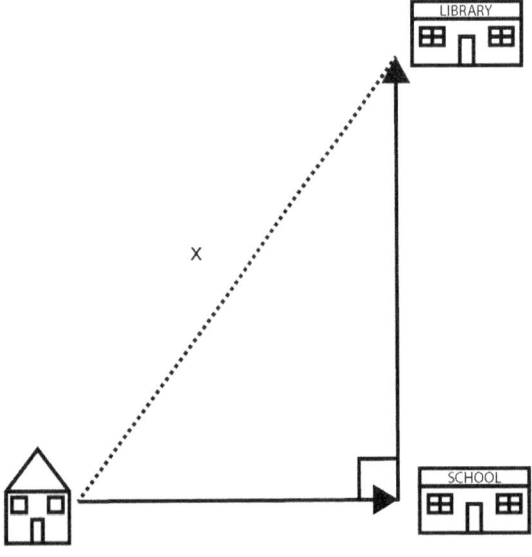

Note: figure not drawn to scale

42. Every day starting from his home Peter travels due east 3 kilometers to the school. After school he travels due north 4 kilometers to the library. What is the distance between Peter's home and the library?

   a. 15 km

   b. 10 km

   c. 5 km

   d. 12 ½ km

43. The width of a rectangle is two thirds of the length. The perimeter of this rectangle is 150 cm. Find the length of this shape.

   a. 30 cm

   b. 45 cm

   c. 60 cm

   d. 75 cm

44. The volume of a sphere with radius r is equal to the volume of a cylinder with radius 3r and height h. What is r/h equal to?

   a. 9/4

   b. 9/2

   c. 5

   d. 27/4

45. The area of a triangle is equal to 32 cm² and the height of this triangle is 4 cm less than 3 times the base. What is the length of the height?

   a. 12

   b. 16

   c. 18

   d. 24

46. The number of cars and corresponding prices in a car exhibition are given in the table below:

Value per car ($)	Number of cars
200,000	8
350,000	2
470,000	5
650,000	5

Which measure of central tendency; mean or median best represents the value of these 40 cars?

    a. The median

    b. The mean

    c. Both of them

    d. None of them

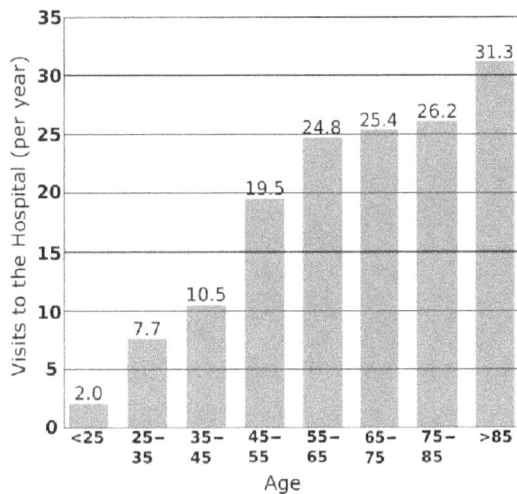

47. Consider the graph above.

How many hospital visits per year does a person aged 85 or more make?

    a. 26.2

    b. 31.3

    c. More than 31.3

    d. A decision cannot be made from this graph.

48. Based on this graph, how many visits per year do you expect a person that is 95 or older to make?

    a. 31.3 or more

    b. Less than 31.3

    c. 31.3

    d. A decision cannot be made from this graph.

49. Consider the following population growth chart.

Country	Population 2000	Population 2005
Japan	122,251,000	128,057,000
China	1,145,195,000	1,341,335,000
United States	253,339,000	310,384,000
Indonesia	184,346,000	239,871,000

What country is growing the fastest?

a. Japan
b. China
c. United States
d. Indonesia

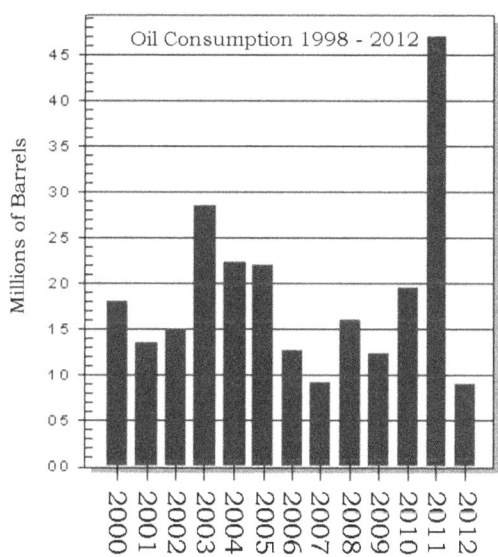

50. The graph above shows oil consumption in millions of barrels for the period, 1998 - 2012. What year did oil consumption peak?

a. 2011
b. 2010
c. 2008
d. 2009

Language Arts - Writing

Abuse of Science: The Atom Bomb

Questions 1 - 4 refer to the following passage

The cost of the two World Wars – not to mention the lives lost – could have easily paid for the entire energy consumption of the nations which waged them. [1] Even today, world powers are spending hundreds of billions of dollars sponsoring wars in a bid to control oil-rich areas. [2] Spending such astronomic sums on peaceful, environment friendly sources of energy would certainly produce results that would limit the energy needs of the planet as a whole. [3] Not to mention, resolving the conflicts between warring nations. [4]

For instance the atom bomb was developed during the Second World War by the recommendations of the great Albert Einstein - who is accepted as the father of modern physics; in fear of the Germans developing it and using on the Allies. [5] No matter what, the technology behind the atom bomb essentially had the power to resolve the war. [6] Using it to produce energy for power was an option wide open to be explored by scientists. [7] Today, as many as forty countries including countries like Egypt, harness nuclear energy as a dominant source of power alongside mainstream carbon sources. [8]

The two atom bombs dropped at Hiroshima and Nagasaki, as the consequence of the tragedy at Pearl Harbor, left catastrophic legacies to the generations that followed. [9] The generations that followed still have not recovered from the genetic disorders. [10] Almost seven decades passing later, abnormal births and birth defects continue to occur. [11]

1. Which sentence from the passage is an example of a sentence fragment?

    a. 3
    b. 4
    c. 5
    d. 6

2. Which of the following changes would focus attention on the main idea of the second paragraph?

    a. Yet, the technology behind the atom bomb essentially had the power of resolving the war itself which scientists like him failed to convey.
    b. As a result of that, the technology behind the atom bomb essentially had the power of resolving the war itself which scientists like him failed to convey.
    c. With respect to that, the technology behind the atom bomb essentially had the power of resolving the war itself which scientists like him failed to convey.
    d. Additionally, the technology behind the atom bomb essentially had the power of resolving the war itself which scientists like him failed to convey.

3. Which of the following changes are needed in sentence 5?

a. For instance the atom bomb was developed during the Second World War by the recommendations of the great Albert Einstein - who is accepted as the father of modern physics - in fear of the Germans developing it and using on the Allies.

b. For instance, the atom bomb was developed during the Second World War by the recommendations of the great Albert Einstein - who is accepted as the father of modern physics - in fear of the Germans developing it and using on the Allies.

c. For instance, the atom bomb was developed during the Second World War by the recommendations of the great Albert Einstein; who is accepted as the father of modern physics - in fear of the Germans developing it and using on the Allies.

d. For instance, the atom bomb was developed during the Second World War by the recommendations of the great Albert Einstein; who is accepted as the father of modern physics, in fear of the Germans developing it and using on the Allies.

4. Which of the following sentences, if inserted before sentence 7, would best illustrate the main idea of the passage?

a. The name of the technology is widely referred to in current science books published worldwide as nuclear fission.

b. This technology is, however, misused by many irresponsible states in the world today.

c. Nuclear fission that is used in the fuelling of the bomb, has the capacity to produce electrical energy which has turned out to be a major alternative later in the Twentieth Century.

d. Nuclear fission, which is the main technology behind the development of the atom bomb can also be used to produce gamma rays which has many applications in medical science.

Leg Surgery

Questions 5 - 8 refer to the following passage

The main reason many young women opt for surgery, despite the pain, inconvenience and cost, is the height discrimination in an increasingly competitive job market. [1] Almost all firms put certain height criteria for the candidates who apply. [2] For example, for an air stewardess position, women must be no more than 163 cm tall; whereas for jobs in foreign affairs, Chinese diplomats are required to match their foreign counterparts. [3] Height concerns also effect routine citizenship privileges such as driving licenses, which require a height of at least 157 cm to be eligible for taking the test in some places. [4]

The urge to undergo surgery is becoming increasingly popular among Chinese males as well. [5] "It offers me a 10 cm increase in my height, which can dramatically change my future," says Jing Yong, an interpreter working in Hong Kong. [6] "This will allow me better opportunities in the competitive job market here," adds the young multilingual who couldn't make it to the foreign ministry for being below 168 cm. [7]

Even parents approve of the idea, being fully aware of all the complexity and they are willing to finance such a labyrinth surgery. [8] "It's something that will give her confidence and achieve her goals in life. [9] Her height used to bother her tremendously, now this can change that," comments Swee Jing's father by her bedside as she is recovering from the eighteen-months process that involves elongating her tibia and fibula by placing two rods that will stimulate the extra growth of the bones. [10] They too are hopeful about the possibilities the surgery would affect the life of their daughter. [11]

5. Which sentence in the second paragraph is least relevant to the main idea of the first paragraph?

    a. 2

    b. 3

    c. 4

    d. 5

6. Which sentence is not consistent with the author's purpose?

    a. 3

    b. 6

    c. 9

    d. 12

7. Which of the following sentences, if inserted after sentence 7, would best illustrate the main idea of the passage?

    a. This is the main reason I am willing to undergo this surgery

    b. This artificial way of gaining height is turning out to be a new trend among the new generation in height conscious China.

    c. Height is a very big problem for Chinese people, particularly for those who wish to go abroad and carry the flag of China there.

    d. Young people like Yong will have to spend the rest of their lives with a fake pair of legs though.

8. Which of the following changes are needed in sentence 8?

    a. Even parents approve of the idea, being fully aware of all the sophistications and they are willing to finance such a labyrinth surgery.

    b. Even parents approve of the idea, being fully aware of all the complications and they are willing to finance such a sophisticated surgery.

    c. Even parents approve of the idea, being fully aware of the complexity and they are willing to finance such a sophisticated surgery.

    d. Even parents approve of the idea, being fully aware of all the complexity and they are willing to finance such a sophisticated surgery.

My Friend Luke

Questions 9 - 12 refer to the following passage

My forty-year old friend Luke is possibly the sweetest, shyest person enjoying his life on the entire Earth. [1] He is somewhat short, skinny and upright; has a thin moustache and a thinner trace of hair covering his head. [2] And since he has problems seeing distant things, he wears glasses that are small, thick and frameless; the round coffee-brown colored glasses give him a cool appearance uniquely suited to his personality. [3] Which I doubt belongs to any other person. [4]

There are traits in him seldom found in others. [5] While in a crowd, he walks sideways so as not to trouble others. [6] Instead of requesting a space to move ahead, he glides past to one side of the person blocking in his way. [7] If the gap turns out to be so narrow that it does not permit his bony frame to pass, he waits patiently for the person to move out of the way. [8] He is panicked by street dogs and neighbors' cats and to avoid them, he crosses to the other side of the street every now and then. [9]

Luke never speaks, as he thinks speaking is a waste of energy; something he is vehemently dedicated to saving. [10] Whenever he does, in order not to interrupt anybody, he speaks with a very soft, low tone – in a way no one ever notices him speaking in the first place. [11] Quite ironically, when he gets a rare chance to speak, he never succeeds in speaking more than two words before being interrupted by others. [12]

9. What sentence from the passage is an example of a sentence fragment?

    a. 4
    b. 5
    c. 6
    d. 7

10. Which sentence in the second paragraph is least relevant to the main idea of the second paragraph?

    a. 6
    b. 7
    c. 8
    d. 9

11. Which of the following sentences should be modified to reduce redundancy?

    a. 2
    b. 3
    c. 4
    d. 5

12. Which of the following sentences, if inserted before sentence 1, would best illustrate the main idea of the passage?

   a. But that does not bother him; rather he always seems to be happy in being able to utter those two words.

   b. Interestingly, he never insists in speaking with people more eloquently.

   c. What is more ironic, he never worked on his social skills and diction to be more communicative.

   d. As a result, Luke feels like hitting those interrupting him in their face.

Of Ease and Discipline

Questions 13 - 16 refer to the following passage

Looking at his watch, Ray thought it was time for a break. [1] So, he let the kids wrap their things up and head out of the classroom. [2] They seemed to like the idea of an extra five minutes before they would start with the boring recitation, turning page after page as one of them stood and read through the old Shakespearean dialect. [3] Some were interested in chatting with him as they approached him with the usual curiosity about a new teacher joining their class. [4] What they didn't know was he was their new music teacher just replacing the dull Mr. Drodsky who happened to be an 'expert' in American Literature with his dreadful Eastern European accent. [5] But for a day only. [6]

They were excited about the rhetoric that they finally have been spared of Mr. Drodsky's shrieking inquiries of "Aa you wiss me, chilsren?" [7] But as they came to know him closely, they were disappointed he would only occupy Mr. Drodsky's position for two weeks. [8] Mr. Drodsky was ill and would be away for the next fifteen days. [9] They seemed to like the news, but were also reluctant to be happy about it. [10] Nevertheless, they were happy about the substitution today and the arrival of their new music teacher. [11] The school would return to their jolly old days with regular music lessons and the parties. [12]

With ring of the bell, all the boys and girls started filling their seats as Ray continued chatting with the ones who had asked him about himself. [13] In a moment all the students – out of their old habits – were ready with their books open, waiting for the teacher to dictate who was in queue to read. [14] Ray was somewhat perplexed as he found this obedience unusual, especially in this century. [15] Coming from a public school in New Jersey, Ray had never seen students 'tamed' to such narrow, desperate discipline in his six years of experience as a music teacher. [16]

13. What sentence from the passage is an example of a sentence fragment?

   a. 3
   b. 4
   c. 5
   d. 6

Practice Test Questions 2

14. Which sentence is not consistent with the author's purpose?

   a. 6

   b. 7

   c. 9

   d. 10

15. Which of the following changes are needed in sentence 16?

   a. Coming from a public school in New Jersey, Ray had never seen students 'tamed' to such narrow, disparate discipline in his six years of experience as a music teacher.

   b. Coming from a public school in New Jersey, Ray had never seen students 'tanned' to such narrow, disparate discipline in his six years of experience as a music teacher.

   c. Coming from a public school in New Jersey, Ray had never seen students 'turned' to such narrow, desperate discipline in his six years of experience as a music teacher.

   d. No change.

16. Which of the following sentences contains non-standard usage?

   a. 4

   b. 5

   c. 6

   d. 7

Spiderman

Questions 17 - 20 refer to the following passage

Spiders have always fascinated Johnson. [1] Ever since his childhood visit to his grandfather's farm in Vancouver where he first saw them in a large web that almost covered the gate of the granary warehouse, he looked for spiders everywhere he visited. [2] He would search for spider webs even in the high rise apartments such as the one he lives in now. [3] He would find them there too. [4] Hanging between two walls near one corner of the store room, a magnificent piece of art left half woven and still being worked on. [5]

It is not the life of the spiders itself that attracted Johnson, rather their art. [6] He likes their delicate webs. [7] The amazing shape and sizes of the webs. [8] The symmetry, the balance, the intricate design and the detailed network fascinates him. [9] He wanders how they manage to create something unique like this with such a little brain that they have. [10] That is why he likes to catch them in action, while they are weaving. [11]

When he opened the store room this week, he saw the huge web in the left corner touching the roof. [12] That has been there for almost six months now and it lay there as it were last month. [13] No strands added. [14] It took on a grayish shade from the dust it gathered over the weeks, making it obvious that Binny has stopped working on it. [15] Hanging here and there in the web are some dry mosquitoes that were spared by the monster that owns the trap. [16]

In the far left, on the wall adjacent to the door, Johnson is trying to build a web out of string and glue -without much success! [17] "Incredible, you little genius!" Johnson murmurs to himself. [18]

17. What sentence from the passage is an example of a sentence fragment?

    a. 2

    b. 3

    c. 4

    d. 5

18. Which of the following changes would focus attention on the main idea of the second paragraph?

    a. He finds the webs to be magnificent piece of art.

    b. He is more interested in the web that they weave.

    c. He enjoys the webs that they weave.

    d. He wanders about the webs that they weave.

19. Which of the following are needed in the sentence 10?

    a. He wonders how they manage to create something so unique with such a tiny brain.

    b. He ponders how they manage to create something unique like this with such a tiny brain.

    c. He imagines how they manage to create something unique like this with such a tiny brain.

    d. He questions how they manage to create something unique like this with such a little brain that they have.

20. Which of the following changes are needed in sentence 13?

    a. That has been there for almost six months now and it lay there as it was last month.

    b. It has been there for almost six months now and it lay there as it were last month.

    c. It has been there for almost six months now and it lay there as it was last month.

    d. No change.

Survival

Questions 21 - 24 refer to the following passage

Aaron Ralston's case was an extraordinary case of adaptation and decision making in extreme conditions. [1] Fortunately, Ralston managed to make the right decision and was rescued with the help of some luck. [2] Thanks to the arrival of the rescue helicopter just as he pulled himself out of the canyon into the open desert. [3]

As he had been stuck in the cave for almost a week, he was aware that he would soon run out of energy to do any work and that would lean the chances of getting himself out of the canyon. [4] Staying in the cave, he would surely die of hunger in the following days. [5] So, he looked at the broader picture and correctly figured out the main threat to his survival. [6] It turned out that the object that he was trying to save was in fact the very challenge to his existence: his right hand, that was stuck under a large rock that rolled on to him as he entered the cave. [7]

As he walked into the hospital steady and upright, it was evident how he managed to adopt himself to the harsh conditions of the desert for six unending days without proper food and sleep; surviving on just a couple of litters of water. [8] One of the doctors who received him recalls being overwhelmed at the impression he had made and describes the amputation as remarkable. [9] "It's a perfect example of someone improvising in a dire situation," he said. [10] "He took a small knife and was able to amputate his arm in such a way that he did not bleed to death." [12]

21. What sentence from the passage is an example of a sentence fragment?

    a. 1
    b. 2
    c. 3
    d. 4

22. Which of the following sentences should be modified to reduce redundancy?

    a. 1
    b. 2
    c. 3
    d. 4

23. Which of the following sentences, if inserted after sentence 7, would best illustrate the main idea of the passage?

a. He was encountered with the dilemma of forsaking either his arm or his life.

b. He had to make a tough decision of choosing between his arm that was under the rock and his life that was in imminent danger.

c. He was face to face with two major threats which he had to overcome in a short period of time.

d. His ingenuity has helped him make the right decision even though it was very traumatic.

24. Which of the following changes are needed in sentence 8?

a. As he walked into the hospital steady and upright, it was evident how he managed to adapt himself to the harsh conditions of the desert for six unending days without proper food and sleep; surviving on just a couple of litters of water.

b. As he walked into the hospital steady and upright, it was evident how he managed to adapt himself to the harsh conditions of the dessert for six unending days without proper food and sleep; surviving on just a couple of litters of water.

c. As he walked into the hospital steady and upright, it was evident how he managed to adapt himself to the harsh conditions of the desert for six unending days without proper food and sleep; surviving on just a couple of litters of water.

d. As he walked into the hospital steady and upright, it was evident how he managed to adapt himself to the harsh conditions of the desert for six unending days without proper food and sleep; surviving on just a couple of liters of water.

The Jump Shot

Questions 25 - 28 refer to the following passage

Bending his one knee, he adjusted his posture to take the shot. [1] He had to be in a position which would allow his shoulder to be level with the table so that his eyes would be at some elevation as the four ball. [2] This would allow the cue to strike the ball at the perfect angle, make the jump and spin it into the pocket. [3] The challenge was the narrow gap between the seven and the black ball through which he had to fine tune his spin. [4] And he was up for it. [5]

Everyone in the club knew Rey was the master of the jump shot and that is what they come to watch. [6] The elegance with which he takes the shot with the cue even touching the surface and also covers any distance around the table is truly amazing. [7] And the sleight-of-hand with which he bounces the ball and directs the spin towards the pocket gives the illusion of a miracle. [8] Rey takes in their applause with modesty, and never takes his attention off his next shot. [9]

He chalks his cue with his usual yellow as he spots the gap in between the seven and the black. [10] Anything fast will need a wider space given the margin of error here. [11] He had to think of a slow roll, retarded enough and yet keep the impact strong enough to allow the jump. [12] Added to that, was the timing of the spin which complicated everything. [13]

Practice Test Questions 2

The crowd knew exactly what was going through his mind. [14] That is why they come to watch him. [15] They enjoy watching him. [16] Not because he plays great shots but because he let them think with him how to do things others think are impossible. [17]

25. Which of the following changes would focus attention on the main idea of the first paragraph?

  a. The challenge was that the narrow gap between the seven and the black through which he had to fine tune his spin.
  b. The only challenge was the narrow gap between the seven and the black through which he had to fine tune his spin.
  c. The only challenge was that the narrow gap between the seven and the black through which he had to fine tune his spin.
  d. No change.

26. Which of the following sentences should be modified to reduce redundancy?

  a. 9
  b. 10
  c. 11
  d. 12

27. Which of the following are needed in sentence 17?

  a. Not because he plays great shots, but because he let them think with him how to do things others think are impossible.
  b. Not because he plays great shots but, because he let them think with him how to do things others think are impossible.
  c. Not because he plays great shots but because, he let them think with him how to do things others think are impossible.
  d. No change.

28. Which of the following changes are needed in sentence 7?

  a. The elegance with which he takes the shot without the cue even touching the surface and also covers any distance around the table is truly amazing.
  b. The elegance with which he takes the shot with the cue even touching the surface and yet covers any distance around the table is truly amazing.
  c. The elegance with which he takes the shot without the cue even touching the surface and yet covers any distance around the table is truly amazing.
  d. No change.

Mother's Love? Or not?

Questions 29 - 32 refer to the following passage

His relationship with his mom was always undefined. [1] He could never quite put his finger on it. [2] In fact, he could never even think what it really was like. [3] He simply never had the chance to think about it. [4] While Alan tried to establish connections with people he met, everything came to a grinding halt when it came to dealings with his mother. [5] As if his world would stop spinning. [6] He would feel suffocated by the temptation of initiating a long-term relationship. [7] For some reason he never knew. [8]

He always felt he was deprived of his mother's love and attention, but could never accept that he was deprived of his only parent's love. [9] Although it was tough to remember painful experiences he had repressed for so long, he decided to give it a try. [10]

But as he was trying to visualize happy memories of his mom holding his hand taking him to the candy store; and the security he felt holding her hand, he was struck by images of a tyrant woman beating him mercilessly for breaking the window. [11] These two different images of the same individual left him confused and perplexed. [12]

29. What sentence from the passage is an example of a sentence fragment?

    a. 4
    b. 5
    c. 6
    d. 7

30. Which of the following sentences should be modified to reduce redundancy?

    a. 9
    b. 10
    c. 11
    d. 12

31. Which of the following are needed in sentence 11?

    a. But as he was trying to visualize happy memories of his mom holding his hand taking him to the candy store, and the security he felt holding her hand, he was struck by the images of a tyrant woman beating him mercilessly for breaking the window.

    b. But as he was trying to visualize happy memories of his mom holding his hand while taking him to the candy shop; amid the security he felt in the hand that was grabbing him strongly, he was struck by the tumultuous pictures of a tyrant woman who was beating him mercilessly for breaking the window.

    c. But as he was trying to visualize his happy memories of his mom holding his hand while taking him to the candy store, and the security he felt holding her hand, he was struck by the images of a tyrant woman beating him mercilessly for breaking the window.

d. But as he was trying to visualize his happy memories of his mom holding his hand while taking him to the candy store - and the security he felt holding her hand - he was struck by the image of a tyrant woman beating him mercilessly for breaking the window.

32. Which of the following changes are needed in sentence 7?

a. He would feel suffocated by the urge to initiate a long-term relationship.

b. He would feel suffocated by the desire of initiating a long-term relationship.

c. He would feel suffocated by the desire to initiate something long-term.

d. He would feel suffocated by the desire to start something perpetual.

A Contrast of Cultures

Questions 33 - 36 refer to the following passage

Apart from the white walls, the living room was burgundy leather, deep colors, heavy cream and browns. [1] The rich patterns of rugs and the art: the photos, handmade woolen tapestries and prints of classical Norwegian paintings on every wall wherever there was space, gave the house warmth.[2] In Australia, our living room was painted yellow and had just one painting in it.[3]

At meal times, Gunborg lit a candle in an old candleholder they'd bought in Pompeii, a Roman replica. [4] Back home, most rooms were lit by just one or a few ceiling bulbs that cast a harsh white light and in Haiti - I would see later- kerosene lamps and candles on the ground as there was no other place to put them.[5] But in Norway each room had numerous sources of light. [6] There were lamps with metal arms that could be bent in strained configurations for reading or sewing; table and free standing lamps in classical or modern design- of ceramic, copper or glass, and candles- regularly lit on shelves, tables and windowsills. [7]

On the ceilings as often as not were no lights at all. [8] My Aussie father was forever telling us to turn off the lights as we left each room, to conserve power. [9] It wasn't the environment that he was concerned about- but the bill; and candles were out of the question save for blackouts since they would have burnt the house down if we forgot about them. [10] In Norway, nobody cared about it. "Its such a dark in winter," they said, "We always need of light." [11]

The Norwegian way of light was initially annoying, without the convenience of a single switch, especially when looking for something in luggage for example; and because every lamp seemed to have its switch in a different place. [12] The grades of shadow from lamp to lamp, the meeting of light arcs and the flickering ceiling patterns of the candles were like people gathering, mimicking the changing shades and arrangements of life. [13]

33. Which sentence in the third paragraph is least relevant to the main idea of the third paragraph?

    a. 8

    b. 9

    c. 10

    d. 11

34. Which of the following sentence fragments, if inserted at the beginning of sentence 13, would best illustrate the main idea of the passage?

    a. But after a while I reconsidered:

    b. Then I realized that something was fishy about this place:

    c. Suddenly, I was struck with the light of wisdom:

    d. Then I was surprised to find myself in the following thought:

35. Which of the following changes are needed in sentence 10?

    a. It wasn't the environment that he was concerned about- but the bill; and candles were out of the question save for blackouts since they should burn the house down if we forgot about them.

    b. It wasn't the environment that he was concerned about- but the bill; and candles were out of the question save for blackouts since they would burn the house down if we forgot about them.

    c. It wasn't the environment that he was concerned about- but the bill; and candles were out of the question save for blackouts since they would have burnt the house down if we had forgotten about them.

    d. It wasn't the environment that he was concerned about- but the bill; and candles were out of the question save for blackouts since they will burn the house down if we forget about them.

36. Which of the following sentences contains non-standard usage?

    a. 4

    b. 5

    c. 9

    d. 11

Directions: Select the best version of the underlined portion of the sentence

37. **Who** won first place in the Western Division?

   a. Whom won first place in the Western Division?
   b. Which won first place in the Western Division?
   c. What won first place in the Western Division?
   d. No change is necessary?

38. **There are now several ways to listen to music, including radio, CDs, and MP3 files which you can download onto an MP3 player.**

   a. There are now several ways to listen to music, including radio, CDs, and MP3 files on which you can download onto an MP3 player.
   b. There are now several ways to listen to music, including radio, CDs, and MP3 files who you can download onto an MP3 player.
   c. There are now several ways to listen to music, including radio, CDs, and MP3 files whom you can download onto an MP3 player.
   d. No change is necessary.

39. **As the tallest monument in the United States, the St. Louis Arch was rose to an impressive 630 feet.**

   a. As the tallest monument in the United States, the St. Louis Arch has rose to an impressive 630 feet.
   b. As the tallest monument in the United States, the St. Louis Arch is risen to an impressive 630 feet.
   c. As the tallest monument in the United States, the St. Louis Arch rises to an impressive 630 feet.
   d. No change is necessary.

40. **The tired, old woman should lain on the sofa.**

   a. The tired, old woman should lie on the sofa.
   b. The tired, old woman should lays on the sofa.
   c. The tired, old woman should laid on the sofa.
   d. No changes are necessary.

41. Did the students understand that Thanksgiving always <u>fallen</u> on the fourth Thursday in November?

    a No change is necessary.

    b. Did the students understand that Thanksgiving always falling on the fourth Thursday in November.

    c. Did the students understand that Thanksgiving always has fell on the fourth Thursday in November.

    d. Did the students understand that Thanksgiving always falls on the fourth Thursday in November.

42. Collecting stamps, <u>build models</u>, and listening to shortwave radio were Rick's main hobbies.

    a. Collecting stamps, building models, and listening to shortwave radio were Rick's main hobbies.

    b. Collecting stamps, to build models, and listening to shortwave radio were Rick's main hobbies.

    c. Collecting stamps, having built models, and listening to shortwave radio were Rick's main hobbies.

    d. No change is necessary.

43. This morning, <u>after the kids will leave for school</u> and before the sun came up, my mother makes herself a cup of cocoa.

    a. This morning, after the kids had left for school and before the sun came up, my mother makes herself a cup of cocoa.

    b. This morning, after the kids leave for school and before the sun came up, my mother makes herself a cup of cocoa.

    c. This morning, after the kids have left for school and before the sun came up, my mother makes herself a cup of cocoa.

    d. No change is necessary.

44. Elaine promised to bring the camera <u>to me</u> at the mall yesterday.

    a. Elaine promised to bring the camera by me at the mall yesterday.

    b. Elaine promised to bring the camera with me at the mall yesterday.

    c. Elaine promised to bring the camera at mc at the mall yesterday.

    d. No changes are necessary.

45. Last night, he <u>laid</u> the sleeping bag down beside my mattress.

   a. Last night, he lay the sleeping bag down beside my mattress.
   b. Last night, he lain
   c. Last night, he has laid
   d. No change is necessary.

46. I would have bought the shirt for you <u>if I know</u> you liked it.

   a. I would have bought the shirt for you if I had known you liked it.
   b. I would have bought the shirt for you if I have known you liked it.
   c. I would have bought the shirt for you if I would know you liked it.
   d. No change is necessary.

47. Jessica's father was in the Navy, so she attended schools in <u>Newark; New Jersey, Key West; Florida, San Diego, California, and Fairbanks, Alaska.</u>

   a. Jessica's father was in the Navy, so she attended schools in Newark, New Jersey, Key West, Florida, San Diego, California, and Fairbanks, Alaska.
   b. Jessica's father was in the Navy, so she attended schools in: Newark, New Jersey, Key West, Florida, San Diego, California, and Fairbanks, Alaska.
   c. Jessica's father was in the Navy, so she attended schools in Newark, New Jersey; Key West, Florida; San Diego, California; and Fairbanks, Alaska.
   d. None of the choices are correct.

48. George wrecked John's <u>car; that</u> was the end of their friendship.

   a. George wrecked John's car that was the end of their friendship.
   b. George wrecked John's car. that was the end of their friendship.
   c. The sentence is correct.
   d. None of the choices are correct.

49. The dress was not Gina's <u>favorite, however,</u> she wore it to the dance.

   a. The dress was not Gina's favorite; however, she wore it to the dance.
   b. None of the choices are correct.
   c. The dress was not Gina's favorite, however; she wore it to the dance.
   d. The dress was not Gina's favorite however, she wore it to the dance.

50. Chris showed his dedication to golf in many <u>ways; for</u> example, he watched all the tournaments on television.

    a. Chris showed his dedication to golf in many ways, for example, he watched all the tournaments on television.

    b. The sentence is correct.

    c. Chris showed his dedication to golf in many ways, for example; he watched all the tournaments on television.

    d. Chris showed his dedication to golf in many ways for example he watched all the tournaments on television.

Science

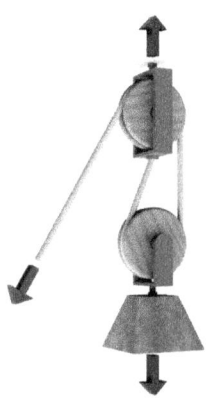

1. Consider the arrangement of pulleys above. If the weight shown is 150 pounds, how much force much be exerted to lift the weight?

    a. 150 pounds

    b. 100 pounds

    c. 75 pounds

    d. 50 pounds

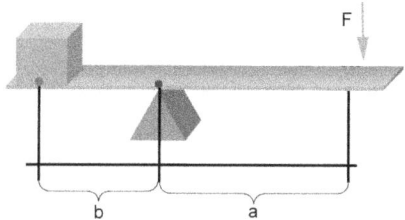

2. Consider the illustration above and the corresponding data:

Weight = W = 100 pounds
Distance from fulcrum to Weight = b = 5 feet
Distance from fulcrum to point where force is applied = a = 10 feet
How much force (F) must be applied to lift the weight?

   a. 100
   b. 50
   c. 25
   d. 10

The Periodic Table of Elements

Questions 3 - 7 refer to the periodic table below.

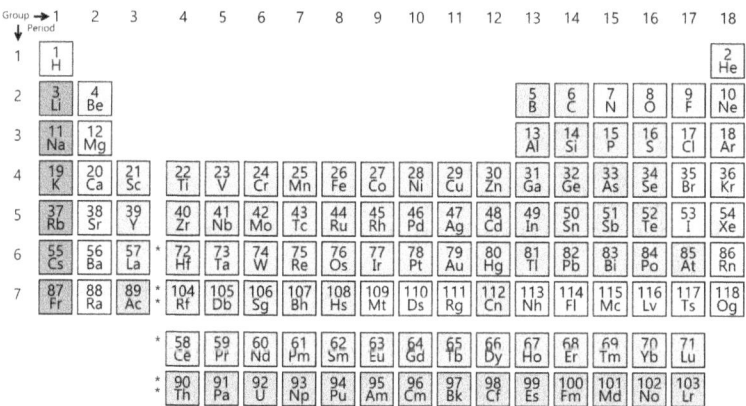

3. How many protons and electrons are in the element carbon?

   a. 6
   b. 12
   c. 2
   d. 14

4. Identify the electron configuration of oxygen:

   a. 2,8

   b. 2,16

   c. 2, 6

   d. 2,8,16

5. Identify the element found in group 2, period 4:

   a. Beryllium

   b. Calcium

   c. Oxygen

   d. Titanium

6. Which of the following does not form a positive ion?

   a. Lithium

   b. Magnesium

   c. Fluorine

   d. Boron

7. The reactivity of alkali metals (group 1) increases as the atomic number increases. Which of the following statements is the correct explanation for this fact?

   a. The atoms only have one electron in their valence (outer) shell.

   b. They are the most reactive group in the periodic table.

   c. Their atomic mass increases.

   d. The valence (outer) shell is farther from the nucleus.

8. A substance containing atoms of more than one element in a definite ratio is called a(n)

   a. Compound

   b. Element

   c. Mixture

   d. Molecule

9. The equation E = mc² is based on the _____, and states that _____ equals _____ times the _____².

a. The equation E = mc² is based on the 2nd Law of Thermodynamics, and states that Mass equals Energy times (the Velocity of light)².

b. The equation E = mc² is based on the Law of Conservation of Mass and Energy, and states that Energy equals Mass times (the Velocity of light)².

c. The equation E = mc² is based on the 1st Law of Thermodynamics, and states that Mass equals Energy times (the Velocity of sound)².

d. The equation E = mc² is based on the Law of Conservation of Mass and Energy, and states that the Velocity of light equals Energy times (the Mass)².

10. Which, if any, of the following statements are true?

a. Water boils at approximately 100 °C (212 °F) at standard atmospheric pressure.

b. The boiling point is the temperature at which the vapor pressure is higher than the atmospheric pressure around the water.

c. Water boils at a higher temperature in areas of lower pressure.

d. All of the above statements are true.

Atmospheric Science

Questions 11 - 14 refer to the following passage.

The atmosphere is an important transitional zone between the solid planetary surface and the higher rarefied ionizing and radiation belts. Not all planets have atmospheres: their existence depends on the mass of the planet, its gravity, and the planet's distance from the Sun — too distant and frozen atmospheres occur. Besides the four gas giant planets, almost all of the terrestrial planets (Earth, Venus, and Mars) have significant atmospheres. Two moons have significant atmospheres: Saturn's moon Titan and Neptune's moon Triton. A tenuous atmosphere exists around Mercury.

The effects of the rotation rate of a planet about its axis can be seen in atmospheric streams and currents. When viewed from space, they appear as bands and eddies in the cloud system and are especially visible on Jupiter and Saturn. Heat from the interior of Jupiter causes circulation patterns in the atmosphere, with warm gas rising and cooling, before sinking back into the depths of the planet. This process is called convection and results in the formation of different colored bands in Jupiter's atmosphere. The light colored bands, called "zones," are the rising areas, while the dark colored regions, or "belts," are the sinking gas. The different colors come from their different chemical compositions; astronomers think that the darker colored belts contain hydrocarbons - molecules that are made of hydrogen, carbon, and oxygen, which turn a darker color when exposed to the Sun's ultraviolet light.

11. Which of the following factors determine if a planet has an atmosphere?

    a. It's mass

    b. It's temperature

    c. It's gravity

    d. All of the above

12. Which choice gives the best definition of the phrase: "a tenuous atmosphere exists around Mercury."

    a. Mercury has a very thin atmosphere

    b. Mercury has a very thick atmosphere

    c. Mercury has no atmosphere

    d. Mercury has a volatile atmosphere

13. What causes the zones in Jupiter's atmosphere?

    a. Cool gas sinking

    b. Warm gas rising

    c. The hydrocarbons exposed to UV light

    d. None of the above

14. Which of the following phrases in the article could be considered an opinion rather than fact?

    a. Earth, Venus, and Mars all have atmospheres

    b. Convection causes the bands in Jupiter's atmosphere

    c. The darker colored bands contain hydrocarbons

    d. Hydrocarbons contain hydrogen, carbon, and oxygen

15. Which of the following is not a habitat where bacteria commonly grow?

    a. Soil

    b. The vacuum of space

    c. Radioactive waste

    d. Deep in the earth's crust

16. Within taxonomy, plants and animals are considered two basic

    a. Families

    b. Kingdoms

    c. Domains

    d. Genus

17. Most of the elements on the periodic table can be classified as

    a. Nonmetals

    b. Metals

    c. Metalloids

    d. Gas

18. Which of these statements about metals are true?

    a. A metal is a substance that conducts heat and electricity.

    b. A metal is shiny and reflects many colors of light, and can be hammered into sheets or drawn into wire.

    c. All of these statements are true.

    d. About 80% of the known chemical elements are metals.

Mars

Questions 19 - 22 refer to the following passage.

Although Mars has no evidence of a structured global magnetic field, observations show that parts of the planet's crust have been magnetized, suggesting that alternating polarity reversals of its dipole field have occurred in the past. This paleomagnetism of magnetically susceptible minerals is similar to the alternating bands found on Earth's ocean floors. One theory, published in 1999 and re-examined in October 2005 (with the help of the Mars Global Surveyor), is that these bands suggest plate tectonic activity on Mars around four billion years ago before the planetary dynamo ceased to function and the planet's magnetic field faded.

Many believe Mars was created as the result of a stochastic process of run-away accumulations of material from the protoplanetary disk that orbited the Sun during the Solar System's formation. Mars has many distinctive chemical features caused by its position in the Solar System including an abundant supply of elements with comparatively low boiling points, such as chlorine, phosphorus, and sulfur. These elements are much more common on Mars than Earth and were probably pushed outward by the young Sun's energetic solar wind.

19. Scientist suspect "tectonic activity" on Mars, to which phenomena are they referring?

    a. Earthquakes

    b. Volcanoes

    c. Mountains building

    d. All of the above

20. Given the absence of a global magnetic field on Mars, which of the following can we infer regarding the planet's core?

    a. It is liquid which is in constant motion

    b. It is solid which does not move

    c. It is liquid which does not move

    d. It is a solid which is in constant motion

21. Which elements is Mars rich in, compared to Earth?

    a. Chlorine

    b. Phosphorous

    c. Sulfur

    d. All of the above.

22. What is the planetary dynamo referring to in the passage above?

    a. The convection currents and movements that occur inside a planet

    b. The nuclear power generated inside a planet

    c. A magnetic field found around a planet

    d. The rotation of the planet

23. Define a biological class.

    a. A collection of similar or like living entities.

    b. Two or more animals in a group, all having the same parent.

    c. All animals sharing the same living environment.

    d. All plant life that share the same physical properties.

24. The mass number of an atom is

    a. The total number of particles that make it up.

    b. The total weight of an atom.

    c. The total mass of an atom.

    d. None of the above.

25. Which of these statements about mechanical energy is/are true?

    a. Mechanical energy is the energy that is possessed by an object due to its motion or due to its position.

    b. Mechanical energy can be either kinetic energy (energy of motion) or potential energy (stored energy of position).

    c. Objects have mechanical energy if they are in motion.

    d. All of the above.

Pluto

Questions 26 - 29 refer to the following passage.

Pluto was discovered by Clyde Tombaugh in 1930 and was originally considered to be the ninth planet from the Sun. After 1992, its status as a planet was questioned following the discovery of several objects of similar size in the Kuiper belt. In 2005, Eris, a dwarf planet in the scattered disc beyond the Kuiper belt which is 27% larger than Pluto, was discovered. This led the International Astronomical Union (IAU) to define the term "planet" formally in 2006, during their 26th General Assembly. The definition excluded Pluto and reclassified it as a dwarf planet. Although Pluto orbits the sun and is nearly spherical, it is not gravitationally dominant as its orbit is influenced by Neptune's gravity and it shares its orbital neighborhood with Kuiper belt objects (termed clearing its neighborhood).

Pluto is the largest and second-most-massive known dwarf planet in the Solar System and the ninth-largest and tenth-most-massive known object directly orbiting the Sun. It is the largest known trans-Neptunian object by volume but is less massive than Eris. Like other Kuiper belt objects, Pluto is primarily made of ice and rock and is relatively small—about one-sixth the mass of the Moon and one-third its volume. It has a moderately eccentric and inclined orbit during which it ranges from 30 to 49 astronomical units or AU (4.4–7.4 billion km) from the Sun. This means that Pluto periodically comes closer to the Sun than Neptune, but a stable orbital resonance with Neptune prevents them from colliding. Light from the Sun takes about 5.5 hours to reach Pluto at its average distance (39.5 AU).

26. Which planet influences Pluto's orbit?

    a. Kuiper

    b. Neptune

    c. Eris

    d. The sun

27. Order the celestial bodies from smallest to largest.

    a. The Moon, Pluto, Neptune, Eris

    b. Pluto, Neptune, Eris, The Moon

    c. Pluto, The Moon, Eris, Neptune

    d. Pluto, Eris, The Moon, Neptune

28. Which one of the following is not one of the three criteria used to determine if a celestial body should be called a planet:

   a. It orbits the sun

   b. A moderately eccentric and inclined orbit

   c. It has cleared the neighborhood

   d. It has a near round shape

29. Order the celestial objects starting with the closest to the sun to the farthest.

   a. Pluto, Kuiper belt, Eris, Neptune

   b. Neptune, Kuiper belt, Pluto, Eris

   c. Neptune, Pluto, Kuiper belt, Eris

   d. Eris, Kuiper belt, Pluto, Neptune

30. How much force is needed to accelerate a car that weights 200 kg to 5 m/s^2?

   a. 40 N

   b. 200 N

   c. 1000 N

   d. 1500 N

31. Strong chemical bonds include

   a. Dipole - dipole interactions

   b. Hydrogen bonding

   c. Covalent or ionic bonds

   d. None of the above

32. A javelin is thrown into a field at 18 m/s. if the Javelin weighs 1.5 kg, what is the momentum?

   a. 1.2 kg x m/s into the field

   b. 12 kg x m/s into the field

   c. 27 kg x m/s into the field

   d. 2.7 kg x m/s into the field

33. Which of these object has greater momentum, a 2 kg truck moving east at 3.5 m/s or a 4.3 kg truck moving south at 1.5 m/s?

   a. The first truck at 7 kg x m/s moving east

   b. The second truck at 7.45 kg x m/s due south

   c. The first truck at 6.45 kg x m/s due east

   d. The second truck at 7 kg x m/s due south

Gravity

Questions 34 - 37 refer to the following passage.

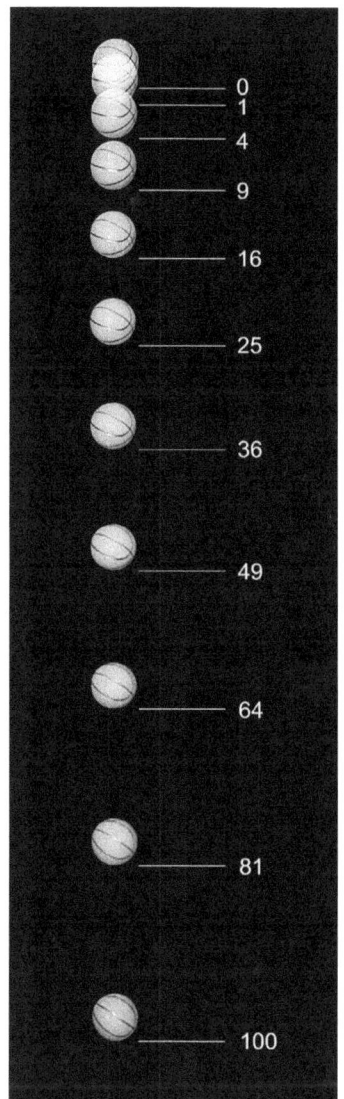

An initially-stationary object which is allowed to fall freely under gravity drops a distance which is proportional to the square of the elapsed time. During the first 1/20th of a second the ball drops one unit of distance (here, a unit is about 12 mm); by 2/20ths it has dropped at total of 4 units; by 3/20ths, nine units and so on. This image spans half a second and was captured at 20 flashes per second.[37]

34. Which of the following applies to the ball?

a. The ball's speed in constant
b. The ball's speed is increasing
c. The ball's speed is decreasing
d. The ball is stationary

35. When is the ball traveling at its fastest speed?

a. Between 6 and 7/20ths of a second
b. Between 7 and 8/20ths of a second
c. Between 8 and 9/20ths of a second
d. Between 9 and 10/20ths of a second

36. Assuming that the ball hit the ground at the distance of 100 units, what was the initial drop height of the ball in mm?

a. 1200 mm
b. 120 mm
c. 12 mmd
d. 1.2 mm

37. Gravitational potential energy can be calculated using the equation Ep = mgh, where Ep is gravitational potential energy in Joules (J), m is the mass (kg) g is the gravitational constant of 10 N/kg, and h is the height (m). If the ball has a mass of 50 grams and drops from 1 meter, what would its gravitational potential energy be?

a. 0.5J
b. 500J
d. 5J
d. 50J

Centipedes

Questions 38 - 41 refer to the following passage.

Centipedes (from Latin prefix centi-, "hundred," and pes, pedis, "foot") are arthropods belonging to the class Chilopoda of the subphylum Myriapoda. They are elongated creatures with one pair of legs per body segment. Centipedes are known to be highly venomous, and often inject paralyzing venom. Despite the name, centipedes can have a varying number of legs, ranging from 30 to 354. Centipedes always have an odd number of pairs of legs. Therefore, no centipede has exactly 100 legs. A key trait uniting this group is a pair of venomous claws or forcipules formed from a modified first appendage, which allow them to capture prey. Centipedes can be found in a wide variety of environments. They normally have a dull coloration combining shades of brown and red. Cavernicolous (cave-dwelling) and subterranean species often lack pigmentation, and many tropical scolopendromorphs have bright aposematic (warning) colors. [39]

38. If a centipede has 99 body segments how many legs will it have?

    a. 198

    b. 98

    c. 99

    d. 200

39. Based on the information above, centipedes are most likely:

    a. Herbivores

    b. Decomposers

    c. Omnivores

    d. Carnivores

40. Centipedes are often dull colors, allowing them to blend into their environment. Give the term for this ability.

    a. Mimicry

    b. Disruptive colouration

    d. Camouflage

    d. Concealing colouration

41. Centipedes are arthropods. Which of the following animals is not a member of this phylum?

   a. Spiders
   b. Snails
   c. Scorpions
   d. Shrimp

Geological Time

Questions 42 - 46 refer picture below depicting geological time scale.

42. According to this image, what is the approximate age of the Earth?

   a. 4.5 billion years old
   b. 1 billion years old
   c. 2 billion years old
   d. 2 million years old

43. Which of the following can be used to determine the age of the Earth?

   a. Fossils

   b. Radioactive elements found in rocks

   c. Layers of rocks

   d. All of the above

44. In which era do we find Dinosaurs?

   a. Paleozoic Era

   b. Mesozoic era

   c. Cenozoic era

   d. All of the above

45. Which period could be known as the "age of reptiles?"

   a. Tertiary

   b. Jurassic

   c. Cambrian

   d. Devonian

46. Earth has known to have undergone four major extinctions so far. Which of the following is likely to be the cause of these extinctions:

   a. Lack of mates

   b. Food shortages

   c. Climate change

   d. Severe weather, e.g., flooding and volcanic eruptions

Origin of Space

The picture below is one proposed timeline of the origin of space. It represents the evolution of the universe over 13.77 billion years, beginning with the Big Bang. Use the image to answer the questions that follow.

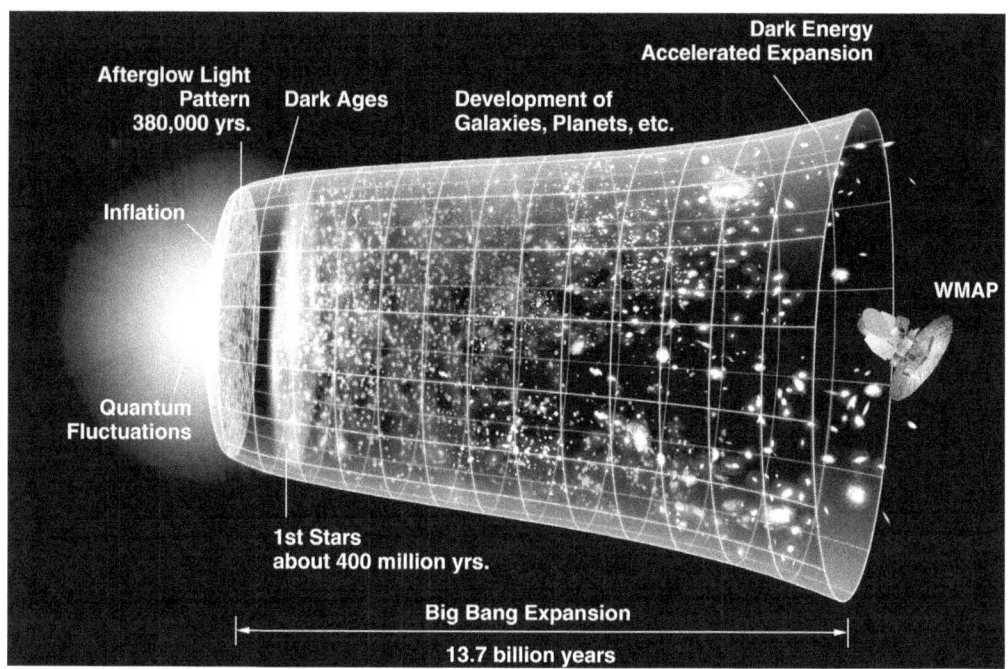

47. Where on the picture above marks the beginning of exponential growth in the universe?

   a. Afterglow light patterns
   b. Dark age expansion
   c. Inflation
   d. The Dark ages

48. Describe the rate that occurs after the period of exponential growth

   a. Exponential
   b. Gradual
   c. Negative
   d. No growth

49. Which is the correct order of evolution starting from earliest to latest?

   a. First stars, dark ages, first galaxies and planets
   b. First galaxies and planets, first stars, dark ages
   c. Dark ages, first planets, and galaxies, first stars
   d. Dark ages, first stars, first galaxies, and planets

50. What can we infer about the dark ages?

    a. There were no galaxies or stars in existence

    b. It occurred before the big bang

    c. It preceded a period of exponential growth

    d. The temperature of the universe was increasing

Answer Key

Social Studies

1. B
The British Parliament passed the British North America Act in 1867.

2. A
Canada's first prime minister, Sir John A. Macdonald, was named in 1867. Scotland-born had come to Canada as a child.

3. C
Louis Riel was the leader of the uprising.

4. A
A major development of the late 19th century was joining the East and West by railroad.

5. C
The British renamed the colony at Québec City "The Province of Quebec."

6. A
Canadians remember veterans each year on November 11th, which is called Remembrance Day.

7. A
Canada's government is known as a Parliamentary Democracy.

8. C
These three branches are the Sovereign (King or Queen), the Senate, and the House of Commons.

9. B
This cartoon was published in response the Intolerable Acts and shows members of the British government holding America down while forcing tea down her throat. Tea was, of course, symbolic of the Intolerable Acts on both sides of the conflict.
Choice A is incorrect. This cartoon is focused on forcing something upon the Americans, not taking from them. This is depicted by the tea being forced down the American's throat.
Choice C is incorrect. This piece was published before the war truly started and the torture in the image is symbolic vs literal.
Choice D is incorrect. This piece was published before the war and is distinctly anti-British.

10. A
Britain has a significant amount of territory, including territory conceded by the Spanish in modern day Florida. This concession indicated that they were actively pursuing expansion and attempting to preempt threats to the territory.
Choice B is incorrect. France is not pictured on this map, and while students may

remember that France does own a lot of New World territory at different times, it is not evident here.
Choice C is incorrect. Spain probably has more land, if the comparison were to be made. Britain has more cities, however, and they have territory taken from the Spanish.

11. B
France has significantly more large towns and forts than the other two world powers.
Choice A is incorrect. Great Britain has a relatively few major towns in comparison with France
Choice C is incorrect. Spain only has two major towns and no forts.

12. B
Fact. The lack of access to digital resources increases the economic inequality in a population.

13. A
The article explains that intra-personal relationships and trust are important in the High Tech world, because creating software is complex and has several complex aspects. This means that there have to be several companies cooperatively working together to create new products, unlike in manufacturing, where products can be created by just one company.
Choice B is incorrect. While the competition between High Tech companies is excellent for the consumer, as mentioned in the article, it's not why there are so many high tech companies compared to manufacturing companies.
Choice C is incorrect. While it's true that the High Tech sector has been around for a significantly shorter time period, it's not why there are more successful companies in High Tech than in manufacturing.

Choice D is incorrect. The article actually explains that High Tech companies are creating more complex products, which is why there are more High Tech companies, each differentiated to take on different tasks.

14. B
The text states that humans have had a negative impact on climate change and that those changes are dangerous to all living creatures.

15. C
Earthquakes are not related to climate and are considered geophysical disasters.
Choice A is incorrect. Floods are directly related to climate changes, especially as part of increased rainfall, which is mentioned in the text.
Choice B is incorrect and mentioned specifically in text. Droughts are caused by changes in rainfall.
Choice D is incorrect. Droughts and Wildfires are linked and both relate to climate change.

16. B
The United States stock market collapse of 1929 started the downfall of many financial institutions and the start of the Great Depression.
Choice C is incorrect, while Germany did default on its loans to the United States after World War I, the Great Depression occurred a number of years after this event.
Choice A is incorrect, Prohibition started in the 1920s, the Great Depression did not start until 1929.

Choice D is incorrect, the Dust Bowl happened during the Great Depression, it did not precipitate it.

17. D
A culmination of the answers given and a few others caused the Great Depression.
Choice A is incorrect, excessive borrowing was partly to blame for causing the Great Depression, but it would not have been as severe if other things had not also happened.
Choice B is incorrect, restricting the amount of money ensured that people would not be able to pay off their debts as easily, but even that by itself would not have caused the Great Depression.
Choice C is incorrect, with people not spending money the economy continued to slump, but that would not have been severe enough to cause the Great Depression.

18. B
Choice A in incorrect. Regional scientists wanted to move to a more analytical understanding
Choice C is incorrect. While regional scientists do want to use analytic language, that's not the traditional language of geography
Choice D is incorrect. Analytical language is not the traditional language of geography.

19. D
Each of the examples is extrapolated from the list and a regional scientist would be interested in each.

20. B
While choice A is covered under geomorphology, it's not a good definition for the concept as a whole.
While choice C is covered under geomorphology, it's not a good definition for the concept as a whole.
Choice D is covered under geomorphology, it's not a good definition for the concept as a whole.

21. D
The Baseline suggested by the theory would never happen because mountains are continually reforming through rejuvenation. Thus the cycle continuously works, but a return to a starting point, does not occur.
A is incorrect. Tectonic activity creates mountains and the accompanying natural disasters.
Choice B is incorrect. Rivers and run off do create valleys.
Choice C is incorrect. Valleys do become canyons if the conditions are correct.

22. D
The three territories have a different governmental setup.
Choice A is incorrect because provinces and territories are not named differently based on when they joined Canada.
Choice B is incorrect because provinces and territories are not organized into categories based on size.
Choice C is incorrect because the 10 provinces and three territories are separate.

23. B
Maintaining roads and highways is a responsibility that falls under the provinces and

territories.
Choice A is incorrect because maintaining the Canadian border falls under immigration and is therefore a responsibility of the Federal government.
Choice C is incorrect because environmental regulation happens on the Federal level.

24. C
Regulating immigration is a jointly held responsibility.
Choice A is incorrect because educating the public is a right reserved by the provinces and territories
Choice B is incorrect because providing Health Care for its citizens is a responsibility of the provinces and territories

25. D
Each of the different assemblies have different names but the same level of power. Names just differ from place to place.

26. B
Districts are assigned based on population. Because of this, the number of districts can increase or decrease as population increases or decreases
Choice A is incorrect because districts are not based on size.
Choice C is incorrect because Canada holds democratic elections not based on monetary wealth
Choice D is incorrect because the Queen does not play a large role in politics.

27. A
A popular vote is taken to elect candidates.
Choice B is incorrect because a majority vote requires the winner to receive a majority of the ballots while a popular vote does not require at least 51%.
Choice C is incorrect because an Electoral College vote happens in the United States.
Choice D is incorrect because the Prime Minister is not involved with elections for the House of Commons.

28. A
A Snap election is the colloquial term for an election that happens or earlier than it's supposed to.
Choice B is incorrect because a re-election is when a person is elected for a second time.
Choice C is incorrect because a recall election is called for by the people.

29. D
Maintaining a vote of confidence is important because it requires the Prime Minister two consider the opinions of others when leading the country

30. A
The opposition parties do play an important role in the government. The opposition parties exist to offer different perspectives and new ideas to the party in power. They also serve as a check and balance for the in power party

31. D
Unless a Prime Minister has a vote of no confidence, there is not a limit on the amount of time that they can serve. The longest serving Prime Minister served for a term of 21 years.

32. C
The style of the signs, including the bare bulbs is distinctively 1960s. The clothing and photograph quality also indicate the 1960s.

33. C
The purpose is to show the aftermath of a fire and the success of modern fire fighting. Choices A, B and D are all incorrect based on the timing of the picture.

34. C
The earliest Canadians were fur trappers.
Choice A is incorrect because the mode of transportation would not work for timber harvesting. While trees were often transported by river, the river pictured is too violent for easy transportation. The boat also doesn't provide enough space for tools and other necessities.
Choice B is incorrect because tobacco did not grow prevalently as far north as Canada.
Choice D is incorrect because gold wasn't discovered in Canada until the late 1800s

35. D
All of the examples are different forms of federations.

36. B
Canada is still a dominion because they still recognize the monarchy of Great Britain as the Head of State, even though it's mostly ceremonial.
Choice A is incorrect because Canada is not an absolute monarchy.
Choice C and D are incorrect because Canada is a Constitutional Monarchy.

37. D
According to the text, choices A and B supported a strong provincial government.

38. B
The passage mentions American expansion and increased nationalism directly. The need to increase government speed for decision making is not mentioned directly but the text does say Canadians desired the "...elimination of the legislative deadlock between Upper and Lower Canada."

39. B
This is a technical monopoly. The company owns the treatment and its means of production. It cannot be replicated which means it's a technical monopoly.

40. A
This is an example of a practical monopoly. This type of monopoly is formed when one company pays for the overhead for major construction which leads to them often becoming the only resource provider in an area.

41. D
Movie Theatres, Mass Transit, and Grocery Stores are all Club Goods. Public broadcasting is an example of a public good.

42. C
While choices A, B, and D are impacts of having public roads, a negative externality must impact those who choose not to use the public good. Taxes are often used to offset negative externalities as described in the text.

43. C
The housing market collapse signalled a period of recession, but the economy was artificially re-inflated by the American Recovery and Reinvestment Act of 2009 before a depression could occur.

44. B
Decreased demand leads to a surplus of product that the market cannot afford and a surplus of labor which leads to layoffs.
Choice A is incorrect because When demand decreases, supply increases.
Choice C is incorrect because The text explains that demand decreased.
Choice D is incorrect. The text explains that demand decreased.

45. A
The text explain that Keynes acknowledged that sometimes there would need to be artificial interference to stabilize the market.
Choice B is incorrect because the market would have moved from a recession to a depression and according to the text "Keynes advocated that the public sector should take active steps to formulate policies to respond to economic downturns."
Choice C is incorrect because the Bailout (The American Recovery and Reinvestment Act) was an economic stimulus package focused on rejuvenating the economy.
D is incorrect. This answer is explicit in the text.

46. A
The model shows that as the distance from the origin (0, 0) increases along the vertical axis (i) it also increases along the horizontal axis (y). Higher interest rates (i) lead to an increase in the GDP (y)

47. B
As price moves up the y-axis quantity moves down the x-axis.
Choice A is incorrect because As price moves up the y-axis quantity moves down the x-axis
Choice C is incorrect because As price moves up the y-axis demand also increases
Choice D is incorrect. As price moves up the y-axis supply decreases

48. C
When production is limited, a choice to produce one item means that another item cannot be produced.
Choice A is incorrect because The graph shows that as one product increases, the other decreases.
Choice B is incorrect because While investors should diversify, this graph represents that production opportunity impacts all markets.

49. C
The federal government can print more money to stimulate the economy, however, increasing the money supply decreases the value of money, ergo inflation. Choice A is incorrect; deflation is an increase in the value of money. Choice B is incorrect; stagflation is a possibility, but does not normally take place. Choice D is incorrect; stagnation is a stalling of the economy, while increasing the money supply stimulates the economy.

50. B

Classical economics holds that over time, economic problems will be corrected by the invisible hand of the market. Adam Smith's theory of the invisible hand is an important part of classical economics. Choice A is incorrect; classical economics was a free market school of thought. Choice C is incorrect; the people's role in classical economics is simply to be consumers. Choice D is incorrect; classical economists would virtually never recommend raising taxes.

Language Arts - Reading

1. D

Choice D is the only possibility. The author refers to Terkoz as a beast, and twice describes him as an ape.

2. D

Animal imagery is used to qualify Tarzan's strength, appearance, and behavior. Simultaneously, Tarzan's humanity is not forgotten: Terkoz identifies Tarzan's pale skin and hairlessness, and the greatness of Terkoz's teeth (natural) are contrasted with the thinness or weakness of Tarzan's knife (man-made). Animal imagery weaves in Tarzan's humanity un-manlike characteristics. He is both a man and not a man, an animal, yet not fully animal. There is no indication that Tarzan actually becomes the animals he resembles: choice A is incorrect. Choice B is probably true, but in this passage no inference can be made about Tarzan's past or childhood. Choice C is a weak answer, as the animal imagery qualifies Tarzan's prowess, rather than his lack of civilization.

3. D

Evidence for choices A is scant or based on subjective interpretation. The narrator mentions that Doolittle did look as pleased as when he saw the Jabizri beetle, but there is no way of knowing if the "snail" reminds him of the beetle (and given the description of the "snail," the resemblance seems unlikely). Choice A can be eliminated. The reader likewise finds no mention of the Doctor's love, specifically, for monster-like creatures — choice B is not viable, either. The reader is aware of the great size of the creature, its long neck and horns, but can find no mention of the "innate beauty" which compels the Doctor's attraction. Choice C is therefore inaccurate. Whether he derives special pleasure in rescuing animals, however, is again subject to interpretation. Therefore the reader will arrive at choice D. It is irrefutable that the Doctor expresses a keenness for the "snail" creature, and this taken with the narrator's inability to name it, as well as his physical description of a monstrous, sea-faring, long-necked and horned snail, indicates the animal's weirdness.

4. D

The key phrase is "this unbelievable monster," which will indicate to the reader that choice D is the correct answer, while choices A and B merely support the description of it and its unbelievable-ness. Choice C is out of place, the narrator does not base his reaction on the Doctor's.

5. D

The passage ends with the mention of the island on which the action takes place, and throughout the passage the narrator frequently cites the water, beach, and sea. Choice C may seem close, but do not satisfy the "island" description. Choices A and B, impossible to ascertain and admittedly unlikely, can be eliminated.

6. A

Choice A is the best choice: Roland believes the Coppins are practically obsessed with owning things. He thinks Mr. Coppin ought to have other interests than in "gauds and trinkets," and that Mr. Coppin would have lived life just fine without a gold watch. His observations extend to the rest of the family: Mrs. Coppin's "indecent" silk petticoat, Frank and Percy's hoarding of money (specie), and of course Muriel's penchant for hiring motor-cars, which Roland seems to find unconscionable. Choice B may seem close, as the description of Mr. Coppin's "gauds and trinkets" does imply a critique of style. Nevertheless, the reader has no way of knowing if Roland's dislike of the rest of the Coppins' material wants is based on their outdatedness. Choice C is incorrect, in fact to lead such clearly lavish lifestyles the Coppins appear well-endowed. Choice D has no evidence; Roland seems to critique the family's drive for material wants, but not as the sole determinant of their personalities.

7. A

Choice A should be the obvious answer. The unfortunate circumstance of Roland's dislike of cars, compounded by the fact that the car Muriel hires is driven by a man intensely jealous of Roland and Muriel's relationship, and his hyperbolic expression of that jealousy through road rage, is no doubt intended to elicit comedy. While sarcasm can potentially describe Roland's thoughts on the Coppins' materialism, the tone does not persist throughout, and is in general not derisive, hence choice B is incorrect. The humor and lightheartedness of the passage make choice C a negligible choice, while choice D is vague and without evidence.

8. B

Choice B has direct evidence: "Disappointed love was giving Albert a good deal of discomfort at this time." The reader could conclude that some other heartbreak weighs on Albert, though the fact that Muriel sits next to him, and that he is not given a chance to forget his agony on this trip, will lead the reader to infer that he has feelings for Muriel, feelings which now torment him. Choice A is irrelevant, choice C is a consequence and not a cause of his torments, while the reader has no reason to know or infer that Roland or Muriel's feelings about cars affect Albert in any way.

9. C

Frank is described as having a "generous, unspoiled" (e.g. sincere, innocent) nature. The reader will immediately disqualify choices A and D. Choice B is possible, but lacks proof. It is known for certain that Frank thrills to see displays of danger and stunning feats, from which the reader will infer that choice C is the choice most apt.

10. B

Choices A and C do occur throughout the passage, though they do not capture the whole idea of it. Choice D is misleading, as little action occurs, and nothing of the kind to suggest rising action which precipitates a climax. The perceptive reader will note that the first paragraph ends on Muriel's habit of hiring motor-cars, which then becomes the vehicle (so to speak) at the end of the passage that conveys the characters to Lexingham.

11. D

In this story, Grandfather Frog tells of how frogs came to lose their tails. His story speaks nothing to the purpose of the frogs' tails, so choice A is untenable, and his story is fictitious — clearly not dealing with facts — so choice B can be eliminated. Readers may estimate that the story is mythical, but ought to be aware that Grandfather Frog is merely retelling, not qualifying or explicating, the myth, so choice C is inaccurate. This leaves only choice D. The moral message which is the point of Grandfather Frog's story is not to be vain.

12. D
Choice A is false: heredity does not play a role in the loss of the tails. Though vanity is central to the tale, subjectivity is not — choice B is off-topic. Choices C and D are likewise off-topic. Choice D is closest to the tale's main message; readers will infer that, beauty being a surface-level experience, it should not be given undue weight, just as the frog king ought not have become prepossessed by his tail.

13. D
Choices B is an illogical choices. Choices A and C are the most likely choices, and the astute reader will determine that while the Grandfather Frog does indeed effect a tone of authority, his attitude towards the story seems primarily instructional, e.g. he seeks to instruct and educate his audience about his topic, rather than assert his authority on it.

14. B
Choice A has no proof, while choice C offers no explanation as to reason why the eagle's head is white. Choice D likewise is unconnected to the significance of the whiteness. Choice B is the best answer, and has ample evidence, including Sammy Jay and Peter Rabbit's references to the eagle's royalty, and that becoming white-headed was a direct consequence of Mother Nature making the eagle king.

15. D
Innovation has no role to play in this tale, and tradition is deemed paramount, as when Sammy Jay refers to the eagle's white head as a sign of royal lineage, bestowed upon him ages ago by Mother Nature herself. Thus, A is incorrect. Choice B is circumstantial, moreover, an explanation for a characteristic and arrangement (e.g. the eagle's white head and his being made king of birds) does not describe any law of the animal kingdom, per se. Choices C is irrelevant. Choice D is the best choice: Mother Nature makes the eagle king based on his being one of the biggest and strongest birds, and on how he garners respect from his claws and beak (i.e. his ability to submit others to his will).

16. D
Choice A is inaccurate; the tale's retelling does not conclude with Peter Rabbit admitting his jealousy. Choices B and C are both wrong: Mother Nature has a logical, considered reason for choosing the eagle to be king, and this choice has apparently been upheld for generations. Choice D is therefore the remaining choice, and is supported by Sammy Jay's observation that he believed everybody knew the story — the reader may thus infer that the tales of one species are not necessarily told by another.

17. B
A preheated oven is an oven heated to the correct temperature, here,, 350 degrees F (175 degrees C).

18. C
The mixture will need to be stirred 6 times. From the instructions,

Bring to a boil, and cook for 3 minutes, stirring every 30 seconds.

19. A

Pat is this sentence means to

Spread the filling over the base, and pat the remaining crumb mixture on top.

20. B

The total brown sugar is 1 1/3 cups.

21. D

The poem is clearly intended to detail the wondrous qualities of a rural town and its natural setting. Comparisons are made to classical European places and objects of great worth. Choices A and C are off-topic. Maintaining comparisons between Italy and the voice's hometown, the tone is not uncanny, curious, or bemused — choice B can be rejected.

22. A

Choices C is irrelevant. Choice B may be partially true, insofar as widely known and celebrated classical Italian cities are in the estimation of the voice no greater than the humble setting of his home. Yet the poem expresses much in favor of that home, which evokes more than criticism and dismissal. Choice D is vague and inaccurate — the voice waxes poetically on the sights and sounds, and seems passionately to advocate for the goodness of his environment. A is therefore the best choice.

23. B

Choice A is incorrect, the mistress in question is not aboriginal wisdom, and those doing the leaving behind are not Americans per se. Choices C, D, and E are likewise off-topic and can only be advanced on subjective grounds. The reader will therefore choose B. The poem deals mainly with the unspoiled beauty of nature, and how it easily rivals Man's loveliest creations. In these lines, the voice suggests that nature was the primordial inspiration for capturing beauty through art, yet those most highly regarded for artistry have failed to attend to this delineation.

24. C

Choice A may be a possible, but the reader will dismiss it for lack of further proof. Choice B is incorrect — poets in the main have not built up their craft by wasting words. Choice D is again possible, but without further allusion or direct comparison is impossible to verify. Choice C is the best fit: the poem seeks to enlighten readers as to the natural beauty of the voice's rural setting. The poem opens with a river, and in the second stanza introduces the Musketaquid, whose travels make up the bulk of the poem.

25. B

All thunderstorms will go through three stages. This is taken directly from the text, "All thunderstorms, regardless of type, go through three stages: the cumulus stage, the mature stage, and the dissipation stage."

26. D

Condensation. From the passage, "As the warm air rises, it cools. The moist water vapor begins to condense as the temperature cools."

27. A
The correct order of the process is seen in this passage:
"Clouds form as warm air carrying moisture rises. As the warm air rises, it cools. The moist water vapor begins to condense as the temperature cools. This releases energy that keeps the air warmer than its surroundings. The result is that it continues to rise."

28. C
From the passage, we see that "if enough instability is present in the atmosphere, this process will continue long enough for cumulonimbus clouds to form," where 'this process' is the process of rising air, condensing water drops generating heat, causing the air to rise farther.

29. B
Choice A is possible, but cannot be proven. Choice B is the simplest and best choice: there is clearly a storm, many different characters are weathering it, and several of them seem to be in some kind of suffering. Choice C is inaccurate. Savva may appear peculiar, but there is nothing to suggest Efimovna or Nazirovna are estranged from society. Choice D is too fanciful, and choice E cannot be confirmed.

30. D
Choice A is incorrect, Savva himself suggests otherwise. Choice B may be confusing, as Savva calls Nazirovna "mother," while she calls him "father" in return. The reader must accept that these are terms of affection, and do not actually suggest blood ties. As for choice C, Savva demonstrates a grounded-ness in reality and the capacity to interact with others; if he is a little weary and morbid, he is not delusional. Choice D is the best choice, and Savva himself declares, "A sinner doesn't deserve to be given rest."

31. D
Savva would have the reader choose A, but there is no evidence for this. In this scene, the reader sees no harmful act by Tihon against Savva, so choice B is incorrect. There is likewise no evidence for choice C. The inn does appear run-down, but how this has contributed to Savva's pain cannot be verified. Choice D is thus the best choice, and supported by Savva's being a pilgrim, and his request that Nazirovna wrap his feet.

32. C
The reader should be aware that choice B is irrelevant and not a description of mood here. Choice A seems likely, but is too extreme. Choice D may come across as a viable choice, but religion's role is confined to characterization. Furthermore, "holy" is an awkward label to apply to mood — spiritual, rapturous, or ecstatic may have served better in this regard. Choice C is therefore the correct answer, and properly reflects the storm weighing down on the suffering cast.

33. B
The reader can easily reject choice C, as both the Sheriff's wife and Mr. Hale's have accompanied the men to the kitchen. Choice A is a tempting choice, but note that it is not clear what event, murder or otherwise, has taken place. Choice D may also seem probable, but the reader will choose B as the best answer, as both the Sheriff and County Attorney place emphasis on Hale's account of what he saw.

34. D
Choice B and C lack proper evidence. The Sheriff appears perturbed at the Attorney's instruction that he ought to have had someone remain at the crime scene, but it is not reasonable to read the Sheriff's response as critical. Choice A, therefore, appears plausible, yet there is no obvious object the two are competing for, nor pervasive spirit of competition. Moreover, both are collaborating to get Hale's witness statement, and neither inhibits the other's progress. Choice D is the best choice.

35. D
Choice A has evidence to the contrary, Mr. Wright was not a fan of talking, and was disinclined to join the investment. Choice B may be a reasonable assumption, save that the reader does not know if Mr. Wright is dead, nor if a murder has even taken place. Choice C is irrelevant. Choice D is the best choice: from Hale and his neighbor's loading of potatoes, to the fact that neither Hale, his neighbor, nor the Wrights have a telephone line in their homes, the scene evidently occurs in the countryside.

36. C
Choice A agrees with the meaning of "done up" as in having applied make-up and jewelry, but here, is inaccurate and does not connect with her "queer" appearance. Choices B and D are irrelevant. Choice E is a contender, as surely exposure to some horrible crime would distract, yet choice E is the second-best choice to C, as the actual meaning of "done up" is indeed "tired out."

37. B
Choice A has been impossible to establish for the reader, while choices C and D are circumstantial and do not necessarily evince the wrong feeling about the kitchen. Choice B is the best choice. The reactions of the women, that allude the reader to the nature of the kitchen. Though it is cold outside and a fire burns in the kitchen, they nervously wait by the door, refusing to come any closer.

38. B
The correct answer can be found in the fourth sentence of the first paragraph.

Choice A is incorrect because repenting begins the day AFTER Mardi Gras. Choice C is incorrect because you can celebrate Mardi Gras without being a member of a Krewe. Choice D is incorrect because exploration does not play any role in a modern Mardi Gras celebration.

39. A
The second sentence is the last paragraph states that Krewes are led by the Kings and Queens. Therefore, you must have to be part of a Krewe to be its King or its Queen.

Choice B is incorrect because it never states in the passage that only people from France can be Kings and Queen of Mardi Gras. Choice C is incorrect because the passage says nothing about having to speak French. Choice D is incorrect because the passage does state that the Kings and Queens throw doubloons, which is fake money.

40. C
The first sentences of BOTH the 2nd and 3rd paragraphs mention that French explorers started this tradition in New Orleans.
Choices A, B and D are incorrect because they are names of cities or countries listed in the 2nd paragraph.

Mathematics - Parts I and II

1. B
1 inch on map = 100,000 inches on ground. So 3 inches on map = 3 x 100,000 = 300,000 inches on ground.

2. B
9.60/3.2 = 3

3. D
84/231 = 12/33 > 1/3
6/35 = 1/5 < 1/3
3/22 = 1/7 < 1/3

4. B
$\sqrt{2}$ is the largest number.
Here are the choices:

    a. 1

    b. $\sqrt{2}$ = 1.414

    c. 3/22 = .1563

    d. 4/3 = 1.33

5. B
We are told that driver B is 20 km/h faster than driver A. So: $V_B = V_A + 20$ where V is the velocity. Also, driver B traveled 480 km 2 hours before driver A. So:

x = 480 km

$t_A - 2 = t_B$ where t is the time. Now we know the relationship between A and B drivers in terms of time and velocity. We need to write an equation only depending on V_A (the speed of driver A) which we are asked to find.

Since distance = velocity * time: $480 = V_A * t_A = V_B * t_B$

$480 = (V_A + 20)(t_A - 2)$

$480 = (V_A + 20)(480/V_A - 2)$

$480 = 480 - 2V_A + 20 * 480/V_A - 40$

$0 = -2V_A + 9600/V_A - 40$ ... Multiplying the equation by V_A eliminates the denominator:

$2V_A^2 + 40V_A - 9600 = 0$ ... Simplifying the equation by 2:

$V_A^2 + 20V_A - 4800 = 0$

$V_{A1,2} = [-20 \pm \sqrt{(400 + 4 * 4800)}] / 2$

$V_{A1,2} = [-20 \pm 140] / 2$

$V_A = [-20 - 140]/2 = -80$ km/h and $V_A = [-20 + 140]/2 = 60$ km/h

We need to check our answers. It is easy to make a table:

t_A	V_A	V_B	t_B	$t_A - t_B$
480/80 = 6	-80	-80 - 20 = -100 B is 20 km/h faster than A. - sign only mentions the direction of the velocity. For magnitude, we need to add -20.	480/100 = 4.8	6 - 4.8 = 1.2 This should be 2!
480/60 = 8	60	60 + 20 = 80	480/80 = 6	8 - 6 = 2 This is correct !

So, V_A = 60 km/h is the only answer satisfying the question.

6. C

1 hour is equal to 3,600 seconds and 1 kilometer is equal to 1000 meters.

Since this train travels 72 kilometers per hour, this means that it covers 72,000 meters in 3,600 seconds.

If it travels 72,000 meters in 3,600 seconds

It travels x meters in 12 seconds

By Cross multiply: x = 72,000 * 12 / 3,600

x = 240 meters

7. A

Let us first mention the money Tony spent: $80

Now we need to find the money Tony earned:

He had 15 dozen eggs = 15 * 12 = 180 eggs. 16 eggs were broken. So,

Remaining number of eggs that Tony sold = 180 – 16 = 164.

Total amount he earned for selling 164 eggs = 164 * 0.54 = $88.56.

As a summary, he spent $80 and earned $88.56.

The profit is the difference: 88.56 - 80 = $8.56

Percentage profit is found by proportioning the profit to the money he spent:

8.56 * 100/80 = 10.7%

Checking the answers, we round 10.7 to the nearest whole number: 11%

8. B

Number of absent students = 83 – 72 = 11

Percentage of absent students is found by proportioning the number of absent students to the total number of students in the class = 11 * 100/83 = 13.25

Checking the answers, we round 13.25 to the nearest whole number: 13%

Practice Test Questions 2

9. D
To find the total turnout in all three polling stations, we need to proportion the number of voters to the number of all registered voters.

Total number of voters = 945 + 860 + 1210 = 3015

Total number of registered voters = 1270 + 1050 + 1440 = 3760

Percentage turnout in all three polling stations = 3015 * 100/3760 = 80.19%

Check the answer, round 80.19 to the nearest whole number: 80%

10. C
The approximate answer to 5205 ÷ 25 is 208. The exact answer is 208.2.

11. A
A common denominator is needed, a number which both 15 and 10 will divide into. So 14-9/30 = 5/30 = 1/6

12. D
The jacket costs $545.00 so we can round up to $550. 10% of $550 is 55. We can round down to $50, which is easier to work with. $550 - $50 is $500. The jacket will cost about $500.

The actual cost is 545 - 54.50 = 490.50.

13. C
Area of Type B consists of two rectangles and a half circle. We can find these three areas and sum them up to find the total area:

Area of the left rectangle: (4 + 8) * 8 = 96 m²

Area of the right rectangle: 14 * 8 = 112 m²

The diameter of the circle is equal to 14 m. So, the radius is 14/2 = 7:

Area of the half circle = (1/2) * πr^2 = (1/2) * (22/7) * $(7)^2$ = (1 * 22 * 49)/(2 * 7) = 77 m²

Area of Type B = 96 + 112 + 77 = 285 m²

Converting this area to ft²: 285 m² = 285 * 10.76 ft² = 3066.6 ft²

Type B is (3066.6 - 1300 = 1766.6 ft²) 1766.6 ft² larger than type A.

14. D
2009 x 108 is about 210,000. The exact answer is 216,972.

15. B
0.12 + 2/5 + 3/5, Convert decimal to fraction to get 3/25 + (1 2/5 = 7/5 = 35/25) + (1 3/5 = 8/5 = 40/25), = (3 + 35 + 40)/25, = 78/25 = 3 3/25

16. B
To solve the equation, we need the equation in the form ax^2 + bx + c = 0.
0.9x^2 + 1.8x - 2.7 = 0 is already in this form.

The quadratic formula to find the roots of a quadratic equation is:

$x_{1,2} = (-b \pm \sqrt{\Delta}) / 2a$ where $\Delta = b^2 - 4ac$ and is called the discriminant of the quadratic equation.

In our question, the equation is $0.9x^2 + 1.8x - 2.7 = 0$. To eliminate the decimals, let us multiply the equation by 10:

$9x^2 + 18x - 27 = 0$ ... This equation can be simplified by 9 since each term contains 9:

$x^2 + 2x - 3 = 0$

By remembering the form $ax^2 + bx + c = 0$:

$a = 1, b = 2, c = -3$

So, we can find the discriminant first, and then the roots of the equation:

$\Delta = b^2 - 4ac = (2)^2 - 4 * 1 * (-3) = 4 + 12 = 16$

$x_{1,2} = (-b \pm \sqrt{\Delta}) / 2a = (-2 \pm \sqrt{16}) / 2 = (-2 \pm 4) / 2$

This means that the roots are,

$x_1 = (-2 - 4)/2 = -3$ and $x_2 = (-2 + 4)/2 = 1$

17. A

We are asked to subtract polynomials. By paying attention to the sign distribution; we write the polynomials and operate:

$4x^3 - 2x^2 - 10 - (5x^3 + x^2 + x + 5) = 4x^3 - 2x^2 - 10 - 5x^3 - x^2 - x - 5$

$= 4x^3 - 5x^3 - 2x^2 - x^2 - x - 10 - 5$ ... similar terms written together to ease summing/substituting.

$x - 15$

18. C

First, we need to arrange the two equations to obtain the form $ax + by = c$. We see that there are 3 and 2 in the denominators of both equations. If we equate all at 6, then we can cancel all 6 in the denominators and have straight equations:

Equate all denominators at 6:

$2(4x + 5y)/6 = 3(x - 3y)/6 + 4 * 6/6$ ... Now we can cancel 6 in the denominators:

$8x + 10y = 3x - 9y + 24$ ... We can collect x and y terms on left side of the equation:

$8x + 10y - 3x + 9y = 24$

$5x + 19y = 24$ ... Equation (I)

Let us arrange the second equation:

$3(3x + y)/6 = 2(2x + 7y)/6 - 1 * 6/6$ ... Now we can cancel 6 in the denominators:

$9x + 3y = 4x + 14y - 6$ ... We can collect x and y terms on left side of the equation:

$9x + 3y - 4x - 14y = -6$

$5x - 11y = -6$ ... Equation (II)

Now, we have two equations and two unknowns x and y. By writing the two equations one under the other and operating, we can find one unknowns first, and find the other next:

$\quad 5x + 19y = 24$

$\underline{-1/\ 5x - 11y = -6}$ ... If we substitute this equation from the upper one, 5x cancels -5x:

$\quad 5x + 19y = 24$

$\underline{-5x + 11y = 6}$ ... Summing side-by-side:

$5x - 5x + 19y + 11y = 24 + 6$

$30y = 30$ ... Dividing both sides by 30:

$y = 1$

Inserting y = 1 into either of the equations, we can find the value of x. Choosing equation I:

$5x + 19 * 1 = 24$

$5x = 24 - 19$

$5x = 5$ ... Dividing both sides by 5:

$x = 1$

So, x = 1 and y = 1 is the solution; it is shown as (1, 1).

19. A

$x^2 + 12x - 13 = 0$ ... We try to separate the middle term 12x to find common factors with x^2 and -13 separately:

$x^2 + 13x - x - 13 = 0$ ... Here, we see that x is a common factor for x^2 and 13x, and -1 is a common factor for -x and -13:

$x(x + 13) - 1(x + 13) = 0$ ... Here, we have x times x + 13 and -1 times x + 13 summed up. This means that we have x - 1 times x + 13:

$(x - 1)(x + 13) = 0$

This is true when either or, both of the expressions in the parenthesis are equal to zero:

$x - 1 = 0$ ... $x = 1$

$x + 13 = 0$ ... $x = -13$

1 and -13 are the solutions for this quadratic equation.

20. C
First, we need to simplify the equation:
$((x^2 + 4x + 4) + (x^2 - 4x + 4)) / (x^2 - 4) = 0$

$(x^2 + 4x + 4 + x^2 - 4x + 4) / (x^2 - 4) = 0$ ... 4x and -4x in the numerator cancel each other.

Note that $x^2 - 4$ is two square difference and is equal to $x^2 - 2^2 = (x - 2)(x + 2)$:

$(2x^2 + 8)/((x - 2)(x + 2)) = 0$

The denominator tells us that if x - 2 or x + 2 equals to zero, there will be no solution. So, we will need to eliminate x = 2 and x = -2 from our solution which will be found considering the numerator:

$2x^2 + 8 = 0$

$2(x^2 + 4) = 0$

$x^2 + 4 = 0$

$x^2 = -4$ ... We know that, a square cannot be equal to a negative number. Solution for the square root of -4 is not a real number, so this equation has no solution.

21. D
We need to distribute the factors to the terms inside the related parenthesis:

$5(3x^2 - 2) - x^2(2 - 3x) = 15x^2 - 10 - (2x^2 - 3x^3)$

$= 15x^2 - 10 - 2x^2 + 3x^3$

$= 3x^3 + 15x^2 - 2x^2 - 10$ ... similar terms written together to ease summing/substituting.

$= 3x^3 + 13x^2 - 10$

22. B
We need to distribute the factors to the terms inside the related parenthesis:

$(x^3 + 2)(x^2 - x) - x^5 = x^5 - x^4 + (2x^2 - 2x) - x^5$

$= x^5 - x^4 + 2x^2 - 2x - x^5$

$= x^5 - x^5 - x^4 + 2x^2 - 2x$ ... similar terms written together to ease summing/substituting.

$= -x^4 + 2x^2 - 2x$

23. B
To simplify the expression, we need to find common factors. We see that both terms contain the term ab^2. So, we can take this term out of each term as a factor:

$9ab^2 + 8ab^2 = (9 + 8) ab^2 = 17ab^2$

24. C
$x^2 - 7x - 30 = 0$ ... We try to separate the middle term -7x to find common factors with x^2 and -30 separately:

$x^2 - 10x + 3x - 30 = 0$ ... Here, we see that x is a common factor for x^2 and -10x, and 3 is a common factor for 3x and -30:

$x(x - 10) + 3(x - 10) = 0$ ... Here, we have x times x - 10 and 3 times x - 10 summed up. This means that we have x + 3 times x - 10:

$(x + 3)(x - 10) = 0$ or $(x - 10)(x + 3) = 0$

25. C
To obtain a polynomial, we should remove the parenthesis by distributing the related factors to the terms inside the parenthesis:
$1 - x(1 - x(1 - x)) = 1 - x(1 - (x - x * x)) = 1 - x(1 - x + x^2)$

$= 1 - (x - x * x + x * x^2) = 1 - x + x^2 - x^3$ ... Writing this result in descending order of powers:

$= - x^3 + x^2 - x + 1$

26. D
To simplify the expression, remove the parenthesis by distributing the related factors to the terms inside the parenthesis:

$7(2y + 8) + 1 - 4(y + 5) = (7 * 2y + 7 * 8) + 1 - (4 * y + 4 * 5)$

$= 14y + 56 + 1 - 4y - 20$

$= 14y - 4y + 56 + 1 - 20$ ... similar terms written together to ease summing/substituting.

$= 10y + 37$

27. D
We understand that each of the n employees earn 's' amount of salary weekly. This means that one employee earns s salary weekly. So; Richard has ns amount of money to employ n employees for a week.

We are asked to find the number of days n employees can be employed with x amount of money. We can do simple direct proportion:

If Richard can employ n employees for 7 days with ns amount of money,

Richard can employ n employees for y days with x amount of money ... y is the number of days we need to find.

So we have two values for b, which means we

$y = (x * 7)/(ns)$

$y = 7x/ns$

28. A
$x^2 - 3x - 4$ ... We try to separate the middle term -3x to find common factors with x^2 and -4 separately:

$x^2 + x - 4x - 4$ ... Here, we see that x is a common factor for x^2 and x, and -4 is a common factor for -4x and -4:

= x(x + 1) - 4(x + 1) ... Here, we have x times x + 1 and -4 times x + 1 summed up. This means that we have x - 4 times x + 1:

= (x - 4)(x + 1) or (x + 1)(x - 4)

29. D

We need to simplify and have x alone and on one side to solve the inequality:

(2x + 1)/(2x - 1) < 1

(2x + 1)/(2x - 1) - 1 < 0 ... We need to write the left side at the common denominator 2x - 1:

(2x + 1)/(2x - 1) - (2x - 1)/(2x - 1) < 0

(2x + 1 - 2x + 1)/(2x - 1) < 0 ... 2x and -2x terms cancel each other in the numerator:

2/(2x - 1) < 0

2 is a positive number; so,

2x - 1 < 0

2x < 1

x < 1/2 ... This means that x should be smaller than 1/2 and not equal to 1/2. This is shown as (-∞, 1/2).

30. B

Total Volume = Volume of large cylinder - Volume of small cylinder

Volume of a cylinder = area of base * height = $πr^2$ * h

Total Volume = (π * 12^2 * 10) - (π * 6^2•5) = 1440π - 180π

= 1260π in^3

31. A

If we know the coordinates of two points on a line, we can find the slope (m) with the below formula:

m = $(y_2 - y_1)/(x_2 - x_1)$ where (x_1, y_1) represent the coordinates of one point and (x_2, y_2) the other.

In this question:

(-9, 6) : x_1 = -9, y_1 = 6

(18, -18) : x_2 = 18, y_2 = -18

Inserting these values into the formula:

m = (-18 - 6)/(18 - (-9)) = (-24)/(27) ... Simplifying by 3:

m = -8/9

Practice Test Questions 2

32. A

If we know the coordinates of two points on a line, we can find the slope (m) with the below formula:

$m = (y_2 - y_1)/(x_2 - x_1)$ where (x_1, y_1) represent the coordinates of one point and (x_2, y_2) the other.

In this question:

$(-4, y_1) : x_1 = -4, y_1 =$ we will find

$(-8, 7) : x_2 = -8, y_2 = 7$

$m = -7/4$

Inserting these values into the formula:

$-7/4 = (7 - y_1)/(-8 - (-4))$

$-7/4 = (7 - y_1)/(-8 + 4)$

$7/(-4) = (7 - y_1)/(-4)$ ... Simplifying the denominators of both sides by -4:

$7 = 7 - y_1$

$0 = -y_1$

$y_1 = 0$

33. D

The area of a rectangle is found by multiplying the width to the length. If we call these sides with "a" and "b"; the area is = a * b.

We are given that a * b = 20 cm² ... Equation I

One side is increased by 1 and the other by 2 cm. So new side lengths are "a + 1" and "b + 2."

The new area is (a + 1)(b + 2) = 35 cm² ... Equation II

Using equations I and II, we can find a and b:

ab = 20

(a + 1)(b + 2) = 35 ... We need to distribute the terms in parenthesis:

ab + 2a + b + 2 = 35

We can insert ab = 20 to the above equation:

20 + 2a + b + 2 = 35

2a + b = 35 - 2 - 20

2a + b = 13 ... This is one equation with two unknowns. We need to use another information to have two equations with two unknowns which leads us to the solution. We know that ab = 20. So, we can use a = 20/b:

2(20/b) + b = 13

40/b + b = 13 ... We equate all denominators to "b" and eliminate it:

40 + b² = 13b

b2 - 13b + 40 = 0 ... We can use the roots by factoring. We try to separate the middle term -13b to find common factors with b2 and 40 separately:

b2 - 8b - 5b + 40 = 0 ... Here, we see that b is a common factor for b2 and -8b, and -5 is a common factor for -5b and 40:

b(b - 8) - 5(b - 8) = 0 Here, we have b times b - 8 and -5 times b - 8 summed up. This means that we have b - 5 times b - 8:

(b - 5)(b - 8) = 0

This is true when either or both expressions in the parenthesis are equal to zero:

b - 5 = 0 ... b = 5

b - 8 = 0 ... b = 8

So we have two values for b, which means we have two values for a as well. To find a, we can use any equation we have. Let us use a = 20/b.

If b = 5, a = 20/b → a = 4

If b = 8, a = 20/b → a = 2.5

So, (a, b) pairs for the sides of the original rectangle are: (4, 5) and (2.5, 8). These are found in (b) and (c) answer choices.

34. D
1/(4x - 2) = 5/6 ... Cross multiply:

5(4x - 2) = 1 * 6 ... Now, we distribute 5 to the parenthesis:

20x - 10 = 6 ... We need x term alone on one side:

20x = 6 + 10

20x = 16 ... Dividing both sides by 20:

x = 16/20 ... Simplifying by 2, and 10 in the denominator gives the decimal equivalent of x:

x = 8/10 = 0.8

35. B
If we know the coordinates of two points on a line, we can find the slope (m) with the below formula:
m = $(y_2 - y_1)/(x_2 - x_1)$ where (x_1, y_1) represent the coordinates of one point and (x_2, y_2) the other.

In this question:

$(-4, -4) : x_1 = -4, y_1 = -4$

$(-1, 2) : x_2 = -1, y_2 = 2$

Inserting these values into the formula:

$m = (2 - (-4))/(-1 - (-4)) = (2 + 4)/(-1 + 4) = 6/3$ ... Simplifying by 3:

$m = 2$

36. A

The formula of the volume of cylinder is the base area multiplied by the height. As the formula:

Volume of a cylinder = $\pi r^2 h$. Where π is 3.142, r is radius of the cross sectional area, and h is the height.

We know that the diameter is 5 meters, so the radius is 5/2 = 2.5 meters.

The volume is: $V = 3.142 * 2.5^2 * 12 = 235.65$ m^3.

37. C

The large cube is made up of 8 smaller cubes with 5 cm sides. The volume of a cube is found by the third power of the length of one side.

Volume of the large cube = Volume of the small cube * 8

$= (5^3) * 8 = 125 * 8$

$= 1000$ cm^3

There is another solution for this question. Find the side length of the large cube. There are two cubes rows with 5 cm length for each. So, one side of the large cube is 10 cm.

The volume of this large cube is equal to $10^3 = 1000$ cm^3

38. A

First write the two equations one under the other. Our aim is to multiply equations with appropriate factors to eliminate one unknown and find the other, and then find the eliminated one using the found value.

$-\sqrt{5}/ x\sqrt{5} - y = \sqrt{5}$ ... If we multiply this equation by $\sqrt{5}$, y terms will cancel:

$\underline{x - y\sqrt{5} = 5}$

$-x\sqrt{5}\sqrt{5} + y\sqrt{5} = -\sqrt{5}\sqrt{5}$ ... using $\sqrt{5}\sqrt{5} = 5$:

$\underline{x - y\sqrt{5} = 5}$

$-5x + y\sqrt{5} = -5$

$\underline{x - y\sqrt{5} = 5}$ ... Summing side-by-side:

-5x + y√5 + x - y√5 = -5 + 5 ... + y√5 and - y√5, -5 and + 5 cancel:

-4x = 0

x = 0

Now, using either of the equations gives us the value of y. Let us choose equation 1:

x√5 - y = √5

0√5 - y = √5

-y = √5

y = -√5

The solution to the system is (0, -√5)

39. D

As shown in the figure, two parallel lines intersecting with a third line with angle of 75°.

x = 75° (corresponding angles)

x + y = 180° (supplementary angles) ... inserting the value of x here:

y = 180° - 75°
y = 105°

40. D

Two parallel lines (m & side AB) intersected by side AC. This means that 50° and a angles are interior angles. So:
a = 50° (interior angles).

41. D

We have a circle given with diameter 8 cm and a square located within the circle. We are asked to find the area of the circle for which we only need to know the length of the radius that is the half of the diameter.
Area of circle = πr² ... r = 8/2 = 4 cm

Area of circle = π * 4²

= 16π cm² ... As we notice, the inner square has no role in this question.

42. C

We see that two legs of a right triangle form by Peter's movements and we are asked to find the length of the hypotenuse. We use the Pythagorean Theorem:
(Hypotenuse)² = (Perpendicular)² + (Base)²
h² = a² + b²

Given: 3² + 4² = h²
h² = 9 + 16
h = √25
h = 5

Practice Test Questions 2

43. B
The width of the rectangle is given to be two thirds of the length. So, if we call the length by a, the width should be (2/3)a. In order not to deal with fractions, let us say that:
length = 3x
Then, width = (2/3)3x = 2x
Remember that the perimeter of a rectangle is found by summing all edges up which means summing two lengths and two widths up.
Perimeter = 2.3x + 2.2x = 150
6x + 4x = 150
10x = 150
x = 15
We are asked to find the length, that is 3x = 3.15 = 45 cm.

44. D
The volume of a sphere is found by $V_{sphere} = (4/3)\pi r^3$
The volume of a cylinder is found by $V = \pi r^2 h$ ... In the question, the radius of the cylinder is 3r. Then,
$V_{cylinder} = \pi(3r)^2 h = 9\pi r^2 h$
Since in this question $V_{sphere} = V_{cylinder}$,
$(4/3)\pi r^3 = 9\pi r^2 h$ ... Eliminating πr^2 from both sides:
$(4/3)r = 9h$ ... By Cross multiply:
4r = 27h
We are asked to find r/h. From the above equation, we can say that if r = 27k, then h = 4k.
r/h = 27k / 4k = 27/4.

45. A
The area of a triangle is found by the formula, Area = (1/2) X base X height
Let us say that base = x
The height of this triangle is 4 cm less than 3 times the base; so, height = 3x – 4
Applying these to the equation above:
Area = 32 = (1/2)·x·(3x – 4)
By cross multiplication and distributing the parenthesis,
64 = 3x² – 4x
3x² – 4x – 64 = 0 ... By factorization,
3x   – 16
x   4
(3x - 16)(x + 4) = 0
There are two solutions for x:
1) 3x – 16 = 0 → x = 16/3
2) x + 4 = 0 → x = - 4 ... Since a length measure cannot be negative, this cannot be a possible solution.
Then, the only solution for x is 16/3.

We are asked to find the height, that is 3x – 4 = 3(16/3) – 4 = 16 – 4 = 12 cm.

46. B
To compare, calculate the mean and median of this set of data:

mean = (8 . 200,000 + 2 . 350,000 + 5 . 470,000 + 5 . 650,000) / (8 + 2 + 5 + 5) = 395,000

The data set can be shown as:

200,000/8 ... ... 350,000/2 ... 470,000/3 ... 470,000/5 ... 650,000/5 ... ...

Since there are 20 terms in this set, the median is the 11th term; that is 470,000.

The mean best represents the values of the cars since the median value has only one car price higher than it.

47. A
Based on this graph, a person that is 85 or older will make 26.2 visits to the hospital every year.

48. A
A person aged 95 or older would make 31.3 or more visits.

49. D
Indonesia is growing the fastest at about 30%.

50. A
According to the graph, oil consumption peaked in 2011.

Language Arts - Writing

1. B
Sentence 4 is a fragment. "Not to mention resolving the conflicts between warring nations."

This sentence is essentially a verbal phrase of the word "resolve" which does not have a main clause as part of the sentence. It is the extension of the sentence preceding it which contains the main clause and does make sense as it stands after the sentence with the main clause. However, since it does not have the main clause in its own structure, it is a sentence fragment.

2. A
The following changes to sentence 6 would focus attention on the main idea in paragraph 2. "Yet, the technology behind the atom bomb essentially had the power of resolving the war itself which scientists like him failed to convey."

The use of the connector "No matter what" in the original sentence is irrelevant given the sense expressed in both the sentences it connects. Taking the context of paragraph into consideration, the use of the connector "Yet" complements the sense expressed in both the sentences.

3. B
Suggested changes for sentence 5, "For instance, the atom bomb was developed during the Second World War by the recommendations of the great Albert Einstein - who is accepted as the father of modern physics - in fear of the Germans developing it and using on the Allies."

The original sentence lacks a comma after the thought extension phrase "For instance."

Also, the use of dash to link two or more ideas and make a point has been incomplete.

4. C

The following sentence, if inserted before sentence 7, would best illustrate the main idea of the passage, "Nuclear fission that is used in the fuelling of the bomb, has the capacity to produce electrical energy which has turned out to be a major alternative later in the Twentieth Century."

The main idea of the passage is the misuse of science regarding the development of the atom bomb during the Second World War, whereas it could effectively be used in meeting the energy demands of the countries involved in the war. This is expressed explicitly in the sentence offered in choice C, which is at the same time coherent with the seventh and eighth sentence between which it is being suggested to be placed. Other choices either lack coherence or are less relevant.

5. A

Sentence 4 is a fragment. "Which I doubt belongs to any <u>other</u> person."

This sentence is an extension of the sentence preceding it. It does not complete the thought when alone, and is thus a sentence fragment.

6. A

Sentence 3 sentence is not consistent with the author's purpose. "For example, for an air stewardess position, girls have to be no more than 163 cm tall; whereas for jobs in foreign affairs, Chinese diplomats are required to match their foreign counterparts."

The passage talks about the people who want to increase their height by undergoing a surgery and points out the minimum height requirements for getting a job that they wish to work in. However, the expression "no more than 163 cm tall" is a statement about a maximum not a minimum. In addition, the sentence refers to Chinese diplomats who must 'match' the height of their foreign counterparts, which could be taller, and hence require surgery, or could be shorter and not require surgery.

7. B

The following sentence, if inserted after sentence 7, would best illustrate the main idea of the passage, "This artificial way of gaining height is turning out to be a new trend among the new generation in height conscious China."

The paragraph discusses about the application of leg surgery among Chinese young people to increase their height. This is best reflected in the sentence suggested in choice B which also contributes to the cohesion of the second paragraph as well as allowing a smooth transition between the second and third paragraph.

8. B

Suggested changes to sentence 8, "Even parents approve of the idea, being fully aware of all the complications and they are willing to finance such a sophisticated surgery."

The usage of vocabulary is incorrect in this sentence. The word "complexity" is an adjective noun used to describe detailed aspects of a given subject which is less relevant here. The word "labyrinth" is also incorrect in this context. The correct counterpart for "complexity" here, would be "complications" which takes into account the length of the surgery itself and the agony, sacrifice and the commitment associated with it, all in one. Also the word "sophisticated", as suggested in choices B and C in the place of "labyrinth" is more appropriate as it hints about the details of the surgery. Choice B offers both changes.

9. A
Sentence 4 is a fragment. "Which I doubt belongs to any other person. "

This sentence is an extension of the sentence preceding it. It does not complete the thought when alone and is thus a sentence fragment.

10. D
Sentence 9 is the least relevant to the main idea of the second paragraph. "He is panicked by street dogs and neighbors' cats and to avoid them, he crosses to the other side of the street every now and then."

The second paragraph mainly talks about Luke's odd behavior while in a moving in a crowd, but sentence 9 shifts the subject to his strategy when he encounters cats and dog in the streets.

11. C
Sentence 4 contains a redundant phrase. "Which I doubt any other person belongs to other than him."

In this sentence the second "other" is redundant. It can be omitted.

12. B
The following sentence, if inserted before sentence 1, would best illustrate the main idea of the passage. "But that does not bother him; rather he always seems to be happy in being able to utter those two words."

The passage starts with the speculation that Luke is probably the only person happy with his peculiar character and style of living. This is reflected in the sentence which is suggested to be added as the last sentence. Other choices do not offer the same relevance and coherence.

13. D
Sentence 6 is a fragment, "But for a day only."

This sentence fails to complete a thought when it stands alone. It is complementary as a thought extension to the previous sentence though and makes perfect sense when it is preceded by that. Since it neither has a noun clause, nor a verbal, it is a sentence fragment.

14. C
Sentence 8 is not consistent with author's purpose. "But as they came to know him closely, they were disappointed he would only occupy Mr. Drodsky's position for two weeks."

In sentence 6, the author indicates that the new teacher is replacing Mr. Drodsky for one day only. However, in sentence 8, it is clearly stated that he will be replacing him for two weeks, contradicting his earlier statement.

15. A
Suggested changes to sentence 16, "Coming from a public school in New Jersey, Ray had never seen students 'tamed' to such narrow, disparate discipline in his six years of experience as a music teacher."

The original sentence contains the wrong usage of the word "desperate." The use of the homophone "disparate" is more suited to express the distinct trait of the students in the new school he has joined. The right modification is suggested in choice A and all other choices offer incorrect changes.

16. D
Sentence 7 contains non-standard usage, "Aa you wiss me, chilsren?"

This sentence refers to Mr. Drodsky's Eastern European accent that can be considered as non-standard usage. Although strictly incorrect, it is permissible stylistically to illustrate his accent.

17. D
Sentence 5 is a fragment. "Hanging in between two sides of the wall near one corner of the store room which they rarely open, a magnificent piece of art left half woven and still being worked on."

This sentence does not express a complete thought since it does not have a verbal clause. A possible revision would be: "Hanging between two walls near one corner of the store room , lies a magnificent piece of art left half woven and still being worked on."

18. B
The following changes to sentence 7 would focus attention on the main idea of the second paragraph, "He is more interested in the web that they weave."

The style of the original sentence lacks cohesion with the passage. Choice B uses a relative comparison with the words "more interested in." The other choices offer changes which does not differ greatly from the original sentence.

19. A
Suggested changes to sentence 10 are, "He wonders how they manage to create something unique like this with such a little brain that they have."

The change here, is related to the use of the word "wander" which is inappropriate here. "Wonder" is the correct word.

20. C
Suggested changes to sentence 13 are, "It has been there for almost six months now and it lay there as it was last month."

The change in this sentence is related to the correct use of grammar. The original sentence uses "that" and "it" to represent the subject, as well as "were" which is also incorrect. "That" in the beginning of the sentence must be replaced with "it" and the singular form of the verb "be" must be used.

21. D
Sentence 4 is a fragment. "Thanks to the arrival of the rescue helicopter just as he pulled himself out of the canyon into the open desert."

This sentence does not complete a thought individually since it expresses a cause only. It expresses meaning when it is used with the effect. It is in fact preceded by the sentence that expresses the effect having the main clause. Without the main clause, this sentence is a sentence fragment.

22. A
Sentence 1 contains redundancy. "Aaron Ralston's case was an extraordinary case of adaptation and decision making in extreme conditions."

The word "case" in this sentence has been used excessively which must be replaced with equivalent synonyms. A possible revision would be: "Aaron Ralston's story is an extraordinary example of adaptation and decision making in extreme conditions."

23. B
The following sentence, if inserted after sentence 7, would best illustrate the main idea of the passage, "He had to make a tough decision of choosing between his arm that was under the rock and his life that was in imminent danger."

The passage exemplifies Ralston's presence of mind under harsh conditions and his exceptional decision-making. It is best reflected in the sentence suggested in choice B which also offers cohesion and consistency with the seventh, or previous sentence.

24. D
The following changes are needed in sentence 8. "As he walked into the hospital steady and upright, it was evident how he managed to <u>adapt</u> himself to the harsh conditions of the desert for six unending days without proper food and sleep; surviving on just a couple of <u>liters</u> of water."

The changes in this sentence are related to vocabulary usage. The use of the words "adopt" and "litter" is incorrect and should be replace with "adapt" and "liter."

25. B
The following changes would focus attention on the main idea of the first paragraph, "The only challenge was the narrow gap between the seven and the black through which he had to fine tune his spin."

The addition of the adjective "only" brings the focus of the sentence to the main idea of the first paragraph. Both choices B and C offer this change. However, choice C is a sentence fragment.

26. D
Sentence 12 contains redundancy.
"He had to think of a slow roll, retarded enough and yet keep the impact strong enough to allow the jump."

The expression "retarded enough" used here, is useless, contributes to redundancy, and should be removed. A possible revision would be: "He had to think of a slow roll and yet keep the impact strong enough to allow the jump."

27. A
Suggested changes to sentence 17 are, "Not because he plays great shots, but because he let them think with him how to do things others think are impossible."

The original sentence does not have a comma after "but" which is preferable in cases when emphasis is intended on alternative propositions. Here, the correct change is suggested in choice A only.

28. C
Suggested changes to sentence 7 are, "The elegance with which he takes the shot without the cue even touching the surface and yet covers any distance around the table is truly amazing."

The original sentence contains an inconsistency in the sentence as well as confusion as to what the author tries to argue.

29. C
Sentence 6 is a sentence fragment. "As if his world would stop spinning.

This sentence contains only an "if" clause and does not have a main and verbal clause. Therefore, it fails to express a complete thought and as a result is a sentence fragment. A possible revision would be as follows: "It was as if his world would stop spinning.

30. A
Suggested changes to Sentence 9 to reduce redundancy are, "He always felt he was deprived of his mother's love and attention, but could never accept that he was deprived of his only parent's love."

The idiom "deprived of" is used twice in the same sentence. It can be improved by replacing one of them with an equivalent expression and making the sentence shorter. A possible revision would be: "He always felt deprived of his mother's love and attention, but could never accept that."

31. D
Sentence 11 - But as he was trying to visualize his happy memories of his mom holding his hand while taking him to the candy store - and the security he felt holding her hand - he was struck by the image of a tyrant woman beating him mercilessly for breaking the window.

The semi-colon-comma construction is complex and unnecessary. Replacing with dashes makes the point more forcefully.

32. A
The following changes are needed to sentence 7. "He would feel suffocated by the urge to initiate a long-term relationship."

The original sentence requires adjustment related to vocabulary usage. The word "temptation" is used to express the inclination to do something uncontrollable and negative. Two synonyms, "urge" and "desire" has been proposed, but since desires are controllable to some extent, the suggestion that has the word "urge" would be more appropriate.

33. A
Sentence 8 is least relevant to the main idea of the third paragraph. "On the ceilings as often as not were no lights at all."

All the other sentences in the paragraph talk about keeping lights on or off. Sentence 8 talks about the positioning of lights on the ceiling.

34. A
The following sentence fragment, if inserted at the beginning of sentence 13 would best illustrate the main idea, "But after a while I reconsidered:"

The answer must be in the context of the author's experience. The author intends to find the contrasting features between cultures and the word "consider" is vital in doing so. Therefore, choice A, having a derivative of the word "consider" provides the best answer in this context.

35. B
The following changes are needed to sentence 10, "It wasn't the environment that he was concerned about- but the bill; and candles were out of the question save for blackouts since they would burn the house down if we forgot about them."

The sentence is a second conditional since the condition clause is in past progressive. Therefore, the main clause should have "would+V2." Only choice B has the past simple of the verb "burn" after "would" in the main clause.

36. D
Sentence 11 contains non-standard usage. "Its such a dark in winter," they said, "We always need of light."

Apparently, the speaker is not a native speaker of English, so while grammatically incorrect, it is stylistically acceptable.

37. D
"Who" is correct because the question uses an active construction. "To whom was first place given?" is passive construction.

38. D
"Which" is correct, because the files are objects and not people.

39. C
The simple present tense, "rises," is correct.

40. A
"Lie" does not require a direct object, while "lay" does. The old woman might lie on the couch, which has no direct object, or she might lay the book down, which has the direct object, "the book."

41. D
The simple present tense, "falls," is correct because it is repeated action.

42. A
The present progressive, "building models," is correct in this sentence; it is required to match the other present progressive verbs.

43. C
Past Perfect tense describes a completed action in the past, before another action in the past.

44. D
The preposition "to" is the correct preposition to use with "bring."

45. D
"Laid" is the past tense.

46. A
This is a past unreal conditional sentence. It requires an 'if' clause and a result clause, and either clause can appear first. The 'if' clause uses the past perfect, while the result clause uses the past participle.

47. C
The semicolon is used in a list where the list items have internal punctuation, such as "Key West, Florida."

48. C
The semicolon links independent clauses. An independent clause can form a complete sentence by itself.

49. A
The semicolon links independent clauses with a conjunction (However).

50. B
The sentence is correct. The semicolon links independent clauses. An independent clause can form a complete sentence by itself.

Science

1. C
75 pounds of force much be exerted downward on the rope to lift the 150 pound weight.

2. B
To solve for F, Weight X b (distance from fulcrum to weight) = Force X a (distance from fulcrum to point where force is applied)
100 X 5 = F X 10
500/10 = F
F =50

3. A
Carbon has an atomic number of 6 this means that it has 6 protons and 6 electrons

4. C
Oxygen has 8 electrons in total. Therefore its configuration is 2,6 (2 in the first shell and then the remaining 6 in the valence shell.

5. B
Groups move across, while period moves down the periodic table, therefore the correct element is 2 across, 4 down.

6. C
Features of positive ions are: that they are usually metal (hydrogen is the exception) and have less than 4 electrons in their outer (valence) shells. Therefore choices A, B, and D all form positive ions, making these answers incorrect. Choice C is correct because fluorine is a non-metal and has 7 electrons in its outer (valence) shell; therefore it will form a negative ion.

7. D
All answers are true statements; however, choice D is the best explanation and therefore correct. With each successive period in the table the elements gain another shell of electrons, it is the valence electron which is donated during a chemical reaction. Each time a shell is added the valence electron gets farther away from the positive nucleus which means that the nucleus had less ability to hold it in place.

8. A
A chemical compound is a chemical substance comprising atoms from two or more elements in a specific ration as expressed in the chemical formula i.e., H2O

9. B
The equation $E = mc^2$ is based on the Law of Conservation of Mass and Energy, and states that Energy equals Mass times the Velocity of light.

10. A
Water boils at approximately 100 °C (212 °F) at standard atmospheric pressure.

11. D
All three choices determine if a planet has an atmosphere. D is the best choice.

12. A
Tenuous means thin, flimsy or weak, therefore choice A is the correct answer.

13. B
the warm air rising causes the light colored bands or "zones." Choice A is incorrect as the cool gas sinking causes the dark colored regions. Choice C is also incorrect as these are found in the darker colored belts.

14. C
Choice C is an opinion, as the passage suggests that "astronomers think that the dark bands contain hydrocarbons" which suggests it may be a hypothesis, rather than a fact supported by evidence.

15. B
The vacuum of space is an environment where bacteria do not commonly exit. The nature of outer space, including intense cold and lack of oxygen, makes it difficult for even most bacteria to grow.

16. B
Plants and animals are kingdoms. There are six recognized kingdoms: Animalia, Plantae, Protista, Fungi, Bacteria, and Archaea.

17. B
The elements on the periodic table can be classified as metals, metalloids and non-metals. Most of the elements on the table can be classified as metals.

18. C
All of these statements are true.

> A metal is a substance that conducts heat and electricity.
>
> A metal is shiny and reflects many colors of light, and can be hammered into sheets or drawn into wire.
>
> About 80% of the known chemical elements are metals.

19. D
Choice D is the correct as all three of these phenomena are due to the movement of tectonic plates, sliding past each other or colliding.

20. B
A functional dynamo and magnetic field suggest a liquid core which is in motion. Therefore choice B is the correct answer.

21. D
The passage states that Mars is richer in these elements than Earth.

22. A
Choice A is correct because the planetary dynamo is the constant movement which occurs inside the planet. Choice B is incorrect as this is the internal power source for the dynamo. Choice C is incorrect as this is the effect the dynamo has on the Earth. Choice D is incorrect as this provides the kinetic energy to maintain the dynamo.

23. A
A biological class is a collection of similar or like living entities. Class has the same meaning in biology as rank. Common classes or ranks include species, order, and phylum.

24. A
The mass number of an atom is the total number of particles (protons and neutrons) that make it up.

25. A
All of the statements are true.

> a. Mechanical energy is the energy that is possessed by an object due to its motion or due to its position.
>
> b. Mechanical energy can be either kinetic energy (energy of motion) or potential energy (stored energy of position).
>
> c. Objects have mechanical energy if they are in motion

26. B
Choice A is incorrect as the Kuiper belt is not a planet but a collection of icy bodies, outside Neptune's orbit. Choice C is incorrect as it is a dwarf planet. Choice D is incorrect as it is a star, not a planet.

27. D
We know that Pluto is 1/6 the size of the moon and Eris is 27% (or just over ¼) bigger than Pluto. Therefore it must also be smaller than the moon. Neptune is a Gas Giant. Therefore it must be the largest.

28. B
According to the IAU, the three criteria for determining if an object is a planet are that it must:

- Orbits the sun (Choice A can be eliminated)

- Choice B is the correct answer as many celestial bodies have a moderately eccentric and inclined orbit, irrespective of if they are planets or not.

- Has cleared the neighborhood – it is not influenced by the gravity of any other objects in space, and apart from its satellites, does not have other objects sharing its orbital path (Choice C can be eliminated).

- Has a nearly round shape (D can also be eliminated).

29. C
Neptune is closer to the sun than Pluto. The passage tells us that "Eris…is beyond the Kuiper belt", suggesting that the Kuiper belt lies in between Pluto and Eris.

30. C
Force = Mass times Acceleration Measured in Newtons. F = 200 X 5 = 1000 N

31. C
Covalent or ionic bonds are considered "strong bonds."

32. C
P = 1.5 x 18 = 27 kg x m/s into the field.

33. A
Momentum of first object = 2 x 3.5 = 7; momentum of second truck = 4.3 x 1.5 = 6.45. First truck has more momentum at 7 kg x m/s moving east.

34. B
there is an increase in the distance covered each second. Choice A is incorrect because the ball is not covering the same distance each second. Choice C is incorrect as the ball is covering a greater distance each second, a decrease in speed indicates less distance each second. Choice D is incorrect because stationary implies no distance covered.

35. D
To work out the where the ball is traveling the fastest, we need to consider the distance covered in each 20th of a second. Choice D is correct because 19 units of distance have been covered between 9 and 10/20ths of a second compared to choice C, where it is 17, B where it is 15, and A where it is 13.

36. A
According to the passage, 1 unit of distance =12mm. The ball falls 100 units in total, therefore 12 x 100 = 1200mm

37. A
We first need to convert 50 g into kg = 50/1000 = 0.05kg.
Then the information can be substituted into the equation Ep = mgh
Ep = 0.05 x 10 x 1
Ep = 0.5 J

38. A
The passage tells us that a centipede has a pair of legs for each body segment. Therefore 99 body segments x 2 legs = 198 legs total.

39. D
The passage tells us that the centipede has venomous claws suggesting that it is predatory.

40. C
Choice C is correct because it includes all methods of blending into one's surroundings. Choice A is incorrect - this is when an animal resembles another animal, plant or non-living object. Choice B is incorrect as this is a form of camouflage, which acts to break up the lines of the animal so it cannot be seen, e.g., stripes on a Zebra. Choice D is incorrect as this is where an animal is the same color as its background, e.g., white polar bears.

41. B
Arthropods have jointed legs, an exoskeleton, and segmented bodies. Snails lack all three of these features.

42. A
4.5 billion years is the earliest date on the spiral.

43. D
Choice A is radiometric dating: a process which looks at the ratio between the number of carbon-14 and carbon-12 isotopes in any dead organism to indicate how long it's been since it was alive.

Choice B - Earth and Moon rocks are measured by the decay of long-lived radioactive isotopes of elements that occur naturally in rocks and minerals and that have half lives of 700 million to more than 100 billion years.
Choice C – rock layers or strata can give scientists an idea of the changes that the Earth has gone through, based on the fossils found in them, their thickness, the type of rock they are, etc.

44. B
Dinosaurs can be found in the Triassic, Jurassic and Cretaceous periods. These three periods are known as the Mesozoic era

45. B
Choice B is correct because it is in the middle of the Mesozoic area, where the diversity of reptiles. Choice A is incorrect because dinosaurs and many other reptiles were extinct by this point. Choices C and D are incorrect because most organisms which existed were sea dwelling, sponge-like creatures, not reptiles.

46. C
Rapid cooling and heating of the Earth's climate would affect choices A, B, and D. Therefore, C is the best answer.

47. C
Choice C is the best choice as it occurs before the other choices listed (reading from left to right) and shows a sharp incline.

48. B
The shape of the diagram is slowly increasing in width.
Choice A is incorrect as this is the growth rate seen in the inflation stage of the picture, where there is a steep incline.
Choice C is incorrect as we would expect to see the chart becoming more narrow over time
Choice D is incorrect as we would expect to the outlines of the chart remaining parallel, rather than increasing in width.

49. D
The diagram moves from left to right

50. A
The dark ages as the name suggests was a period of no light meaning no stars or planets etc.

Conclusion

CONGRATULATIONS! You have made it this far because you have applied yourself diligently to practicing for the exam and no doubt improved your potential score considerably! Getting into a good school is a huge step in a journey that might be challenging at times but will be many times more rewarding and fulfilling. That is why being prepared is so important.

Good Luck!

Register for Free Updates and More Practice Test Questions

Register your purchase at https://www.test-preparation.ca/register/

for updates, free test tips and more practice test questions.

https://www.facebook.com/CompleteTestPreparation/

https://www.youtube.com/user/MrTestPreparation

Online Resources

How to Prepare for a Test - The Ultimate Guide

https://www.test-preparation.ca/prepare-test/

Learning Styles - The Complete Guide

https://www.test-preparation.ca/learning-style/

Test Anxiety Secrets!

https://www.test-preparation.ca/test-anxiety/

Time Management on a Test

https://www.test-preparation.ca/time-management/

Flash Cards - The Complete Guide

https://www.test-preparation.ca/flash-cards/

Test Preparation Video Series

https://www.test-preparation.ca/test-video/

How to Memorize - The Complete Guide

https://www.test-preparation.ca/memorize/

Online Library of Student Tips and Strategies

https://www.test-preparation.ca/students-say/